Library of
Davidson College

Westview Replica Editions

The concept of Westview Replica Editions is a response to the continuing crisis in academic and informational publishing. Library budgets for books have been severely curtailed. Ever larger portions of general library budgets are being diverted from the purchase of books and used for data banks, computers, micromedia, and other methods of information retrieval. Interlibrary loan structures further reduce the edition sizes required to satisfy the needs of the scholarly community. Economic pressures on the university presses and the few private scholarly publishing companies have severely limited the capacity of the industry to properly serve the academic and research communities. As a result, many manuscripts dealing with important subjects, often representing the highest level of scholarship, are no longer economically viable publishing projects—or, if accepted for publication, are typically subject to lead times ranging from one to three years.

Westview Replica Editions are our practical solution to the problem. We accept a manuscript in camera-ready form, typed according to our specifications, and move it immediately into the production process. As always, the selection criteria include the importance of the subject, the work's contribution to scholarship, and its insight, originality of thought, and excellence of exposition. The responsibility for editing and proofreading lies with the author or sponsoring institution. We prepare chapter headings and display pages, file for copyright, and obtain Library of Congress Cataloging in Publication Data. A detailed manual contains simple instructions for preparing the final typescript, and our editorial staff is always available to answer questions.

The end result is a book printed on acid-free paper and bound in sturdy library-quality soft covers. We manufacture these books ourselves using equipment that does not require a lengthy make-ready process and that allows us to publish first editions of 300 to 600 copies and to reprint even smaller quantities as needed. Thus, we can produce Replica Editions quickly and can keep even very specialized books in print as long as there is a demand for them.

The Federal Republic of Germany and the United States

About the Book and Editors

The Federal Republic of Germany and the United States: Changing Political, Social, and Economic Relations
edited by James A. Cooney, Gordon A. Craig,
Hans Peter Schwarz, and Fritz Stern

This book examines the current and historical dimensions of relations between the United States and the Federal Republic of Germany, focusing on the complex economic issues that make the two countries interdependent and on the resulting policy implications. The contributors analyze the reasons for increasingly problematic relations between the United States and West Germany, arguing that the situation is exacerbated by the inadequate understanding Americans often have of the changing nature of society, politics, and culture in West Germany.

James A. Cooney is executive director of the McCloy German Scholars Program and adjunct lecturer in public policy at the Kennedy School of Government at Harvard University. Gordon A. Craig is J. E. Wallace Sterling Professor of the Humanities at Stanford University. Hans Peter Schwarz is professor of political science and director of the Institute for Political Science and European Issues at the University of Cologne. Fritz Stern is past provost and Seth Low Professor of History at Columbia University.

Published in cooperation with the
Woodrow Wilson International Center for Scholars

The Federal Republic of Germany and the United States
Changing Political, Social, and Economic Relations

edited by James A. Cooney, Gordon A. Craig,
Hans Peter Schwarz, and Fritz Stern

Westview Press / Boulder and London

A *Westview Replica Edition*

All rights reserved. No part of this publication may be reproduced or transmitted in any form or by any means, electronic or mechanical, including photocopy, recording, or any information storage and retrieval system, without permission in writing from the publisher.

Copyright © 1984 by the Woodrow Wilson International Center for Scholars

Published in 1984 in the United States of America by
  Westview Press, Inc.
  5500 Central Avenue
  Boulder, Colorado 80301
  Frederick A. Praeger, Publisher

Library of Congress Cataloging in Publication Data
Main entry under title:
The Federal Republic of Germany and the United States.
  (A Westview replica edition)
  Papers from a conference sponsored by the Woodrow Wilson International Center for Scholars and held in Washington in Sept. 1983.
  1. United States—Foreign relations—Germany (West)—Congresses. 2. Germany (West)—Foreign Relations—United States—Congresses. 3. United States—Foreign economic relations—Germany (West)—Congresses. 4. Germany (West)—Foreign economic relations—United States—Congresses.
I. Cooney, James A. II. Woodrow Wilson International Center for Scholars.
E183.8.G3F43   1984   327.43073   84-19630
ISBN: 0-8133-7004-3

Printed and bound in the United States of America

10   9   8   7   6   5   4   3

CONTENTS

LIST OF CONTRIBUTORS   ix

FOREWORD by James H. Billington   xi

INTRODUCTION: THE CONTEXT OF GERMAN-AMERICAN RELATIONS *by James A. Cooney*   1

GERMANY AND THE UNITED STATES: SOME HISTORICAL PARALLELS AND DIFFERENCES AND THEIR REFLECTION IN ATTITUDES TOWARD FOREIGN POLICY *by Gordon A. Craig*   16

CULTURAL CHANGE AND GENERATION CHANGE IN POSTWAR WESTERN GERMANY *by Richard Löwenthal*   34

THE WEST GERMANS, WESTERN DEMOCRACY, AND WESTERN TIES IN THE LIGHT OF PUBLIC OPINION RESEARCH *by Hans Peter Schwarz*   56

RELIGION AND POLITICS IN GERMANY AND IN GERMAN-AMERICAN RELATIONS *by Jürgen Moltmann*   98

THE INTEGRATION AND DIVERGENCE OF GERMAN AND AMERICAN ECONOMIC INTERESTS *by Sidney L. Jones*   109

THE ECONOMIC RELATIONS OF THE FEDERAL REPUBLIC OF GERMANY AND THE UNITED STATES OF AMERICA *by Reimut Jochimsen*   130

AMERICAN FORCES IN THE FEDERAL REPUBLIC: PAST, CURRENT AND FUTURE *by Ernest May*   153

SQUARING MANY CIRCLES: WEST GERMAN SECURITY POLICY BETWEEN DETERRENCE, DETENTE AND ALLIANCE *by Josef Joffe*   174

POLICY IMPLICATIONS OF DEVELOPMENT AND THE PRESENT STATUS OF U.S.-GERMAN RELATIONS: A GERMAN POINT OF VIEW by Kurt H. Biedenkopf   **204**

SUSTAINING THE AMERICAN-GERMAN RELATIONSHIP IN A TIME OF STRATEGIC AND ATTITUDINAL CHANGE by James R. Schlesinger   **219**

CONCLUSION: GERMAN-AMERICAN RELATIONS AND "THE RETURN OF THE REPRESSED" by Fritz Stern   **234**

CONTRIBUTORS

KURT BIEDENKOPF, *Chairman, Christian Democratic Union in Westphalen-Lippe*

JAMES H. BILLINGTON, *Director, Woodrow Wilson International Center for Scholars*

JAMES A. COONEY, *Adjunct Lecturer and Executive Director, McCloy German Scholars Program, Kennedy School of Government, Harvard University*

GORDON A. CRAIG, *J.E. Wallace Sterling Professor of the Humanities Emeritus, Stanford University*

REIMUT JOCHIMSEN, *Minister for Economics, Business, and Transportation, North Rhine-Westphalia*

JOSEF JOFFE, *Senior Associate, Carnegie Endowment for International Peace; former Fellow, The Wilson Center*

SIDNEY L. JONES, *Undersecretary for Economic Affairs, U.S. Department of Commerce; former Fellow, The Wilson Center*

RICHARD LÖWENTHAL, *Professor of International Relations Emeritus, Free University, Berlin*

ERNEST MAY, *Charles Warren Professor of History, Harvard University; former Fellow, The Wilson Center*

JÜRGEN MOLTMANN, *Professor of Theology, University of Tübingen*

JAMES R. SCHLESINGER, *Senior Advisor, Center for Strategic and International Studies, Georgetown University; former U.S. Secretary of Defense*

HANS PETER SCHWARZ, *Professor of Political Science and Director, Research Institute for Political Science and European Issues, University of Cologne; former Fellow, The Wilson Center*

FRITZ STERN, *Seth Low Professor of History, Columbia University*

FOREWORD

by James H. Billington

This volume on German-American relations is the culmination of a project that began in the early 1980s and has involved many people. It originated in the general awareness that the long postwar era of relatively secure consensus in North Atlantic relations was ending — and the specific belief that the Wilson Center should begin to consider a new program on Europe. European scholars and European problems have always played a large part in the life of the Wilson Center. Because the Federal Republic plays such a critical role within Europe and the Atlantic Alliance, it seemed fitting to focus first on Germany. Thus, the Wilson Center organized and convened in Washington on September 21-23, 1983 a conference for 40 German and American core participants on "German-American Relations and the Future Role of the Federal Republic in Europe and the World," which produced the papers that led to this volume.

As a "living memorial" to a scholar-president, the Woodrow Wilson International Center for Scholars seeks to provide scholarly perspective in a present-minded city — not merely to recycle anguish about current events with fashionable phrases. In originally conceiving of such a gathering I was specially guided by the advice and example of the many great German scholars who fled from Nazism and deepened the perspective of our own country in the postwar era: Theodor Mommsen, who introduced me to serious scholarship as my first faculty adviser in college, and Klaus Epstein, who introduced me to scholarly collegiality when I first began to teach a decade later. It is my hope that both the conference and the volume will be worthy of such people.

The key role among many on the Wilson Center staff was played by Samuel Wells, secretary of the International Security Studies Program at the Center, who provided the basic plan for the conference and watched over it from beginning to end. Jim Cooney, from Harvard University, was the project coordinator during the 12-month planning phase and is the general editor of this book, bringing good humor and expertise on German-American relations to the task. Initial support and major funding came from the Thyssen Foundation; special thanks are due to Kurt Birrenbach, who helped shape plans for the conference at every stage. Additional support was provided by the German Marshall Fund of the United States and the United States Information Agency, thanks to the personal interest of the heads of these organizations: President Frank Loy and Director Charles Wick. Robert Mosbacher, vice chairman of the Board of Trustees of the Wilson Center, hosted conference participants and members of the Wilson Center Board and Wilson Council at the opening dinner addressed by Senate Majority Leader Howard Baker in the diplomatic reception rooms of the U.S. State Department. George McGhee, a former U.S. ambassador to Germany and lively participant in the conference, graciously received all the conference participants for dinner at his home in Middleburg, Virginia. Senators, Congressmen and other political leaders participated in all or part of the conference as did the press and other media.

Gordon A. Craig, Hans Peter Schwarz, and Fritz Stern — as the other editors for the book and consultants for the project — have guided us in our overall plans. Elizabeth Dixon, of the Center's publications office, has coordinated the publication process. General Andrew J. Goodpaster, Distinguished Senior Scholar at the Wilson Center, did an outstanding and effective job as chairman of the conference.

THE CONTEXT OF GERMAN-AMERICAN RELATIONS: AN INTRODUCTION

by James A. Cooney

Conferences and projects on German-American relations are not rare, nor are books on the topic.[1] The Wilson Center Conference on "German-American Relations and the Future Role of the Federal Republic in Europe and the World" was one of the first times, however, that such a meeting was held in Washington, and the conference intentionally included several Americans who do not have expertise on Germany.

The striking feature of the conference was the absence of harsh words and accusations which have characterized other German-American meetings in recent years. Differences were not so much between Germans and Americans as *within* each group.

Because German-U.S. relations seem to be beset by deep and complex problems, the Wilson Center project proposed to look carefully at the policies and fundamental values of each country. The goal of the project was to stimulate an examination of the historical roots of present values held in the two countries, to consider present policy differences in this light, and to make suggestions for policy alternatives in the future which might influence bilateral and alliance relations positively. The two-fold emphasis on historical values and suggestions for future policy formulation was particularly crucial for the project. In short, the authors in this volume were given the difficult task of dealing with "basic orientations" in the areas which they were covering.

The papers were grouped into four areas: historical assessments of the social and political values influencing German-American policies; economic issues; security issues; and policy implications for the future. The papers were prepared and distributed before the conference in Washington and served as the basis for discussion at the meetings. Significant revisions have been made since then in light of both the discussions which took place and subsequent events. If any one topic dominated discussion, it was security — but in relation to long term challenges as opposed to the short term issue of INF deployment. There are also genuine differences in economic policy which are likely to pose difficult problems in the future. At least in the economic sphere, however, the disagreements are structural, rather than philosophical or ideological, so that common interests will set limits to how far the disagreements go.

One of the surprises at the conference was the presence of one theme through nearly all the discussions — namely, the "German Question." The whole topic of national identity in Germany (including the relationship between the two Germanys, the rise of the peace movement, and the significance of neo-nationalism, neutralism and pacifism in Germany) is timely and may make this volume particularly valuable because these issues are examined by authors from several fields — academics, political leaders, journalists, and a leading German theologian. The role of the churches in Germany, in fact, figured importantly in our dicussions. Several of the authors for this volume grappled with the underlying patterns in German-American relations, and that necessitated consideration of this "German Question." I will return to this in the last part of this chapter, after looking first at German-U.S. relations in the broader framework of European-U.S. relations, then introducing the other chapters in this volume and relating them to the discussion at the Wilson Center conference. In his conclusion to the book Fritz Stern also focuses on new stirrings of national awareness in the Federal Republic. These stirrings, incidentally, were seen as normal and predictable by the conference participants; the challenge will be to channel them within the context of the Western Alliance.

German-American Relations in the European Context

The United States is the Federal Republic's most important ally, and the Federal Republic is arguably the most important ally of the U.S. as well. An observer of German-American relations in recent years, however, would be hard-pressed to recognize this closeness based on the rhetoric of the two sides. The public ups-and-downs of the relationship, especially under Helmut Schmidt, were frontpage material for the press. Fortunately, the overall relationship is based much more on the common interests which have evolved in the postwar era and is therefore much more stable.

German-U.S. ties are an integral part of the European-U.S. alliance, which has also been beset with angry rhetoric. Dieter Buhl's assessment in *Die Zeit*, that European-American disagreement is so acute that "thorough therapy" is necessary for the partnership, is overstated.[2] Josef Joffe has put the problems in more balanced perspective in several articles.[3] Still, there are signs that the U.S. and Europe are moving in separate dircetions. Some say that the United States is governed by a new determination and self-confidence while Europe is embroiled in self-doubt; others see the U.S. following a unilateralist course while Europe toys with neutralist ideas.

The ambiguous nature of European reactions to American policies in the last decade is unmistakable. In the early 1970s the Europeans feared superpower domination, in the late 1970s they criticized the U.S. for lack of leadership, and now in the 1980s they fear that the U.S. has abandoned efforts at compromise with the Soviets. These frictions will not disappear quickly, but they are outweighed by common interests. Future relations should be based on these good relations, and not on any sense of duty to the European-American alliance. What is needed on both sides of the Atlantic is a clearer sense of self-identity — a self-identity which will make it possible for both Europeans and Americans to pursue their interests in cooperation with each other, without seeing disaster in every disagreement or in every development which does not fit entirely into their respective pictures of the world. Neither side is confident enough with the other.

This lack of confidence may be the main reason for the current "anti-American" phase in Europe. (Obviously, there is a counterpart phase in the U.S. — it manifests itself in isolationist tendencies, talk of a "decadent Europe," and calls for withdrawing troops from Europe unilaterally.) The anti-American label is difficult to pin on countries or groups in the population because there is disagreement on its meaning, but new feelings are emerging in Europe which are perhaps best described as "anti-American tendencies."

Not surprisingly, the causes of the anti-American tendencies are complex. First, a general fear that governments have lost control of major issues — military and economic — pervades Western, and especially European, thinking. Second, the young generation does not automatically accept the assumptions of the older generations, and many youth are alienated from the political system. Their impact on the system is considerably greater in Europe. Third, differences in economic policies threaten to destroy postwar economic cooperation — which has remained even through severe recessions — and bring in new protectionist measures. Fourth, the relevance of the NATO Alliance, symbolized by the debate about new American intermediate range missiles, stands at the heart of the dispute. This ties in with the Soviet build-up and the differing assessments of its impact.

The anti-American tendencies relate partly to European attitudes about themselves, partly to European history and cultural resentments against the U.S., and partly to the Reagan Administration. The Europeans prefer to describe the present atmosphere not as anti-Americanism but as a reflection of deep-seated uncertainty about the future of the modern industrial state.

Among the major European powers, these tendencies seem to be strongest in the Federal Republic. Germans point out that the feelings, to the degree they exist, are mostly an elite affair, widespread among but limited to the disaffected young generation, intellectual circles, and the churches. The vociferous minority espousing these views is not so much anti-American as anti-modernism, but the U.S. offers a visible target for what the supporters oppose. A certain historical anti-Americanism must also be acknowledged, whether it relates to German history (the Federal Republic is without question the most "Western" German state in history: in some respects Catholic Poland is more Western than Germany) or to a response to the incredible "pro-American" attitudes in the first postwar decades.

The Federal Republic has most exemplified the systematic "de-demonization" of the Soviet Union evident in Europe in the past 10 years. The Social Democrats had to do this — they had to say we can talk to the Soviets — in order to justify their foreign policy. The problem with the de-demonization idea is that it has been turned 180° to lead to questions about the ability and judgment of the U.S. to use its military arsenal. After the invasion of Afghanistan, the Germans — and other Europeans — raised more questions about American intentions than Soviet intentions. This puzzled many Americans.

In the Federal Republic, the question is not whether people think it is important to be on good terms with the U.S. (polls reflect how strongly people still agree on this), but whether the country should stay out of world conflicts. New attitudes are evident regarding this question; a majority would probably favor a position between the superpowers.

The different sources of anti-American tendencies are evident. On the elite level, the feelings are tied to inconsistent American leadership. On the youth level, they are tied to an attitude of "we don't care about the superpowers." Youth protests in the past were closely associated with trends in the U.S., but the present neutralist tendencies are new and independent. Alienated youth in the U.S. view the political problems confronting them as strictly domestic, and their response is to drop out of the political system. In Europe, alienated youth see the problems as more international, and youth are able to exert more influence on the system. The predominant world role of the U.S. guarantees that protest inevitably turns against the U.S.

The tensions in the German-American relationship stem from a wide range of factors. Several authors in this book cite the educational system, especially the universities, as a cause for growing criticism of the U.S. (and of the West German system too). The media, particularly television networks and weekly magazines like *Stern* and *Spiegel*, is also subject to criticism for biased reporting. Michel Meyer, the respected French representative in Bonn for the French TV network Antenne-2, conducted a two month review of German news coverage of U.S.-European relations in 1981 for the Aspen Institute Berlin; his report that he did not see a single positive report about the U.S. in that period received considerable publicity, including in *Time*.[4] TV jobs are usually awarded on the basis of party affiliation, and the two major parties have overwhelming leverage on TV news. Because of German labor laws and the unhappy historical experiences with limits to the freedom of expression, German editors for television and the press are more severely constrained in managing the news than their American counterparts. Committee decisionmaking is more the rule, and this increases the pressure to hire staff members of the same political persuasion. In contrast to the American and British tradition of separating fact and opinion, the line is more blurred in West German reporting. In brief, the critical coverage of the U.S. is likely to continue.

Another factor for the tensions in the German-U.S. relationship is fear about the future — the German word *Angst* gives a more complete description. Helmut Schmidt has written about the meaning of *Angst* in his new capacity as a senior editorial member of the weekly newspaper, *Die Zeit*.[5] Fundamental value changes are taking place and citizens — especially Germans, according to Schmidt, because of their lack of national identity and their historical burden — need anchoring points.

The one criticism which Europeans and Germans are too quick to make is to blame problems on specific American presidents. The same people who criticize Ronald Reagan also criticized Jimmy Carter. One of the most astute German observers of the U.S., Marion Gräfin Dönhoff, argues in an article both that the "old relationship of trust" will return once another Administration takes office in Washington, but that "neither the party-political system nor the electoral process in the United States is likely to bring the best man to the top."[6] Countess Dönhoff and Europeans may not like it, but the U.S. has a decentralized political system where power is shared, not concentrated as in parliamentary systems; the European complaint is with the system rather than the individuals, and the system is not likely to change.

The picture that is drawn in this section may be overly bleak because it does not emphasize enough the commonalities that are likely to prevail in European-U.S. relations in the face of any crises. Present differences in German-American relations, however, do need to be explored from an historical perspective, and that was a major purpose of the papers in this volume. The following section introduces them in terms of socio-cultural trends, economic policies, security issues, and policy implications for the future.

Introduction to the Project and the Conference

1. *Socio-cultural Trends*   The first task for this project on "German-American Relations and the Future Role of the Federal Republic in Europe and the World" was to provide an historical assessment of social, cultural and political values. Gordon Craig in his chapter offers long-term perspectives on political and cultural values in Germany and the U.S. to show how these values affect the formulation of foreign policy. Richard Löwenthal outlines cultural and generation changes in postwar West Germany to analyze the degree to which Western thinking has sunk in for the Federal Republic. Hans Peter Schwarz uses public opinion data to show how strongly West Germans have absorbed Western ideas and political concepts. He stresses the positive postwar developments which led to a nearly unanimous consensus on the merits of constitutional government, and then he assesses present trends in light of these beliefs. Finally, Jürgen Moltmann uses the peace and security issue to focus on the interaction of politics and religion in German-American relations. The Christian churches are taking on a new role, more independent from the State, and churches are increasingly pushing their own visions of the future.

The major dispute in the discussion of these papers on socio-cultural trends was how to assess the Peace Movement. Views ranged from those who perceive it as another variant of German romanticism which will disappear shortly, to those who distinguish it as a fundamental turning point in German politics due to its grass roots strength and religious zeal. One participant called it the most Americanized political movement yet seen in Germany: it represents a coalition of single issue groups which agree only on wanting to refuse deployment of new missiles and which will fall apart if the issue is settled. Some see renewed German nationalism at the root of the peace movement. The consensus at the conference was that increased nationalism was not an issue at present but is likely to be evident in the future. After all, nationalist tendencies are manifest in France and Great Britain, yet only Germany has a legitimate historical grievance. On the other hand, caution is needed so that the label of nationalism is not attached too quickly to developments in Germany which might be rationalized as something else — such as part of the youth culture or the environmental movement — in other countries. The U.S. may have grown too accustomed to a compliant German partner, but steps away from compliance should not be confused with German nationalism. The reunification issue fits here too: no one expects it or demands it, but Germans want it to remain paramount on the detente agenda. Any move toward reunification of Germany, though, would depend on a move toward European unification — but this would raise the thorny issue of Eastern Europe.

Gordon Craig traces the special German-American relationship back three centuries. Both sides have experienced long periods of isolation in foreign policy, as well as strong feelings of exceptionalism accompanied by manifestations of xenophobia. Craig points out that the reaction to the Enlightenment in America was political and led to the establishment of a constitutional system based on popular sovereignty. The reaction to the Enlightenment in Germany, in contrast, was moral and the result was a strengthening of existing authoritarian structures. Fundamental differences in the German-U.S. relationship are evident through this response to the Enlightenment. Individuality in the U.S. came to be seen in pragmatic, political and egalitarian terms whereas it was seen in Germany in a metaphysical way which viewed an interest in politics as a harmful distraction.

Craig argues that a nation's foreign policy is necessarily influenced by its history and political development. In Germany, except for Hitler, foreign policy has been considered to be the "sphere of the State"; hence, it is left to professionals. In the U.S., the approach has been to avoid having a foreign policy if possible, but if not, then to have one which expresses the popular will — whatever the cost of incoherence or discontinuity. Idealism, not realism, tends to motivate American policies which are expected to be not only effective but also correct.

World War II marked a break in continuity for both countries: exceptionalism diminished in West Germany and the U.S. reconciled itself to a world role. Craig's key point is that just as isolationism is repudiated by most Americans today, so too is old-fashioned, neutralist sentiment currently rejected by the majority of West Germans. The possibility of a reversion to pre-1945 forms of thought and behavior by either the U.S. or West Germany seems reasonably remote in the current context.

Richard Löwenthal analyzes the problem somewhat differently. He looks back as far as the Middle Ages to show Germany's doubts about whether the country fits in as part of the Western world, but this *Zwischenkultur* (in-between culture) disappeared from Germany both politically and culturally after 1945. Hitler produced the collapse of the *Zwischenkultur* concept by driving its antidemocratic nationalism to its most absurd conclusions. The end of the war in 1945 thus was a "cultural watershed" for Germany. The first vote was made by those emigrating from the East — i.e., with their feet.

Löwenthal feels that the Federal Republic is now indelibly linked to the Western Alliance and is no longer burdened with the idea of being an intermediary between the East and West. Löwenthal believes that it is not the Greens but rather the Peace movement which constitutes the first substantial threat to the Federal Republic's ties to the Atlantic Alliance and the U.S. The Green movement typically combines proposals which are often sensible with an irrational anti-industrialism; it is anarchic rather than revolutionary. The Peace movement encompasses more of the population and is motivated by "stark fear." The emergence of the Peace movement relates to the unstable balance between the superpowers which for the first time has given rise to fears that confrontation may indeed explode into nuclear war. That feeling, rather than any pro-Soviet sentiments, explains the strength of the Peace movement. The rhetoric of the Reagan Administration has only served to increase this fear even though that was not the intention. The one consolation for Löwenthal is that the real danger — the Peace Movement — is not cultural and hence not fundamental; instead, it is linked to a particular political situation and thus apt to be ephemeral. The Western outlook is solidly entrenched in the Federal Republic, but steady efforts to maintain it are needed.

Hans Peter Schwarz concentrates on the positive side of the Federal Republic's postwar integration into the West. His major point is that the concerns expressed today about neo-nationalism, neutralism and pacifism must be considered in terms of the basic values which exist in German society. According to Schwarz, the Germans have a "neurotic" tendency to question repeatedly whether democracy in the FRG is secure. He faults those concerned about stability in West Germany for overlooking a basic orientation: a nearly unanimous consensus on the merits of constitutional government. The parties and public opinion both reflect this. Using empirical evidence, Schwarz outlines the stability of democracy in the FRG, evaluates the basic foreign policy orientation in light of this stability, and finally considers the "new tradition" evident in the 1980s. Schwarz identifies two major political cultures which live in peaceful coexistence but are separated by a deep cleavage. The majority of the electorate belongs largely to the productive classes and is committed to the values of industrial society and Western constitutional democracy. Challenging this culture is an activist, politicized minority of university-trained, middle-class radicals, largely alienated from industrial society and uncertain about constitutional democracy and Western orientation. There is a confrontation between the apolitical, productive classes and a politicized, non-productive class.

Schwarz looks at the attractions of nationalism, neutralism and pacifism for Germans. He points out that West Germans throughout the 1950s expressed a general preference for reunification with East Germany rather than with Europe. In addition, the CDU/CSU saw itself in opposition as the "custodian of the national idea." Still, he doubts that any danger is posed today even though the feelings of support in the Federal Republic for a neutralist stance remain strong, as they have throughout the postwar era. Throughout the 1950s there was support for a "reunification-neutralism" along the lines of the Austrian model. The present neutralist yearnings, in contrast, are for West German disentanglement from superpower politics. Sympathy exists for these feelings, particularly within the SPD, but the support is not pronounced. Despite its recent rhetoric, the SPD would probably uphold NATO positions if it returned to power.

Pacifist unilateralism has greater support in the FRG than nationalism or neutralism. In part, this results from unilateralism being perceived as a vague mood; in part, it results from the different views of unilateralism. Schwarz distinguishes among "radical unilateralists" (very ideological and alienated from society), "specific unilateralists" (frustrated supporters of detente who may even be pro-West and pro-U.S.), and "apolitical peace lovers" (probably pro-West but emotionally concerned about peace; often church-related).

Schwarz concludes that the empirical evidence of the past 35 years of German history disproves the skeptical question of *incertitude allemandes*. Even today there is no indication of a sharp break in long-term stable opinions. Having a subculture of alienated radicals is not abnormal, and although there is a national consciousness in Germany, no other divided country displays such moderate national feelings, according to Schwarz. The Western ties are firmly rooted.

Jürgen Moltmann presents a very different, important and controversial perspective in his chapter on religion and politics in Germany and in German-American relations. Security for Moltmann has to be understood in more than just a military sense or else it is too defensive. He outlines the special role of the churches in the two Germanys, and then goes on to say that a disengagement between church and society in our time is making the churches free to realize their own visions of the future. The Christian discussion about peace demonstrates the new political importance of religion; the discussion about security shows the religious importance of politics. Moltmann's argument that the church in the GDR "expresses itself much more freely and critically about the government's rearmament policy, and on behalf of peace, than the churches in the Federal Republic" was hotly disputed, mainly with the claim that the East German Church is critical because it has to be.

Moltmann's paper draws a clear line between idealists and realists. He maintains that the danger of the present security policy is that all the political problems of the world are reduced to pro- or anti-communism. Problems of the Third World are essentially ignored. In Moltmann's words, the American dream — which originally was Europe's dream of America as well — "will become a nightmare for other nations if it is turned into the ideology of American hegemony, and if it is not extended to all nations as a humane dream."

2. *Economic Issues*   The discussion of economic issues was the most sobering of the conference because fundamental differences are visible and likely to remain. The differences stem not just from policy questions like interest rates, but from America's role as a global power compared to Europe's role as a regional power. In summarizing the debate, one participant talked about the grave implications of economic differences since they can have consequences of an attitudinal or emotional nature. These in turn, could injure the social-political stability on which the security consensus in the Alliance is dependent.

Sidney Jones, now Undersecretary of Economic Affairs in the Department of Commerce, argues that German-American economic relations will be characterized in the coming years by increasing competition accompanied by increasing integration. The two countries share views on an open economic system, the importance of bilateral trade, and the need for economic growth. They differ, though, on the proper mix of domestic fiscal and monetary policies, the purposes and processes of East-West trade, and the balance of regional and global economic strategies.

The golden era of German-American economic relations disappeared during the 1970s, but the trendy predictions of disaster seen recently should not be overestimated because the fundamental bilateral relationship remains strong. Both countries pursue similar economic policies: they both subscribe to a "dogmatic liberalism" and avoid "concerted action" programs to achieve regional and international objectives; at the same time, neither country is willing to give up sovereign control of its economic policies, and that is unfortunate since economic problems are increasingly multinational. The Federal Republic faces somewhat of a quandary because it is under pressure to conform to the consensus policies of the European Community even though the results are sometimes contrary to its global interests and relations with the U.S. The United States would do well to learn from the German success in balancing regional and global interests. Opportunities and responsibilities in Latin America and the Pacific Basin should be pursued; that would not imply a turning away from global priorities and the central role of Western Europe by the U.S. Both German and American regional priorities deserve recognition. Such policy initiatives would reflect a positive broadening of interests and a more realistic recognition of bilateral power and responsibilities.

Reimut Jochimsen, the Minister for Economics in the largest German state (North Rhine-Westphalia), emphasizes that the Federal Republic and the U.S. are *not* on equal footing. Capital flows and new jobs are noticeably lower in Germany, and the manufacturing sector lags behind much of Europe. In the past, an expanding German economy led to "extensive" growth, but now growth is almost entirely "intensive." The Germans recognize the limits of sovereignty in economic policy; the U.S. still has freedom here, especially since a strong dollar provides more options for Americans.

Jochimsen calls for a "renewed stewardship" among countries rather than a fallback to the "locomotive" theories of the 1970s. Macroeconomic policies are of primary concern to Germans who view their unemployment problems and balance of payment difficulties as directly related to American interest rates. Although there was no expectation of sharp changes in American policy, the Germans feel that common policy and actions by the major trading nations on an international level provide the best bet for coping with international economic problems — but the United States must take the lead. More attention must be given to the political aspects of the world economic system. Jochimsen criticizes America economic policy on several counts and claims that it is high time for this policy to pay more attention to its inevitable leading role in the world economy.

3. *Security Issues* Security issues dominated the discussions at the conference but surprisingly little attention was given to missile deployment and the *heisse Herbst* of 1983. The focus was more on changing values and perceptions and their implications. Ernest May outlined that although the development of the American commitment to the Federal Republic was "improvisational," the U.S. has always defined its security interests in the FRG as vital. The definition of security has remained the same even though major changes have occurred: originally, Americans were concerned about militant German nationalism, but now the concern is about neutralism.

May addressed two questions in his chapter: What historical circumstances shaped the Alliance? Will the nature of the Alliance stay the same in the future? Immediately after World War II the U.S. had no plans for an alliance with Europe. Several types of relationships were tried out before the "deterrent alliance" concept was accepted. The efforts to make NATO an "armed alliance" in the 1950s were especially hard due to French objections. The MLF idea in the early 1960s was a cockeyed idea militarily, according to May, but a creation of genius politically because it bought time until agreement evolved on a "deterrent alliance" with the doctrine of flexible response. That posture has basically been maintained since 1967.

May envisions three possibilities for the Alliance in the future. First, it could continue in its present mold as a deterrent alliance. Second, it could become more of an armed alliance, genuinely prepared for sustained non-nuclear combat. Third, it could turn to other concepts such as a dependence on threats of strategic nuclear retaliation, an alliance based on promises of liberation rather than protection, or no alliance at all. May elaborates on these possibilities, looking especially at the pro's and con's of continuing with the present shape of the Alliance, and he predicts that the U.S.-German relationship may look very similar even in the 21st century primarily because there is no reasonable and feasible alternative.

On a shorter term basis, Josef Joffe looks at the present stability of German security policy and also predicts it will continue because the Federal Republic enjoys the "blessings of non-autonomy." Germans are net importers of security — and not having to make security choices helped solidify democracy domestically. The comfort of the Federal Republic's insulated power and lack of foreign involvement contrasts with the French and British postwar security commitments and burdens. Germans, in fact, worry more about having too much power rather than too little.

Questions arose, though, about whether Germans will continue to see limited autonomy as a blessing, particularly if American and German views on the Soviet Union and the fear of nuclear war diverge. The Federal Republic may like to carve out a role aimed not at independence but at least at allowing more maneuverability and choices. Joffe also presents a controversial view about the peace movement which he says may well be a *cyclical* rather than a secular phenomenon. The question is not only why peace movements arise, but also why they vanish. Joffe feels that there may be relevant lessons from the peace movements of the 1950s which had a short life.

4. *Policy Implications for the Future*   To conclude the project, Kurt Biedenkopf and James Schlesinger were each asked to identify a short list of policy options for the future. The discussion on this topic stressed the need to heed the changing values underlying our defense and alliance consensus. Germany requires a European framework to deal with its national interests, and the need for the Federal Republic to cooperate with the Soviet Union should not be forgotten. Certain compromises between relations with the U.S. and within the European alliance may be necessary.

Critical differences are apparent in American and European approaches to military problems. The U.S. sees the Soviet threat as considerably greater than do the Europeans. Europe is content with a "low-confidence" deterrent; the U.S. prefers a "high-confidence" deterrent. The Americans worry more about the Soviet potential for disrupting the political cohesion of the Alliance, but the Europeans should not believe that the U.S. maintains its presence in Europe out of balance of power considerations. According to Schlesinger, the U.S. is there out of belief and confidence in the European nations, but there is still need for more understanding of Germany and German feelings. Less emphasis on global unilateralism would be a step in the right direction. The U.S. should also recognize that the search for identity among young Germans is inevitable. The U.S. should be aware that the search in itself should not be equated with rising German nationalism. The entire process can, in fact, be strengthening rather than destructive.

Biedenkopf points out that the postwar German-U.S. relationship is without historical precedent, but also that the Atlantic Alliance is the institutional answer to conditions that no longer exist. Reappraisal is thus needed in three areas: (1) the present structure, objectives and purpose of NATO; (2) economic and social policy; (3) the European and American value systems. Biedenkopf's startling recommendations all relate to developing a European identity, not because of dissatisfaction with the U.S. but because it is a natural step for the Europeans to take. The first issue addresses the problem of "loss of will" in Europe; Biedenkopf shares the views of some American critics that more European willingness to share the defense burden must be demonstrated. He is prepared to start thinking constructively about the time when some U.S. troops may withdraw from Europe.

On the second issue, Biedenkopf feels that the overhaul of economic doctrine may be just as essential for the future cohesion of the Alliance as a reexamination of military doctrine. Now that European economics have achieved parity of sorts with the U.S. economy, the issue of "burden-sharing" should be squarely faced; no longer should the U.S. bear a disproportionate share of the costs. Biedenkopf directs attention to the social dimension of economic policy and to the relation of these economic and social issues to defense efforts. On the third issue of changing values, Biedenkopf brings in the element of religion. It is providing guidance and stability for those who are looking for a new authority to fill the vacuum created by the shaken authority of present experts. The discussions on this point and on the Moltmann paper highlighted the importance of will and morale, especially in the security debate.

Biedenkopf states plainly, "The key to the future U.S.-German relations lies in Europe, not Germany." Europe needs to develop its own political identity and assume the corresponding responsibilities. The present relation between Europe and the U.S. is not a stable one. According to Biedenkopf, "Germany's main political goals require a European policy," and he feels that German or European reunification fits in with these objectives too.

James Schlesinger also proposes three issues to consider for the future. He begins, though, by expounding on the underlying American attitudes about foreign affairs which he says the Europeans need to recognize. The American impulse in foreign affairs is "quintessentially idealist-romantic" and the policy oscillates between missionary zeal and periodic withdrawal. Schlesinger's first priority for solidifying German-American and European-American relations is to preserve cohesion among the allies. The need for cohesion should transcend any political or military differences; Alliance unity should not be sacrificed because of European attitudes on an issue such as Nicaragua. Schlesinger finds it ironic that the U.S. has taken European security problems more seriously than Europeans for over 25 years.

The second issue which Schlesinger points to is the new consensus within the Alliance to diminish reliance on the early recourse to nuclear weapons. The Alliance should develop plans to reflect this new consensus; he calls for the creation of a new body of "wise men" within NATO for the first time since the 1950s. The purpose of that body would be to improve the conventional posture of NATO, and hence the confidence of its members in the overall deterrent. Such an independent body needs to be formed because the formal NATO councils are unlikely to effect the needed changes.

Schlesinger's third issue is directed to Americans: above all, they must pay attention to the requirements of coalition politics. This pertains to arms control negotiations, economic policies, Alliance disputes, and certainly the national needs of the Germans. The search for German identity and the revival of German nationalism are unavoidable; the U.S. and other Alliance members can work, however, to channel these emotions so that they do not question fundamental Alliance ties. On the other hand, Europeans and particularly Germans should recognize that the support of the American public for U.S. involvement has to be earned anew in each era. The efforts will cease if they are not appreciated, according to Schlesinger.

Challenges Facing the Federal Republic

The charge to the authors in this volume and to the participants at the Wilson Center conference was to consider *basic values* in the German-American relationship. The topic that received the most attention was security: Ernest May and Josef Joffe covered it explicitly, Jürgen Moltmann and James Schlesinger dwelt primarily on it, and several other authors referred to it at length. Interestingly, the potential for dispute on economic issues may be just as high as on security questions. Prospects for resolving U.S. and German economic differences were, in fact, viewed pessimistically, but the nature of the problem is more structural than ideological. The papers by Sidney Jones and Reimut Jochimsen indicate the areas of disagreement but also the common interests which are likely to keep economic disputes from permanently damaging the German-U.S. alliance.

Throughout the papers and the discussion at the conference, however, one major theme emerged repeatedly: the German Question. In a sense, the papers that looked at the processes of development in the German-American relationship (e.g., Gordon Craig, Richard Löwenthal, Hans Peter Schwarz and Kurt Biedenkopf) were all trying to cope with where the German Question fits. Schwarz labels the concern *incertitude allemandes*; others ask "whither Germany?" *Business Week* laments that "the German Question has returned to haunt Western Europe and the U.S.," and the *New York Times* says that German "nationalist sentiment has pushed a major party [the SPD] to an anti-NATO line."[7] In the last year, without doubt, there has been an upsurge in the West German willingness to talk about German interests, needs and relations with the GDR — but this in itself is hardly ominous.

The CDU/CSU government of Helmut Kohl has shown a pro-American stance in its policies and has established good working relations with the Reagan Administration. At the same time, it may also have concluded that the Federal Republic is reaching the moment when it becomes legitimate to express German national feeling openly and bring it into play politically.[8] West Germans are trying to be more "German" which is only natural after 40 years.[9] Jonathan Dean claims that, among the major German parties, a broader definition of the Federal Republic's international position has appeared; it combines close ties to the U.S. and Europe with a sustained effort to reach accommodation on political issues and arms control with the Soviet Union, the GDR and the other Warsaw Pact states.[10] These feelings make for strange political combinations at times — e.g., the conservative CSU leader Franz Josef Strauss and the liberal SPD defense expert Karsten Voigt both favor some sort of "double key" system for nuclear weapons on German soil in order to increase the German influence on the use of such weapons.[11]

The biggest surprise of the Kohl government policy is the emphasis it has placed on relations with the GDR. Even though the CDU claimed in opposition that it was the protector of German national interests, few suspected that Kohl's biggest success would be in his *Deutschlandpolitik*. (This term, which means literally "German policy," has supplanted the word

Ostpolitik with its historical connotation. *Deutschlandpolitik* is not narrowly defined to German-German relations; it includes them as well as relations with the rest of the East bloc, but it does not include East-West bloc relations.) The CDU criticized the SPD in the last federal election for campaigning on the theme "in the German interest," yet the government deliberately revived the theme of German unity — the most German of these national interests. Marion Dönhoff, in recent articles in *Die Zeit*, has asked whether the Germans are in the "waiting room of history," and "what is happening to the Germans?"[12]

These issues tie in with the question of neo-nationalism, neutralism and pacifism. Hans Peter Schwarz's chapter indicates the complexity of these questions and shows that they cannot easily be dismissed. A certain ambiguity surrounds them, but there are no calls for German reunification. Petra Kelly of the Greens expresses her dislike for the term "nationalism," and a meeting sponsored by the Greens on the *Deutschlandfrage* drew a poor turnout.[13] Participants at the Wilson Center conference echoed James Schlesinger's feeling that German nationalism is not a concern if it is channeled correctly to assure Alliance ties.

The tendencies toward neutralism provide a tougher case. Schwarz documents the continual underlying attraction of neutralism for parts of the West German population, and other observers of German-American relations — including Jonathan Dean, Karl Kaiser and Elizabeth Pond — note the same tendencies. Josef Joffee describes the Greens as "inward bound, almost escapist"; their message is not *Deutschland über alles*, but "leave us alone."[14] The fundamental debate is Germany's role in the East-West debate and this applies to the pacifist-unilateralists as well.[15]

Fritz Stern, in the conclusion to this volume which he wrote as a postscript to the conference, is struck by the same themes mentioned here. He uses Freud's term "return of the repressed" (which Richard Löwenthal has also used in his writings) in relation to the reappearance of the German Question. Stern portrays the fall 1983 German debate surrounding deployment of new American missiles as one of the "moments of crisis (in the lives of nations) which jolt people into greater awareness of self and into greater recognition of earlier, barely noticed subterranean changes." The core of the Alliance and German-American relations is security. Although the Alliance serves economic interests too, its *raison d'etre* is security, and this is where the changes have been most striking. Germans know that their security rests in American hands — they know it, depend on it, but resent it.

The challenge for the German government then — at a time when German-German relations are the closest ever, but when it is hard to see that the East German leadership can continue its accommodations — is to assure its allies that *Deutschlandpolitik* is compatible with Alliance responsibilities. Any progress in German-German ties is likely to be slow. James Schlesinger's advice is relevant here and certainly seems to be accepted totally by the Kohl government: the political cohesion of the Alliance has to be the top priority. The "return of the repressed" should not be lamented but rather incorporated into Western policies.

NOTES

[1] The American Council on Germany and Atlantik Brücke co-sponsor significant biennial meetings; the Aspen Institute Berlin and the Chicago Council on Foreign Relations both take an active interest in German-American relations, as do the German political foundations. The new American Institute for Contemporary German Studies will undoubtedly make a significant contribution to the field. For recent books on the role of the Federal Republic, see Wolfram Hanrieder (ed.), *West German Foreign Policy: 1949-1979*, (Boulder: Westview Press, 1980); Peter Merkl (ed.) *West German Foreign Policy: Dilemmas and Directions* (Chicago Council on Foreign Relations, 1982); Viola Herms Drath (ed.), *Germany in World Politics*, (New York: Cyro Press, 1979).

[2] Dieter Buhl, *Die Zeit*, December 30, 1983; also translated in *The German Tribune*, January 8, 1984, p.3.

[3] Josef Joffe, "European-American Relations: the Enduring Crisis," *Foreign Affairs*, vol. 59, no. 4, Spring 1981, pp. 835-881; Joffe, "Europe and America: the Politics of Resentment (cont'd)" *Foreign Affairs*, vol. 61, no. 3, pp. 569-590; Joffe, "Europe's American Pacifier," *Foreign Policy*, no. 54, Spring 1984, pp. 64-82.

[4] The project was organized by the Aspen Institute Berlin and is described in "Mass Media and the Public: Europe and the United States," *Report from Aspen Institute Berlin 1/82*.

[5] Helmut Schmidt, "Fürchtet Euch nicht," *Die Zeit*, Dec. 30, 1983, p.1 (North American edition).

[6] Marion Dönhoff, *Die Zeit*, September 30, 1983, p.1 (North American edition).

[7] Viola Drath, "The Pershing Debate is Deepening Germany's Identity Crisis," *Business Week*, December 12, 1983, p. 55; *New York Times* editorial, "Germany, Uber (sic) Alles," November 27, 1983.

[8] Robert Gerald Livingston, "Once Again, the German Question," *German Studies Newsletter* No. 2, Harvard University, April, 1984.

[9] Michael Sturmer, "Nation and State in a Divided Germany," paper and talk at the Center for International Affairs, Harvard University, March 22, 1984.

[10] Jonathan Dean, "Federal Germany after the Euromissiles," *Bulletin of the Atomic Scientists*, vol. 39, no. 10, December 1983, p. 37.

[11] Strauss wants to have a group surrounding the U.S. President to represent European interests; Voigt wants to have a German finger on the safety catch.

[12] *Die Zeit*, January 13, 1984, p.1; March 23, 1984, p. 1 (North American edition).

[13] Writing in the *Wall Street Journal*, Diane Coutu said that Petra Kelly taught a generation of young Germans how to clamor for greater distance from the United States by importing the phrase "grass roots democracy" from the U.S. rather than using taboo expressions like "German nationalism."

[14] Josef Joffe, "The Greening of Germany," *The New Republic*, February 14, 1983, pp. 18-22.

[15] I use the word "Germany" consciously here to include both Germanys. It is interesting to note how the different authors in this volume are inconsistent in their terms for the Federal Republic — some are ready to call it "Germany" but most are not; nearly everyone will apply the adjective "German" to the Federal Republic. It is not always clear how they would refer to the East Germans. The East Germans solve this in their own language by using their initials — e.g., *DDR-Bürger* (East German Citizen), *die DDR Mannschaft* (the East German team) . They apply the same use of initials to the Federal Republic — using BRD from the words Bundesrepublik Deutschland), and that explains the West German objection to being described by those initials, for example, at the Olympics.

GERMANY AND THE UNITED STATES: SOME HISTORICAL PARALLELS AND DIFFERENCES AND THEIR REFLECTION IN ATTITUDES TOWARD FOREIGN POLICY

by Gordon A. Craig

It is surely appropriate, in a book that will deal extensively with relations between the United States and Germany, to begin with some consideration of the similarities between the two nations. This was a theme that, in the first half of the nineteenth century, before our mutual relations had ever been troubled by considerations of power or the ravages of war, fascinated American intellectuals, theologians, scholars and educators. The historians William Hickling Prescott, John Lothrop Motley, and George Bancroft, for example, who were all interested in the history of the spread of liberty in the world, convinced themselves, not only that great movement had culminated in the establishment of the United States of America, but that its origins were to be found in Germany, in the centuries-old struggle between Teuton and Celt, German and Gaul.

Germany and the United States were, therefore, if not natural allies, then at least bound by a special relationship. Bancroft elaborated this idea with enthusiasm in his *History of the United States*, in which he discovered correspondences between Frederick the Great and George Washington, Immanuel Kant and Benjamin Franklin, and, more improbably, between Martin Luther and Thomas Jefferson, and in which he described the two nations as protagonists in a great drama in which Protestantism was vindicated and saved from its enemies. This had begun, he wrote,[1]

> In 1613, when the congregation of Pilgrims at Leyden was growing by comers from England, (and) the elector of Brandenburg, John Sigismund, after eight years of reflection, adopted the faith of those who were to plant Massachusetts.

In the century and more that has passed since Bancroft's time, our historical experience has broadened and our perspective changed, becoming both more differentiated and less optimistic. The similarities that we find as we look at the histories of our two countries now seem to be more problematical than the likenesses that appealed to his fancy and that of Prescott and Motley, and they are offset by profounder dissimilarities that escaped their attention but that we can recognize, with our greater powers of hindsight, as being the causes both of misunderstanding and friction between our two peoples.

Of the similarities, certainly the most salient is the fact that, for significantly long periods of their history, Germany and the United States were outsiders in world politics. It is understandable that Bancroft, with his narrower perspective and his religious bias, should have regarded the two countries as being in the vanguard of progress, but no detached observer of the international scene in the seventeenth and eighteenth centuries, or even at the beginning of the nineteenth, could have entertained a similar notion. The Peace of Westphalia, which ended the Thirty Years War, was the first settlement imposed upon the German states by foreign powers, and its political and psychological effects were more protracted than those of the settlements made after the two great conflicts of the twentieth century. In 1648, Germany was in effect excluded from all of the main lines of European development for an indefinite period. By the simple process of denying it any access to the sea, the stronger powers turned it into a land-locked island in the center of the continent, while at the same time confirming its internal atomization by legitimizing its more than three hundred sovereignties and subsequently maintaining that to try to reduce their number would be considered an affront to "German liberties" and a violation of international law. In the period that followed, the greater part of Germany was a remote and backward area, so much so that, when Madame de Stael made her first journey to it in 1803, she felt that she was leaving the confines of the civilized world and entering a region that was unknown and exotic.[2]

Europeans who visited America in the same period found it possibly even more exotic. It was certainly more remote, both physically and politically, and this was the result of volition rather than of foreign decree. The Americans were outsiders by choice. Most of them had crossed the wide Atlantic to escape from the restrictions and prohibitions, the wars and the hierarchies of the old world. Once established in their new homes, they set about the long process of detaching themselves from the administrative connections that had facilitated their emigration while tying them to their lands of origin; and when they had won their independence, they lived in constant suspicion lest they be drawn back into the world from which they had escaped with such effort. Even before the break with England was final, Benjamin Franklin was justifying it in a letter from that country in words that would be repeated with variations by countless Americans after him.

> When I consider the extreme corruption prevalent among all orders of men in this old rotten state, and the glorious public virtue so predominant in our rising country, I cannot but apprehend more mischief than benefit from a closer union. I fear they will drag us after them in all the plundering wars which their desperate circumstances, injustice, and rapacity may prompt

them to undertake; and their wide-wasting prodigality and profusion is a gulf that will swallow up every aid we may distress ourselves to afford them. Here numberless and needless places, enormous salaries, pensions, prerequisites, bribes, groundless quarrels, foolish expections . . . devour all revenue and produce continual necessity in the midst of natural plenty. I apprehend, therefore, that to unite us intimately will only be to corrupt and poison us also.³

If the causes of the separation from the world of international politics were different, the results were in important respects much the same. In both countries, there arose a feeling of *exceptionalism* or uniqueness. The leaders of the young American republic never doubted that their country was destined to be different from others and that they had indeed founded a *novum ordinem saeculorum*, and the millenarian strain of Puritan thought found exuberant expression in their speeches and in patriotic outbursts like Freneau and Brackenridge's *Poem, On the Rising Glory of America*, which proclaimed:

This is a land where the more noble light
Of holy resolution beams, the star
Which rose from Judah lights our skies.

The great result of all our labors here,
The last day's glory and the world renew'd.⁴

This faith was transmitted from generation to generation and influenced not only the rhetoric of American politicians in the nineteenth and twentieth centuries but the self-image of ordinary American citizens. Similarly, in Germany, particularly in the area that stretched from Westphalia to the Danube and from the Rhine to Upper Saxony, which W. H. Riehl called "the motley encyclopedia of our society,"⁵ belief in German uniqueness was a consequence of isolation and was reflected, as I have written elsewhere,⁶ in the excessive use of the adjective "German" to suggest the special quality of native attributes (German valor, German loyalty, a German maiden, and the like). It was also reflected in the preoccupation with the nature and meaning of Germanness that Heine derided⁷ but which Wagner shrewdly recognized as being the result of the devastation wrought by the Thirty Years War, the experience of being thrown back upon one's own resources, and a memory of, and longing for, lost glories.⁸

Not unnaturally, this feeling of exceptionalism was accompanied by manifestations of xenophobia that differed in intensity according to time and circumstance. Suspicion and dislike of foreign ideas and influences found their most extreme expression in Germany among spokesmen of the lunatic fringe of the Romantic movement, but they were also part of the culture of the communities of middle Germany throughout the eighteenth and early nineteenth centuries. Indeed, even after the profound social changes of the Bismarck and Wilhelmine periods had broken down the walls between these communities and the outside world, their psychology persisted in muted forms. The fact that xenophobic behavior was characteristic also of middle America hardly needs to be proven to anyone who has read *Martin Chuzzlewit* or H. L. Mencken's corrosive analyses of what used to be called the Bible Belt. In his brilliant study of the towns of middle Germany from 1648 to 1871, Mack Walker had written that "belief in the primacy of communal membership, mistrust of floating individuals, and righteous hostility toward the outside were the hometown legacy to the Germany of the late nineteenth century and at least the first half of the twentieth century."[9] With the change of a single word, this would describe the American situation as well.

A second notable correspondence between Germany and the United States was that, in their progress toward national unity, they followed surprisingly parallel courses and passed through similar crises with similar results. In each case, full integration of the nation was preceded by a long period during which vain attempts were made to solve the problem of the relationship between the collectivity and its components, between the aggregate and its separate parts, by means of compromises between the claimants, a process in which the Articles of Confederation, the Missouri Compromise and the Dred Scott Decision, the Germanic Confederation, and the Frankfurt Parliament were unhappy episodes. The problem was finally settled in both countries, although not until the seventh decade of the nineteenth century, by means of civil war, a drastic solution with some unhappy results. R. C. Binkley once wrote that both nations were profoundly altered by passing through this "crisis of federative polity." "Even the American Union saved at Gettysburg," he wrote, "was no longer the same as that which the fathers had brought forth upon the continent fourscore and seven years before. Government of the people, by the people, and for the people survived the Civil War in America, just as monarchic government survived the civil war in Germany, but in both cases the fine balance of federative compromise was ended, in America by the triumph of the Unionists, in Germany by the victory of the Prussian secessionists."[10]

To push Binkley's point a bit further, the period that opened in the 1870s was, for both America and Germany, one of heightened centralization and enhanced power of the government over the individual. It was a period of tumultuous economic development (the German *Gründerzeit* had its American equivalent) and of unrestrained competition in which cartels and monopolies had the advantage over individual traders. It was an age of bigness. It was an age in which power was sought after and idealized and made an end in itself and, for that very reason, an age of which the most incisive critics were Nietzsche and Henry Adams, who realized that power makes for ruthlessness and unconditionality but also, as the German philosopher said, for stupidity.[11] In the hundred or so years that followed the crisis of the 1860s, both countries were to learn that sad, and ultimately sobering, lesson.

Despite this similarity of pattern, however, the national development of Germany and the United States was marked by a fundamental difference, and this arose from the way in which the great intellectual movement of the eighteenth century that we call the Enlightenment — and the Germans call the *Aufklärung* — was experienced in the two countries. In America, its emphasis was political and its result the establishment of a constitutional system based upon popular sovereignty. In Germany its emphasis was moral and its result the strengthening of existing authoritarian structures.

The generation that made the revolution of 1776 in America — and by that is meant not only the men who have been called the great *virtuosi* of the American Enlightenment, Franklin, Adams, and Jefferson,[12] but leaders amd opinion-makers in every one of the colonies —was literally steeped in the ideas of the Enlightenment rationalism. They were familiar with the writings of social reformers and critics like Voltaire, Rousseau and Montesquieu, with Beccaria's ideas concerning the reform of criminal law, with what Grotius and Pufendorf and Vattel had written about the laws of nature and of nations, and, above all, with Locke's views on natural rights and social contract. Nor did they consider their reading a mere diversion or an intellectual exercise to delight the mind. They were eminently practical men who aspired to make a new commonwealth, and to them ideas were tools in their great enterprise. Locke's theories were, therefore, given institutional form, his concept of atomistic social freedom[13] transformed into the revolutionary idea of the people as a constituent power, of a constitutional assembly chosen by the people, not to govern, but to set up the institutions of government, a convention that would at the same time define the rights of the citizen and the powers of government, that could be recalled and replaced by the procedures that it had delineated.[14]

Nothing of this kind occurred in Germany. The ideas of the *philosophes* circulated in parts of the country, although their penetration of the heartland was not extensive, and Germany had its own great representatives of the Enlightenment in Kant and Lessing and Lichtenberg, to say nothing of Frederick II of Prussia, whose institutional reforms reflected the rationalism of the French Enlightenment. But this had little effect on a country that did not respond easily to outside influences, and where local communities clung to custom and tradition. Moreover, the influence of religion, stronger at least in this respect than in the West, succeeded in blunting the ideas of social contract and popular sovereignty that were characteristic of the Western Enlightenment and in shifting the emphasis of the movement to questions of morality and self-improvement.[15] There were no atheists in the German *Aufklärung* and, perhaps in large part because of that, there were no political revolutionaries either. As Hajo Holborn once wrote, "the entire intellectual bent of eighteenth century Germany was in the direction of the education and cultivation of the individual. All political demands were secondary, if they were considered at all."[16]

The failure of the Enlightenment in Germany and the subsequent dominance of Herder's cultural nationalism and the ideas of the Romantic movement resulted in a view of humanity that was basically antithetical to that in America, one that came to regard individuality not in pragmatic, political, egalitarian terms, but mystically and metaphysically "as meaning the particular embodiment assumed, from time to time, by the Divine Spirit, whether in individual persons or in the super-personal organizations of community life."[17] The result was that German thinking became not only unpolitical, but anti-political. The emphasis upon individual *Bildung* became so excessive as to make interest in politics a harmful distraction. German intellectuals would have agreed with Maistre's dictum, "In philosophy, contempt for Locke is the beginning of wisdom."[18] Much of Nietzsche is little more than variations on that theme, and Thomas Mann's *Reflections of an Unpolitical Man* is filled with shrill insistence that politics is incompatible with true humanism and participatory democracy alien to the German temperament.[19] Decisions affecting communal life were properly the function of civil servants (*Beamten*) and ultimately of that remote but all-powerful organism of which they were the agents and in whose being all subjects realized their own significance, the State.

This was a true parting of the ways and was the cause of mutual incomprehension. It was as difficult for Americans to understand what Germans meant when they talked about the State as it was for the latter to comprehend what Americans meant when they talked about a government of the people, by the people, and for the people.[20] As Ernst Tröltsch once wrote, anyone who believed in natural law, the equality of men, and their destined aspiration to form a more perfect union could hardly avoid regarding German Romantic nationalism as a mixture of mysticism and brutality; while anyone who regarded the historical process as the progress of God's will mirrored in the spirit of individual peoples (*Volksgeistern*) and as an abundance of national individualities fulfilling their highest potentialities in competition with each other would see nothing in Western ideas but barren rationalism and egalitarian atomization, a combination of insipidity and pharisaism.[21]

A nation's foreign policy is necessarily influenced by its history and the nature of its political development, and it is not difficult to illustrate this in the case of Germany and the United States by considering, first, prevailing attitudes toward foreign affairs and, second, the way in which the two countries have conducted their external relations.

In Germany foreign policy has traditionally been considered to be the sphere of the State; at least, this was so until 1933, when it became once more, as in the time before the emergence of the modern state, a matter of personal caprice and inspiration of the ruler. In a classical treatment of politics, Leopold von Ranke wrote of the Great Powers as individual organisms, responding to the laws of their own nature, "progressing amid all the turmoil of the world, . . . each in its own way, . . . celestial bodies, in their cycles, their mutual gravitation, their systems."[22] What this meant in practical terms was that the State was the embodiment of the national identity and purpose, whose actions were determined by the sovereign and his agents on the basis of a rational system of rules and precepts drawn from experience and reflection and intended to give guidance in the identification, protection and advancement of the State's vital interests. This system was variously called *ragione di stato*, *raison d'etat*, and *Staatsraison*. The modalities available for the defense and promotion of interest were varied and included negotiation of differences, alliances, system-building (leagues, coalitions, balance of power), and war. Foreign policy was not a matter for the plebs, but for professionals; there was no real measure of parliamentary control over it in Germany before 1914, and relatively little thereafter. In this sense, the State was as autonomous as Ranke suggested.

To the American way of thinking, all this was objectionable. From earliest times, there had been the gravest doubt about the legitimacy of foreign policy as an activity for Americans.[23] Colonel George Harvey was voicing a deep-seated prejudice when he said, in the 1920s, "The foreign policy of the United States is to have no foreign policy"; and twenty-five years later, when Demaree Bess wrote an article with the title "Why Americans Hate the State Department," he was making the point, among others, that they regarded it as an agency that was offensive because otiose.[24] As they looked at the world outside, Americans saw no clear distinction between negotiation, alliances, systems, and war; the earlier processes seemed to tend inevitably toward the last. Balance of power had a particularly threatening quality; from John Adams ("It is obvious that all the powers of Europe will be maneuvering with us to work us into their real or imaginary balances")[25] to Woodrow Wilson and Cordell Hull, it was regarded, as Hull said in 1943, as an expedient fraught with "iniquitous consequences";[26] and this view was so firmly imbedded in the popular consciousness that, in the 1970s, Henry Kissinger believed that the principal challenge of the Nixon Administration was "to educate the American people in the requirements of the balance of power."[27]

The degree of freedom in foreign affairs that was enjoyed by the State in Germany was impermissible in the eyes of Americans. If it was unavoidable that the United States have a foreign policy, and this was by no means clear, then it must be the expression, not of any autonomous body, but of the popular will, whatever the cost might be in incoherence and discontinuity and whatever the risk of making policy the plaything of all the winds of fashionable doctrine.

It must, moreover, express not only the will of the American people but their moral excellence, if not superiority, as well. This was a requirement of policy that did not bulk so large in Germany, not, of course, because German statesmen were more immoral than their American colleagues, but rather because they were readier to admit the primacy in foreign affairs of what is today called situational ethics and the futility, if not the danger, of seeking to apply absolute moral standards. Prince Bismarck, who dominated German foreign policy for thirty years and whose methods and characteristic style had continuing influence, considered himself to be a Christian but recognized that, in the conduct of his office, he was forced to do things that were hardly compatible with the precepts of the Sermon on the Mount. He seems to have resolved the dilemma by means of Luther's distinction between *Personalethik* and *Berufsethik*, the idea that the vocation to which one is called by God also has an ethic that requires obedience.[28] It was, in his view, the duty of the statesman not to question the dynamics of the State that he had been chosen to serve but to understand them, not to doubt its requirements of power and growth, but to find ways of satisfying them.

The moral conflict between personal conscience and responsibility to his office was reduced in Bismarck's case to the somewhat simpler problem of persuading himself, on any given occasion, that he was performing his duties as a statesman well. And since, like Hegel, he believed that all States were equal under God, the question of morality did not otherwise concern him.[29] His successors seem to have made similar adjustments, and there is no record of their having been accused of immorality for having done so.[30]

But Americans have always felt a compulsion to believe that their policies were not merely effective, but good — there was a decided difference between what Bismarck expected from the Diety and the hopes of John Quincy Adams, who, upon becoming Secretary of State, wrote:

> Extend, all-seeing God, Thy hand.
> In mercy still decree,
> And make, to bless my native land,
> An instrument of me[31] —

and that their actions in foreign affairs were prompted by idealistic rather than merely realistic motives.[32] Behavior that smacked too blatantly of old-world *Realpolitik* was, and still is, apt to elicit astonishing public outcries (during a recent furor over the activities of the CIA, an English journalist said, "You haven't got a country over there; you've got a great big church!"), and American statesmen felt constantly compelled to reassure the republic with respect to its essential nobility, as Woodrow Wilson did in a speech in Boston in February 1919, when he said, "Speaking with perfect frankness in the name of the people of the United States, I have uttered as the object of this great war ideals, and nothing but ideals, and the war has been won by that inspiration."[33] Although himself prone to this kind of Wilsonian excess as a young man, Walter Lippmann later suggested that Americans might make more friends and get along better with their allies if they did not always seem to claim that the United States was not only the strongest and richest nation in the world but also the best, in the spiritual sense; but in this respect they seem to be incorrigible.

Connected with this attitude was their tendency to see foreign policy ideologically, in terms of sharp dichotomies: good and evil, friend and foe, peace and war. This was alien to the very spirit of German *Realpolitik*, which was always interest-oriented,[34] and to the style of its greatest practitioners. Between 1871 and 1933, the Germans never deluded themselves with the thought that they had a responsibility to save the rest of the world or to support causes abroad that seemed to represent Germanic values or beliefs. Their statesmen saw the world in which they moved in terms not of natural alliances and fixed oppositions, but of shifting combinations, of mergings and meldings. Friendships and antagonisms were generally impermanent and often ambiguous. One could sometimes deal more profitably with an antagonist than with an associate. Circumstances altered cases, and the cardinal sin was for the statesman to sentimentalize his political attachments and invest them with personal feeling.

Bismarck expressed this attitude in one of his letters to Leopold von Gerlach in the 1850s:[35]

> Sympathies and antipathies with respect to foreign powers and persons I cannot justify to my sense of duty to the foreign service of my country, either in myself or in others. Therein lies the embryo of disloyalty toward one's master or the land one serves. And especially when one's current diplomatic connections and the maintenance of friendly relations in peacetime in accordance with those things, one ceases in my opinion to conduct politics and begins to act according to personal caprice. In my view, not even the King has the right to subordinate the interests of the fatherland to personal feelings of love and hate toward the foreigner.

Gustav Stresemann, in an age when international ideologies had begun to complicate the diplomatic process, had no doubt that Bismarck was right. His personal predilection for a Western orientation of policy did not prevent him from balancing the Locarno Pact of 1925 with the Berlin Treaty of 1926, which renewed the Soviet-German agreement made at Rapallo four years earlier.[36] It was at about the same time that the political scientist Carl Schmitt, in a series of lectures at the University of Bonn, began to elaborate his theory that "the specific political distinction to which political actions and motives can be reduced is the distinction between friend and foe," but it is worth noting that he was careful to state that the political enemy was not necessarily morally evil ("he is merely the other, the stranger") and that his theory did not imply that any nation or group was the natural or perpetual enemy of any other nation or group.[37]

The attitude toward the relationship between peace and war was much the same, at least in nineteenth century German statecraft. If war was an instrument of policy — as Clausewitz insisted it must be and Bismarck demonstrated it could be — then it was a process that both originated in and aspired to peace. This continuum would be disturbed if war were allowed to assume its absolute form through the dissolution of the political restraints upon it and its transformation into a religious cause. It was not the least of Bismarck's considerable achievements that, during the wars against Austria and France, he was able to prevent his sovereign and the military high command from exceeding the political objectives of the struggle in the heat of victory.

On all of these questions, American attitudes differed markedly, largely because the original separateness of the country, its sense of exceptionalism, and its Enlightenment heritage encouraged a more ideological approach to them. Even in the revolutionary period, the desire to remain detached from international politics had been ambivalent, for inherent in it was the idea that such detachment would provide time for the gathering of the strength that one day would change the whole world for the better. When Samuel Williams wrote in 1775 that the cause of America was "the cause of self-defense and public faith," he added "and of the liberties of mankind"; and in 1784 Richard Price expressed the conviction that the American revolution "in favor of universal liberty . . . begins a new era in the history of mankind."[39]

If the dominant characteristic of American foreign policy in the nineteenth century was isolationism, just below the surface there lay a thwarted missionary impulse that stirred whenever there were embattled movements abroad that seemed at least potentially to typify American ideals. The Greek revolution of the 1820s and the European revolutions of 1830 and 1848 aroused enthusiasm in the United States and inspired movements that called for assistance and intervention; in 1848, Congressman Alexander Buell did not hesitate to speak of the "higher mission of his country" to spread its own principles over the whole world.[40] It was this spirit that found its fullest expression in the speeches and proclamations of Woodrow Wilson in 1918 and 1919 ("I do not mean any disrespect to any other great people when I say that America is the hope of the world");[41] and, if the nation recoiled from his high enthusiasm in the decade that followed, it was not a permanent retreat. As American power has grown, so has its sense of having a global mission to defend the cause of freedom, and this has been couched increasingly in ideological terms.

Ideological also is the American approach to the questions of friends and foes and peace and war. The fortunes of the policy of detente in the United States illustrate how uncongenial Bismarckian relativism is to most Americans. After the public rejection of his plan for establishing a tolerable *modus vivendi* with the Soviet Union, Henry Kissinger wrote that, since "detente is the mitigation of conflict among some adversaries, not the cultivation of friendship," it was particularly hard for Americans to understand. "The American perception of international affairs has traditionally been Manichaean. Relations among states are either peaceful or warlike — there is no comfortable in-between."[42]

American insistence upon seeing a sharp dichotomy between peace and war probably had its roots in the strong Lockean tradition in American political thought. Locke viewed the international system (and the founding fathers followed him in this) as a rudimentary order in which the law of nature or reason prevailed. An attack upon another nation was possible only through violation of the law of reason, and the offender, by placing himself beyond the pale, became a legitimate target for destruction, so that the law and the normal condition of nations, which was peace, could be restored.[43] There was no place in this scheme for twilight zones or limited wars; and it is understandable that with this intellectual heritage — and the additional strong belief that democracies are constitutionally incapable of aggressive action[44] — Americans would tend to do exactly what Clausewitz warned against: to expect their wars to be fought, not as an extension of politics, but as crusades, to be impatient with political planning in wartime lest it divert energy from operations, to tolerate an excessive degree of military intervention in the planning of over-all strategy, and to believe that there was no substitute for victory.

That their historical evolution and the nature of their political institutions have affected the way in which Germany and the United States have conducted their foreign relations goes almost without saying. One illustration of this is the way in which their relatively late arrival upon the international scene invested their diplomacy with forms of maladroitness that resembled social parvenuism.

In *Democracy in America*, Alexis de Tocqueville commented at some length upon the social awkwardness of Americans in the early nineteenth century.

> An American leaves his country with a heart swollen with pride; on arriving in Europe, he at once finds that we are not so engrossed by the United States and the great people who inhabit it as he had supposed, and this begins to annoy him. . . . (In society) he is afraid of ranking himself too high; still more is he afraid of being ranked too low. This twofold peril keeps his mind constantly on the stretch and embarrasses all he says or does. . . . He is like a man surrounded by traps; society is not a recreation for him but a serious toil; he weighs your least actions, interrogates your looks, and scrutinizes all you say lest there should be some hidden allusion to affront him. . . . He is full of scruples and at the same time of pretensions; he wishes to do enough, but fears to do too much, and as he does not very well know the limits of the one or the other, he keeps up a haughty and embarrassed air of reserve.[45]

Much of what Tocqueville said of Americans in the 1830s was documented for a later period in the novels of Henry James. Much also applies to American diplomacy in the nineteenth and twentieth centuries, which tended — not, certainly, in the case of our greatest diplomats, but frequently and notably enough among the rest to warrant the generalization — toward a brashness and assertiveness that was in part the result of insecurity. Connected with this was an impatience with diplomatic formality and etiquette and a disregard of accepted procedures that began in revolutionary times. Our first envoys sought to dramatize American uniqueness in their behavior, Benjamin Franklin by the studied plainness of his dress and his insistence upon appearing at the French court in a simple brown coat, a cloth cap, and unpowdered hair, John Adams by his penchant for lecturing to his hosts and informing them tartly that "the dignity of North America does not consist in diplomatic ceremonials or any of the subtleties of etiquette; it consists solely in reason, justice, truth, the rights of mankind, and the interests of the nations of Europe."[46] These early attempts to put the United States upon the diplomatic map were not unsuccessful. At a later and less appropriate time, excessiveness of this kind became tedious and self-defeating.

It was never, however, as harmful in its effects as it was in Germany, particularly during the Empire, when German manners in intercourse with other governments became at times as offensive as they were when the

Third Reich was at its height. It is unfair to talk, as some writers have done,[47] about a consistent emphasis upon violence, threats, pressures and surprises as being characteristic of imperial policy and to attribute this to a desire to impose German *Kultur* on the rest of the world, for there is, as has already been indicated, little evidence to prove the existence of such desire. But Gerhard Weinberg is certainly correct in detecting "an adolescent assertiveness accompanied by a preference for bullying and drama, a preference so deep and abiding as to be unaffected by the weakness or strength of Germany's position in the world at any given moment" and in perceiving that this rose out of "concern over not being taken seriously enough by others," especially as a new actor in international politics.[48]

Bismarck himself, despite his long years of diplomatic experience before becoming Chancellor of the Reich, was not immune to this kind of behavior, as is shown by his treatment of the representatives of lesser powers and, particularly, by the gratuitous insolence of his behavior toward England during the dispute over *Angra Pequena*. His son Herbert outdid his father in discourtesy and outright rudeness, both as envoy and as Secretary of State for Foreign Affairs. And the personal diplomacy of William II was a classical illustration on parvenuism at its worst, for the Emperor spoke incessantly and bombastically about the mission of the Hohenzollern dynasty and the superiority of German virtues, industry, and power, gave unwanted advice to other governments, claimed credit for their successes, and did not hesitate to threaten them with dire consequences when their policies displeased him. All of this decisively worsened Germany's image in the eyes of foreign governments, including that of the United States, who tended to take William at his own valuation and regard even his most impulsive statements as reflecting Germany's policy and intentions, and this led to a growing conviction that it was ambitious, unpredictable and dangerous.[49] There was a decided modification of this style during the Weimar Republic, but it is worth noting that the change was not universally approved and that Reich President Paul von Hindenburg complained of Stresemann that he did not pound the table enough.

The fact that the United States was a democracy and Germany, before 1919, was not affected their diplomacy in markedly divergent ways. Tocqueville wrote in 1835, "I do not hesitate to say that it is especially in the conduct of their foreign relations that democracies appear to me decidedly inferior to other governments.... A democracy can only with great difficulty regulate the details of an important undertaking, persevere in a fixed design, and work out its execution in spite of serious obstacles. It cannot combine its measures with secrecy or await their consequences with patience."[50] How relevant this is to conduct of American policy will be apparent to anyone who reflects upon the historical proliferation of agencies participating in, or having a share in reviewing, policy decisions in the United States and the jurisdictional fragmentation that has resulted, in our own time, in the existence of more than eighty congressional committees and sub-committees, often without staff with experience in foreign affairs, which have some right to be consulted on complex foreign problems.[51] Even the process of negotiation, once reserved to professional diplomats, has been increasingly affected by this monstrous bureaucratic growth. In the Conference on Security and Cooperation in Europe in the early 1970s, the head of the American delegation had little influence on the development of negotiating strategy, which was prepared in Washington in the National Security Council and the Departments of State, Defense, Commerce and the Treasury, which intermittently sent experts to advise the delegation. Before the conference was over, its sessions had been attended by a number of congressmen and it was being examined by several congressional sub-committees.[52]

Even in a simpler age, the vigilance of Congress on the one hand and the widespread distrust of the diplomatic process on the other created serious obstacles to effective practice. The strong prejudice against secrecy after 1919 and the ever-present impatience with protracted negotiation, natural to a people that derived, from its conquest of a continent, the belief that all problems have solutions and that delay in finding them betokens a lack of energy and imagination, gave a premium to public forms of diplomacy that was more productive of rhetoric than tangible results. A deep-seated distrust of diplomats (who were variously described in Congress as elitist, "cookie-pusher," sexual deviates, and persons whose service abroad rendered them incapable of recognizing, and unwilling to defend the true interest of their country) led to an unhealthy dependence upon amateur negotiators of one kind or another. Finally, administrations that were worried about public support for their policies were tempted to try to drum it up by exaggerating their expected results (a tactic known as "selling the sizzle instead of the steak") or by hortatory diplomacy, sloganry, and the declaration of doctrines.[53] These expedients often confused even the persons charged with implementing them.

Since it was never subjected to the same degree of public or parliamentary examination and interference, the conduct of German foreign relations during the Empire and even during the Republic tended to be more consistent, more disciplined, and more professional. The advantages that this brought, however, were offset by the tendency toward irresponsibility. In the Wilhelmine period, cliques and individuals close to the emperor exercised an influence upon policy that was often the despair of the leadership of the Foreign Ministry. This was particularly true of the military, because of the privileged position accorded it in the constitutional structure of the Empire. Even Bismarck had difficulty in controlling policy initiatives and private diplomacy by the General Staff and the military attaches, and his successors were less successful than he, with the result that Germany's freedom of diplomatic maneuver before 1914 was seriously restricted by military plans and commitments. Nor did this end during the Republic. It is perhaps an exaggeration to say that the *Reichswehr* had its own foreign relations, and we now know that the army's dissatisfaction with Heinrich Brüning's diplomatic priorities was an important reason for that statesman's dismissal from office.[54]

Finally, those charged with the conduct of foreign relations in both countries had to operate under the shadow of history or, more properly, of exaggerated or glorified visions of the past. In 1865, Richard Wagner wrote that "in his longing for German glory, the German can usually dream of nothing else but something similar to the restoration of the Roman Empire,"[55] and to the extent that this was true it may explain the grandiosity of William II's policy and his frantic attempt to fit reality to myth, to live up to his insistence that "there is only one true emperor in the world, and that is the German Kaiser, not in relation to his person and character but by virtue of the right of a thousand-year tradition."[56] During the Weimar Republic, the glorified past was embodied in the Bismarckian Reich, and those charged with the formulation and execution of policy were expected by large sections of the population to match its performance, despite Germany's radically reduced power and resources. The Americans had their myth too — the fixed belief, legitimized by quotations from the founding fathers and arguments drawn from the history of the 19th century, that ocean-girt America had no need to concern itself with foreign quarrels, since it could defend itself against any eventuality by its own resources — and policy-makers who were aware that even in the 19th century American safety had been adventitious, since the country was protected from foreign menaces by the distractions of the European powers and the supremacy of the British fleet, and who realized that the changed conditions of the twentieth century called for new measures, soon discovered how formidable a grip that historical legacy had upon the American imagination. A false sense of security based upon a misreading of the past not only served as an underpinning of isolationism in the United States and an invincible argument against alliance diplomacy and balance of power politics but was also the basis of what Bayliss Manning has called "a national ineptitude for calibrating accurately what the nation's security interests really [were]."[57] In the case of Germany, the tendency to glorify the past at the expense of the present caused a similar lack of perspective. In both countries, popular tribunes whose slogans promised a return to the values and independence of the past ("America First!", "Deutschland erwache!") were successful in defeating those whose policies looked to the future and sought to avert its dangers. In the crucial years between 1929 and 1933, when the slide toward dictatorship and war might still have been prevented, initiatives by the Hoover Administration on the one hand and by Stresemann and Brüning on the other were blunted and eventually defeated by necessary concessions to popular mythology.[58]

In both Germany and the United States, the Second World War marked a decisive breaking of historical continuity, and after it was over attitudes on many things had changed. In both countries, the emphasis on exceptionalism was diminished, a change signalized by Konrad Adenauer's statement, "In the lands of the German West, there is a natural longing to escape from the confines of national narrowness into the fullness of the European consciousness,"[59] and by clear signs that the majority of Americans were becoming reconciled to their country's being permanently involved in world politics. In Germany, the State, that mysterious entity that had traditionally served to condone domestic absolutism and foreign adventurism, was demythologized and depersonalized. The relationship between government and the individual became pragmatic rather than romantic and a democratic political and social system was established and quickly demonstrated its effectiveness. This made it easier for the United States to win domestic support, not only for the return of sovereignty to the Federal Republic, but also for its rearmament and admission to the NATO alliance as a full partner. What was once a perceptible cultural gap between the two countries was noticeably reduced, and a relationship that in earlier times had been nervous even when friendly, frequently tense, and sometimes hostile in the most extreme degree took on the intimacy of collaboration.

It would be surprising if this friendship were not, even after thirty years, occasionally troubled by misunderstandings, maladroit behavior, and sporadic manifestations of doubt and self-examination, and whenever this happens fears are expressed of a possible return to the attitudes and behavior of an earlier time. The United States government is sometimes less than attentive to the feelings and interests of its German ally, failing to consult it properly in advance of actions it intends to take, as if harking back to the days when the United States had no allies and needed none. Indeed, it has been known on occasion to intimate that if the government of the Federal Republic does not show more understanding of American views about security requirements, it may, in Franklin Roosevelt's phrase, pick up its dishes and go home. The former kind of behavior has recently elicited some caustic remarks from Helmut Schmidt about indignities that he suffered at the hands of the Carter and Reagan Administrations;[60] the latter has caused Rudolf Augstein of *Der Spiegel* to accuse the United States of blackmail.[61] At the same time, Washington's coolness toward any renewal of the detente policy and, more particularly, President Reagan's "Empire of Evil" speech at Orlando has seemed to many Germans to signify a revival of the dichotomized thinking of the past and has led Gräfin Dönhoff to ask worriedly, "Why is America so ideological?"[62] On the other side of the Atlantic, the considerable amount of discussion in the Federal Republic in the last few years about German identity and problem of a *Sonderbewusstsein* and the recent furor about the spurious Hitler diaries have led some Americans to become concerned about the possibility of a revival of German nationalism and the awakening of old myths and traditions long thought buried.[63]

But this, as has been said already, was to be expected, and it is worth remembering when we confront it that old-fashioned nationalist sentiment is clearly rejected by the majority of West Germans, just as isolationism is repudiated by most Americans. The possibility of a reversion on the part of either of the allies to pre-1945 forms of thought and behavior seems, in the present state of the world, to be reasonably remote. The acceleration of change since the end of the Second World War has made the world that lay before it seem infinitely distant from us and bereft of many discernible points of reference. If there is a danger to the alliance, it would appear to lie elsewhere, in the possibility of the partners becoming imprisoned in the assumptions and procedures of their more recent past. This is what is most disturbing about the Orlando speech. It would be an unhappy ending to much fruitful collaboration if the United States and Germany allowed themselves to become rigid in their thinking and uncritical of the international system that their joint efforts have helped to maintain for almost thirty-five years, and if they failed to appreciate the inevitability of change and the necessity of adjustment to new realities and opportunities.

NOTES

[1] George Bancroft, *History of the United States*, (13th ed., Boston, 1874), X, p. 81; David Levin, *History as Romantic Art: Bancroft, Prescott, Motley and Parkman* (Stanford, 1959), *passim*; Gordon A. Craig, "Preussen und die Vereinigten Staaten," in *Preussen und das Ausland*, ed. Otto Busch (Berlin, 1982), pp. 54-55.

[2] Madame de Stael, *De l'Allemagne*, ed. Comtesse J. de Ponge (4 vols., Paris, 1958-59), Observations générales; Pt. 1, chapter 2, p. 13.

[3] *Writings of Benjamin Franklin*, ed. Albert H. Smyth, VI, pp. 311-12, cited in Bernard Bailyn, *The Ideological Origins of the American Revolution* (Cambridge, Mass., 1967), p. 136.

[4] Cited in Sacvan Bercovitch, *The Puritan Origins of the American Self* (New Haven, 1975), p. 146.

[5] W. H. Riehl, *Land und Leute* (9th ed., Stuttgart, 1899), p. 155.

[6] Gordon A Craig, *The Germans* (New York, 1982), p. 25.

[7] "On Ludwig Börne," Part IV, in Heinrich Heine, *Werke*, ed. Martin Greiner (2 vols., Cologne, 1962), p. 752 ff.

[8] Richard Wagner, "Was ist deutsch?" in *Ausgewählte Schriften und Briefe*, ed. Alfred Lorenz (2 vols., Berlin, 1938), II, p. 332.

[9] Mack Walker, *German Home Towns: Community, State, and General Estate, 1648-1871* (Ithaca, 1971), pp. 405 ff.

[10] R. C. Brinkley, *Realism and Nationalism, 1850-1871* (New York, 1935), p. 183.

[11] Friedrich Nietzsche, *Götzendämmerung* (Kroner ed., Stuttgart, 1964), p. 122.

[12] Bailyn, *Ideological Origins*, p. 27.

[13] Louis Hartz, *The Liberal Tradition in America* (New York, 1955), p. 62.

[14] R. R. Palmer, *The Age of the Democratic Revolution* (2 vols., Princeton, 1959, 1964), I, pp. 214 ff.

[15] Wilhelm Dilthey, *Leben Schleiermachers*, I/1 (Göttingen, 1970) (*Gesammelte Schriften*, XIII/1), pp. 84-86.

[16] Hajo Holborn, "Der deutsche Idealismus in sozialgeschichtlicher Beleuchtung," *Historische Zeitschrift*, CLXXIV (1952), p. 365. See also, in stronger terms, Friedrich Nietzsche, *Morgenröte* (Kroner ed., Stuttgart, 1976), p. 166.

[17] Ernst Tröltsch, "Naturrecht und Humanität in der Weltpolitik," in *Deutscher Geist und Westeuropa* (Stuttgart, 1925), pp. 14ff.

[18] Hans Aarsleff, "Language and Victorian Ideology," *The American Scholar*, LII, No. 3 (Summer, 1983), p. 367.

[19] Thomas Mann, *Betrachtungen eines Unpolitischen* (Frankfurt am Main, 1956), pp. 22, 24, 103.

[20] Thorstein Veblen, *Imperial Germany and the Industrial Revolution* (1915; new ed., New York, 1939), pp. 160, 162.

[21] Tröltsch, *Deutscher Geist*, pp. 7, 15.

[22] Leopold von Ranke, "A Dialogue on Politics" (1836), in Theodore Von Laue, *Leopold von Ranke: The Formative Years* (Princeton, 1950), pp. 168, 180.

[23] See Felix Gilbert, *Towards the Farewell Address: Ideas of Early American Foreign Policy* (Princeton, 1961), p. 17.

[24] Demaree Bess, "Why Americans Hate the State Department," *Saturday Evening Post* CCXXIII, pp. 22 ff. (August 19, 1950).

[25] *The Works of John Adams*, C. F. Adams (ed.),(Boston, 1865 ff), III, p. 316.

[26] Cordell Hull, *Memoirs*, II (New York, 1948), p. 1452.

[27] Henry Kissinger, *Years of Upheaval* (Boston, 1982), p. 50.

[28] Karl Holl, *Gesammelte Aufsätze zur Kirchengeschichte*. I. *Luther* (6th ed., Tübingen, 1932), pp. 282 ff.

[29] For a fuller discussion, see Gordon A. Craig and Alexander L. George, *Force and Statecraft: Diplomatic Problems of Our Time* (New York, 1983), pp. 255-78.

[30] On Bismarck's answer to such accusation, the famous letter to Andrae-Roman, see Otto von Bismarck, *Die gesammelten Werke* (15 vols., in 19, Berlin, 1924 ff.), XIV/2, p. 709; and Otto Vossler, "Bismarck's Ethos," *Historische Zeitschrift*, CLXXI (1951), p. 286.

[31] Samuel Flagg Bemis, *John Quincy Adams and the Foundations of American Foreign Policy* (New York, 1949), p. 244.

[32] In general, see Robert Endicott Osgood, *Ideals and Self-Interest in America's Foreign Relations* (Chicago, 1953).

[33] *The Messages and Papers of Woodrow Wilson*, ed. Albert Shaw, II (New York, 1924), p. 642.

[34] See Ludwig August von Rochau, *Grundsätze der Realpolitik*, ed. Hans-Ulrich Wehler, (Frankfurt am Main, 1972), especially Part I (1853), chapter 1 and, on idealism and realism, Part II (1869), chapter 4.

[35] Bismarck, *Gesammelte Werke*, XIV/1, p. 465.

[36] Gordon A. Craig, *From Bismarck to Adenauer: Aspects of German Statecraft* (Baltimore, 1958), pp. 80-82.

[37] Carl Schmitt, *Der Begriff des Politischen* (new ed., Hamburg, 1963), pp. 26, 27, 35; Joseph W. Bendersky, *Carl Schmitt: Theorist for the Reich* (Princeton, 1983), pp. 88-95.

[38] Bailyn, *Ideological Origins*, pp. 139 ff.

[39] Cited in Knud Krakau, "American Foreign Relations — an American Style?" in *Oceans Apart? Comparing Germany and the United States. Studies in Commemoration of the 150th Anniversary of the Birth of Carl Schurz*, ed. Erich Angermann and Marie-Luise Frings (Stuttgart, 1981), p. 125.

[40] Günter Moltmann, *Atlantische Blockpolitik im 19. Jahrhundert: Die Vereinigten Staaten und der deutsche Liberalismus und die deutsche Revolution von 1848/49* (Düsseldorf, 1973), pp. 336 ff., 350 ff.

[41] *The Messages of Woodrow Wilson*, II, p. 644.

[42] Kissinger, *Years of Upheaval*, pp. 753, 980.

[43] Krakau, in *Oceans Apart?*, pp. 127 ff.; Roger D. Masters, *The Nation is Burdened: American Foreign Policy in a Changing World* (New York, 1967), chapter 9.

[44] Bayliss Manning, "246 Years of American Foreign Policy: Doric, Ionian — and Corinthian?" in *The Americans: 1976*, ed. Irving Kristol and Paul Weaver (Toronto, 1976), p. 256.

[45] Alexis de Tocqueville, *Democracy in America*. The Henry Reeve Text as revised by Francis Bowen, further corrected and edited by Phillips Bradley (2 vols., New York, 1945, 1954), II, Book 3, chapter 3.

[46] Gilbert, *To the Farewell Address*, p. 67.

[47] Harold Nicolson, *Diplomacy* (London, 1939) pp. 146-48.

[48] Gerhard L. Weinberg, "National Style in Diplomacy: Germany," in *Oceans Apart?*, p. 149.

[49] Paul Kennedy, "The Kaiser and German Weltpolitik: Reflections on Wilhelm II's Place in the Making of German Foreign Policy," in John C. G. Rohl and Nicolaus Sombart (eds.), *Kaiser Wilhelm II: New Interpretations* (Cambridge, 1982), pp. 143-48; and on American reactions, Gordon A. Craig, "The United States and the European Balance," *Foreign Affairs*, LV, No. 1 (October, 1976), pp. 190-91.

[50] Tocqueville, *Democracy*, I, p. 234.

[51] Krakau, in *Oceans Apart?*, p. 141.

[52] Craig and George, *Force and Statecraft*, p. 167.

[53] See Stanley Hoffmann, "The American Style: Our Past and Our Principles," *Foreign Affairs*, XLVI No. 2 (January, 1968), p. 365; George F. Kennan, *Memoirs, 1925-1950* (Boston, 1967), p. 322.

[54] Gordon A, Craig, *The Politics of the Prussian Army, 1640-1945* (Oxford, 1955), chapters X, XI; Gaines Post, Jr. *The Civil-Military Fabric of Weimar Foreign Policy* (Princeton, 1973), *passim*; Michael Geyer, "Reichswehr, NSDAP, and the Seizure of Power," in *The Nazi Machtergreifung*, Peter D. Stachura (ed.), (London,1983), pp. 101-23.

[55] Wagner, *Ausgewählte Schriften*, II, p. 332.

[56] Elizabeth Fehrenbach, *Wandlung des deutschen Kaisergedankens, 1871-1918* (Munich, 1969), pp. 89 ff.

[57] Manning, in *The Americans: 1976*, p. 258.

[58] Gordon A. Craig, "Die Regierung Hoover und die Abrüstungskonferenz," in *Internationale Beziehungen in der Weltwirtschaftskrise 1929-1933*, Josef Becker and Klaus Hildebrand (eds.) (Munich, 1980), pp. 101-127.

[59] Golo Mann, "Konrad Adenauer: Staatsmann der Sorge," *Frankfurter Allgemeine Zeitung*, February 14, 1976.

[60] "Schmidt Talks about U.S., Nuclear Plans and Europe," *San Francisco Chronicle*, May 28, 1983, p. 10.

[61] Rudolf Augstein, "The Germans to the Front," *Der Spiegel*, 37:22 (May 30, 1983), p. 18.

[62] Marion Gräfin Dönhoff, "Warum ist Amerika so ideologisch?," *Die Zeit*, June 17, 1983, p. 1.

[63] See David Gress, "What the West Should Know about German Neutralism," *Commentary*, January, 1983, pp. 26-31.

CULTURAL CHANGE AND GENERATION CHANGE IN POSTWAR WESTERN GERMANY

by Richard Löwenthal

The purpose of this essay is to discuss the value changes in the Federal Republic of Germany from the angle of the relation of "Western" and "non-Western" elements in its culture. The underlying assumption is that this relation is of crucial importance for the long-term development of West Germany's attitudes towards the Western democracies in general and the United States in particular.

In order to understand the postwar evolution of West German culture, we must start from the fact that the defeat of Hitler's Third Reich and the ensuing partition of Germany marked not only the political collapse of a Great Power, but a cultural watershed for its people. From its origin in the early Middle Ages, the German nation had at first developed as an integral part — in its own consciousness, a central part — of the Western civilization then emerging from the fusion of the heritage of classical antiquity and of the contributions of the Germanic and Celtic "Barbarians" of the North under the influence of the Western form of Christianity. Medieval Germany fully shared both (1) in the pluralistic structure of that civilization with its dualism of secular and spiritual authority, its plurality of estates, it autonomous cities and early universities, and (2) in its cultural values stressing the role of reason as a key to an understanding of the world order, the inalienable rights of the individual with the corresponding responsibilities, the binding force of voluntarily entered communities and of the legal order, and the importance of work as a fulfilment of man's role in society. Germany therefore also shared in the unique dynamic potential of Western civilization based on its pluralistic structures and cultural values. A first loosening of Germany's Western ties arose during the Lutheran reformation with its rejection of the medieval morality of pious works. Elsewhere this led to a new, "bourgeois" moral code sanctifying the duties of the daily round, but it was frozen here at an early stage producing no new moral code beyond the double emphasis on the inner voice of conscience and the obedience to secular authority. Germany, thrown back in its economic and social development by the Thirty Years' War and retarded in the growth of its middle class, continued to make major contributions to Western culture by its music, poetry and philosophy. The widespread emphasis on a combination of inward-looking faith and outward obedience, however, began to show some kinship with the life style created by Russian orthodoxy rather than with the self-confident activism of the emerging Western bourgeoisie.

If German culture may thus be said to have been in a peculiar fringe situation within the Western fold by the time of the French political and the British industrial revolutions, a more and more divergent emphasis led to its increasingly separate development in the course of the 19th century. The impact first of the rise of an active German national consciousness in the course of resistance to the conquests of Napoleon, and second of the growth of German industry and the restoration of German national unity under an authoritarian regime with a privileged military class was instrumental. At the end of that century, the sense of belonging to a common Western civilization had largely disappeared in Germany. On the eve of World War I, a man of the worldwide horizon of Max Weber was able to speak of a special mission of German culture "between Anglo-Saxon materialism and Russian barbarism."

The resulting *Zwischenkultur* (in-between culture), in the name of which the Germans may be said to have fought in two world wars, was characterized not only by a belated and correspondingly aggressive form of messianic nationalism, but also — contrary to the intentions of liberal men like Max Weber — by a strongly anti-liberal and anti-democratic bias. It survived the defeat of 1918 and the collapse of the empire and soon reemerged as the dominant cultural current in the Weimar Republic. True, the creators of the Weimar constitution and the only reliable democratic forces supporting it throughout — the Social Democrats and the main part of the Catholic Center — were looking to the West. They, however, got little encouragement from there in the formative years of the young republic, and by 1920 they no longer represented a majority. The negative majority of conservative nationalists and Communists was anti-Western not only politically, but also culturally. While the Communists looked to a Russia of which they knew little, the nationalists, including the small, elitist groups of "national revolutionaries," remained in the tradition of the *Zwischenkultur*. It was from its ideas also that Adolf Hitler concocted his ideological brew, and from its followers that he recruited the bulk of his movement.

By driving the anti-democratic nationalism of the *Zwischenkultur* to its most absurd and inhuman conclusions, Hitler produced its collapse along with that of his regime. After his "mission" of mass destruction and mass annihilation, the idea of a special German cultural mission between West and East is literally no longer imaginable. But it is important for our historical understanding to be aware that the conversion of important numbers of Germans away from the tenets of anti-democratic nationalism and towards a return to Western values *preceded* the collapse of the Third Reich; it was a product of the experience of its regime, not only of its *defeat*.

I am using the term of conversion deliberately, because one of its early and formative elements was a religious phenomenon; I am speaking of what can only be described as the moral revival within the Protestant Church. At least in its Lutheran main branch, its dignitaries had preserved its traditional authoritarian attitude and supported the anti-democratic Right throughout the Weimar Republic. When the new Nazi regime decided to destroy its autonomy by creating a pro-nazi movement of "German Christians" and appointing a "Reich bishop" from its own rank, the old leadership tried to oppose the change but was decisively defeated in Nazi-organized "church elections." Now, though, a counter-movement of independent-minded theologians and regional church leaders, partly influenced by the smaller "reformed" (Calvinist) branch and by the teachings of Karl Barth, rose to defend not only the formal autonomy of the church, but also the substance of Christian ethics against the new regime. The voice of conscience could no longer be reconciled with obedience to an authority with an increasingly obvious anti-Christian character. The *"Pfarrernotbund"* (Pastoral Emergency League) and the *"Bekennende Kirche"* (Confessional Church) included hard-boiled conservative nationalists like Niemöller as well as reforming innovators close to the ideas of a Reinhold Niebuhr. Still, they all helped Nazi victims and risked the concentration camps, where quite a few suffered and some of them were killed. Yet the survivors of this movement were to exert a formative influence on German Protestantism in the postwar period.

Both Protestant and Catholic churchmen and believers were also to take part, as individuals, in the conspiratorial circles in which traditional conservatives from the nobility and the military establishment met with prominent Social Democratic and trade union leaders before and during the war in unsuccessful but brave attempts first to preserve peace and finally to overthrow Hitler. Their attempts culminated in the preparations for the failed coup of July 20, 1944. In our context, the symptomatic importance of those circles is that many conservatives of the traditional upper classes (which had accepted if not positively welcomed Hitler's rise to power for nationalist reasons while expecting from him an authoritarian regime preserving the rule of law) had been profoundly shocked both by his reckless aggressiveness without and his terrorist rule within. They had come to realize that a rule of law in modern conditions could only be restored in a democracy — and peace only by an understanding with the West. The story has not yet been written of how many once prominent trade unionists and Social Democrats survived Hitler's rule thanks to the quiet protection by conservative acquaintances in the army or the bureaucracy — and how many of the latter have come through the mill of postwar de-nazification thanks to the testimony of those one-time proteges.

The statement that Germany arose out of the debacle "without elites" would make the rise of the Federal Republic inexplicable if it were true, but it is not. Owing to the subterranean process described here, both more experienced democrats and more formerly anti-democratic conservatives converted to democracy survived the collapse than anybody outside Germany could have expected. And they survived not only with a basic democratic consensus that had never existed before, but also with a common Western orientation.

Finally, the followers of the Soviet-oriented and anti-democratic mass-movement of the Communist party, which had counted millions of voters at the end of the Weimar Republic, had also undergone a profound change.

This applied less to those leaders who had survived Stalin's purges in the Soviet Union or Hitler's concentration camps at home, and more to the rank and file who had served in his armies, particularly at the Eastern front. The less they had believed in the anti-Soviet propaganda of Goebbels, the more they had been shocked by what they saw of the living conditions in the Russian countryside; moreover, what they learned about the atrocities committed in Russia by the SS and sections of the German armies was sufficient to fill them with a justified fear of Russian retaliation. When they returned, it was no longer their hopes but rather their fears that pointed Eastward. They were no longer Communists.

So far, I have concentrated on changes that occurred underground before and during Hitler's war. But the moment of return was also the moment of visible choice. Long before any Germans were offered a chance to cast their ballots under the occupying powers, millions of them voted with their feet by a gigantic trek from East to West. Not only families fled from their ransacked and burned homes in the Eastern territories in search of shelter in the Western part of the country; soliders, too, left their units in the East whenever they had a chance and hurried West in the hope of falling into Western rather than Russian captivity. There was no propaganda that told them to do so; the Cold War had not yet started, and Hitler wanted nobody to leave the front line while he was alive.

In the hour of despair, though, millions of Germans put their last hope in that "Western humanity" they had been told for many years to despise. And on the whole, despite occasional excesses in the West as well (for instance, by American soldiers who had never believed the "atrocity stories" about Hitler's concentration camps, and grew mad with rage when they actually saw them) their hope was justified.

The tremendous physical upheaval of defeat, destruction and mass flight was followed by a no less profound mental upheaval, no longer confined to intellectual elites. The terrible urgency of the struggle for survival and the search for lost family members in a thoroughly disorganized country did not prevent the effort to rethink, but rather stimulated it in the early period of misery. In the years before the currency reform, Germans read more serious books and periodicals and conducted more serious discussions in small, private circles than for many years before or after.

The most effective contribution of the "re-education" effort of the Western powers to this rethinking was the spread of detailed knowledge of the crimes of the Nazi regime among the millions of Germans who had known little about the concentration camps except that they existed, and that they themselves wished on no account to become their inmates. The full extent of the policy of mass annihilation, finally accepted as fact by the overwhelming majority of Germans, caused a shock that not only destroyed the former nationalist world view, but for a considerable time numbed the national consciousness particularly among the younger generation returning from the war. While the drama of total defeat after years of victories convinced them that Germany would never again play the role of a Great Power, the horror of Hitler's crimes made many of them wish to see themselves no longer as

Germans, but simply as decent human beings or possibly good Europeans. They wanted to turn their eyes and minds away from their German identity and indeed from German history. In the great majority of cases, this was not yet an active moral decision to prevent forever a repetition of such crimes — that was to come much later — but a flight from the unbearable vision.

The Western powers were far from wishing that the defeated Germans should make a choice among the victors. In fact, for years they banished any criticism of the Soviets from the licensed German press. Nonetheless, the Germans, soon after the physical choice of the Great Trek, had to make a political choice as well. The Soviets had gone ahead in licensing German political parties, and before the end of 1945 began to press for a fusion of the Social Democrats with the Communists, who proved less attractive despite all the official favors showered on them. In the Soviet zone that fusion was forced through, in some cases by sending reluctant Social Democrats back to the concentration camps. In Berlin, still undivided under four-power control, this was less easy, but the Soviets wanted a unified party for the whole of occupied Germany to be led from Berlin. Though some Western journalists and labor officials of the controlling authorities understood the danger, their leading personalities were at first indifferent to such *"querelles allemandes"* or even thought it inevitable that "Communism would come to the Rhine." But the Berlin Social Democrats insisted on a ballot of all members which, carried out in the Western sectors, yielded a decisive majority against fusion with the Communists in early 1946. In October of the same year, the only free elections ever held in postwar Germany under four-power control made the anti-fusion Social Democrats the strongest party in Berlin (where the Communists had been the strongest party in the last years before Hitler seized power!). The Communist "fusion party" lagged far behind. It was a signal indicating how the Germans in the Soviet zone would vote if free to choose, and the later elections in the Western zones soon confirmed the weakness of the Communists.

We are thus entitled to say that the postwar Germans, wherever they were free to make a political choice, made a choice for the West and for a democratic party system in the early period of misery and furious rethinking. This was all *before* the appearance of visible conflict between the powers, before the Truman doctrine and Marshall plan, and of course before the West German currency reform, the Berlin blockade and the calling of a West German constituent assembly, none of which would have been possible without that choice. It was a decision for Western freedom under law, produced by the absence of both under Hitler's rule — and Stalin's.

In the circumstances, that decision implied the partition of Germany, as the Soviets were clearly unwilling to permit democratic institutions of the Western type in their zone. A number of West German leaders, aware of that danger, hesitated to make use of the Western powers' offer that the West German State government should call a constituent assembly. Still, the argument that democratic self-government in the greater part of Germany was better than none at all, and that the attraction of the new state might make an impact on the Soviet zone as well, led them to agree. Parallel with the assembly's work, cooperation with Western Europe and the United States started in the framework of the Marshall Plan, while the Berliners' steadfastness under Stalin's blockade and their decisive support by the Anglo-American airlift created a strong emotional tie between the free Germans and the Western powers. The period of postwar chaos and postwar isolation was over for the West Germans, even before the Federal Republic was founded in May 1949 and formed its first government later in the same year. The period of postwar economic misery was also over once the currency reform was introduced, as a necessary pre-condition for West Germany's role in the Marshall Plan, in June 1948. Price controls and rationing were abolished on West German initiative at the same time.

The end of postwar chaos and postwar misery ended also the period of furious rethinking and opened the period of furious rebuilding — the Adenauer era. The electoral victory of the Christian Democrats under predominantly Catholic leadership made the new state a conservative democracy, criticized by many intellectuals of the Left as a "restoration regime." Yet in fact it was a type of regime, and governed a type of society, that Germany had not known in the past. It was radically different from Hitler's dictatorship in its rule of law and pluralism of parties. Because the Conservatives, including quite a few former servants of the Nazi government, had become convinced supporters of the democratic constitution, it was also utterly different from the precarious Weimar Republic. Its armed forces, when they came to be created in the framework of NATO after a long political fight, never attempted to become a state within the state, as they had been under the empire or the Weimar Republic.

In its social structure and in its manners, the new state was both more mobile than any German society before Hitler, and more bourgeois and civil than any previous Germany at all. Several factors made for a far less rigid stratification than in the German past: the economic and social upheavals caused first by Hitler's regime and then by its collapse; the breaking up of the cohesion of the nobility first by Hitler and then by the Communist regime of East Germany; the rise of a new managerial generation in the war economy and the postwar industrial reorganization; the renewal of the high judiciary and police in the course of de-nazification and the much more limited shake-up of the high bureaucracy in general; and last but not least the co-determination rights granted to the trade unions in the coal and steel industry. At the same time, a deep-seated reaction against the universal rudeness and lack of manners in the omni-present Nazi organizations, from the army to the SA and Hitler youth, made for an increased sense of distance, of respect for one's fellow man, in short for civility which Germany had not known before. This was true even on the part of policemen and officials facing the public behind a window. Altogether, German society had become much more bourgeois and thus much more similar to other Western societies. The outward "Americanization" of many aspects of the style of life, to which the Germans could oppose less traditional reserves than the French or the

British, was one superficial indicator for this profound change.

Yet while there was no restoration of pre-democratic institutions and pre-modern social stratification, there was indeed in the years of West German recovery a restoration of elements of traditional authority, less in economic life, but more in the courts and bureaucracy, in schools and universities and in family life. This was, of course, an expression of the fact that the late achievement of a German democracy had come about without a democratic revolution.

It was not, in the main, imposed from above, but was largely based on a deep longing among the people for stability and certainty after all the shocks and all the frightening confusion of the last decades. Part of the secret of Dr. Adenauer's ascendancy for more than a decade was that his personality, with it aura of calm, consistency and clarity of decision, corresponded ideally to this longing. Yet there was something artificial in the restoration of traditional forms of authority to fill the gap left first by the profound disorientation of an older generation homesick for a distant past and second by the exclusive preoccupation of a middle generation with its private effort to regain security and well-being. Soon, a younger generation was to rise in protest against it.

Adenauer's foreign policy of Western integration proved far-sighted as well as consistently popular with the majority of West Germans. The Social Democrats — who had opposed the treaties rearming the Federal Republic as part of the Atlantic Alliance not on principle, but on the grounds that further attempts at Western negotiations with the Soviets in the hope of achieving the reunification of both German states in freedom should first be made — loyally accepted the treaties after ratification. And by 1960 they also admitted that the decision had been right. Adenauer, though, had supported his justified pro-Western policy by the doubtful argument that Western integration, including military integration, was also the surest way to achieve unification. When the East Germans, during the international crisis produced by Khrushchev's "Berlin Ultimatum" (1958), divided the city of Berlin by a wall in August 1961 in order to stop the growing escape of East German subjects through this loophole to the West, that argument thoroughly lost its credibility.

Many of the younger Germans began to conclude that as reunification seemed unobtainable, it was better to improve relations with the East German state by recognizing its international status in order to restore at least human contacts with it inhabitants. In fact, the West German government's insistence on non-recognition both of the East German, non-democratic state and of the Polish rights to the former German territories handed to them by the Soviets in 1945 had been a concession to the national feelings of the refugees from Eastern Germany and the expellees from the newly Polandized territories. This amounted to a tactical concession to nationalism by a man who himself was anything but a nationalist. It backfired, however, with a young generation that began to ask more questions about the share of its elders in Hitler's crimes and to call for reconciliation with the Polish people on the basis of mutual forgiveness, as a remarkable memorandum of the German Evangelical Church put it in 1965. For most Germans, 1945 had brought a turning away from the horrors of Nazism and a numbed acceptance of the new realities. It had taken a generation for the moral conclusions to be consciously drawn, and the "Westernized" Lutheran Church was to play an important part in the process.

The same young generation also began to raise persistent questions about the Nazi past which the teachers surviving from that period tended to ignore. For some years, these young people had begun to rebel against their elders in family, school and university, and doubt about the unanswered questions quickly turned into a general attack on what I have called the "restoration of traditional authority." As reform had been too long delayed, and as many of the exponents of traditional authority had what appeared to the young as a tarnished past, the student movement in particular quickly assumed features of a militant anti-authoritarianism. Moreover, while German postwar anti-Communism lost its traditional national legitimation in the eyes of the young critics, international resistance to Communism appeared discredited at the same time by the war in Vietnam. The critique of American policy was eagerly picked up from the American student protest movement. Among the theoretically-minded German protesters, the critique of particular policies quickly led to the spread of neo-Marxist doctrines "explaining" those policies as the necessary products of a declining capitalism turning into fascism. While the influence of the Communist party on the movement remained limited, it adopted Ho Chi Minh and "Che" Guevara as its heroes and Herbert Marcuse, whose neo-Marxism had acquired marked neo-Bakuninist features in his old age, as its guru. Altogether, a movement which had begun its protest against traditional authority under the Frankfurt school's banner of a belated Enlightenment for Germany came to show increasing features of a romantic relapse into a cult of naked force. At first, it appeared as the first serious anti-Western movement in postwar Germany; yet it was rather the manifestation of a general Western malaise in the special conditions of the German borderland of the West.

The German student protest reached its high point after 1966, when a temporary economic recession had given rise to the formation of a "National Democratic Party" on the Right and its early successes in a number of state elections. This party expressed the homesickness mainly of a number of older people for the less unsavory aspects of the Nazi past, but lacked the militancy of a true neo-Nazi movement. The same recession also led to the fall of the government of Adenauer's successor Ludwig Erhard, and to the formation of a "Grand Coalition" government of Christian Democrats and Social Democrats.

The Grand Coalition succeeded in overcoming the recession and taking the first steps towards a normalization of relations with Germany's Eastern neighbors. Its progress, though, was minimal owing partly to Soviet, Polish and East German distrust of its intentions and partly to the strength of resistance within the CDU to anything smacking of recognition of the postwar territorial status quo. At the same time, the Grand Coalition passed the long-prepared "emergency legislation" intended to make West German sovereignty more complete by making the rights of emergency action still reserved by the former occupying powers superfluous. Nobody in the government believed for a moment that an emergency was near or that the law was needed to justify exceptional measures in the foreseeable future; the text of the law also contained safeguards against an abuse of the new powers that could stand comparison with the best similar provisions in other democracies. The radical Left, nevertheless, with the student movement in the vanguard, interpreted it as a preparation for suppressing democratic freedoms. This combined with the rise of "National Democrats" seemed like proof to them that the Federal Republic was faced with an impending decisive struggle between the supporters of the new fascist regime they feared and the revolution of which they dreamed. It was in this situation that the student movement undertook to reach out beyond the universities and create an "extra-parliamentary opposition"; its demonstrations caused much violence on the streets, but they failed in their chief aim to win substantial numbers of industrial workers as allies for the radical students.

The movement was effectively ended by the outcome of the federal elections of the fall of 1969. They not only demonstrated the waning of the "National Democrats" who failed to win a single seat, but led to the formation of the Social-Liberal coalition under Willy Brandt. Instead of the final battle between fascism and revolution imagined by the young radicals, the West German voters had once more demonstrated the irrelevance of fascist tendencies in their country, and had installed a government of democratic reform. While a remnant of the student movement ossified in the ranks of the Communist party and of Maoist or other dissident Communist sects, most of its activists reacted to the dramatic refutation of their prophecies differently. They interpreted their formula of a "march through the institutions" by joining the Social-Democratic party in order to fight for a Marxist revival there, or by seeking jobs as teachers or in the organs of public opinion. In fact, the radical students quickly conquered the Young Socialists organization, which soon assured its decline. Within a few years, though, the most able among them had turned into authentic Social Democrats committed to Western democracy. On the opposite pole, the tiny band of terrorists drew the extreme conclusion of the attempt to make a revolution without support among the people.

The direct political effect of the student revolt was confined to a series of university reforms conceded by state governments and later both moderated and generalized by a federal "framework law." These reforms combined necessary and useful corrections of authoritarian structures with forms of political student influence on curriculum, examination standards and professorial appointments which lowered the level of many German universities for a number of years. There were also more general effects of a more lasting character: the student revolt had been the most dramatic demonstration of value changes in important parts of the young generation of the Federal Republic. These changes affected both political and private attitudes and were to exert continued influence on the climate of West German life.

Among the political changes, the new moral concern about the Nazi past and distrust of people who appeared as its surviving representatives was widespread. The anti-authoritarian emphasis was less particular to Germany, though probably strongest here, because the dusty atmosphere of restored traditional authority had been most strongly resented by the young. A related attitude was the growing longing for a more direct democracy than the representative parliamentary institutions could offer. While the student ideologue had dreamed of the model of the Paris Commune of 1871 or of the Russian Soviets before they came under Bolshevik party control, what actually developed in the following years was a widespread tendency not to replace representative democracy, but to supplement it by a welter of local "citizen's initiatives." On international issues, while the student cult of revolutionary heroes did not catch on among the younger generation at large, the criticism of the Vietnam war was gradually accepted more widely. This left behind the potential for a more critical attitude towards the United States.

Most of the value changes were not specifically German; instead, they represented common developments throughout the Western world. In many cases they were clearly taken over from the United States, but with "German thoroughness" added. This applies, on one side, to the "sexual revolution" in actual behavior, in the frank public discussion and presentation of sexual detail, and the widespread toleration of sexual "deviations" down to the spreading of tolerated pornography. Yet in apparent contrast to this breakthrough of a hedonism freed from many traditional moral inhibitions, though by no means generally excluding a new morality, there was also a noticeable tendency among the young to despise many of the venal pleasures of the "consumer society" and particularly their conspicuous display. It did not last with most of the young when they grew older, and thus had no measurable influence on the market of such "mass luxuries" as cars or motorbikes or television sets or on the prosperity of restaurants or bars.

But the fact that it had become fashionable to look down on the amenities of the capitalist world — the radical student leaders had spoken of "consumption terror" — had a noticeable effect on the zeal to earn the money needed to buy them. It became equally fashionable to deprecate the value of performance in work (*Leistung*), particularly, but not only, in its competitive aspect. This, too, did not last when industrial workers grew older and had families; at least I am aware of little evidence for a decline of performance in German industry, and its export figures tend to contradict it. Still, the anti-performance attitude was quite visible in the schools, often encouraged by teachers from the student movement, and for a time in the universities. It was also noticeable in branches of work where the individual worker's responsibility was reduced by new technology, such as that of bookkeepers and bank employees by computers. And it was rampant among people holding jobs from which they could not be dismissed, as in the civil service and parts of the public services.

Besides the contradictory tendencies towards unfettered hedonism, contempt of the "consumers' society" and decline of working zeal, West Germany in the 1960s also got its share of such international phenomena as drug addiction, violent non-political youth gangs and pseudo-religious youth sects. Behind all those aspects of youth disorientation, of change in values or plain loss of values, two more basic changes could be noticed. One was the "generation gap" which is apparent in the tangible sense that both the loosening of family ties and the speed of change in living conditions made it (1) more difficult for the young to discuss their problems with elders who had not grown up with car trips, television and the pill, and (2) more natural for them to develop "other-directed characters," in David Riesman's description, taking their cues from the "peer group." The other basic change was, possibly more in Germany than elsewhere, the loss of the unthinking faith in more or less automatic progress which in the course of the 19th century had come to shape the world view of many millions of "secularized" Westerners more effectively than any religious traditions. The experience of the steady progress of science and technology and the long-run progress of the economy had for a number of Western generations seemed to offer a guarantee also for progress towards more freedom, reasonableness, security and peace. It had taken two world wars, the tyrannies of Hitler and Stalin, and the threat of the atomic bomb to shake that optimistic world view; even then, it seemed still to have revived for a time in the generation engaged in the rebuilding after Hitler's war and Germany's defeat. But I notice little of such trust in the future and much thinly hidden despair in the German generation of the students' revolt, for all its brave talk about revolution.

The degree of value change that had taken place in the West German population in general by the time the Social-Liberal government assumed power in late 1969 was, of course, far less radical than that of the rebellious students, but the majority had moved somewhat in the same direction. The wish for a more liberal and less traditional atmosphere, for greater scope for people to shape the style of their own lives, was shared by millions of solid citizens who had no sympathy whatever for rioting in the streets. The sexual revolution was clearly a majority phenomenon, and so was a fairly strong tendency of the young to emancipate themselves from the advice of their elders. There was widespread pessimism about the future, but a growing awareness that freedom and peace were not guaranteed by any automatism of history but depended on conscious action. In short, there was a mood favoring a government of reform: a government that believed (1) that an orderly and secure life for the citizens of the Federal Republic could by now be maintained with less traditional authority and more democratic participation, and (2) that the country's role in the world in general and in the Western Alliance in particular would be better served if, in its relations with its Eastern neighbors, it ceased to make concessions to the out-of-date nationalism of a minority.

The *Ostpolitik* of the Social-Liberal government had one aspect connected with the general policies of the Atlantic Alliance, a second aspect concerning West Germany's relations with its Eastern neighbors, and a third aspect concerning West German domestic politics. For the Atlantic Alliance, which under American leadership wished to stabilize the European situation as part of a policy of detente corresponding to the arrival of an approximate nuclear parity between the superpowers, West German non-recognition of the German Democratic Republic (GDR) and of the German-Polish frontier had become an obstacle to this policy, particularly as the three Western powers were bound by treaty with the Federal Republic not to recognize the GDR against Bonn's will. West German acceptance of a *modus vivendi* with the Soviet bloc on the basis of the territorial status quo would therefore be a welcome aid to Western detente policy in general and to the negotiation of a more secure status for West Berlin by the four powers in particular.

From the aspect of West German relations with the East, such a *modus vivendi* on the basis of the status quo had the minimum aim of increasing West Germany's and West Berlin's security by both avoiding isolation from the Western allies and normalizing relations with the Soviet bloc. In the case of the GDR, such normalization would also help "to maintain the substance of the German nation" by restoring, in the absence of a reunification of the two German states, at least the human contacts among Germans on both sides of the border. In the view of some early advocates of *Ostpolitik*, it could also have the maximum aim of "change by *rapprochement*" — of promoting liberalizing changes in the Communist regimes by removing the popular fear of "German revanchism" so far deliberately maintained by those regimes. In fact, even before the full unfolding of *Ostpolitik*, the "Prague Spring" of 1968 and its crushing by Soviet bloc military intervention had shown both the potential for such liberalizing change and the determination of the Soviet leadership to prevent it by every means in its power, but the minimum aim of normalization remained valid.

From the aspect of German domestic politics, *Ostpolitik* required the overcoming of the traditional nationalist resistance of the German expellees from the East and those other West German citizens who still believed that the German cause could be served by standing pat on the "legality" of the frontiers of 1937 pending a peace treaty. This resistance had effectively prevented the government of the Grand Coalition from getting into serious negotiations with the East, and the same resistance led in 1972 to a parliamentary crisis in which the Brandt government was nearly overthrown. It was effectively broken by the subsequent general elections which made Brandt's party the strongest in the Bundestag for the first time in the history of the Federal Republic.

The negotiations with the East, independently initiated by Bonn to the early dismay of the U.S. government, were then carried out in close understanding with the Western powers. Indeed, they could not have achieved final success without full cooperation with the Allies. The Federal Republic could not have risked permitting international recognition of the GDR without a satisfactory agreement on the status of and access to West Berlin; such an agreement could only be negotiated between the four victorious powers. The net result of the negotiations was thus that while West German relations with the Soviet bloc were for the first time becoming as nearly normal as those of the other nations of the Atlantic Alliance, West Germany's ties to that alliance became even closer than before, and its role within it more influential. Bonn's role in bringing about the acceptance of Britain's entry into the European Community, which France had previously resisted, was one expression of that increased influence. In sum, it may be said that the Federal Republic managed in the Social-Liberal period (including the important later role of Helmut Schmidt's government in world affairs) to reduce the strength of nationalist tendencies among its population, to improve national ties between the ordinary citizens of West and East Germany, and to increase its weight in world politics in general and in the Atlantic Alliance and the European Community in particular.

The domestic reforms of this period chiefly dealt with changes in the code of law, social relations and education. The changes in the code of law primarily concerned an improvement of the position of women in family law, an easing of conditions for legal abortion and in the legal status of homosexuals in penal law, as well as adjustments to the sexual revolution concerning publications and the cinema. In another field, freedom of non-violent demonstrations was considerably extended despite much opposition. During the height of the terrorist campaign, however, some limitations of the contacts of imprisoned terrorists with the outside world were also imposed.

In social relations, the Federal Republic continued, both before and after the onset of the world economic recession, to have a remarkable degree of industrial peace. Particularly under the Schmidt government, the Chancellor's close relations to trade union leaders and the custom of regular meetings between them and the employers' leaders contributed significantly to this. During this period, too, the principle of co-determination by representation of the labor side on the boards of industrial firms was extended by law from the coal and steel industries, where it had been in force since Adenauer's time, to other major industrial works. The social insurance system, remarkably well developed even in the period of conservative rule and still somewhat expanded in the early years of the Social-Liberal coalition, began to suffer increasing financial difficulties in the years of recession as the decline of employment both reduced its income and increased its burdens.

Most controversial were the reforms in educational policy, in which primary competence rests with the states. One field in which West Germany had been lagging behind many other Western states was the effort to equalize educational chances for children from different family backgrounds — to avoid a situation in which all children from rich and academic families should get access to higher education and nearly all from poorer and less educated families should remain outside, regardless of their talents and efforts. The creation of comprehensive schools in which the admission to higher levels is only gradually decided has made an important beginning here, and despite much criticism due partly to class prejudice, but partly also to initial mistakes in detail, I believe it is likely to last.

Far more doubtful is the value of some of the changes in the curriculum. While the tendency to attach reduced importance to classical studies is an international trend in the Western world, the attempts to abolish history as a separate subject in the school progam may be unique to some West German states in the 1970s. It was justified by government ministers concerned with the need to expand the time allotted to basic social and political education, within which a certain amount of historical information would also find its place. In fact, this happened at a moment when much of the social and political education had fallen into the hands of "radical" teachers formed by the students' revolt. These teachers told their pupils little about the purpose and functioning of democratic institutions, much about the need to criticize them, and nothing about history except isolated examples to justify their own political views. Those irresponsible experiments have in the meantime been largely corrected, but the victims remain with us, with their shocking lack of historical and political knowledge, as part of the young generation of today.

Finally, the attempt to "democratize" educational institutions, sanctioned by legislation for new university statutes, took the unfortunate form of handing university self-government to separate and more or less equal elected bodies representing the professors, the teaching assistants, the students and the non-academic staff. Introduced while the student revolt was in full swing and with the undisguised intent to appease it, these statutes led for years to a climate of factional political intrigue and bitterness in most universities, to a substantial decline in examination standards, and to quite a number of appointments of incompetent candidates to tenured positions. At the same time, they also led to the appointment of a few highly qualified scholars who might have had difficulty succeeding in the traditional university because of their left-wing views. As the student revolt receded, most of the students lost interest in the election of their representatives — leaving the influential positions to what was now a declining radical minority. In the end, after the German Supreme Court had forced some correction in the laws, the state governments developed the habit of interfering more and more in university decisions, often without convincing justification: damage to the autonomy of German universities has been a major long-run effect of the failed reform.

The years during which the Social-Liberal coalition governed the Federal Republic of Germany coincided with a period of major changes both in public thinking about economic problems and in the economic problems of the advanced industrial countries themselves. The change in thinking began with the emerging public consciousness of the ecological dangers inherent in modern industrial technology and agricultural chemistry: dangers of the gradual poisoning of air, water and land, which during the postwar period of rapid and steady economic growth had reached a point which by the end of the 1960s was causing general concern throughout the Western world. It was followed by the debate about the "limits of growth," started by the book published by the Club of Rome with that title. Its claim that the exhaustion of raw materials and energy resources on a limited planet would force, within a foreseeable time, an absolute end of economic growth was rejected by most economists; the grounds were that not only the discovery of additional resources, but above all the use of alternative materials with the help of new technology would always be possible. Still, the importance of the fact that even the *temporary* exhaustion of *particular* resources was likely to impose repeatedly at least particular and temporary limits on growth was made obvious with the first "oil shock." The first shock, caused by the Arab boycott in the course of the Yom Kippur war, and the subsequent shocks, caused by the price increases of the OPEC monopoly, were to become major causes — though not, of course, the only cause of a lasting worldwide recession.

The West German government did more than most other Western governments to protect the natural environment from pollution, but it did not do enough to keep pace with the growing danger. It also was more successful in limiting, for a number of years, the recession and the mass unemployment due to it than were most other Western countries. In the end, though, it too succumbed to its full force. While the impact of actual economic suffering was thus delayed in the Federal Republic to a remarkable degree, discussion of both the ecological dangers and the limits of growth had a major intellectual impact from an early date. They merged with the earlier factors of value change among the young generation (or rather, considering the lapse of time since the student revolt, generations).

It seems characteristic of such value change in flux that it assumes highly contradictory forms, at least for a time. At times the value change can be a constructive adjustment of earlier norms of behavior to new conditions in the basic values of modern Western societies; at other times it can be a romantic rejection of those basic values. Thus, few would deny that the importance of individual and competitive material success and corresponding conspicuous consumption has, in the course of the unfolding of industrial capitalism, been overstressed to a degree harmful to other human values. A greater stress on communal solidarity and mutual aid, as frequently found among the critical youth, is a healthy corrective tendency. Note, though, that it is clearly a quite different and socially harmful conclusion to jump from a lesser valuation of individual material success and consumption to a lesser valuation of performance in work. Equally, the new consciousness of man's responsibility for his natural environment, on which the future of mankind depends, is clearly a constructive and important value change. Yet it is absurd if critical young people condemn the entire age of "industrialism" as a wicked war against nature and juxtapose it with a "hippy" ideal on the grand scale. Similarly, there are compelling arguments for a policy of more selective economic growth which would be unlikely to restore the unprecedented pace of growth of the "golden age" that lasted through the quarter century from 1947 to 1972, but could effectively overcome the actual prolonged recession. There is no sense in rejecting economic growth in principle in favor of dreams of a stationary economy in a world in which the huge majority of mankind still lives in miserable conditions. The one set of new ideas aims at a realistic adjustment to changes in our conditions of existence; the other, at a romantic relapse from modernity.

This mixture of often sensible concrete proposals, put forward in many cases by local citizens' initiatives, and an irrational anti-industrialism ignoring the real conditions for the economic survival of humanity is characteristic of the "Green" movement in West Germany. It is a mixed movement also in its composition. Frustrated survivors of the Communist splinter groups are looking for a new political role in its ranks, and asocial addicts of street violence demonstrate on its fringes. The bulk of the movement, in contrast, is distinct from the generation of the students' revolt through its opposition to violence and lack of interest in communism or even Marxism. It detests the Marxist belief in an endless development of the "productive forces" and is utterly indifferent to the "achievements" of the Communist powers. Here again we see something typical for the critical part of today's West German young generation: it turned its back on the Young Socialists and preferred the Greens precisely because the Young Socialists ("Jusos") were led by neo-Marxist survivors of the student revolt. Finally, the "Jusos" themselves began to turn Green with envy.

More generally, the Green movement is anarchic rather than revolutionary. It has no centralist organization adapted to a struggle for power. The one thing it has taken over from the student movement is a belief in "basis democracy." This makes its internal life difficult but encourages local democratic initiatives on the one hand and diverse local conflicts with the democratically elected federal and state authorities on the other. Their idea of democratic participation is that all issues within a particular institution or locality should be decided by "those concerned." This is applied primarily to local issues of an ecological character, and it may often be useful where the issue is really local. Wherever the "local" issue is important in a context transcending the locality and has therefore to be decided from the angle of a broader economic interest or by the democratic organs of the state or federal government, the Greens oppose such decisions and call for "peaceful resistance" to their execution. Conflicts of this kind have arisen, for instance, over the building of nuclear power stations and the extension of the Frankfurt airport. This famous case involved a federal plan for the development of West German air traffic; the inhabitants of the surrounding localities opposed it because it deprived them of a wooded recreation area. As usual in such cases, the resistance did not remain peaceful and was finally overcome by police action.

Despite limited successes in a number of state elections as well as the latest federal election, the new Green party is suffering from growing internal troubles. It would certainly remain a fringe phenomenon of passing importance except for the rise of a much bigger issue: the national and international dispute about the stationing of American intermediate range missiles on West German soil, and the "Peace Movement" directed against it. For while the Green party gives determined support to the "Peace Movement," the actual and potential following of that movement considerably exceeds the following of the Greens. It is that movement that constitutes the first substantial threat ever to the Federal Republic's ties with the Atlantic Alliance in general and the United States in particular.

In order to understand the rise and impact of the peace movement in the Federal Republic of Germany, one has to keep in mind two basic facts about postwar Germany and two new developments of the last few years. The first basic fact is that Germany is divided into two states by the East-West conflict. The second is that although the superpowers have long kept large nuclear arsenals on the territories of their respective German allies, the German states have no nuclear weapons of their own and no control over those of the great powers.

The first new development relevant to our context is that since the late 1970s, the nuclear balance between the superpowers has become unstable. The second relevant new development is that the mood of an important part of the West German young generation has for some time been characterized by fear of imminent catastrophe, either ecological or nuclear.

What I have called the two basic facts about postwar Germany are statements of the obvious. The German people have lived for more than thirty years in a divided country, with nuclear weapons on their soil in the hands of opposing powers over whose actions they have no control. What is remarkable is the comparative equanimity with which they have lived in those conditions until a few years ago. We have to understand the reasons for that long equanimity in order to see the two new developments in context.

Until at least the middle 1960s, the United States possessed a clear nuclear superiority. This meant that the Soviets had no prospect of success in a nuclear war and the United States had no motive for it. It meant also that the Soviets could not risk a conventional attack in Europe because of the risk of American nuclear retaliation: deterrence in Europe worked all around. Even after the development of intercontinental missiles caused Khrushchev to believe for a time, during the Berlin and Cuban crises of 1958-62, that the U.S. superiority had sufficiently diminished to give him a chance for political advances in Europe short of war, President Kennedy was able to convince him that this had been an illusion. During this entire period, then, West German equanimity in the midst of the nuclear weapons of both superpowers was amply justified by American nuclear superiority.

When in the late 1960s the Soviets began to approach nuclear parity, the American administration of President Richard Nixon and security adviser Henry Kissinger decided to attempt to stabilize the strategic nuclear balance by negotiations rather than engage in a nuclear arms race in unstable conditions. The resulting first SALT agreement, while imperfect, became the core of the policy of detente, of which the *Ostpolitik* of the Federal Republic was a part. Instead of the former American nuclear superiority, the apparent stability of the nuclear balance together with the new general climate of East-West detente became a new reason for equanimity in the West German situation.

From the middle 1970s, however, while negotiations about SALT II proceeded, the stability of the strategic nuclear balance began to appear doubtful, while the nuclear balance in Europe was clearly upset by the Soviet development of the SS-20. From the West European and particularly the

West German point of view, acceptance of the new situation meant becoming open to nuclear blackmail. Countermeasures such as stationing corresponding weapons in Western Europe, including West Germany, carried the risk of a nuclear arms race in a situation of unstable balance — a situation that had never before existed. NATO's "double-track decision" of December 1979, urged by the West Europeans including the West German government of Helmut Schmidt, was an attempt to avoid both dangers by convincing the Soviets that their nuclear superiority in Europe would not be tolerated, but that an arms race could still be avoided by agreeing on a stable nuclear balance in that theater.

Yet from the moment that the threat of the SS-20 had become obvious, the threat of a nuclear arms race in a situation of unstable balance has remained and is bound to remain until some agreement on a stable balance takes place. But a nuclear arms race in a situation of unstable balance implies the fear of either side that the opponent may be tempted to a nuclear first strike in a situation when he feels temporarily superior, and there is the corresponding temptation to either side in apparently favorable conditions. Owing to the improbability of either side becoming sufficiently superior to the other for an annihilating first strike, and the necessary uncertainty of each side's estimates of the strength of its opponent, it remains highly *unlikely* that either would actually yield to a temptation implying such tremendous risks — but it is no longer *strictly impossible* in logic, as it was during the past decades of the conflicts.

It is the vague feeling of this ultimate uncertainty implied in a nuclear arms race in a situation of unstable balance which explains why the past equanimity has disappeared in many West German minds, and why fear of a nuclear holocaust has taken its place. That fear is strengthened by the general tendency of a young generation which has thoroughly lost the traditional optimism of the belief in automatic progress of modern humanity. It has already become, by the teachings of the ecologists, used to thinking in terms of ecological catastrophes due to the unforeseen consequences of modern technologies in general and of nuclear power stations in particular. That is where the second new development mentioned above converges with the first.

If the above analysis is correct, it follows that the decisive motive of the German peace movement is stark fear. This does not imply, however, that it is a mean, self-seeking motive: in most cases it is a moral fear for one's fellows as well, including the enemy — as the great influence of the movement in the churches underlines. With the vast majority of its followers, the demand for *unilateral* renunciation of armaments (which is common to the West German peace movement as distinct, for instance, from the American one) is *not* based on ideological sympathy with the Communist powers. The pious wish that they, too, should disarm unilaterally is not based on much hope, and the argument that the Soviets are models of peaceful conduct is much less heard than the argument that American medium-range missiles stationed in Germany would become the first targets for Soviet bombs.

Yet while there is little sympathy with the Soviet system in the peace movement, there is marked indifference to the threat of its expansion. The danger of annihilation of mankind by nuclear war is constantly stressed, the danger of a loss of freedom by Soviet blackmail is hardly ever mentioned by the spokesmen of the peace movement — including those of the substantial part of the Social Democratic party which supports them. Despite the geographical closeness of the Polish events, there is a lack of awareness of the human importance of the difference of democratic and dictatorial political systems in important sections of West German youth. Responsibility for this must be partly attributd to the defects of recent political and historical school education mentioned earlier, including the role of teachers from the student movement of the late 1960s. These teachers generally failed to pass on their own neo-Marxist ideas to their pupils effectively, but they often succeeded in making them skeptical about their democratic institutions. In part, the Social-Liberal governments of the past decade, which deserve praise for steadily increasing the West German defense effort along with the diplomacy of detente, must take some blame for paying too little attention to educating public opinion on the nature of the continuing East-West conflict.

Outside Germany, this problem is often oversimplified as a rising West German tendency towards "neutralism" or even "neutralist nationalism." There are very few West Germans, even within the peace movement, who would wish to leave the Western Alliance. Even fewer are sufficiently naive to think that such a move would cause the Soviets to release the GDR from its empire and thus become the prelude to German national reunification. But a considerably larger number, while taking the Alliance for granted, sees the conflict now merely as a rivalry between the superpowers, both of which are regarded as using ideological principles only as a disguise for naked power politics. Parallels between Soviet policies in Afghanistan and United States policies in Central America are frequently drawn, and not only on the radical Left. The wish is widespread that the Europeans should be left out of the troubles caused by superpower rivalry in other continents. This is neither neutralist nor nationalist, and least of all a tendency to detach Germany from Western culture; indeed, it is remarkable how much, despite all the difficulties of economic cooperation in the European Community, the ties to Western Europe are taken for granted. But it is true that, as during the Vietnam war and perhaps more strongly today, there is a fairly widespread critical detachment from the current policy of the United States, producing in a substantial minority a tendency towards "equidistance" from the superpowers.

This decline of confidence in American leadership, to use the broadest formula for the phenomenon, now becomes important in relation to the Geneva negotiations on the intermediate range missiles. For all the impact of the peace movement, a large majority of West Germans wishes for success at the Geneva negotiations. That represents the only safe alternative either to accepting Soviet nuclear superiority, with its potential of blackmail and ultimate loss of freedom, or to a nuclear arms race in a situation of unstable balance with its incalculable risks. Almost as large a majority would also accept a limited stationing of U.S. missiles on West German soil as a result of an interim agreement, and I would predict that attempts at resistance to stationing could be kept within manageable proportions in such a case. But in case of total failure of the negotiations, German popular support for a decision to station would depend largely on the impression that the Soviets alone are to be blamed for the failure — hence on the degree of trust in American leadership.

The West German public, of course, knows little and understands less about the course of the negotiations (and this includes myself as part of that public). But it knows all the more about the vagaries of American political rhetoric. While there have been many assurances of peaceful intentions during the period of negotiations, there have been nearly as many manifestos morally condemning the government sitting at the other side of the table — announcements of long-term, giant armament programs and proposals for combining an arms race with deliberate efforts to weaken, if not ruin the Russian economy. Not only West German, but many West European readers wonder whether this is the way to convince the Soviet leaders that the present American administration is a promising partner for the give and take of negotiations, particularly in the absence of readiness for an early top-level meeting as a means to create a minimum of mutual trust. I am afraid that while this impression remains, the readiness of the West German public to blame the Russians *alone* for a failure at Geneva will be less than enthusiastic — and the enforcement of stationing against the resistance of the peace movement will be less than easy.

To avoid any misunderstanding: I have always been convinced that a clear parliamentary majority for stationing would be found even in those unfavorable conditions, and I have always regarded any attempt to prevent the execution of such a democratic decision by physical "mass resistance" as both entirely illegitimate and bound to fail. But it was to be expected that in such conditions there would be, apart from the extremist fringe of violent "resisters" that does not exceed the dimensions of a police problem, a mass movement of peaceful "civil disobedience." This would include substantial numbers of believers from the Christian denominations with leading clergymen in the forefront, as well as substantial numbers of activists from the left wing of the Social Democratic party. Many of those critics who kept aloof both from violent resistance and peaceful civil disobedience would nevertheless blame both the Federal Republic's loyalty to the Alliance and the stability of its democratic institutions to a test in such unnecessarily poor conditions. The critics would blame the West German and American governments for having mismanaged a necessary effort to restore allied and German security.

In the aftermath of the "stationing crisis," one consequence may well be that a number of responsible West German opinion leaders, while reasserting their loyalty to the Atlantic Alliance, will begin to look for possibilities for a closer political cooperation of the leading West European members of the Alliance. This would be aimed at forming a European counterweight *within* the Alliance against what they regard as incalculable elements in the foreign and defense policy of the present United States administration.

It may seem unfortunate that the last section of this attempt to survey the generational and value changes in the Federal Republic of Germany from the angle of their impact on German-American relations since World War II has had to deal with factors that may cause a major crisis in those relations in the near but uncertain future. Hence, I wish to conclude this essay by summing up my general results in a more affirmative spirit.

I have found in all the postwar period no significant tendency for a return to the anti-democratic nationalism of what I have called the German *Zwischenkultur* of the 19th and the first half of the 20th century. On the contrary, the re-found sense of being part of a common Western culture has remained strong through successive German generations, and the important value changes have occurred largely parallel with similar changes throughout the Western world, though of course with national peculiarities. This is true, for instance (1) for the loss of much of the bourgeois distance in human relations new to postwar Germany, which disappeared in the new first-name style of later young generations throughout the West; (2) for the limited outbreaks of political violence in the course of the student revolt and again in the ecological movement; (3) for the widespread demand for a more direct democracy and for the new sense of ecological responsibility; (4) and not least for the emergence of a "peace movement" arising from the new sense of nuclear instability, and including the special role of the churches in that movement.

By contrast, traditional nationalism in the divided nation has tended to get weaker, not stronger, with the lapse of time, and neo-Nazi movements have remained recurrent but marginal. Probably the most dangerous form taken by nationalism in West Germany today appears as violent hostility against foreigners, practiced by unemployed youngsters who have neither finished school nor learned a trade — again a familiar phenomenon in other Western countries. As for Communism and the variants of revolutionary Marxism generally, they had their heyday in the course of the student revolt as, for instance, in France and Italy, and have faded since. The main difference is that in West Germany there exists no significant Eurocommunism, but rather a Soviet-controlled party which, although it exerts some indirect influence by infiltrating other movements has for several years polled an average of one percent of votes under its own name.

It is, of course, legitimate that neo-Nazi activities and other forms of political violence should be watched with greater concern in the country that once produced the unique horrors of Hitlerism. The same applies to abuses of police power, though these are probably less frequent than in most major Western nations. But while watchfulness is always justified, generalization from marginal phenomena is not. The real dangers, then, in my judgment, are not cultural and therefore fundamental; they are linked to particular political situations and therefore apt to prove ephemeral in nature. While the present differences with the United States about strategic and economic policies toward the Soviet Union and the Soviet bloc are potentially more serious than any in the past, not only the federal government in Bonn, but also a solid majority of Germans are convinced of their passing character — not least because they urgently wish them to pass.

Nearly four decades after the end of Hitler's war, I am convinced that the roots of the Western outlook have sunk in deeply in West Germany, and the reknotted ties with Western culture will hold whatever happens. That means that the ties of the Atlantic Alliance will also hold as long as the Soviet Union insists on retaining its European empire. I also remain convinced, however, that the maintenance of the ties of the Alliance will require a steady effort on the part of both our countries: on the German side, an effort to revive again and again the full understanding of the roots of the Alliance in a long-term conflict of systems and principles; and on the American side, a corresponding effort to keep alive the understanding that the forms of this long-term conflict must be kept under control if mankind is to survive.

THE WEST GERMANS, WESTERN DEMOCRACY, AND WESTERN TIES IN THE LIGHT OF PUBLIC OPINION RESEARCH

by Hans Peter Schwarz

"*Incertitudes allemandes*" was the title of a study by Pierre Vienot[1] which has been long forgotten and remains nearly forgotten today. Writing in 1931, the concerned author was fully justified in formulating his doubts. "*Incertitudes allemandes*" — the theme has since been struck repeatedly, heavy with gloomy premonitions, in the Western democracies associated with the Federal Republic as much as in Germany itself.

Usually, two main worries impose themselves. Anxiety as to the stability of West German democracy is one worry, uncertainty as to the West Germans' foreign political reliability the other. Certainly, the two are interconnected. The remarkable talent with which the Germans, early in the 1930s, first wrecked their own democracy and then proceeded to lay in ruins the rest of Europe remains unforgotten. Indeed, one followed the other.

But domestic political foolishness, excessive even by twentieth century standards, must not necessarily coincide with unscrupulousness or idiocy in the conduct of foreign policy. One does not step into the same river twice. It is theoretically possible that the Germans will remain good democrats, while simultaneously leaving nothing untried to upset the European balance by buffoonery in the field of foreign policy. In any event, to separate clearly the questions of democratic stability and basic foreign political orientations in the Federal Republic seems expedient.

It is true that a democracy requires the same tender care as a beautiful garden. But we have probably worried far too often and far too much during the past decades that the Federal Republic might go the way of the Weimar Republic. "Bonn is not Weimar,"[2] but a democracy like most others in Western Europe — with the great advantages inherent to this form of government, though also with the well-known internal tensions and strains. One will reach this conclusion even taking into account the challenges described by catch-phrases like "shifting values," "alternative movement," "alienation," "generation gap," etc.

By contrast, there have been more frequent grounds for worry lest the Federal Republic's integration into the Western security system cede to an irritating lability. Anyone familiar with the conditions for European stability is keenly aware of the key role played by the Federal Republic. Fundamental changes in Bonn's foreign policy, or even irritations of some duration, could shake the overarching system of the Western community and of East-West relations as much as an unlikely collapse of democracy in the Federal Republic.

The suspicion with which West German foreign policy is being observed by the West feeds on this insight throughout the 1950s, the 1960s, the 1970s, and again now in the early 1980s. Vast though the benefit may be which the Western world has derived from the Federal Republic's thirty years of foreign political reasonableness, its potential ability to do harm is equally large.

If endangered at all, Bonn does not face an end like the Weimar Republic in 1933, but rather that of the Czechoslovak Republic in 1938/39 or the French Third Republic in 1940, which, after all, had survived 65 difficult years: not suicide, then, but death by asphyxiation or decapitation at the hands of totalitarian neighbors!

The ensuing analysis is directed at underlying values and orientations observable with regards to the issue areas just outlined: the stability of democracy and basic attitudes in the field of foreign policy. Naturally, basic orientations are only one of many elements determining the politics of a nation. The currents of international affairs, coincidences of domestic politics, even incidents such as the death of a great leader or a personal power-struggle in a ruling party determine the course of history to a large extent.

How might the history of the Federal Republic have unfolded if the neo-National Socialist and authoritarian NPD had not barely missed the 5 percent threshold by a few tenths in the federal elections of 1969? There would have been no social-liberal coalition, no *neue Ostpolitik* by Willy Brandt, though instead perhaps a general shift to the right in German politics! Or, what would have been the effect of a different outcome in the federal elections of March 6, 1983?

A nation's politics, however, are not determined merely by parliamentary constellations, by the international system, and by many and frequently random conditions, but also by long-term values. The more diffuse the domestic and international scenery, the more important become these guiding ideals. They form the subject of the following essay.

Few phenomena which are the object of observation by political scientists and historians are harder to grasp or more ambiguous than basic orientations and their impact. This holds even more true if these vague objects are yet to be analyzed over longer periods of time.

Constraints of time and space prohibit a differentiated discussion of even a few factors in a short essay. A thorough elucidation of all findings is out of the question, but flash exposures are at least revealing. To reduce the observer's subjectivity somewhat, the following exposition will rely to a certain extent on data generated in polls conducted by the EMNID-Institut, the Institut für Demoskopie in Allensbach (IfD), and by the Sozialwissenschaftliches Forschungsinstitut der Konrad-Adenauer-Stiftung.[3]

Two complexes will be singled out:

(1) conditions for stability and critical factors affecting democratic constitional government in the Federal Republic of Germany;
(2) basic orientations relevant to foreign policy, especially tendencies circumscribed by the terms "nationalism," "neutralism," and "pacifist and anti-Western unilateralism."

Using these findings as a starting point, attempts will be made in each case to formulate general statements about the value system in the Federal Republic.

Stability of Democracy

There is a neurotic quality to the uncertainty which causes Germans time and again to wonder whether their democracy is truly secured. The relevant literature would fill a medium-sized library. Since 1949, political opponents have often been reproached for endangering the long-term existence of democracy. From the early years of the Federal Republic, demoscopic institutes, too, have forever been asking questions about systemic stability. From time to time, comforting or disturbing analyses are published which trigger a lively public discussion — for instance, about the time of the NPD's rise during the second half of the 1960s, or regarding leftist radicalism in the first half of the 1970s. Yet, all those who were concerned about democratic stability in postwar Germany have overlooked one basic orientation: the nearly unanimous consensus on the merits of constitutional government which existed not only within the party system but also in the multi-faceted world of published opinion. This consensus was already apparent in the deliberations of the Constituent Assembly, drafting the *Grundgesetz* ("Basic Law") in 1948/1949. It was corroborated throughout the first decades of the Federal Republic and it has held to this very day. Thus, these problems are among the most discussed trends in German politics, and there is no shortage of demoscopic analyses.

Actually, the German public should have been reassured by election results since 1949. Contrary to the Weimar Republic, the parties unequivocally supportive of democratic constitutional government have always been able to garner majorities well in excess of 90 percent. While other Western countries have grown used to large Communist parties as in France and Italy, the rise, in the German case, of smaller parties and movements potentially opposed to the system — the NPD between 1966-1969, the APO in the same period, the "Greens" today — has led to considerable anxiety. Since Hitler started from practically nothing, the reassuring election results did not calm the West Germans. A menacing anti-democratic potential might be lurking behind this ostensibly stable facade, to be activated by unfavorable conditions — by, for example, the disappearance of Adenauer's strong democratic leadership, a recession, or a change of government from center-right to center-left or vice-versa.

The Federal Republic, so it appeared, should be guided by the ideas of "Western democracy." Which elements were to be seen as specifically "Western" remained and remains a moot point. The democratic left pointed to radical-democratic traditions, to certain egalitarian goals in education and, most generally, to pluralism and a high degree of tolerance. The conservatives emphasized primarily Christian-humanist traditions of natural rights, the rule of law, and the separation of powers, not least federalism. The neo-liberals regarded a large measure of economic and societal autonomy as a particularly exemplary element of Western systems. But the political parties which really counted agreed on the whole that humane and cooperative policies should take precedence over power politics and narrow-minded nationalism.

They also agreed that the new democracy, to be conceived as a "Western democracy," should enter into the closest partnership with the free states of the West. From the early beginnings of the postwar period a deep phalanx of liberal, socialist, conservative politicians and intellectuals did their best to reintegrate the Germans, turned cynical and disoriented by Nazism and war, into the mainstream of Western democratic thought.[4]

Most attention was devoted to the temptations emanating from the immediate past. Neo-Nazism and right-wing authoritarianism were at the center of attention in the social sciences and in the liberal camp which, since the 1950s, increasingly set the public trends. Threats from the right were perceived as the main danger.

However, the threat attributable to totalitarian Communism was not overlooked. The constitutional parties and the published opinion distanced themselves from Communism, and the demarcation against Communist totalitarianism was facilitated at that time by the rapid decline in attraction for the West German Communist Party (KPD) observable after the Berlin blockade. Organizationally and as an idea, Communism was totally discredited on a long-term basis by the drama of political oppression in the GDR. But unlike Neo-Nazism, the contemporary totalitarianism of the Communists appeared primarily as an external danger rather than an internal one, and thus it seemed to call for responses chiefly in the realms of foreign and security policy.

From the late 1940s until the late 1960s public opinion in the Federal Republic was characterized by a nearly unanimous anti-totalitarian consensus. In the public debate on the dangers to democratic stability, the late 1960s marked a decisive turning point. As in the United States, torn by the Vietnam War, a radical critique of the established liberal democracy and its socio-economic conditions erupted. To the "New Left," staring more and more at the miseries of the Third World and at the war in Vietnam, most Western democracies looked equally mendacious, unfree, ugly, dissatisfied, and exploitative. This seemed especially true for the U.S.

As everywhere else in the Western world, the student movement in the Federal Republic was also Janus-faced: radical but democratic and by no means incompatible with constitutional government on the one hand; totalitarian in all shades of Marxist convictions on the other. Yet the movement's totalitarian component appeared increasingly bothersome, threatening, and obstructive to healthy democratic development.

The reactions on the part of liberal intellectuals displayed the same basic pattern in the Federal Republic as elsewhere. Many Social Democrats and Liberals who had been wondering critically whether society and politics in the Federal Republic had really and irreversibly left the problematic *Sonderweg* ("special way") of a separate German development,[5] now felt compelled to stress that since 1949 an exemplary, pluralist, sensitive, and generally successful democratic community had been achieved. A main reason for jettisoning previous doubts was the ease with which the change of government to the Social-Liberal Coalition had been effected. Was this not proof that the Anglo-Saxon model of democracy also functioned in the Federal Republic?

Thus, one group of liberals moved politically to the right, even though a majority of those involved would not openly admit this. Another group, however, joined forces with the radical protest movement which prevailed temporarily in universities and the electronic media. Organizationally, the latter found themselves on the SPD's left wing or in the miscellaneous tiny extremist groups and parties of the "lunatic fringe" of the German Left. And when the ecologist movement started gaining momentum in the mid-1970s, it was easy to connect there, too.

Since the mid-1960s, the radical left criticism was directed predominantly against the capitalist character of the Western states, chiefly the U.S. These critics refused to recognize the community of Western democracies as exemplary and felt no sense of affiliation to it. Once again an indefatigable quest for a "Third Way" between capitalism and Communism (which had been typical for the 1930s and the immediate postwar period) was initiated. Several of the critics unconditionally entered the totalitarian camp of orthodox Communism or wore themselves out in the *"action directe"* of anarchic terrorism.

From the point of view of intellectual history, the differences between moderate center-left policies and radical leftism are far from novel. In the German case, the rise of the "New Left" meant a considerable numerical and organizational reinforcement of the German public's radical elements. Perhaps the Federal Republic merely caught up with developments which France and Italy had experienced much earlier. In any event, the force of gravity of the intellectual debate clearly shifted to the left. The ideological differences occurred mainly between liberals, conservatives and Social Democrats on the one side, left-wing radicals of various orientations (including the "Greens") on the other, while not a few democratic socialists and liberals were anxious not to commit themselves too one-sidedly.

Does this imply that democracy in the Federal Republic was more endangered from the Right during the first one-and-a-half decades, while for the past fifteen years it has had to fend off criticism primarily from the nondemocratic Left? Although that may be true of the debate among political activists, a glance at the attitudes of society as a whole reveals a different picture. And since, in the last analysis, elections in democracies are decided by the more apolitical electorate, voters' opinions deserve at least as much attention as those of political activists.

A look at the basic views of the early and mid-1950s reminds us that democracy had to be instituted in the Federal Republic with Germans and against Germans who had followed Hitler until 1942 (and many even later) — Germans, fanatic or opportunistic, either with hope in their hearts or increasingly desperate, disillusioned and cynical. But large parts of the population disassociated themselves soon from the radical politics of Hitler and Nazism — millions already during the fatal last years of the war, millions in the immediate postwar period, and the large remainder in the course of the 1950s. Understanding of democratic government grew steadily, notwithstanding occasional relapses which, fortunately, have always been overcome.

Like X-rays, opinion polls of two decades map the path travelled by the bulk of Germans. Responses such as those mentioned in Table 1, of course, can only serve to illustrate far more complicated opinions and processes. One thing, however, is clear. Support for the system, which has been expressed since 1949 in election results favoring democratic parties, is increasingly corroborated by the views emerging from opinion polls. In the early 1950s, many Germans (albeit not a majority) may still have voted for democratic parties for lack of alternatives or out of opportunism; but now this happens increasingly because the political system as such appears expedient and natural.

After all, it makes sense that the acceptance of democracy should grow the longer this form of government exists and the more it stands the test of time. Senior citizens who previously were Monarchists, National Socialists or Communists have gotten used to democratic constitutional government. Today's intermediate generations as well as the younger age cohorts do not know any other way. This satisfaction with the system, even in periods of economic depression, is undoubtedly one of the most remarkable traits of today's German political culture.

Different explanations have been advanced to account for these positive changes, and they probably have to be combined. Until well into the late 1960s, the opinion was frequently held that the political system derived its legitimacy mainly from economic success.[6] This view probably held true for the 1950s, but fails to convince fully today, even if it may largely explain to a large extent why former Nazis resigned themselves to democracy without decisive resistance in the 1950s. The recession of the period 1980-1983, however, has shown that in an economically critical situation Germans do not hold the system itself but rather the government responsible. It is the opposition which profits most from protest, not the anti-systemic parties. The relatively good showing of the "Greens" does not result from dissatisfaction with the economic situation, but rather reflects a long-term process of alienation within a societal subculture of the middle classes.

A further explanation views the system-support and the overall increase in willingness to partake in democratic life as resulting from thorough processes of modernization which have likewise altered the educational system,

TABLE 1 Changes in Attitudes toward Previous Regimes (Monarchy and Dictatorship) and Key Values of the Bonn Republic (Political Competition and Freedom of Political Expression), 1950–77 (in percentages)

Questions	1950	1951	1952	1953	1954	1955	1956	1957
Restore monarchy?								
Yes	—	32	—	—	22	—	—	16
No	—	36	—	—	51	—	—	60
Don't know	—	32	—	—	27	—	—	24
Hitler one of Germany's greatest statesmen?								
Yes	—	—	—	—	—	48	43	—
No	—	—	—	—	—	36	37	—
Don't know	—	—	—	—	—	16	20	—
A new Nazi Party?								
Support	—	—	—	16	—	—	15	11
Oppose	—	—	—	62	—	—	61	66
Indifferent	—	—	—	22	—	—	24	23
Political competition is better for a country to have								
One party	25	23	21	20	19	15	11	12
Several parties	53	60	68	66	69	74	76	77
Undecided/other/no answer	22	17	11	14	12	11	13	11
Freedom of political expression								
Can speak freely today in West Germany	—	—	—	55	58	71	78	75
Are limitations, better to be careful	—	—	—	35	35	26	17	20
Undecided/no answer	—	—	—	10	7	3	5	5

leisure-time behavior, and information patterns. This, too, is certainly a correct observation. Nevertheless, political activity has grown markedly only in a comparatively circumscribed stratum of university educated, younger Germans, frequently employed in the public service.

Increased political participation is a typically middle class phenomenon, and in the German case it also favors primarily those strata which, like teachers, civil servants, students, journalists or lawyers, have appropriate training to influence politics at least on the local level, on the middle level of political parties, or through participation in citizens' initiatives and protest groups.

Unfortunately, it is precisely these strata which contain a disproportionately high number of individuals alienated from democratic constitutional government or the values of industrial society. The German example here confirms the thesis advanced several years ago by the Princeton school and also Seymour M. Lipset[7] that higher levels of political information or activity alone represent no safe indicator of stability in a constitutional state. In any event, today the large majority of citizens — politically active ones as much as the apolitical "silent majority" — accepts the democracy of the Basic Law. The Federal Republic today differs significantly from the Weimar Republic. Even those who more or less openly strive for fundamental changes realistically present their aims as further development of the democratic system.

1958	1959	1960	1961	1962	1963	1964	1965	1966	1967	1968	1971	1977
—	—	—	—	—	—	10	11	—	—	—	—	—
—	—	—	—	—	—	71	66	—	—	—	—	—
—	—	—	—	—	—	19	23	—	—	—	—	—
—	42	34	30	37	35	29	—	—	32	—	—	—
—	41	43	43	44	44	44	—	—	52	—	—	—
—	17	23	27	19	21	27	—	—	16	—	—	—
11	11	—	—	8	—	—	—	7	6	—	—	7
64	62	—	—	71	—	—	—	74	78	—	—	79
25	27	—	—	21	—	—	—	19	16	—	—	14
12	12	11	11	—	—	—	—	—	8	7	—	6
77	76	79	73	—	—	—	—	—	82	81	—	90
11	12	10	16	—	—	—	—	—	10	12	—	4
70	70	—	—	71	—	—	—	—	—	—	84	—
25	24	—	—	21	—	—	—	—	—	—	13	—
5	6	—	—	8	—	—	—	—	—	—	3	—

Source: Institute für Demoskopie. Allensbach, West Germany. These and all other public opinion polls cited in this study were obtained from the Institut and the Roper Public Opinion Research Center, Williamstown, Massachusetts. I am very grateful to the director of the Allensbach Institute, Dr. Elisabeth Noelle-Neumann, and the Roper Center for making these materials available. Sole responsibility for the presentation, analysis, and interpretation of these data rests with the author. See David P. Conradt, *The German Polity* (New York and London: Longman, 1978), p. 49.

It is conspicious that ideas of radical, albeit not violent, revolutionary change are essentially restricted to the left of the political spectrum. Numerically, the violent radicals are few. Revolutionary leftist groups like the terrorists of the "Red Army Fraction" may temporarily have acted as a scourge, but as a political force they are just as insignificant as similar anti-democratic organizations of the extreme Right.

In this sense, there is much to recommend the supposition that German voters will continue to adhere to the value system of constitutional government not just from political wisdom, but also out of habit, inertia and lack of imagination (which in this case is most welcome).

Still, most observers agree that since the late 1960s a growing political subculture, whose members are alienated from the socio-political system, has established itself. This phenomenon afflicts most Western societies and must be understood as the *malaise* of the educated and semi-educated strata who are somewhat removed from scientific, technical or economic professions. Young working class unemployed, too, often fall under the influence of the alienated strata.

Awareness of the danger of this political alienation first became apparent to the general public and to social scientists during the student unrest of the second half of the 1960s. Opinion polls since have shown that political values in universities diverge markedly from those values broadly prevalent in society. The Institut für Demoskopie, Allensbach, conducted a representative survey during the first months of 1978 at 33 universities in the Federal Republic; only about one-third (36 percent) of the students questioned rejected Communist participation in Western European governments decisively, 30 percent were in favor, the rest expressed no opinion. One-quarter (25 percent) considered "violence against objects" as a legitimate means for the realization of political demands under certain conditions; 8 percent accepted violence against persons and objects. The response to the question posed both in 1968 (at the height of the student movement) and in 1978 is especially revealing: "Do government and parliament no longer represent the interests of the people?" The 12 percent who were in "full and complete agreement" in 1968 had grown to one-fifth (21 percent) by 1978. Thirty-five percent thought this to be "partially" the case in 1968; in 1978, 44 percent marked this answer.[8] For our purpose, the fact that a then nine-year-old reformist Social-Liberal coalition government was unable to overcome the students' alienation is less interesting than the alienation itself.

Undoubtedly, the influence of the university milieu plays a considerable role. This will presumably wear off somewhat upon entering the professions; it already has in many cases. On the other hand, university radicalism radiates into education, the judicial system, and the media. It is evident that at some German universities, especially the big-city universities, an antidemocratic potential, alienated from the institutions of constitutional government, can be found which will make itself felt even after graduates enter the professions.

Deficient socialization processes in the new middle classes (employees other than management, civil servants, non-academic professions) emerge as a main source of radicalization. The father's church or union ties are below average in influence.[9]

This subculture of more or less alienated radicals is distributed across a number of organizations. Since 1981 most of them find their political home with the "Greens." The members of the "Greens" come from a wide range of orientations, but they share a high degree of alienation from the sociopolitical system. To these must be added large numbers of Protestant and Catholic students as well as young union members and finally the Young Socialists in the SPD (aged up to 35 years). These radical tendencies receive strong support from radio and television journalism, from the left wing of the unions, and from the radical wings of the churches. Yet though these organizations believe that they are committed to the values of democracy, they do not hesitate to enter alliances with openly anti-democratic organizations like the Moscow-oriented DKP and miscellaneous other radical left-wing parties and groups.

Perhaps the most important phenomenon is the unwillingness on the part of the more radical groups to admit that strict adherence to the values of liberal constitutionalism must remain the main criterion for political coalitions. Since the late 1960s we observe that the commitment to radical goals such as "democratization," "socialism," anti-nuclear protest, and unilateralism seems to be of primary importance, whereas commitment to ideals and procedures of constitutional democracy seems to be of secondary concern. On the left of the political spectrum the dividing line between strict believers in the values of parliamentary democracy and anti-democratic radicals was diluted. Most of the new radicals still believe in democracy, but it is a brand of democracy far apart from the belief of the majority of voters and not wholly consistent with the basic idea of constitutionalism.

The basic ideological outlook of the mainstream of Germany's "new left" can be sketched in broad strokes as follows: anti-authoritarian, critical toward representative democracy, socialist, hedonistic and frequently opposed to the traditional concept of family, radically or moderately critical of modern technology and a growth-oriented economy, extremely individualistic and simultaneously oriented toward a community of small groups, pessimistic, upset and dissatisfied with the state if not openly opposed to it. Other attributes which remain to be depicted include: critical of America in their international outlook, opposed to NATO, committed to unilateral disarmament by the West, and finally, uncritical receptiveness for Eastern propaganda theses without marked sympathies for the Soviet Union.

Simplifying somewhat, the 1970s and the 1980s have led to a somewhat peaceful coexistence of two or more divergent political cultures. There is a majority of the electorate, largely embracing the productive classes, equally committed to the values of industrial society and Western constitutional democracy. This majority is being challenged by an activist, politicized minority of university-trained, middle-class radicals which is more or less alienated from industrial society and at least uncertain about constitutional democracy and a Western orientation. One may call this a modern class war between the apolitical, productive classes on the one hand, and a politicized non-productive class on the other hand. At least it is a deep cleavage between two political cultures.

The processes of politicization and radicalization which have already lasted for 15 years in education, parts of the social welfare administration, the judicial system, the humanities and social sciences and the electronic media are quite noticeable. It remains to be seen how far-reaching the changes which they are bringing about will be, and how strong the counter-forces which they have provoked will be. In the political realm, the SPD first benefited from the new movement and then started to suffer from it, but whether this is reversible is not yet clear.

It is evident that the election result of March 6, 1983 can prove fateful for the radicalized academic subculture. What began as a movement has turned into a small party in the Bundestag with a relatively clear political profile: critical of technology, opposed to nuclear war, oriented to grass-roots democracy in a complicated way, uncertain about the institutions of constitutional government, pacifist, neutralist, but also heterogeneous and more of an ephemeral phenomenon than a great movement. Perhaps the SPD will assimilate a considerable part of these alienated groups, but it would thereby alienate itself even more than in the past from the majority of voters. In the long run, this would strengthen the predominance of the CDU/CSU and FDP center-right coalition.

A fundamental threat to democratic stability thus is hardly to be feared; at most, there will be those constant adjustments which no vigorous political system can escape. On the whole, Western Europe's postwar democracies are tough. They are capable of digesting most anti-democratic elements. Partisans of constitutional government in the Federal Republic will have to stay on the alert, but they also have grounds for optimism.

Basic Foreign Policy Orientations

Is the picture of the West German's basic foreign policy orientations equally as clear (and reassuring) as their attitudes on constitutional government? To oversimplify a complex reality, the overwhelming majority of West Germans today perceive themselves quite naturally as members of the Western community. This pertains not only to the population as a whole, but also to the predominant part of society's functional elites.

When Germans are asked to identify from a given list those countries with which the Federal Republic should cooperate especially closely, an almost monotonously clear orientation toward Western societies results:

Question: With which of these countries should we cooperate as closely as possible?
(in percentage of affirmative responses)

	Mar. 1953	Sept. 1954	Apr. 1956	Sept. 1963	Oct. 1968	Nov. 1970	Aug. 1972	Sept. 1975	Nov. 1979	Sept. 1980	July 1983
America	83	78	69	90	81	86	78	82	80	80	79
England	62	58	49	65	59	62	55	48	48	46	50
France	55	46	34	71	68	75	63	64	65	69	66
Spain	50	42	26	20	21	23	21	14	20	19	16
Italy	44	34	30	30	32	36	33	26	26	26	31
Japan	41	35	24	31	35	43	44	36	42	40	40
Russia	18	22	23	27	35	52	49	42	29	20	38
Israel	15	13	10	17	24	24	25	25			
Poland	11	11	10	27	25	35	32	22	21	20	21

Source: *Jahrbuch der öffentlichen Meinung*, 1947–1955, 1957, 1958–1964, 1968–1973, 1976 and Allensbach Archiv, IfD-Umfragen 3075, 3087, 4030.

Despite the ups and downs of German-American relations, America is always "number one." This holds true to this very day, and it is also striking in comparison with other European countries. In a poll taken in February 1982 in seven European countries, the Germans displayed by far the most favorable attitude toward the United States:

Question: All in all, what is your opinion of the USA?

	B	D	DK	GB	F	I	CH
	%	%	%	%	%	%	%
Trust very much	8	16	5	6	4	17	4
Trust pretty much	42	41	33	29	36	36	29
Trust very little	19	33	30	39	35	18	51
Trust not at all	10	7	18	21	12	11	12
No opinion/no reply	20	2	14	5	13	18	4

B = Belgium; D = Federal Republic; DK = Denmark; GB = Great Britain; F = France; I = Italy; CH = Switzerland.
Source: Gallup poll, February 1982. EMNID-Informationen Nr. 5/6, 1982.

The table of long-term trends, however, is revealing not only about the German-American relationship. As is evident, West Germans do differentiate — and markedly so — between their Western European neighbors. Since 1954, they obviously value the closest possible cooperation with France higher than with Britain. Italy features somewhat Cinderella-like in German's political consciousness.

Especially interesting, of course, is the changing assessment of Russia. Here several points become apparent. A certain change in the assessment occurred in the mid-1950s after Stalin's death following the establishment of diplomatic relations by Adenauer in September of 1955. A dramatic increase in responses ("should cooperate as closely as possible"), however, does not occur until the early years of the Social-Liberal Government, perhaps indicating how sensitively the electorate is attuned to the government's leadership in the field of foreign policy.

According to other polls, public attitudes toward the Soviet Union change quickly to improvements or deteriorations in official relations between Bonn and Moscow, but equally to world-wide developments involving the Soviet Union.

However the ups and downs unfold, a considerable distance toward Moscow is unmistakable compared to attitudes toward the important Western states. This is evidenced in responses to questions about threat-perceptions, posed time and again since the early 1950s. With a considerable majority of German voters, suspicion of the Soviet Union proved as pronounced a constant as the pro-American orientation. Asked how they would decide if they had to choose *one* of these alternatives, "a good relationship with America or a good relationship with Russia," those questioned responded with a more or less pronounced majority:

	May/June 1954	Oct. 1975	Nov. 1979	May 1981	June 1983
	%	%	%	%	%
America	62	52	63	65	56
Russia	10	12	12	6	6
No Opinion	28	36	25	29	38

Source: Allensbacher Archiv, IfD-Umfragen 074, 3020, 3075, 4130, 4028.

Compared to the 1970s, the pattern of opinions about the U.S. and Russia has become polarized again in the period of renewed tensions between East and West.

Despite a majority's basic mistrust of the Soviet Union, there is still a marked desire for fairly harmonic relations with the East — a simple demand of common sense for a country like the Federal Republic. This desire has grown mainly in the 1970s; since mid-1982 it is growing again (Table 2).

To a certain extent the assessment of the Soviet Union is also reflected in party affiliation. In the 1970s and early 1980s, CDU/CSU-oriented voters were more prone than partisans of the Brandt and Schmidt governments to doubt the sincerity of Soviet rapprochement, and thus were more skeptical of the desirability of close German-Soviet cooperation. Likewise, for nearly a decade voters under 30 tended to be slightly more sanguine about the possibilities of close cooperation with the Soviet Union than the majority of the electorate.

Yet even today, in a period of heightened East-West tensions, when the desire for a certain equidistance runs rather high and when nuclear hardware is being regarded with suspicion, a majority of the electorate, confronted with the hard choice between NATO and the eventual deployment of new missiles, pronounces itself for the Alliance. In August 1983 the following picture emerges:

Question: Suppose we have only the choice to leave NATO or to deploy the new American missiles on our soil, what should we do: leave NATO or deploy the new missiles?

	Total %	Partisanship			
		CDU/CSU %	SPD %	FDP %	Greens %
Deploy the new missiles	46	64	34	60	11
Leave Nato	22	9	30	13	73
Don't know	32	27	36	27	16
	100	100	100	100	100

Source: Institut für Demoskopie, Allensbach. *Frankfurter Allgemeine Zeitung*, Sept. 16, 1983.

It would be easy to analyze the Western ties along different dimensions based on a cornucopia of empirical materials. Simplified, four dimensions enter the picture: (1) the dimension of culture and society; (2) the basic political order; (3) the economic dimension; (4) foreign and security policy.

As is well known, these dimensions do not necessarily coincide. Certain European democracies with pluralist societies are not included in the Western security system (Austria, Switzerland, Finland, Sweden, Ireland). They demonstrate that under propitious circumstances it is possible to remain a Western country without belonging to NATO. Besides, the impulses of Western civilization reach well beyond the Western European/Atlantic states. They are alive in the Eastern bloc, where they are frequently suppressed, but also in many developing countries overseas. On the other hand, there have

TABLE 2   Question: A general question regarding German foreign policy: in the future, should we cooperate equally closely with America and Russia or rather either cooperate more closely with Russia or more closely with America—what do you think?

	May 1973 %	Oct. 1977 %	Sept. 1978 %	Jan. 1980 %	May 1981 %	July 1981 %	Nov. 1981 %	Dec. 1981 %
Cooperate more with America	36	49	51	49	56	50	41	45
Cooperate more with Russia	3	2	1	2	1	2	2	1
Cooperate equally with America and Russia	54	38	36	41	32	37	41	41
Undecided	7	11	12	8	11	11	16	13
	100	100	100	100	100	100	100	100

	Dec./Jan. 1981/82 %	Mar./Apr. 1982 %	June 1982	June 1982	Nov. 1982 %	Jan. 1983 %	Feb./Mar. 1983 %	June 1983 %
Cooperate more with America	42	43	51	54	44	39	40	42
Cooperate more with Russia	2	2	1	1	2	1	1	2
Cooperate equally with America and Russia	44	43	39	39	48	51	49	47
Undecided	12	12	9	6	6	9	10	9
	100	100	100	100	100	100	100	100

TABLE 2 (continued)
Breakdown of Responses from December/January 1981/82

	Total %	Men %	Women %	Age Groups			
				16–29 %	30–44 %	45–59 %	60 years or older %
Cooperate more with America	42	45	40	33	40	49	47
Cooperate more with Russia	2	2	2	4	2	1	2
Cooperate equally with America and Russia	44	45	43	51	49	40	36
Undecided	12	8	15	12	9	10	15
	100	100	100	100	100	100	100

	Partisanship			
	CDU/CSU %	SPD %	FDP %	Greens %
Cooperate more with America	59	35	27	12
Cooperate more with Rusia	1	3	1	9
Cooperate equally with America with Russia	32	53	62	66
Undecided	8	9	10	13
	100	100	100	100

Source: Allensbacher Archiv, IfD-Umfragen 2131, 3049, 3060, 3178, 4103, 3098, 4002, 4003, 4004, 4006, 4010, 4030/II, 4018 B, 4025.

always been, and still are, members of the Western security community which do not have a democratic order (among them Portugal and Greece in the past, Turkey today). By the same token, membership in the free enterprise system of the West is not synonymous with political democracy or even with integration into the intellectual ambit of Western-occidental civilization.

The Federal Republic, though, is one of those instances where *all* dimensions of Western ties coincide and reinforce each other. The concept of Western ties (*Westbindung*) serves to secure the democratic order and the pluralistic society as well as to prevent, or at least defuse, risky conflicts with the Western democracies. In the economic area, Western ties facilitate optimal factor mobility. Naturally, the economic argument for Western ties was especially compelling under conditions of reconstruction, but it has remained so in the public's consciousness.

The integration into a community of Western culture and ideas supplements the political and economic ties. If a powerful passion against Western cosmopolitanism, Western materialism, Western liberalism, Western decadence were to emerge again as it did in the former Reich — chiefly during the First World War as well as in the 1920s and early 1930s — such an anti-Western neo-romanticism and a nervous quest for a German cultural identity would eventually affect the basic political orientation too.

Individual groups in the alternative movement do in fact display rudiments of a cultural anti-Westernism, but they are not yet sufficiently representative to give rise to serious worry. Culturally the Federal Republic remains a thoroughly Western country, probably more cosmopolitan and "Americanized" than the larger and smaller European neighbors. Until now, no enduringly effective tendencies can be felt in the Federal Republic's intellectual life which would steer back onto the anti-Western *Sonderweg* of earlier periods in German history.

Overstating somewhat, for more than 30 years Western ties have come to be understood as a sort of *"raison d' etat* for the Federal Republic." Regardless of all efforts at improving relations with the East, the shaping of intra-Western relations has had, and continues to have, priority. Since 1949 Western ties have been considered as more urgent than the goal of national reunification, and more important (to all the major parties) than good relations with the Communist states.

Explicitly or implicitly, Western ties provide security against the Soviet Union and the East and Central-European Communist party dictatorships under its control. The preconditions for preserving West Germany's and Western Europe's freedom against totalitarianism is the maintenance and strengthening of the Western community system along all dimensions. On this, consensus still exists among the general public and those parties which can be taken seriously, even though the incontestable antagonism between the Western Alliance and the Soviet Union has been occasionally blurred in the past by slogans like "security partnership."

But the underlying reality in the Federal Republic today as earlier is first of all a widespread consensus that the future of Western democracy, the functioning of West Germany's economy, and the future development of pluralist society are only possible in the closest imaginable community with the Western democracies.

Minority groups that reject the basic Western orientation find themselves forced quickly to justify their position. They must seek to prove:

— that their policy would not place the Federal Republic in a position of dependence on Moscow;

— they they do not intend to loosen the friendly bonds with the Western democracies (criticism of the Reagan Administration might be combined with stretching out a hand to the "freeze-movement" which is more in the camp of the Democratic Party);

— that national aspirations do not represent that sort of nationalism which still evokes terrible memories;

— that an *Ostpolitik* committed to the ideals of detente could be accepted by all well-meaning, reasonable sectors of public opinion in friendly Western Europe and in the United States.

Throughout the 1950s, the Social Democrats found themselves compelled to justify their position; since 1980 they are again visibly moving into this position. In the early 1950s even the openly neutralist *Gesamtdeutsche Volkspartei* (GVP) which the eventual Social Democratic Federal President Gustav Heinemann belonged to and which relied primarily on a pacifist and pan-German oriented political subculture of German protestantism could not evade this pressure.

Only the "Greens" and the groups of the so-called peace movement allied to them are an exception. Just as they reject or at least call in question the socio-political system domestically, they have few scruples about cancelling the consensus on the necessity of close Western ties. But this is precisely what weakens their political appeal and represents a major difficulty in the attempt to win large parts of the SPD to their course. In any event, the base of Western ties can be seen as stronger and more solidly joined with the public and the more respectable parties (including the SPD) than is often assumed.

Nevertheless, those groups which since the early 1980s have openly questioned the basic consensus on Western ties deserve careful attention. Consequently, the examination of the tendencies in the electorate fitting into the framework of these initial reflections will analyze three distinguishable attitudes:

— the mainstream of uncontested pro-Western foreign policy orientation;

— positions which interweave principally pro-Western orientation in a complex fashion with elements of an alternative policy *within* the Western system;

— more or less open and fundamental rejection of Western ties in favor of alternative models.

Because basic attitudes in this field are often ambiguous and contradictory, a selected series of findings will be presented and discussed below, primarily by way of illustration.
Three questions are relevant:

1. What are the national motives or alternative tendencies in German public opinion?
2. What is the meaning of West German neutralism?
3. How strong is the pacifist unilateralism?

Anti-Western Neo-Nationalism?

Anyone familiar with German history fears many things, but the ghost of a new German nationalism usually appears most sinister to foreign observers. Could nationalism really be completely extinguished in the depths of the Germans' hearts?

The notion of "nationalism" ranges from an anti-Western belief in the superior uniqueness of "German nature," to resentment about the civilizing and economic superiority of the Western community, to a fanatic determination to reunify and regain the lost Eastern territories at any price, and finally to the moderate will to bring about reunification with Germans in the GDR, even at the price of non-participation in European integration.

In the course of the 1950s, it became more and more evident that haughty, xenophobic, warmongering and risk-taking nationalism was ostracized by West Germans in the wake of their experience with the Third Reich. But there never was any doubt that West Germans would have preferred reunification with the Germans in the Eastern zone to European unification, had a genuine alternative offered itself.

Opinion polls speak out clearly in this respect:

Precedence was assigned to:	1951 %	1953 %	1954 %	1955 %	1956 %	1957 %	1958 %	1959 %
Unification of the Eastern and Western zones	55	57	67	76	73	68	70	70
European unification	27	29	28	21	22	27	25	23
No opinion	18	14	5	3	5	5	5	7

Source: EMNID-Berichte, 21/1959.

For many years, however, the importance of Western ties for foreign policy has been understood as the safest concept for bringing about reunification. Hence, those parties that perceived the policy of integration and reunification as contradictory were never able to get the majority of the population on their side.

But in the 1960s and early 1970s, the German will for reunification seemed to suffer a fate analogous to the veteran in that melancholic song, "Old soldiers never die, they just fade away . . ."

Question: Do you think you will live to see the reunification of East and West Germany?

	Yes	No	Impossible to say
	%	%	%
1966 July	29	47	24
1967 November	21	49	30
1969 November	18	62	20
1970 July	14	66	20
1972 June/July	15	69	16
1976 January	13	65	22

Source: *Jahrbuch der öffentlichen Meinung 1968 bis 1973*, p. 506 and 1976, p. 83.

The belief that national yearnings could be realized evaporated from year to year. West Germans with a high-school diploma tend to assess the situation with even fewer illusions than elementary school graduates, the younger age-classes more than the older ones.

The will to reunify is currently reduced to an inconsequential wish — much as one wishes for a permanently blue sky or life without death and disease. The individuals who articulated their skepticism about realizing reunification respond as follows to the question, "Are you very desirous of reunification, or is it not at all that important to you?": 61 percent "very desirous"; 36 percent "not at all that important"; 3 percent other responses. Again, the seniors are less indifferent to the national question. Political affiliation plays a role, too, although it is negligible overall. But 72 percent of all those questioned (68 percent of whom are SPD-oriented, 82 percent CDU-oriented) were simultaneously opposed to deleting the sentence from the Preamble to the Basic Law, "The entire German people are called upon to achieve in free self-determination the unity and freedom of Germany."[10]

Hence, the national preoccupation plainly rests in a deep-freeze. It may thaw under changed international circumstances because there are still sufficient numbers of younger Germans who respond with corresponding interest, but for the time being the national question no longer represents an effective motive for political orientation. And there has been little change over the past few years.

To put it positively, the West Germans have learned to pursue goals which are difficult to reconcile with a sense of measure and without illusions. They see themselves as part of the Western world, but, in accordance with official policy, they leave the national question open. They wish for closer European integration, too, yet without harboring many illusions in this respect. They belong to the Western world, are citizens of the Federal Republic and Germans all at once — without perceiving this as incompatible. There are no more aspirations to the nation-state's exclusivity, but also there is not complete relinquishment of national self-confidence. Instead, there is a realistic resignation to the facts of European power relations; the Germans have accustomed themselves to these relations even though their results may not be considered satisfactory.

Many maintain that the patent anti-Western tendencies among the SPD's left and the "Greens" are based on a neo-nationalism, ordinarily hidden with care. In his reports from Bonn for the *New York Times*, John Vinocur often pointed this out in the early 1980s. He realized sooner than others that the intra-party base for Helmut Schmidt's foreign policy of loyalty to NATO was eroding, but he was wrong in interpreting this as a symptom of a new nationalism.

In the last years of the Social-Liberal Coalition Helmut Schmidt and large groups of the SPD frequently justified their criticism of the U.S.'s abandonment of detente by invoking the imperative of intra-German detente (human contacts, Berlin, etc.). Up to a point, this was fully appropriate. On the other hand, the argument of "national interest" was overextended since the continuation of a policy of detente 1970s style — increasingly considered obsolete in the U.S., Great Britain, and France since Mitterand came into office — seemed unexplainable in any other way.

However, far too wide-reaching conclusions have been drawn from the fact that a plausible argument has been employed for a German *Ostpolitik* which was becoming more difficult to explain to other Western countries. In fact, the Schmidt Government and the SPD could not be accused of seeking to reverse the partition of Germany. Rather, uneasiness has been voiced time and again in the SPD as to whether the recognition of the GDR should not go even further than the narrow restrictions of West German constitutional law permit.

Among the more radical leftists on the SPD's fringe and in the ranks of the "Greens" there currently is a comparatively minute group of intellectuals (Rudolf Bahro, Peter Brandt) that is fascinated by the idea of a national socialism and a rapprochement of the Federal Republic to the GDR under the banner of neutralism. Yet "Greens" in their majority are much more dogmatic about the recognition of a strict "two-states doctrine" than some SPD members of parliament who are not overly happy with the Basic Law's reunification provisions and with the narrow bounds which the Federal Constitutional Court has drawn for recognition of the GDR. On the occasion of the discussion of Chancellor Kohl's Government Declaration of May 4, 1983, the "Greens" turned vehemently to criticizing even the Wall and the *Schiessbefehl* ("order to shoot") which forces GDR border guards to use live ammunition against their fleeing compatriots.

Certain signs of national socialist xenophobia which are occasionally expressed in the agitation of leftist groups against the decision to modernize the INF and against the U.S. armaments policy should be taken more seriously. Spokesmen for the left say that Germany is a country occupied by Russian and American troops; they impute to the superpowers an inclination to engage in limited nuclear warfare at the Germans' expense; as a result they claim that a "new patriotism" is the order of the day. Anti-Americanism, anti-capitalist Socialism, nuclear pacifism and neutralism are brought into close connection with the sense of nationhood of a German national allegedly enslaved by the blocs and threatened with death; the whole concoction is enriched by anti-technical cultural criticism directed against consumer society.

All that is still a thoroughly artificial product of intellectuals and, for the time being, appears almost not at all in representative opinion polls, but presumably this ideological mixture will continue to remain alive. The radical Left may succeed in establishing a lasting reunification-nationalism with a neutralist point, but currently no viable concept can be ascertained — only statements of nationalist resentment.

Is there any chance that neo-nationalism will emerge from the center or the right? Since its return to the government, the CDU, which has seen itself throughout the opposition period as the custodian of the national idea, has articulated more clearly than previous governments that the German question remains open. The party at large thinks primarily of the East Germans' right to freedom, though there are no precise ideas as to the form of a possible solution. The territories lost to Poland seem to play no role in these far-reaching goals. The whole concept is vague — a frustrated hope, not a policy. Partially, the purpose is to occupy positions which a radical and anti-Western leftist nationalism might assume later; for some, it is traditionalism.

Yet this will not develop into more than a *ceterum censeo*, to be heard from previous CDU governments as well, so long as the Eastern bloc in general and the GDR in particular show no signs of internal decay. What might happen in a period of Eastern weakness, what the political center and the democratic right would do if the GDR entered a critical state as in Communist Poland since 1980 (today, such a possibility is no longer as irrevelant as in the past) is not clear. But aversion to risk and love of peace at nearly any price are such a strong part of the political psychology of the West German people and parties that even a historian finds it reasonably difficult to imagine a late twentieth century Bismarck who would seek to reunify Germany with ingenuity, unscrupulous in his choice of means, and, in the final analysis, through "blood and iron."

Given a crisis in the Eastern bloc and the GDR, the democratic parties of the center and the moderate right probably would display that responsible bourgeois prudence which has also been characteristic of cabinets led by Adenauer, Erhard, and Kiesinger. "Bismarck in Bonn"[11] — the title of a book from the 1960s — is an unimaginable idea.

Nothing needs to be said in this context about the "silent majority" of German voters. Together with the parties that articulate its wishes, the "silent majority" has firmly established itself psychologically in the postwar system of Europe and displays no inclination whatsoever to rock the luxuriously equipped boat of West German statehood with an irrational "new nationalism."

Anti-Western Neutralism? Unlike Sweden and Switzerland or, since the postwar period, also Finland and Austria, Germany does not belong to the Western European countries with a tradition of neutrality. It has always been too large and too important for the European balance of power to make a policy of neutralism plausible. To the extent that a neutral Germany was discussed after the Second World War, the protagonists have always taken their cues from a foreign policy-making use of Germany's central geographic position — albeit non-aligned, in the nature of things still much more along the lines of German foreign policy during the Weimar Republic than that of Switzerland, Sweden or Austria.

Neutralism, then, can denote two different concepts in the German case: non-alignment of a reunified Germany or "neutralistic" foreign policy by the Federal Republic, whatever that means.

The neutralism of the 1950s corresponded to the first concept. It was a reunification-neutralism. The reinstitution of the German Reich was to be made acceptable to the Soviet Union by committing it (like Austria in 1955) to non-alignment, or — which was deemed more likely at the time — to a position of guaranteed non-alignment by the Four Powers. Neutralism and national aspirations thus coincided.

From 1953 to 1960, the SPD in its majority subscribed to such a concept. Nothing was ostracized as passionately by Adenauer as this form of neutralism. He recognized it as the great mortal sin of his opponents on the opposition benches, and he feared the further evils which might flow from it:

— American withdrawal from Europe (where was the 7th Army to be positioned, and how was a rump-Europe without Germany to be defended?);

— decay of the Western European community which had just started growing together (for fear of a much stronger, reunified Germany, France would probably be driven to the Soviet side!);

— internal instability of German democracy in a precarious and lengthy transition period;

— preponderance of the sole World Power remaining in Europe, the Soviet Union, with the effect — as it came to be called — of the "Finlandization" of a Germany kept nonaligned.

There still is little else which Adenauer's party, the CDU, instinctively detests as much as the idea of a German neutralism. And since neutrality even of a reunited Germany has been rejected, neutralist tendencies aiming solely at the considerably weaker Federal Republic seem all the more illusory.

Tiny groups of intellectuals are now resurrecting the issue of pan-German neutralism for the first time in years. Individual intellectuals, who take a liking to old errors, seem to appear in every young political generation, but these outsiders carry no political weight.

Conceptions aimed at disentangling the Federal Republic fully or in part from the superpower antagonism must be differentiated in principle from reunification-neutralism. Insofar as this is advocated, a formally neutral status is viewed at best as a final objective (here, too, currently only groups of the "lunatic fringe" of the radical Left or the radical Right are relevant). But because a disentanglement of the Federal Republic alone from the blocs is hard to imagine, internal logic bends this West German neutralism, too, in the direction of pan-German concepts.

To be sure, even in the late 1960s and the 1970s there have been notions of disentangling the Federal Republic, in conjunction with several Eastern and Western neighbors, from one-sided ties within the framework of a lengthy process of detente. Even though the blocs would not disappear for some time to come, all-European structures were supposed to be increasingly superimposed on them. This was a time when Gaullist ideas found some resonance even among Germany's moderate left, and Zbigniew Brzezinski's essay in *Foreign Affairs*, "A Framework for East-West Reconciliation,"[13] was also discussed in Bonn.

Non-aligned status for the Federal Republic, however, would have meant non-aligned status for the GDR (both as long-range objectives) — but without aiming at reunification in the sense of restoring Bismarck's *Reich*. Thus, while the first concept of neutralism was inextricably wedded to the national aspirations in a divided Germany, the second was equally inextricably wedded to detente.

But there are many intermediate steps between a basic line of Western ties and a course designed to overcome the blocs — and these are the most interesting from the perspective of *Realpolitik*. Partial distancing from the U.S. or NATO on basic questions of security policy can be presented as intermediate steps, especially an openly proclaimed line of "equidistance" from Moscow and Washington regarding controversies as to Third World conflicts or unsolicited efforts at "honest brokerage" between the U.S. and the Soviet Union.

That German statesmen occasionally feel compelled to aid in pouring oil on troubled waters at times of sharp East-West tensions is neither surprising nor problematic in itself. After all, there are good reasons for members in a league of free states to steer their own course on certain questions. But if occasional disputes turn into a habit, if they concern vital issue-areas and if they are being used in a systematic way to cast a particular profile of German foreign policy, this could be interpreted as an intermediate step in the direction of the Alliance's fringes. In the last years of Helmut Schmidt's chancellorship many observers asked themselves whether such a strategy was being pursued.

Since a "neutralism" on Bonn's part has been feared in Western capitals over the past years, such a policy of deliberately linked intermediate steps seemed the most likely possibility. There would not be withdrawal from NATO or the protective relationship with the U.S.; there would be no thought of formal neutrality; but there would still be an *Ostpolitik* along the Eastern fringes of the Alliance. Formulas such as "mediatorship" or "security partnership with the East" gave rise to suspicions that the Federal Republic sees itself on the one hand as a firm component of the West, but on the other as a sort of bridge where Western reconnaissance moves are to cross — e.g., Eastern arms control proposals were to be transported into the Alliance via this bridge while the pipeline installations for Siberian gas were being constructed underneath. "Neutralism" in this sense no longer appeared as a status precisely delimited by international law, but rather as a mentality of anxious indecisiveness and unreliable wavering — an attempt to remain in the Western Alliance without really participating.

We shall dispense with a discussion of whether and how such tendencies manifested themselves in the Federal Republic's party spectrum, and ask instead what sort of backing neutralist tendencies have had, and continue to have, among the electorate.

Although there is no tradition of neutrality in Germany, the echo which the idea of neutralism has found among the general public during the nearly 35 years of history for the Federal Republic is still striking. This reception is not just for reunification-neutralism, but for a neutral status for the Federal Republic modeled on Austria's. Even today, though the idea of a reunified, neutral Germany apparently has been gathering dust on the shelves of history since the mid-1950s, such a neutralism still evokes sympathy.

An Allensbach poll even shows that this sympathy is still growing:

Question: What is your opinion about the following proposal for German reunification? Conditions for reunification are the following demands:

— the GDR leaves the Warsaw Pact, the Federal Republic leaves NATO;
— there must be a guarantee that the reunified Germany is neutral and enters no alliances;
— the reunified Germany can decide on its social system in free and secret elections.

Here it is again. What is your view? Would you welcome a reunification of Germany under these conditions or not welcome it under these conditions?

Federal Republic and West Berlin
(Population over 16)

	Sept. 1978 %	May 1979 %	June 1980 %	May 1981 %	Nov. 1981 %
Welcome	38	49	47	54	53
Don't welcome	34	26	27	24	20
Undecided	28	25	26	22	27
	100	100	100	100	100

Source: Allensbacher Archiv, IfD-Umfragen 3060, 3070, 3183, 4103, 4002.

Whether this indicates a reawakening of the national idea, however, seems doubtful. Rather, it is to be surmised that the renewed East-West confrontation leads to growing sympathy for this conceivable idea; few harbor illusions as to its utopian character.[14] The idea of a neutralist Federal Republic has always been capable of attracting much support on the part of the electorate.

Since 1951 (albeit interrupted between 1968 and 1979) EMNID has regularly presented a representative sample of the population with the question, "Which do you personally think important: that we as Germans get on good terms with the Americans — that we get on good terms with the Russians — or that we should act neutrally toward both?" The responses are revealing.

We should:	1951 %	1952 %	1953 %	1955 %	1956 %	1957 %	1959 %
get on good terms with the Americans	39	41	46	48	31	39	41
get on good terms with the Russians	1	1	1	3	2	2	2
remain neutral	48	44	42	45	62	55	54
no clear opinion	12	14	11	4	5	4	3

We should:	1960 %	1961 %	1964 %	1965 %	1967 %	1980 %
get on good terms with the Americans	45	55	49	50	35	80
get on good terms with the Russians	2	1	2	3	6	4
remain neutral	48	34	42	42	57	43
no clear opinion	5	10	7	5	4	1

Source: EMNID-Berichte, 5/1980.

There are several notable points in this longitudinal examination:

1. The vigor and long-term nature of this sub-tendency of West German foreign policy is clear, although none of the significant parties pleaded for a neutral status for the Federal Republic during this period.

2. The sympathy for a neutral status is by no means synonymous with a preference for the Soviet Union. (This leaves out of consideration that such a position would benefit the USSR.) But for all intents and purposes, sympathy for a neuralist foreign policy would decrease if respondents were to find out that neutralism, albeit not in its intent, is a pro-Soviet option in its effect.

3. There are reasons for the assumption that the predisposition toward neutralism always grows in periods of vehement overseas tensions between the superpowers (Middle East since 1956, Vietnam 1967). If this is correct, the neutralism expressed here would represent a sort of escapism which is

trying not to get out of the Alliance, but definitely out of superpower tensions.

What effect do the current tensions have? In the beginning, the peace movement's impact was only slight. An EMNID poll of early October 1981 — i.e., the month of the large peace demonstration in Bonn — shows that just at a time of sharpest confrontation the number of those advocating neutrality along the Austrian model amounted to a mere 35 percent, while 63 percent rejected it — a value, then, which was nearly as low as in 1961 when a Third World War threatened to break out over Berlin! As the figures show, responses can readily be correlated positively with preference for the CDU/CSU, FDP, and SPD. But most interesting is the fact that 82 percent of potential "Green" voters were in favor. If there is a party in the Federal Republic today whose supporters overwhelmingly advocate a neutral status, it is the "Greens."

	Total West Germans %	Partisanship			
		CDU/CSU %	SPD %	FDP %	Greens %
Approve neutrality	35	30	37	24	82
Reject neutrality	63				

Source: Der Spiegel, Nov. 30, 1981, p. 94.

The picture of the Federal Republic emerging from a previously mentioned Gallup Poll taken in seven Western European countries is unequivocal; confronted with several alternative questions on security policy, a large majority of West Germans chose the continuation of the pro-Alliance policy:

	Federal Republic %
The NATO Alliance to the Western European countries, the USA and Canada should be maintained	53
Form a European defensive alliance inside NATO under European command but allied to NATO	22
Withdraw our forces from NATO but remain allied politically to NATO	7
Form an independent European defensive alliance under European command without alliance to the USA	8
Rely on the Bundeswehr without any alliance	2
Reduce our military defensive capability and trust in greater agreement with the Soviet Union	4
Don't know/no response	4

Source: Gallup-Umfrage, February 1982. EMNID-Informationen, Nr. 5/6, 1982.

This does not contradict the fact that, notwithstanding a basic affirmation of Western ties, there is a strong desire to reduce the confrontation between East and West. Chancellor Schmidt's willingness to engage in dialogue during the tensions following the invasion of Afghanistan found as much of a positive echo in the population as the Kohl government's readiness to engage in dialogue.[15] Similarly, the East-West negotiations on INF and START in Geneva received positive assessment. A majority of West Germans tend to look first for a negotiated settlement before finding themselves forced to prepare for confrontation, standing reliably by the U.S.

This tendency could be abused by a cleverly maneuvering Federal Government looking for intermediate steps toward the objectives of a neutralist policy — but only up to a certain point and at the risk of hefty reverses.

Abroad, though, a certain caution in the policy of confrontation is frequently misunderstood as neutralism, the more so if relevant suspicions are provoked by the coalition parties or in official statements (as in the last years of Chancellor Schmidt). In reality, neutralism in its wider or restricted meanings forms the program only of a minority party, currently supported by five percent of the voters. The SPD acts tactically; but there are reasons to assume that given the difficulties of any party in opposition, and in view of the rejection of neutralist concepts in all those Western states which count, it will not go beyond tactical or partial rejection of NATO positions.

Anti-Western and Pacifist Unilateralism? Neutralism is no more of a clear concept than the tendencies which have collected in the so-called peace movement. Their objectives are heterogeneous. The hard core is quite evidently composed of groups which reject any policy of balance based on military power, and once again speak out for unilateral emasculation in the face of totalitarian rearmament. In this, even those unilateralist organizations which are far from pro-Soviet are often influenced by Communist functionaries acting openly, or by organizations controlled by Eastern propaganda machines operated more covertly.

These hard-line unilateralist or more or less openly pro-Soviet organizations are often joined by individuals and groups who take sides mainly against certain Western military measures, but who would not, upon serious consideration, reject a policy of military balance within a NATO framework. But they do demand a continuation of the policy of detente, renunciation of Pershing II and cruise missile deployment in the NATO countries, and the removal of chemical weapons. Emotionally and for reasons of moral conviction, they reject high armaments spending as well as weapons exports to the Third World or an extension of NATO commitments beyond the European theater.

This trend among the champions of detente who, however, are not radical unilateralists, extends beyond the pacifist unilateralists and the pronouncedly anti-Western radicals. Since the late 1970s, it finds political expression among the Social Democratic rank and file, but also among influential party leaders, especially Willy Brandt. Along the left perimeter, it meets with the radical groups of the so-called peace movement. But under certain circumstances, it can also be persuaded to accept the Federal Government's official policy of military balance so long as it is tied to credible initiatives of detente. The discussion on security policy which for years has been fragmenting the SPD reflects this openness for both sides.

It is well known and quite understandable that since the big peace demonstration in Bonn in the fall of 1980 the attention of Western publics is riveted with a certain one-sidedness on the pacifist tendencies as well as on those retaining the primacy of detente. Up to the collapse of the Social-Liberal Coalition in the fall of 1982, this was well justified by the SPD's inability, as the largest government party, to define clearly its own position vis-a-vis pacifist and anti-NATO unilateralism. In addition the interest fed on the deliberate drama about the so-called peace movement that many televison journalists created. The audio-visual media have played a decisive part in publicizing the issue and legitimizing protest.

The fascination with the phenomenon, however, has caused the political weight of the unilateralists to be overrated. In fact, pacifist and anti-NATO unilateralists in the Federal Republic articulate the opinion of a comparatively small minority. And in the meantime, a new government has established itself in Bonn, presumably for a longer term, which has no corresponding problems with its rank and file. This should not lead one to disregard the internal difficulties of the Social Democrats — after all, in a more distant future they will at some point become a governing party again. But for the current and medium-term discussion on defense, the SPD's internal situation is of secondary importance.

In reality, the official security policy is supported by a broad majority of voters — not only according to the federal elections of March 6, 1983, but also according to findings emerging from opinion polls.

In this regard the attitudes of the population — precisely at the time when excitement in the media and among the partisans of the peace movement peaked during the period of the Bonn demonstration of October 1981 — are revealing.

Question: There are many different opinions on the questions of armament and disarmament. Several of them are on this page. Which of these most clearly approximates your opinion?

    1. The West should initiate disarmament, regardless of whether or not the East goes along.
    2. The West should disarm, but only to the same extent as the East.
    3. Before the West disarms, the East must start disarming since it has a clear military advantage.
    4. The West should not disarm at all; peace can be guaranteed only by Western superiority.
    5. I can't say much about armament and disarmament; in the final analysis, I'm not quite clear about what is best.

	Total	Opinion Number: (in percent)					No response
		1	2	3	4	5	
Altogether	2,009	5.8	39.5	26.4	8.8	18.6	0.8
SPD	616	5.8	41.6	23.5	9.6	18.8	0.8
CDU/CSU	814	1.6	37.1	33.8	9.3	17.4	0.7
FDP	167	4.7	46.7	21.6	6.6	19.8	0.6
GLU ("Greens")	87	28.7	49.4	9.2	4.6	8.0	0.0
NPD	3	0.0	0.0	33.3	66.7	0.0	0.0
DKP	5	80.0	0.0	0.0	0.0	0.0	0.0
Others	10	20.0	40.0	10.0	0.0	20.0	0.0
Don't know	56	19.6	37.5	16.1	5.4	19.6	0.0
Refuses answer/no response	250	6.8	36.0	22.8	8.8	24.8	1.2

Source: S.F.K. der Konrad-Adenauer-Stiftung (KAS). October 1981.

The findings are relatively baffling: with 5.8 percent, the unilateralists find themselves markedly in the minority position. Those who championed a military policy of Western superiority (which does not correspond to the official position of the Federal Government) are visibly more numerous with 8.8 percent.

Most impressive, though, is the vast middle group — all in all 65.9 percent of respondents. These citizens (one-third of respondents) either plead for balanced mutual arms reduction, or they (one-quarter) assume the harder position that Western disarmament should be initiated only after the East has begun reducing its superiority.

Respondents' political partisanship is also revealing. On the middle ground of the "silent majority," CDU/SCU voters do differ markedly from SPD voters, but not very significantly. It is also remarkable that nearly one-third of "Green" (GLU) partisans favor unilateral action, whereas half of them still support the official government concept of balanced arms reduction.

The optimism of those believing in the long-term commitment of a majority of German voters to NATO's defense policy of upholding the military balance is somewhat dashed by two observations. First, we can analyze a certain strain on the part of those voters who are in favor of official policies. Secondly, there has always been a tendency to favor a fundamental commitment to the West but with caution when it came to concrete and controversial decisions to go ahead with plans for deploying nuclear weapons.

Since late 1982, the number of those sympathetic to a certain degree of unilateral disarmament is increasing. According to an Allensbach poll, the number of those favoring cautious first steps toward disarmament on the part of the West rose from 34 percent in May 1982 to 46 percent in August 1983. At the same time, the number of skeptics fell from 49 percent to 37 percent; 17 percent were undecided each time.[16]

That sounds alarming. But at the same time that the above-mentioned K.A.S. poll in October 1981 showed a rather limited minority of unilaterals

(5.8 percent), their number — according to an Allensbach poll of December 1981 — was already up to 33 percent. The explanation for this contradiction is obvious. Allensbach suggested only a cautious first step ("I think there will be progress toward disarmament only if one side starts the process. That would mean giving a signal of trust to the other side which could not be neglected. That would really lead to peace and detente."); and those interviewed had to decide between polarized arguments. The K.A.S. poll, on the other hand, put the case for unilateralism more bluntly while five differentiated questions served as a reminder that there is no such thing as a clear, polarized distinction between unilateralism on the one hand and opposition to it on the other hand. For the time being one must conclude that there is only a hard core of determined unilateralists, but the number of those favorably inclined to take certain cautious steps in the direction of unilateral disarmament is much larger. Nevertheless, in the swings of German moods concerning security policies, the period from the fall of 1982 to the summer of 1983 was characterized by certain inroads of unilateralism.

This evolution has probably been due to the fact that attention increasingly focused on nuclear hardware. The natural tendency to shy away from concrete armament decisions may have resulted in greater sympathy for unilateralist moves. Anxiety, if it comes to concrete measures, is traditional in Germany. In the first half of the 1950s, when a majority of voters sanctioned Adenauer's foreign policy of Western ties in every federal election, support for the establishment of the *Bundeswehr* rallied a majority only slowly at first but then more rapidly starting in the Fall of 1956.

Question: Basically, are you for or against our deploying a *Bundeswehr*?

	1954 %	1955 %	1956 %	1957 %	1958 %
In favor	45	49	46	55	60
Oppose	50	45	46	39	35
No response	5	6	8	6	5
	100	100	100	100	100

Source: EMNID, 1958.

The willingness to be drafted also grew slowly (for males aged 16 to 65, 59 percent in 1955 responded with "reluctant or unwilling," 45 percent in 1963).[17] Equipping armed forces in the Federal Republic with nuclear weapons and missiles was met with particular hesitation in past decades. In 1958, the movement "against nuclear death" (*Kampf dem Atomtod*) focused public attention on this issue; overwhelming majorities of the same voters who had endorsed Adenauer's Western course in the 1957 and 1958 federal and *Land* elections were opposed to deploying launching pads for nuclear missiles (but also generally to nuclear weapons) on German territory (81 percent opposed, 15 percent in favor, 4 percent no opinion; even 71 percent of CDU supporters were opposed).[18] The systems were installed and the issue calmed down, but future Federal governments saw clearly that the danger of a negative majority exists whenever terrifying modern weapons have to be introduced even in the context of deterrence.

Small wonder, then, that the neutron bomb generated little sympathy during the first heated discussions in 1978. ("West needs neutron bomb," 39 percent; "neutron bomb unnecessary," 29 percent; "undecided, uninformed," 32 percent.[19])

The population's reaction was correspondingly hesitant, although not totally negative, when the question of neutron weapons in 1981 again made waves among the public. Opponents and supporters were approximately balanced. ("Oppose unconditionally," 31 percent; "oppose conditionally — neutron bomb should be produced and deployed in Europe only if it becomes necessary for Western security," 23 percent; "support conditionally," 32 percent; "support unconditionally," 13 percent.[20])

Even more pronounced support is indicated for the double-track decision. The results of several Allensbach polls are as follows:

	May 1981 %	Jan. 1982 %	Dec. 1982 %	Aug.1983 %
Approve	53	52	51	49
Disapprove	20	22	25	23
Undecided	27	26	24	28
	100	100	100	100

Source: Allensbacher Archiv, *Frankfurter Allgemeine Zeitung*, Sept. 16, 1983.

These are snapshots. Naturally, in public opinion the answers often vary considerably according to the precise wording of the question. It is fair to assume that the ratio of supporters to critics as well as the number of undecided will change drastically pending the course of future discussions.

Surprisingly, the West German population proves to be the least defeatist in a European comparison, second only to the Swiss and Britons. This emerges from a provocative question probing the readiness to fight in case of war defending liberty against the Russians.

> *Question*: Some people believe that war today would be so terrible that it would be better to submit to Russian domination than to risk a war. Others believe it would be preferable to fight for the defense [. . . of your country . . .] than to submit to Russian domination. Which opinion would you tend to favor?

	Nation[+]							
	B	D	DK	GB	F	I	CH	USA
	%	%	%	%	%	%	%	%
Prefer accepting Russian domination	15	19	17	12	13	17	8	6
Prefer defense	49	74	51	75	57	48	77	83
Don't know/no response	36	7	32	13	30	35	15	11

[+] B = Belgium; D = Federal Republic; DK = Denmark; GB = Great Britain; F = France; I = Italy; CH = Switzerland; USA = United States
Source: Gallup-Umfrage, February 1982. EMNID-Informationen No. 5/6 1982.

Attitudes on these basic questions of Western defense policy depend closely on perceptions of the East-West power ratio. Time and again the opinion is voiced that unilateralist attitudes essentially express fear of a superior Soviet Union. In fact, a much more complicated picture presents itself.

Few sets of attitudes have undergone such thorough empirical examination since the first half of the 1950s as the German assessment of the power ratio.

Question: Currently, which side do think is stronger, the Americans and the West on the one hand, or the Russians and the East on the other?

	West	East	Both equal	No response
	%	%	%	%
1954	40	23	33	4
1956	33	23	39	5
1958	33	30	34	3
1960	32	22	38	8
1961	34	22	41	3
1962	39	15	29	17
1963	46	10	33	11
1964	54	7	29	10
1965	47	12	31	10
1966	39	15	33	13
1968	34	21	35	10
1974	23	24	43	11
1975	27	29	44	1
1976	16	35	47	2
1981	15	41	43	1
1982 (Nov.)	23	27	49	1

Source: EMNID, APD 12/1981 and EMNID-Informationen 10-1982.

The trend is obvious. During the second half of the 1960s, the cohorts of voters believing either that the West was stronger or that a certain balance had been reached were about equal. In 1966, only 15 percent believed in

Soviet superiority. Due to the trends dominating the entire 1970s, a fundamental shift occurred by 1981. Only 15 percent still believed in Western superiority; those assuming either Eastern superiority or a balance were approximately equal. Meanwhile, confidence in Western strength has grown again. Are we witnessing another change of trends?

Ever since this question has been posed, correlations to political partisanship have been run. CDU/CSU partisanship correlates positively with the assumption of Soviet superiority, SPD partisanship tends to correlate positively with the assumption of balance (but no clear party profile results on either side). By contrast, among the "Greens," the number of those assuming a balance, 50.6 percent, was significantly above that of CDU/CSU adherents (23.6 percent) or SPD adherents (38.5 percent).[21] This was quite logical: those not wanting to modernize in the face of the opponent's armaments can rationalize this readily by assuming the balance to be intact.

If the fear-thesis were correct as an explanation of pacifist unilaterism, the CDU/CSU partisans, 60.8 percent of whom were convinced of Soviet superiority in October 1981, would have had to favor unilateral measures of disarmament matching Eastern demands. Instead, the CDU's supporters stood alone among the sympathizers of the larger parties to plead for a rise in defense expenditures (18.8 percent), even if it necessitated cuts in social services. Still, 56.9 percent of the CDU's supporters who felt that higher defense expenditures were appropriate believed this should be done only if it did not lead to any economizing on social services.

By contrast, 62.1 percent of "Green" supporters unconditionally opposed increasing defense expenditures; one-third was prepared to accept them but (as with the majority of CDU/CSU supporters and SPD supporters — 53.6 percent) only if social expenditures would not suffer.[22]

Quite obviously, then, large parts of the German electorate are rather reluctant to opt for "guns" when faced with the alternative, of "guns or butter." Perception of Soviet superiority or of balance has not thus far produced the willingness to make sacrifices for defense; on the other hand, it has not yet resulted in the defeatism frequently imputed to Germans in Western countries. Again, the inclination to prefer "soft options" is clear.

Similar findings result from the question whether pacifist inclinations in the Federal Republic are conditioned mainly by increased fear of war. In the treatment of this phenomenon, too, we can rely on impressive longitudinal studies.

Question: Do you believe there will be a new world war within the next three years?

	A new world war is:			
	probable %	possible %	improbable %	no opinion %
1950	35	48	17	—
1951	18	56	26	—
1952	16	47	37	—
1953	8	39	53	—
1954	7	45	48	—
1955	3	27	70	—
1956 May	5	35	60	—
1956 Nov.	13	55	32	—
1957 Aug.	5	32	63	—
1958 May	4	35	61	—
1959 June	5	37	58	—
1960 May	5	39	56	—
1961 Sept.	7	37	56	—
1962 Jan.	8	47	45	—
1962 Sept.	4	33	63	—
1964 Sept.	2	16	74	8
1965 Apr.	2	16	53	9
1967 June	6	30	55	9
1968 Oct.	3	29	60	8
1979 July	2	17	80	1
1979 Dec.	4	35	59	2
1980 Jan.	9	40	49	1
1980 Dec.	3	29	68	—
1981 July/Aug.	5	32	63	—
1982 June	6	38	56	1

Source: EMNID, APD 44/1962 and 5/6-1982.

The fear of war evidently relates to tensions in East-West relations. Since the early 1950s, there has been no pronounced fear of war even among small sections of the German population. By the same token, responses as to the "possibility" of a world war within the next three years vary greatly. The Suez and Hungarian crises of 1956, the Berlin crisis 1961/62, the Afghanistan crisis and East-West tensions in 1982 provide obvious peaks, but one must not neglect that even when a sizable minority had a decidedly gloomy assessment, a consistent minority remained imperturbable (except for 1962 when a third world war threatened to erupt over Berlin).

If fear of war had played a primary role, then the 1950s would also have had to produce a very powerful peace movement. There was resistance to rearmament and the movement "against nuclear death" in 1957 and 1958, but intensity and durability were low.

Since early 1980, the fear of superpower clashes has grown markedly. But conjecture as to the extent that conditions of international politics are responsible for swelling the ranks of pacifist unilateralism in the Federal Republic must be qualified. If one alleges that the determinants of the international system are mainly responsible for the protest behavior, the fact that only a small minority of committed Germans participate in the peace movement and consider pacifist unilateralism appropriate could not be explained.

Indeed, the spread of the so-called peace movement in the Federal Republic must be explained in terms of sociological models rather than political conditions. The peace movement is supported primarily by Germans under 35: the mass base is provided by high-school and university students, and the representation of the young unemployed is above average. Although the organization rests in the hands of older individuals (teachers, clergymen, union functionaries, "protest functionaries," professionals, homemakers, journalists), the strongest social base is still comprised of younger Germans with a high level of formal education.

Several theories are proffered to explain this phenomenon:

1. *The group-dynamics explanation.* High-school and university students are characterized by a high degree of direct communication in their fields of activity. As opposed to the normal working person, work and leisure are interwoven. The chance that a high-school or university student is seized completely by the value systems and organizations of his milieu are considerably greater than for most professional groups. Intensive communication, rapid exchange of information, ready availability for organization facilitates formation of political subcultures with their own marks. Now, if there were well-organized and politically ideologized groups in the milieu (student congregations, Socialist or Communist pupils' or students' organizations, pacifist single-purpose movements), then the chance is good that many will temporarily be swept along by the tendencies experienced as mass-movements in the milieu.

2. *The theory of deferred adolescence.* Pupils and students as yet fill no permanent professional roles. They must comply with roles of dependent trainees while at the same time finding themselves in distinctly worse economic circumstances than their working contemporaries. Contrary to these, however, they have more leisure time and see themselves in a position to cogitate the world and society in general, and they are invariably commended for political activity. The unavoidable inclination of working adults to concern themselve primarily with professional tasks, their own family, and specific interests thus far has little effect on students, nor does responsibility for specific tasks. Hence, pupils and students in their irresponsibly long phase of scholastic or academic training tend much more strongly than other groups to engage in general reasoning and involve themselves in the highest causes (world peace, end to hunger and need in the Third World, re-establishment of the ecological balance, taming of technology).

3. *The theory of post-materialist society.* This theory, developed by Ronald Inglehart and much seized upon in Germany,[23] is an ideology of the subculture just described rather than a theory to explain its political orientations.

The effect of saturation with material goods, of course, which is noticeable especially among the young people from the middle class, leads to an ideological glorification of non-material values as well as to an idealistic critique of technology. While still living at the expense of society or parents, a young person does not need to concern himself much with the technical environment or the economic superstructure. And once he finds himself, for example, as a civil servant, a radio journalist or a social worker, in a remarkably well-paid and secure position, as is the case in Germany, then again he can safely give full reign to his critical mistrust of technology and economics. Why such criticism spills over to nuclear deterrence is self-evident.

4. *The theory of "telecracy."* Many of the politically committed Socialists and liberals have moved from the protest generation of the 1968 movement into radio and television stations. A great number of them view their job not as primarily journalistic, but as a political mission. The obligation to inform is joined by the intent to manipulate public consciousness. The so-called peace movement is also a TV movement.

To be sure, international events (end of detente, dramatic rearmament in the U.S. under Reagan, NATO's decision to modernize its INF) have contributed to the activities of these groups. Overall, however, it is fair to say that a generation has not been galvanized by one great theme — danger of war and maintenance of peace. On the contrary, a disposable, excited political subculture, prone to a certain extent to alienation, has found its current theme in the peace issue!

From the mid- to late 1960s up to the 1970s the big theme was "democratization." Beginning in the mid-1970s, the leftist political subculture found its calling chiefly in protests against nuclear power plants and technical mega-projects (Runway West in Frankfurt). Since the early 1980s, the themes have been peace and opposition to INF modernization. Churches have added further impulses on the topic of peace.

What conclusions are to be drawn from these analytical snapshots?

1. The pacifist unilateralists and the anti-NATO radicals who affect them in part form a structural minority in West German society. This is evidenced again and again. In the representative poll of October 1981 mentioned above, a mere 12 percent of respondents between the ages of 18 and 29 favored unilateral disarmament (as opposed to 4.7 percent of the 30-59-year-olds and 2.4 percent of those over 60). But 40.3 percent advocated balanced arms reductions, 20.3 percent pleaded for Russian advances *to precede* Western disarmament, and 7.4 percent desired Western superiority.[24]

Polling produced this picture of younger Germans at the exact time that hundreds of thousands of young people were streaming to the big peace demonstrations in Bonn. Even one million demonstrators amount to a mere 1/25th of the German electorate. They are vocal, they are committed, they are active — but they remain a structural minority.

2. The unilateralists' impact feeds from their great (often fanatical) commitment, their close organizational network, support from television journalism, and most specifically from the fact that the entire German Left has

been concentrating exclusively on this theme since 1981. Future temporary reinforcement cannot be ruled out. But there are socio-structural limits to the movement's growth, and predictably a single-purpose movement will be unable to maintain its activities with full momentum for many years. Frustration, acclimatization to the nuclear age and the recognition that life will continue even after missile deployment might take effect sooner or later.

3. For years, pacifist unilateralism has been profiting from the fact that the SPD is politically neutered by its leftist rank and file. Analogous to the French army following the Dreyfus Affair, the moderate center plays the part of a *grande muette* in today's Social Democracy. The silent majority of sober, non-hysterical functionaries, members of parliament, and even some top politicians tactically play for time, hoping that the rank and file will eventually find a different theme. Thus, that part of the German public sympathizing with moderate center-left positions remains largely leaderless on this issue. This, too, gives rise to the appearance of an alternative movement of near-irresistible explosiveness and moral power.

The New Tradition

Incertitudes allemandes? The empirical evidence of 35 years of German history disproves this skeptical question. Even the in-depth analysis of currently prevalent attitudes produces no sharp breach in long-term, relatively stable opinions.

1. The vast majority of West Germans see their democratic constitutional government as natural. In comparison to other Western European countries, democracy in the Federal Republic is remarkably stable. In its 35 years of existence, it has experienced neither system crises like France in 1958 and 1968 nor a constitutional crisis like Belgium in the 1970s. It knows no large Communist parties as do Italy and France. Unlike Great Britain, it is neither burdened with regional autonomist tendencies nor with an unending civil war in a border province; and unlike Greece it never experienced the interlude of a colonels' dictatorship.

Whoever compares the Federal Republic to the contemporary democracies in Western Europe will judge it more appropriate than those projecting it primarily against the background of a problematic German history. The stability of democratic government at least partially accounts for the evident stability of majority opinions in the electorate. And attitudes marked by experience, custom, and education in turn strengthen the stability of constitutional government.

2. Even contemporary West German democracy must suffer a political subculture of more or less alienated radicals. In this it is not fundamentally different from other Western European democracies in which waves of protest well up, but then retreat again. Distinctly socio-pathological mass movements or activities afflict modern democracies more regularly than friends of moderate politics would care to admit. What Seymour Martin Lipset and Earl Raab have elaborated by means of longitudinal analysis of the American

example can be discerned in European democracies as well — "the politics of unreason," carried by groups of the extreme Left and Right.[25] Though recognizing the phenomenon's ubiquity must not lull the vigilance and assertiveness of the friends of constitutional government, it does draw attention to the fact that sooner or later hysterical movements spring up in any democracy, but they also fade again if a country is fortunate and if it has democratic leaders who will not be bullied and have electoral majorities backing them. In any event, there is reason to doubt that those phenomena of fundamentally or partially alienated political subcultures in the Federal Republic are really sufficiently unprecedented to warrant terms such as "alternative culture," "silent revolution," "crisis of values," etc. Political life in modern societies often just happens to be more hectic, contradictory, and brutal: the values are often less compatible and the conflicts correspondingly sharper than is the case under less dynamic social conditions. But then, modern democracies can stand a considerable measure of anarchy, violence, and madness. The alienation of politically active strata from democratic constitutional government and industrial society is a challenge to all moderate forces, to be sure. But one can live with it; much of it will wear down and dissipate again.

3. The political ties to the West have become a living, new tradition, just as with democratic constitutional government. The great majority of elites and voters recognizes it as a sort of *"raison d'etat* of the Federal Republic."* Of course, how the maxims of a *raison d'etat* are to be interpreted and applied in specific instances is usually controversial. It accounts for much of the foreign political dispute between the government and opposition, but also within the government parties and opposition. In any event, the Western ties are deeply rooted in the party system. To the surprise of radical leftist groups, they have survived 13 years of Social-Liberal Coalition because, naturally, neither the leading Social Democrats nor the Free Democrats wanted to disturb the fundamental orientations. Thus, there is every reason to expect that under a new government, too, they will survive the pacifist movement, even if it grows more hysterical.

4. Probably the most encouraging development in the decades since 1949 was the withering away of German nationalism. As all polls indicate and as statements by German officials reminds us from time to time, the German problem is not a dead issue and national consciousness is still alive, though tempered by awareness of the realities of European power relationships. Yet there is no divided country in modern history where the national feelings are so moderate, so balanced by caution and so impregnated with a sense of responsibility for European peace. In this respect, the change brought about by the experience of Hitler's nationalism and the sufferings of the war is as deep-reaching and as permanent as the conversion to the value system of Western democracy.

A latent national dream still haunts some quarters of public opinion, waiting for dramatic changes in Russia and in the Eastern bloc as a whole which might provide a chance for liberation of the Germans confined in the GDR. But one can definitely rule out, at least for the time being, that the present peace movement and its obvious sympathies for neutralism are motivated by the yearning for reunification. Of course, in a more or less distant future nobody can exclude the danger of a leftist and neutralist nationalism which might regress to the old concept of a reunified Germany. There are abundant examples in modern history that nationalism is not confined to the political Right. But for the time being, this is only a possibility and one cannot expect the moderate majority to be persuaded to embark on a highly risky and uncertain course. An electorate which has kept calm in the 1950s, when the chances for reunification were much better than they are today, will not become reckless in the 1980s.

5. Though the commitment to the community of Western democracies is firmly established, there is nevertheless a certain disposition on the part of the German electorate to consider neutralist policies. Since the 1950s there has been a continuous up and down in the strength of the neutralist mood. From time to time the number of those admitting neutralist sympathies is even greater than the bulk of voters showing unflinching support of NATO.

This neutralism may reflect a yearning for a reunified, neutral Germany (as in the '50s), or it may be concerned exclusively with the Federal Republic (as in the 1970s and early '80s). In either case it indicates uneasiness about East-West tensions and signals a tendency to shy away from the unpleasant realities of power politics. To most of those who confess a certain neutralism, this is much more a vague mood than a determination to abandon the NATO camp. It offers emotional escapism, for example, through flirtation with an illusory equidistance between the superpowers, but there is no serious desire to radically alter an international status which, for 35 years, has provided security and prosperity. This mood could be manipulated, of course, by a Federal Government prepared to weaken the Western ties. But given the determination of the government of Helmut Kohl to stick to the alliance, the escapist mood can hardly be converted into meaningful policies.

6. More or less the same may be true of today's pacificism. Like neutralism, it is much more a mood than a clear concept. Germans who favor some kind of pacifist response to the complexities of international security show various degrees of attachment to pacifist ideas. In those segments of the electorate where the present pacifism gets favorable attention, one may distinguish three different groups:

— first, the hard-core unilateralists;

— second, a much larger group of Germans mainly opposed to the deployment of new American missiles;

— third, a still larger group composed of largely apolitical voters responding primarily with unsophisticated emotionalism to the call for peace, without caring too much about the issues as such, without being aware of the political consequences of certain pacifist policies, but also without any prejudice against a basically pro-Western foreign policy.

One may call these groups the radical unilateralists, the specific unilateralists, and the apolitical peace-lovers.

The radical unilateralists are highly politicized and ideologically motivated. To a large extent, they not only diverge from the foreign policies supported by a majority of the electorate, but they are also alienated from the prevailing social and political system by invoking all kinds of alternative ways of life. They deeply abhor balance-of-power policies, most of them are anti-militarist (with the exception of full-fledged Communists), most of them also show an open or latent anti-American bias.

They are found in all sorts of organizations, including the "Greens," the left wing of the SPD (particularly many of the rank and file members), all blends of orthodox and non-orthodox Communists, fellow-travellers, but also effective organizations from the left wing of the Protestant and Catholic churches, including many clergymen. Sociologically speaking, all these organizations get their main support from the younger generation, and they are to a large extent composed of educated middle class people. Numerically, this hard core of uncompromising radical unilateralists may comprise 5-8 percent of the German electorate. That means that they comprise a structural, if vocal minority.

The second group — the specific unilateralists — is composed of frustrated believers in the detente policies of the 1970s. Most of them are basically pro-Western, maybe even pro-American. But they abhor the idea that the former complementarity of vigorous detente policies, dear to the entire Western Alliance, and a policy of military balance should be defunct. To a large extent, they blame the Reagan Administration for the end of detente and for the deadlock of arms control negotiations. Since they are still in favor of detente policies, they have become more or less susceptible to the idea of equidistance — though they want a more independent German *Ostpolitik* without abandoning NATO, hoping that the U.S. sooner or later might return to the previous detente policies. Needless to say, a majority of these voters adheres to the SPD.

The third group, concerned, but rather apolitical and not particularly sophisticated peace-lovers (many of them practicing Christians), is even less committed to radical pacifist foreign policies. They are basically pro-Western, pro-NATO, many of them relatively conservative people (particularly from the older age cohorts) who simply want to avoid war, domestic strife and international tensions. These Germans do not opt for a weakened NATO, they do not even abandon their basic mistrust of Soviet Russia. But being confronted with hard choices and apocalyptic fears stirred up by the peace movement, they opt for an easy way out of the confrontation — for a kind of moratorium, for an endless continuation of the INF negotiations without deployment, in any case for a negotiated settlement thus avoiding an unpleasant Western rearmament.

7. What the media and the pacifists themselves portray as a mighty peace movement is in fact a mixed bag of elements bound to fall apart sooner or later.

There is no chance of convincing the hard core of the radical pacifists. They must be left aside, and the Alliance must learn to live with them, as it has learned to live with Communist mass parties in France and Italy.

The final stand of the second group — specific unilateralists, detente-minded Germans — will depend largely on the outcome of the struggle inside the SPD. Maybe the leadership of the Social Democrats will put up a brave fight against American missiles, knowing full well that it will be beaten, and then will silently return to Alliance policy. Maybe the missile issue will force the SPD and its electorate more and more toward a policy of equidistance and practical unilateralism, though membership in NATO will not be questioned. The outcome is still open. In the latter case, a considerable part of the German electorate, though not a majority, will be much more open than before to unilateralist and neutralist attitudes.

As to the third group of the undecided — the apolitical, concerned people — one may expect that they will eventually support the policies of the Alliance and of the Kohl Government when the chips are down in Geneva, and when they realize that the future of NATO would be at stake if Germany did not stick to the double-track decision.

Since the Greens represent only a structural minority of the electorate, since the so-called peace movement is torn apart by many internal and organizational tensions, and since the fragmented Social Democrats will have to play the part of the opposition for quite a while, prospects are good that the *raison d'etat* of the Federal Republic, which demands a predictable course amidst the NATO convoy will prevail. Western ties in the Federal Republic have a tenacious life.

NOTES

[1] Pierre Vienot, *Incertitude allemandes*, Paris, 1931.

[2] The title of a volume by the Swiss author Rene Allemann (*Bonn is nicht Weimar*, Köln/Berlin, 1956) which received much attention in the 1950s.

[3] The material has been made available by the Sozialwissenschaftliches Forschungsinstitut der Konrad-Adenauer-Stiftung, where, in accordance with this author's questions, correlations have been run on various relevant polls to permit a more thorough-going analysis of opinions. The author is particularly grateful to Mr. Wolffs, Dipl.-Pol.

[4] For the basic positions of the various schools of thought from a Social Democratic perspective, see Richard Löwenthal (pseudonym: Paul Sering), *Jenseits des Kapitalismus. Ein Beitrag zur sozialistischen Normenorientierung*, Lauf b. Nürnberg, 1946 (reprinted and brought up to date with a new preface: Berlin/Bonn/Bad Godesberg, 1977); from a conservative perspective, Friedrich Meinecke, *Die deutsche Katastrophe*, Zürich, 1946, and Gerhard Ritter, *Europa und die deutsche Frage*, München, 1948. The most important neo-liberal interpretations were published by Wilhelm Röpke, *Die deutsche Frage*, Erlenbach/Zürich, 1945. The most fundamental analysis from a Catholic-conservative position is by F.A. Kramer, *Vor den Ruinen Deutschlands. Ein Aufruf zur geschichtlichen Selbstbestimmung*, Koblenz, 1945. The liberal mainstream of the 1950s and 1960s is marked by the books of Karl Dietrich Bracher, *Das deutsche Dilemma. Leidensweg der politischen Emanzipation*, München, 1971; Ralf Dahrendorf, *Gesellschaft und Demokratie in Deutschland*, München, 1965, and Ernst Fränkel, *Deutschland und die westlichen Demokratien*, Stuttgart, 1964. The historical interpretation of the Catholic left is found in the writings of Eugen Kogon, *Die unvollendete Erneuerung. Deutschland im Kräftefeld 1945-1963*, Frankfurt am Main, 1964, the increasingly important (left-) liberal and radical-democratic view in the anthology by Hans Werner Richter, *Bestandsaufnahme. Eine deutsche Bilanz*

1962, München/Wien/Basel, 1962. The author himself has presented the decisive beginnings of West Germany's relevant discussion in the volume *Vom Reich zur Bundesrepublik. Deutschland im Widerstreit der aussenpolitischen Konzeptionen in den Jahren der Besatzungsherrschaft 1945-1949* (Stuttgart: Klett-Cotta, 1980 [1966]). See also my books on Germany in the Adenauer era: *Die Ära Adenauer. Gründerjahre der Republik, 1949-1957*, Geschichte der Bundesrepublik Deutschland, vol. II, (Stuttgart/ Wiesbaden: Brockhaus, DVA, 1981); *Die Ära Adenauer. Epochenwechsel, 1957-1963* Geschichte der Bundesrepublik Deutschland, vol. III, (Stuttgart/Wiesbaden: Brockhaus, DVA, 1983). For an overview see Gordon Craig, *The Germans* (New York: G.P. Putnam's Sons, 1982).

[5] Regarding the extensive literature on the special way and the current state of the discussion, see the synopsis of Bernd Faulenbach, "Deutscher Sonderweg. Zur Geschichte und Problematik einer zentralen Kategorie des deutschen politischen Bewusstseins," in *Aus Politik und Zeitgeschichte*, vol. 33 (1981), pp. 3-21.

[6] Werner Kaltefleiter, *Wirtschaft und Politik in Deutschland. Konjunktur als Bestimmungsfaktor des Parteiensystems*, Köln/Opladen, 1968 (1966).

[7] Gabriel S. Almond and Sidney Verba, *The Civic Culture. Political Attitudes and Democracy in Five Nations* (Princeton, N.J.: Princeton University Press, 1963), pp. 3-42. Seymour Martin Lipset, *Political Man. The Social Bases of Politics* (New York: Doubleday & Co., 1959).

[8] Source: *Frankfurter Allgemeine Zeitung*, October 2, 1978. Similar, even more critical opinions were brought to light in a 1979 study by the Friedrich-Ebert-Stiftung. See Christian Krause et al., *Zwischen Revolution und Resignation. Alternativkultur, politische Grundströmungen und Hochschulaktivitäten in der Studentenschaft*, Bonn, 1980.

[9] *Ibid.*, pp. 173, 175.

[10] Source: *Allensbacher Jahrbuch der Demoskopie*, 1976, p. 80. The views also changed very little thereafter: Dec. 1977/Jan. 1978, 75 percent; May/June 1979, 76 percent; June 1982, 77 percent opposed to deletion. *Ibid.*, No. 3052, 3070, 4010/II. Apparently, national consciousness has slowly stabilized again.

[11] Hans-Georg von Studnitz, *Bismarck in Bonn. Bemerkungen zur Aussenpolitik*, Stuttgart, 1964.

[12] A handy survey of this leftist and rightist neutralism was provided in the anthology by Wolfgang Venohr (ed.), *Die deutsche Einheit kommt bestimmt* (Bergisch Gladbach: Lübbe, 1982), where Theodor Schweisfurth warms over the ideas of reunification-neutralism, and Peter Brandt and Herbert Ammon plead for a leftist, pacifist, and socialist concept of non-alignment. To be taken seriously is the political potential of Oskar Lafontaine from the left wing of the SPD; he is quite obviously moving towards more and more neutralist positions. See his *Angst vor den Freunden*, Spiegel-Buch, Hamburg, 1983.

[13] Zbigniew Brzezinski, "The Framework of East-West Reconciliation," in *Foreign Affairs*, vol. 46, no. 2 (January 1968), pp. 256-75.

[14] In the corresponding first Allensbach poll of September 1978 just mentioned, 38 percent expressed their sympathy for a neutral, reunified Germany, only 4 percent considered possible a reunification within the next ten years, 53 percent thought it improbable, 8 percent had no opinion, and 35 percent had never heard of a neutralist manifest emanating for dissident circles in the GDR. (*Aktuelle demoskopische Berichte Allensbach*. Manifest des "Bund demokratischer Kommunisten Deutschlands," April 28, 1978.)

[15] Cf. *Aktuelle demoskopische Berichte Allensbach*, 29/31 May, 1980. EMNID, APD June/July 1980.

[16] Source: *Frankfurter Allgemeine Zeitung*, Sept. 16, 1983.

[17] Source: EMNID, 06/1969.

[18] Source: EMNID, 11/1958.

[19] *Aktuelle demoskopische Berichte Allensbach*, June 26, 1978.

[20] Source: *Der Spiegel*, No. 48, 1981, pp. 59-63.

[21] Source for the October 1981 figures: S.F.K. der Konrad Adenauer Stiftung (KAS).

[22] Source: *Ibid*.

[23] Ronald Inglehart, *The Silent Revolution. Changing Values and Political Styles among Western Publics* (Princeton, N.J.: Princeton University Press, 1973). The relevant German discussion is analyzed by Helmut Vogt, *Politische Generationen* (Opladen: Westdeutsche Verlagsgesellschaft, 1982).

[24] See the table on page 84 above. Source: *S.F.K. der KAS*.

[25] Seymour Martin Lipset and Earl Raab, *The Politics of Unreason. Right-wing Extremism in America, 1790-1970* (New York, Evanston, London: Harper & Row, 1970).

RELIGION AND POLITICS IN GERMANY AND IN GERMAN-AMERICAN RELATIONS

by Jürgen Moltmann

I shall be confining myself in this paper to a few comments on (1) the political importance of religion in Germany, (2) the religious importance of politics in Germany, and (3) the religious and moral dimensions of German-American relations. The discussion about peace and security will provide a kind of focal point.[1]

The Political Importance of Religion in Germany

In Germany, the religion which acquires political importance (in the sense of public effectiveness) was, and still is, the organized religion of the churches. This applies both to the Federal Republic of Germany and to the German Democratic Republic. It is true that 1½ million Moslems are now living in the Federal Republic, most of them Turkish immigrant workers. It is also true that the missionaries of the new religions — the so-called youth religions — are penetrating into every suburb. But in spite of this, the Federal Republic, unlike the United States or England, is not as yet a multi-religious society. More than 90 percent of the population still belong to one of the two main Christian denominations. This means that crises and changes in the religious sector (in basic trust, fundamental values, what people hope for in life, and their attitude toward living) are discerned and expressed first and foremost by the two churches, and are also induced by these churches. Anyone who wants to know how the religious foundations of our people are being shaken, and how men and women are being stirred by new religious points of reference, will get the best and most vivid impression from the great General Assemblies (*Kirchentage*) of the Protestant and Catholic churches.

But the churches are in a state of radical transition in their institutional form as well, and this transition clearly reflects the change in the political importance of religion in Germany. Only 65 years ago, Article 137, Section 1, of the Weimar Constitution of 1919 declared: "There is no established state church." Up to that time the Protestant churches, at least, had been established state churches. The prince of each German state was the church's *summepiscopus*; the clergy were his officials; and the established churches were the public institutions of the Christian civil religion which held the dominant position in that particular state. "State church" meant that religion was practiced by church and state together. Attempts have been made in modern times to divide church and state by creating a state which is neutral toward religion. Or the state has been cut off from church and faith by way of civil religion's motto: "Religion is my private affair." But these attempts have hardly done anything to change the political significance of religion as this was once determined through the form of the state church. Times of war have always evoked a great religious unity of church, state and people. The conservative religion of the Holy Alliance emerged from the Wars of Liberation against Napoleon. In the First World War, the political religion of German nationalism mobilized the troops "For God, King and Fatherland." In the Second World War, political messianism drove the Germans into the measureless guilt and mass death "For Führer, People and Fatherland." The state churches were generally the religious instruments of these political movements. It was only under the Hitler dictatorship and its neo-pagan philosophy that for the the first time — and at the cost of severe internal conflicts — Christian resistance grew up in the churches, and even the public significance of church religion changed. And yet Auschwitz and the Holocaust inflicted on the Jewish people remain the appalling accusation that has to be levied against a blind and faint-hearted Christian church in Germany.

Today the internal conflicts in the churches flare up over the question about the consequences of resistance against the state ideology of National Socialism; the question about the consequences of *non*-resistance is more explosive still. Was that resistance conditioned merely by the extraordinary situation? Or does the result for the churches have to be critical freedom *in principle* toward every constitutional form and every government whatsoever? If the church has to withstand every dictatorship which despises human beings and every totalitarian ideology, can it then regard Western parliamentary democracy as its true home, and become the religion sustaining this form of civic community? Or must it here too become the advocate of the weak, and a ferment of liberty for the people? Does this mean that in certain circumstances, if the occasion seems to demand it, it must ally itself with forms of extra-parliamentary opposition such as the peace movement, the ecology movement, Third World groups?

I should like to look at the elements of this transition and the present conflict in the two churches. I shall consider them under four headings, before going on to describe the main conflict at the present moment: the peace question.

1. The alliance between "throne and altar" — i.e., state and church — came to an end in 1919 when "the throne" was abolished. For the churches, "the throne" was replaced by "the people" and "the nation" — but not by the democracy of the Weimar Republic. The church's own prevailing self-questioning came to be that it was "the people's church." Of course this meant a church "belonging to the people," but in actual fact it was merely a continuation of the state church with different instruments. What emerged was a "church *for* the people," a "pastoral" church for looking after the

people, a "religious welfare church," the administered religion of society. For whether our churches see themselves as state churches or people's churches, the premise is the same: religion is *involuntary affiliation*. So 90 percent of the population "belong" to one or another of the major churches and pay taxes to it; only 10-15 percent, however, participate actively in the church's life. The basis on which the churches operate is this affiliation first of all. Participation by the people comes second. With only a little exaggeration one might say that affiliation is involuntary; only secession from the church is voluntary.

At this point the big differences between Germany and the United States become evident. In America democratic "commonwealths" were founded in opposition to European monarchies, and free-church congregations were formed in contrast to the churches of Europe. In the American republic, the system of voluntary religion came into being. This voluntary system is the religious basis of democratic society in America. State churches and people's churches never create a climate friendly toward democracy — this is true in the Federal Republic of Germany too — because they never renounce their claim to dominate the religion and morality of men and women.

But the increasing independence of modern people in moral and political questions, and in religious ones as well, is going to mean that, in the Federal Republic as well, the churches will become congregational churches instead of people's churches, and they will increasingly take over elements from the free churches. If the churches cannot make this change themselves, they will be forced to make it, sooner or later, by the slow movement toward a renunciation of official church affiliation. We can already see this change of structure in the local churches themselves: church attendance is declining, but participation in the Lord's Supper is growing. The quantity of Christian life is diminishing; the quality is increasing. Voluntary participation and involvement are taking the place of passive membership.

2. The churches are moving away from an identification with the "civil" or "political" religion of society to a critical solidarity with the community as a whole. On the Protestant side, this note could be heard for the first time in the "acknowledgement of guilt" made by the German churches in Stuttgart in 1945: the church spoke for the whole people, but it spoke critically and self-critically. It became a politically relevant factor when, in 1965, it laid down its position in a memorandum on the condition of those who had been expelled from former German territories, urging reconciliation with our eastern neighbors. This prepared the ground for the policy toward East Germany pursued by the Social-Liberal coalition.

From the division of Germany in 1945 until the building of the Berlin Wall in 1961, the churches were the strongest forces keeping the unity of the German people alive. The great church assemblies (*Kirchentage*) which took place in Berlin and Leipzig were great all-German demonstrations as well. It is true that, after the building of the Berlin Wall, an independent federation of churches was formed in the German Democratic Republic. But there was still a strong sense that the church in East and West Germany is a unity. This has led to the remarkable fact that a great many Christians —

Protestant Christians especially — have been, and still are, against a one-sided integration of the Federal Republic in the West. Ties with "our brothers and sisters in the GDR" are strong. It is hardly possible for us to talk about German-American relations without talking about German-German relations at the same time.

It has proved easier for the church to maintain its new attitude of critical solidarity toward society and state in the GDR, on the foundation of "socialism as it really exists," than in "the free constitutional state" in the Federal Republic. So, surprisingly enough, the church in the German Democratic Republic expresses itself much more freely and critically about the government's rearmament policy, and on behalf of peace, than the churches in the Federal Republic.

3. A critical detachment toward our own society and our own state goes hand in hand with a new ecumenical awareness among Christians, both Catholic and Protestant. And at church assemblies, synods and conferences the conflict between ecumenical solidarity and national loyalty is an increasingly common experience. Let me give two examples.

a) The "Programme to Combat Racism" which was passed by the World Council of Churches in 1971 drew attention to white racism, and the oppression and exploitation of black people in South Africa. But the practical steps involved led to a continuing conflict in our country. When the help given to the oppressed ceased to be merely humanitarian, when the economic interests of German banks and companies in South Africa were subjected to a critical investigation, and when Christian women's organizations organized a boycott — "Don't buy the fruits of apartheid!" — the churches were accused of illegitimate interference in politics. There is really no problem here: as long as the church gave its blessing to our own weapons, it counted as non-political; but if it once begins to act against our own national interests, it is called political. What really is a problem, however, is the question of priorities. There are more and more involved Christian groups in the churches who are no longer prepared to put national loyalty before ecumenical solidarity. They act contrary to the ruling interests in their own society, in solidarity with the victims of those same interests. Of course this is not merely an ethical problem for individual faith. It is also a financial problem for the churches. Every public act of ecumenical solidarity which is bound up with national disloyalty has to be paid for by a secession of registered members of the church. And this means a loss of the tax legally imposed on these members, which is used to finance much of the church's work and its ministry. Consequently the traditional structure of the church itself is inherently called into question through this conflict.

b) Christians in the Catholic church are faced by a similar conflict through the struggle of the peoples of Nicaragua and El Salvador, Honduras and Guatemala. Are they not bound, in the name of the martyred Bishop Romero, to support the people and the *Iglesia popular*, which has entered the people's struggle for liberation? For these people are Catholics, who declare that they are suffering under the domination of the United States. But German economic interests are involved on the other side; moreover, the Western alliance is directed against the Communist threat wherever it arises — which means in Central America too. Here, as well, more and more involved Christian groups are growing up that put solidarity with the people of Central America before loyalty to the Western world. Here too, in the discussion about the theology of liberation, the person who supports the interest of the rulers counts as "non-political," while the person who seeks for freedom in solidarity with the people is branded as "political."

4. Of course these tendencies have been countered by other conservative movements in all the churches. But this new phenomenon is going to spread: Christians are no longer always "true subjects of his majesty." Nor are they anymore the always law-abiding and obedient citizens of the state. They can become very uncomfortable, critical partners and, in extreme cases, "unreliable elements." This, at least, is the experience of totalitarian powers-that-be with Christians in Eastern Europe, Latin America and Asia. It is also the experience of governments in parliamentary democracies, who are discovering more and more Christians among political dissidents, and who, in certain decisions, are no longer able to rely on the legitimation of even the major churches. One of these critical questions is the application of the threat of mass annihilation through nuclear armaments. No century hitherto has ever seen as many Christians among political martyrs. The ancient Constantinian alliance between political and ecclesiastical power is drawing irrevocably to a close. The era of differences and tensions between church and political rule is beginning. Christians can become "strangers in their own country."

The ever-stronger distinction between Christian morals and the morality of the civic community also belongs to this growing differentiation. As long as the amalgam between church and state still existed, the churches were able to impose the principles of Christian morality on every citizen by way of the criminal code. We only have to think of the laws about adultery, abortion, suicide, euthanasia or blasphemy, to name a few. But if general civic morality now takes its bearings from the general "basic values" of the pluralistic society, then what is specifically and distinctively Christian can emerge, without the compulsion of law, simply through the free testimony of the Christian life. The secularization of general civic morality therefore also leads to the "Christianization" of the morality that is specifically Christian. So the disengagement between church and society in our time is making the churches free to realize their own vision of the future and their own world-wide community.

5. The present discussion about peace provides the test and the proof of the changes I have described in religion and in its political importance in Germany. Remarkably enough, there is no discussion about security in the churches. There is only a discussion about peace. This is significant. So we shall look first at the Christian discussion about peace, in order to make clear to ourselves the new political importance of religion; and we shall then go on to consider the discussion about security, from which we can discern the religious importance of politics.

But first let me point to the double irony of the events which took place in Krefeld in June 1983. Vice President George Bush and Chancellor Helmut Kohl came to Krefeld on the occasion of the 300th anniversary of the first German emigration to Pennsylvania, with the aim of praising the German-American security pact. They proclaimed that only a strong military deterrent secures the Western world. Unfortunately, however, the German emigrants who left Krefeld in 1683 happened to be Mennonites. They were, in fact, the forerunners of today's peace movement. Because they wanted to live without armaments, and rejected Prussian military service, they emigrated to America, where they hoped to find "the land of peace" they dreamed of. The visit of Bush and Kohl was disrupted in a detestable way by a few violent demonstrators among the mass of peaceful ones. The people who resorted to violence evidently did not know anything about the Mennonites either, for the Mennonites did not merely reject the exercise of violence by the state. They rejected personal violence even more emphatically. That was why they emigrated. It would surely have been an act of historical honesty if, at this celebration of German-American relations, an ear had been lent to the testimony of the Mennonite peace churches from which these relations sprang.

The churches in Germany — just like the churches in the United States — are moving away from their traditional doctrine about a just war, in the direction of a new, unequivocal testimony for peace. "Post-Hiroshima" and in the face of new methods of mass annihilation (A-, B-, and C-weapons), there can no longer be any such thing as a just war. All the major Christian churches that have made statements on this subject agree in saying that the employment of these weapons of mass annihilation, and the evoking of a nuclear holocaust, cannot be justified under any circumstances whatsoever. It follows from this that the majority of Christians will not participate in a nuclear war.

What is still controversial, however, is the question whether the present "peace through deterrence" can be justified — that is to say, whether there can be such a thing as "just nuclear rearmament." As long ago as 1958 the Evangelical church in Germany (which is a federation of Protestant churches) threatened to split on this question. The Heidelberg Theses of 1959 by Carl Friedrich von Weizsäcker were an attempt to make the "yes" or "no" response to this question "complementary" answers: "The church must also recognize that participation in the attempt to secure peace in freedom through the existence of atomic weapons is a course of action which is still possible for Christians today. "The Evangelical church's Memorandum of 1981 reiterated these theses 22 years later. But the statement is so formulated that this admission is bound to a time-limit: "still today" is a "period of grace." In explaining the very similarly worded declaration by the German Catholic Episcopal Conference of 1983, Cardinal Höffner called it " reprieve," "a stay of execution." Nuclear deterrence is only justifiable if it gains time, and if that time is used for disarmament negotiations aimed at building up a security system which is not based on mutual terror. The declaration of the American Catholic Episcopal Conference sees this as a limited justification for the possession of weapons of mass annihilation — a justification limited both in time and substance.

The Reformed churches in Holland and Germany went one step further in their Declarations of 1979 and 1981: because the rapidity of rearmament always exceeds the rapidity of disarmament talks, the justification offered is illusory. If this justification ceases to apply, then there is no such thing as just nuclear armaments at all. Even the possession of weapons of mass annihilation, or the threat to use them, must be called "irresponsible" and "unjust"; it can therefore never be supported.

This makes the question of peace a question of creed. "In our attitude to methods of mass destruction, what is at stake is the acknowledgment or denial of the Gospel," says the Declaration of the German Reformed church. The resolution passed by the Synod of the Federation of Protestant Churches in the GDR on September 28, 1982 is very similar: "This threat to all life through excessive armaments is a challenge to our faith. If we accept it in silence, we shall find ourselves in opposition to God the Creator, for his charge lays on us the duty of preserving creation, and excludes the right to destroy it. Consequently the question at stake here is obedience toward God or disobedience toward him." These are the top priorities of the Christian faith. It follows that neither in East nor West can Christians affirm and support a supposed system of security resting on total deterrence and the threat of the apocalyptic destruction of the world. Not only can a security system of this kind lead to the possible nuclear holocaust. In actual, cold fact it is already spreading poverty, hunger and death in the Third World. That is why the Declaration of the German Reformed churches realistically put a name to the costs: "The acknowledgment of our faith is irreconcilable with the affirmation or even toleration of a 'security' system which is maintained at the cost of the hungry and wretched people of this earth, and at the price of their death."

If rearmament in the USSR and the U.S. goes on at the present rate, then, in my view, it is only a question of time until all the major churches take the same step as the Reformed churches, and declare that "the attempt to secure peace in freedom by way of the existence of nuclear weapons" is *no longer today a possible Christian course of action*. Countries that believe that they have to increase their defense budget to the point that they are in a position to wage a nuclear war successfully will provoke a new struggle with the churches — this time a comprehensive one. The defamation of Christian groups and persons as infiltrated by Communism or as the agents of imperialism is probably the beginning of this conflict.

The Religious Importance Of Politics In Germany

Politics have always had a religious dimension, not only in the United States but in Germany too. However, because what is religious can always be demonic as well, this statement itself is an ambiguous one. Here I shall confine myself to the religious side of the present security policy.

Robert Bellah has investigated the ideas of civil religion in the United States. Up to 1945 German politics were determined by a glorification of the German nation, and by the dream of a pan-German Reich. After 1945 the division of Germany dominated the different political ideologies. Konrad Adenauer integrated the Federal Republic in the West with the help of the notion of "the Christian West." Walter Ulbricht integrated the German Democratic Republic in the Eastern bloc as "the first German workers' and peasant-farmers' state." This division of Germany and the integration of its two parts in the two opposing power blocs has had a fateful effect on our political thinking. Germans have in any case always shown an astonishing tendency to think in terms of either/or alternatives. Because they joined the countries of Europe as what Helmuth Plessner calls "a belated nation," German political awareness was always insecure and immature, and therefore on the look-out for compensations. That was the reason the Fascist friend/enemy thinking found such a ready response with us: people made sure of their collective identity best by fighting against their traditional enemies and the enemies of the state. Earlier on, these were "the French"; later, "the Russians"; and today, "the Communists." When Germany was divided into East and West, "public enemy number one" became in each case the other half of Germany: here "the capitalist Federal Republic" — there "the Russian zone," the Communist GDR. Any opposition in either of Germany's two parts can without the slightest effort be denigrated as the Fifth Column of the other part. This has paralyzed political life in both German states.

Ever since 1948, elections in the Federal Republic have always been won on the slogan "security," and with anti-Communist watchwords. Because it expresses and exploits people's deep-lying anxieties, this kind of security policy has religious features too. I do not mean this merely in the general sense of something that goes beyond the possibilities open to practical politics. I mean it quite specifically: this policy of national security is a kind of political Manichaeism. That is to say, it is an apocalyptic policy through and through.

Because total security is unattainable, it is a utopia. And because it demands tremendous sacrifices and is built upon the threat of world annihilation, it is what Erhard Eppler has rightly called *"a deadly utopia."* External security can only be achieved through the nuclear deterrence of "the enemy," and our own invulnerability can only be attained by way of our own military strength. Internal security can only be reached through the total surveillance of one's own population, through the restriction of civil rights and liberties, and through the criminalization of "the enemy within the gates."

In this way the policies of national security can easily become the Moloch of a new sacrificial religion: the price of security is continually growing; the utility is continually declining. The external peace achieved by the nuclear deterrent is destabilizing world politics, and spreading unrest; the measures of internal security are destabilizing own own society and spreading social discord. Because the costs are generally shifted onto the shoulders of the weakest, it is probably the nations of the Third World who have to bear them.

But if total "security" only exists when one is oneself a degree stronger than the enemy (as Colin S. Gray pointed out), then this security policy endangers even the balance of nuclear deterrence between the great powers which up to now we have generally euphemistically termed peace. The striving for total security through superior strength is in tendency unlimited and in principle unfulfillable. In this respect it must be called religious. Because it only seems to be fulfilled when all enemies at home and abroad are potentially eliminated, it is demonic. Because it is an endeavor which is today bringing the world closer and closer to nuclear annihilation, it must be described as apocalyptic.

Christianity, as we all know, is a religion not of anxiety but of faith. It is not a cult of fear, but one of hope. In the perspective of the Christian faith the security policy I have described is an extreme form of godlessness. Now, there is of course a Christian apocalyptic which has penetrated the political ideology of some nations. And there is also a Manichaean Christianity which, instead of seeking for understanding and peace between the nations, looks forward to history's final struggle between "the children of light" and "the children of darkness." Earlier, this was a feature of the marginal sects belonging to the church's underground. Since the Puritan "revolution of the Saints," these ideas have become a part of some political ideology and have lent an apocalyptic coloring to politics.

If the enemy is "the source of all evil," one can neither negotiate with him, nor conclude treaties. One can only fight him. Like Cromwell earlier, modern Manichaean Christians interpret the present "signs of the times" with the help of the Book of Revelation: this is the hour of the horsemen on the red horse, or the red dragon who persecutes the saints; it is the hour of the bowls of wrath poured out on the earth. The saints must gather together in resistance. Mary will lead her "blue army" to victory in the struggle against "the red dragon."

When this religious apocalyptic is linked with political anti-Communism, the result is a political religion which only sees red, and is blind to the motley reality of the world. This seems to me the danger of the present security policy: all the political problems in the world are reduced to pro- or anti-communism. The particular problems of the nations belonging to the Third World are no longer recognized at all. "Communism" is supposed to be at work in every action that is considered undesirable. Neither Ho Chi Min, Fidel Castro nor the Sandinistas started out as Marxists. They were turned into Marxists only when the West joined issue with them. The East-West conflict is limited to the northern hemisphere. Anyone who extends it to the rest of the world does not see the realities of the Third World — or does not want to see them. The North-South conflict and the problem of economic justice cannot be classified under the categories of the conflict between West and East.

Unfortunately the countries of the Eastern bloc show similar tendencies toward a friend/enemy kind of thinking, and toward the apocalyptic of "the last fight," as the Communist "International" puts it. Soviet Marxism is an ideology of struggle no less blind, no less infatuated, than the religious and political apocalyptic I have just described. In the struggle against capitalism and imperialism, the Marxists are Manichaeans too, even though they are atheistic Manichaeans, not religious ones.

Friends on the one side — enemies on the other: this apocalyptically stimulated thinking is diametrically opposed to Christ's Sermon on the Mount, and to the command to love our enemies. It therefore challenges Christians to work out the political reasonableness of love of our enemies. In 1981 rearmament was the center of discussion in the Federal Republic. It is not by chance that 1981 was also "the year of the Sermon on the Mount": President and Chancellor, party committees and the great national newspapers all struggled to find an interpretation of this evidently dangerous Christian document. For centuries, Christians who followed the Sermon on the Mount were viewed as madmen in a normal world. It may well be that today they are the only normal people in a world gone mad.

German-American Relations: The "Dream" of America

The religious and moral dimensions of German-American relations may perhaps best be comprehended in terms of "the American dream." In their declarations on the State of the Nation, American presidents never tire of conjuring up "the bold and splendid dream which inspired the founding fathers of our nation." They call for new faith in this ancient dream, and they promise its realization. It is the dream of freedom: a new nation conceived in liberty; it is the dream of human rights for all; the dream of the unhindered "pursuit of happiness," as the American Declaration of Independence phrases it. The symbols of the Old Testament prophets, the messianism of the Thousand Year Empire and the hopes of the weary and heavy-laden of many nations have all helped to embroider this American dream, turning it into the vision of the greatest experiment of modern times. The American dream was strong enough to inspire the abolition of slavery in the 19th century and the Civil Rights movement of the 1960s. It was so wide open that it motivated the liberation of the black people in its own country too, as Martin Luther King showed in his unforgettable speech, "I have a dream. . . ."

Europeans have one simple point of departure when they try to enter into this dream of the American people: before there was an American dream, "America" was the dream of Europeans. It was the dream of liberty for everyone, of a land of unlimited opportunity, of justice in a community without classes and privileges; it was the dream of a land of peace. This was the dream of men and women in Europe who were bowed down under political oppression, religious persecution, social humiliation and racial discrimination. The American dream is really simply the transformation and expansion of the European dream of America. This means that the American dream did not merely reflect a hope confined to America; it must have a universal meaning for all the men and women who hope for liberty and human rights. But it means too that an international discussion of the American dream is not an illegitimate intervention by foreigners in the internal affairs of the United States of America. For America is the dream of humanity as a whole.

With regard to the first point, I should like to say that the American dream will become a nightmare for other nations if it is turned into the ideology of American hegemony, and if it is not extended to all nations as *a human dream*. The vision of liberty and happiness cannot merely be fulfilled by one nation alone. It can only be realized by the whole of humanity, just as human rights can only be realized by the community of men and women as a whole. As a humane dream, the American dream is a true and necessary dream; as a solely American dream it is an impossible dream.

Where the second point is concerned, I should like to express the expectation that the United States will promote the liberation of the nations from colonialism and dictatorship, and will encourage democracy in the world; that it will follow up its insistence on individual human rights by furthering, too, social and economic rights for men and women everywhere; but that it should cease to surround itself by a protective zone of authoritarian regimes and dictatorships.

"The U.S. Experiment" — the free, just and equal community of men and women of different races, religions, languages and traditions — can only succeed if *humanity's* experiment succeeds in a humane world-wide community. The power and the means to succeed are there. But the power and the means of destruction are ready and waiting too. In spite of some bitter disappointments, the United States is for many people still a hope. Can the United States itself have a future if it disappoints these hopes — the hopes of all humanity? I believe that the future of the United States depends on the hopes of human beings everywhere, because it is in the name of a human hope that it has come forward.

German-American relations came into being when persecuted and oppressed men and women emigrated from Germany in order to seek the land of liberty and the nation of peace. And, in this spirit, German-American relations have a meaning today if they serve to spread peace in the world, and justice for every man and woman.

NOTES

[1] A more detailed account of my views on the first and second points under discussion may be found in my contribution "Theologie heute" in J. Habermas, *Stichworte zur "Geistigen Situation der Zeit,"* vol. II, *Politik und Kultur*, Suhrkamp es 1000, Frankfurt 1979, pp. 754-80. I have expounded my ideas on the third point at more length in "Der amerikanische Traum," *The Center Magazine* IX, 6, 1976, pp. 59-66; and in *Evangelische Theologie* 37, 1977, pp. 166-78.

THE INTEGRATION AND DIVERGENCE OF GERMAN AND AMERICAN ECONOMIC INTERESTS

by Sidney L. Jones

> The ability to accumulate wealth is infinitely more important than the possession of wealth; it guarantees not only possessions and increase in wealth already accumulated, but also ensures the replacement of what is lost. This applies with even greater force to entire nations.
> — *The German economist Friedrich List, writing in 1846 in favor of the commercial association of German states and creation of a customs union.*

Although competition between the Federal Republic of Germany and the United States of America continues to increase, as both nations emphasize domestic, regional, and international goals, their economies are also becoming more integrated through the trading of goods and services, bilateral capital investments, diversified commercial and investment banking activities, coordination of energy and commodity plans, and discussions of stabilization policies at international meetings. Bilateral relations are generally positive because of the mutual benefits from cooperation and the importance of minimizing unwanted trade protectionism, investment barriers, and capital and credit controls. Their fundamental interests and values are compatible and existing problems are manageable despite occasional warnings of impending crises and the natural strains caused by the long postwar transition from a patron-client relationship into one of intense competition between two world-class economic powers. While neither country actually qualifies as the ideal model often described by euphoric analysts, both have created strong economic systems as a necessary foundation for stable political, social, and multilateral military security activities.

Increasing emphasis on economic issues in world affairs has coincided with the rapid development of both nations using similar policies, institutions, and factor inputs. Comparative advantages have resulted from the fortunate mix of skilled labor and management, abundant capital, and efficient commercial application of technology, plus support for an open and competitive international trade and investment system. Fiscal policies have been used to promote economic growth and cyclical stabilization and to provide enough government services and social programs to sustain support for centrist political coalitions. Strong central banks have accommodated reasonable money and credit demands and occasionally initiated anti-inflation monetary restraint. While relying on the private operation of most economic activities, a "mixed economy" approach has combined traditional capitalism with extensive government involvement, including comprehensive subsidies, tax incentives, purchases of goods and services, and public loans and credit guarantees. The dual results are impressive. America has become the most powerful economy in the world, its dollar serves as a reserve and transaction currency for the international economy, and its nuclear deterrent and conventional military forces provide a framework for multilateral security arrangements. Germany has rapidly recovered from the devastation of World War II to become *Modell Deutschland* providing domestic prosperity and stability and serving as the linchpin for European economic and security cooperation.

Policy Background of Bilateral Relations

During the early postwar years bilateral goals were usually compatible and reinforcing. The new Federal Republic concentrated on restoring its shattered economy and entry back into world affairs. The accumulated demand for housing and consumer goods, rapid growth of exports, ready availability of inexpensive energy resources and raw materials, and inflows of investments and technology contributed to the "economic miracle" of recovery. Geopolitical priorities responded to American hegemony and threats of Soviet intervention demonstrated by the brutal Berlin blockade and construction of border barriers to prevent the continued migration of millions of dissatisfied people to the West. The United States concentrated on geopolitical competition with the Soviet Union and global economic development issues while striving to sustain domestic growth and correct its chronic balance-of-payment deficits.

By the mid-1960s bilateral relations were rapidly changing as coerced conformity and narrow preoccupation with commercial success evolved into more reasoned cooperation based on mutual cost/benefit analyses and more diversified national interests. In the subsequent environment, the dominant factors of integration and cooperation have prevailed, but the convergence of interests is no longer automatic or predictable as the power-parity gap has narrowed and the issues have become more complex. Strong economic forces pointing toward integration include: established bilateral trade and investments; promotion of international economic growth creating expanded export markets and access to raw materials at reasonable prices; cooperation among public and private financial institutions in providing necessary investment capital and trade financing; support for international institutions coordinating stabilization policies; and efforts to improve the functions of foreign exchange markets and the stability of important national currency exchange rates.

There are also fragmenting pressures resulting from direct competition between these two dominant economies for the same domestic and foreign markets for their goods and services; investment and financing opportunities; mergers and acquisitions; sources of technology; access to raw materials; tariffs; non-tariff regulations; government subsidies and tax incentives; and relative influence over the policies of international institutions. These economic issues always become more abrasive during periods of sluggish growth and high exchange reflects genuine concerns about the extended period of sluggish unemployment but they are not as ominous as the various political, social, and military security issues that must be resolved.

Examples of such fundamental questions include: the disparate national goals for economic growth, unemployment, inflation, current account balances, and the role of the dollar and Deutsche Mark in international and regional currency exchange markets; the continuing disagreement over the optimum mix of fiscal and monetary policies in the United States, particularly the alleged distortions attributed to the moderate restraint initiated by monetary authorities in the fall of 1979 and the impact of that action on bilateral and international interest rates, currency exchange rates, flows of capital, investments, and the overall pace of economic activity and unemployment; the divergence of interests and responsibilities in regional arrangements, as the Federal Republic strives to be "the best European" by supporting the European Community's expansion and integration and the United States properly emphasizes the increasing relative importance of Latin America and the Pacific Basin as it evaluates its long-term goals; the serious dispute over the purposes and processes of East-West trade, particularly the controversial sales of high-technology goods and services and favorable financing agreements; the eternal debate over agricultural issues as the Federal Republic defends European Community policies against intense pressures from the United States to increase its exports; and continued differences about how to respond to the repetitive demands of many developing nations for increased foreign aid, concessionary development and trade financing, rescheduling or cancellation of debts for countries unable to service existing obligations, preferential trade arrangements, and income stabilization and buffer storage programs for commodity-exploring nations.

The conventional wisdom now assumes that the Federal Republic should increase its participation in international affairs to a level commensurate with the relative strength of its economy. It is similarly argued that the United States will have to reduce its global commitments as part of a general realignment of priorities necessary to revitalize its economy. These controversial propositions will undoubtedly create national, bilateral, and international debates throughout the 1980s. Whatever happens in the future, it appears that the historic "golden era" of German-American relations gradually changed throughout the 1970s for the positive and negative reasons cited above. A fashionable rhetoric has been developed to question the potential capacity and resolve of a "weakened America" to provide substantive and moral leadership. This viewpoint argues that America has lost its moorings and is no longer a worthy model because of its alleged abdication of fiscal and monetary responsibilities, chronic stagflation conditions, wasteful consumption of energy and commodities, and an obsolete technology and industrial base which can no longer compete in a changing world. It follows logically from this analysis, that the claimed erosion of economic strength fatally weakens the credibility of American political and multilateral security initiatives. Variations on this theme can be extrapolated all the way to a future collapse of market economies and the end of Western Civilization.

Part of this escalating criticism reflects the continuing scapegoat role assigned to the United States as the world's most powerful economy with its comprehensive interests and responsibilities. It is usually politically convenient for other nations to blame the United States for their specific domestic and international problems. But at least part of the abrasive exchange reflects genuine concerns about the extended period of sluggish economic activity and resulting unemployment and the increasingly brittle international trade and financial system. These prolonged tensions have prevented the solution of several fundamental problems and caused minor issues to become major disputes. A third difficulty involves misunderstandings about the evolving goals of the Federal Republic as it assumes a different role throughout Europe and the world economy. It must now respond to internal economic and political factors by emphasizing the development of Western Europe and *Ostpolitik* efforts to expand trade and investment opportunities in the Soviet Union and Eastern Europe. From the other side of the Atlantic, the image of *Modell Deutschland* as an economic miracle and reliable political and military ally seems to be eroding. The euphoric descriptions of bilateral relations throughout the postwar era have partially changed into trendy predictions of disaster.

While our current problems create interesting journalistic and geopolitical analyses, fundamental bilateral relations remain strong and mutually beneficial with each partner committed to the same basic goals, including the importance of a liberal domestic and international economic system. Long periods of sustained growth and widespread personal affluence have made both nations somewhat complacent, but the harsh realities of the extended economic recession and intense international competition have reminded them that success is not guaranteed. The necessary adjustment of policies and allocation of resources, toward investment and technology and away from personal and public consumption, will not be easy or politically popular. Existing pressure groups and institutions already have established claims against the prospective distribution of national incomes. History does indicate, however, that when push-turns-to-shove, the Federal Republic and the United States will support economic vitality to preserve political and social stability. In the final analysis, bilateral cooperation and integration will also continue, despite the disruptive pressures of direct competition and divergent interests, because there is no reasonable alternative for either country.

Economic Development

The advantages of cooperation were emphasized in 1947 when occupation officials declared that ". . . an orderly and prosperous Europe requires the economic contribution of a stable and productive Germany." The subsequent economic development summarized in Table 1 is largely the result of policies shared by the two nations. First, they relied upon liberal market principles rather than government controls and monopolistic cartels. Creation of a socially responsible market economy combining the incentives of private ownership with public welfare obligations has been the mutual goal. Second, rapid industrialization has been based on advanced technology, mass production and marketing procedures, and an infrastructure of professional and public services. Third, a large supply of educated, skilled, and disciplined workers and managers has been available to operate the complex economies. Their relatively high compensation costs have been somewhat offset by productivity gains until recent disappointments. In return, the labor force has received rising real incomes and comprehensive private and public welfare and pension benefits. Fourth, both nations have developed sophisticated domestic financial institutions and access to international money and capital markets to finance their large investment and trade requirements. The Federal Republic has a high national savings rate and the United States is trying to increase incentives for savings to finance large private and public financing requirements. Fifth, international trade and investment are a crucial part of

TABLE 1   SELECTED ECONOMIC STATISTICS, 1960–1982
(percent, compounded annual rate of change)

	1960–1970	1970–1980	1978–1981	1982
A. Federal Republic of Germany				
Gross National Product (1975 Deutsche marks)	4.7	2.8	1.9	−1.1
Industrial production	5.2	1.8	0.9	−3.1
Gross National Product implicit price deflator	3.5	5.2	4.3	4.8
Consumer prices	2.6	5.1	5.2	5.3
Employment in industry	0.6	−1.5	−0.4	−3.5
Imports (CIF)	11.4	20.2	10.4	−5.2
Exports (FOB)	11.6	18.9	7.3	0.2
B. United States of America				
Gross National Product (1972 dollars)	3.9	3.2	1.7	−1.7
Industrial production	5.0	3.2	1.1	−8.2
Gross National Product implicit price deflator	2.9	6.8	8.9	6.0
Consumer prices	2.7	7.8	11.7	6.1
Payroll employment	2.7	2.5	1.8	−1.6
Imports (FAS)	10.4	20.1	14.5	−6.4
Exports (FAS)	8.0	18.1	18.5	−10.7

Source: Federal Reserve Bank of St. Louis, *International Economic Conditions Annual Data*, various issues.

both economies. According to OECD reports, from 1960 through 1980 exports totaled 20 percent of the Federal Republic's gross domestic product and the figure has increased in recent years as the basic industries have emphasized foreign sales. The United States is also increasingly dependent upon foreign trade and investments for sustaining its key industrial and agricultural sectors.

A sixth similarity involves the mix of economic programs used for stabilization purposes. Government spending and tax policies have attempted to fine-tune economic growth and neutralize unemployment and welfare strains while the independent central banks have concentrated on controlling inflation and maintaining balanced external accounts. The anticipated equilibrium has eroded, however, as political pressures have increased total government outlays as a percent of the gross national product from 32 percent in 1960 to 47 percent by 1980 in the Federal Republic and from 28 percent to 33 percent in the UnitedStates. The escalation of government budgets and reduced tax revenues have created large fiscal deficits which threaten to crowd out private borrowing needs, particularly if monetary officials attempt to sustain anti-inflation policies. Both nations face excruciating budget priority decisions during the 1980s as they allocate funds to defense, income security, health, education, public works and government interest payments.

The sharp cyclical deterioration of economic activity since 1978 is also summarized in Table 1. During this extended stagflation period, overall economic activity declined, inflation pressures increased (particularly in the United States), and the unemployment rate rose to double-digit levels (an average rate of 10.2 percent in the United States and 9.9 percent in the Federal Republic during the first three months of 1983). The sharp erosion of domestic private business and residential housing investment and disappointing exports were the major negative factors. A strong cyclical recovery is now underway in the United States, led by improving personal consumption, housing construction, inventory replenishment, and government spending. Progress is also expected in the Federal Republic during 1983, but skepticism persists about the sustainability of the recovery as long as high interest rates discourage investment, international trade conditions remain distorted and large prospective government budget deficits continue to threaten the stability of monetary policies. The current expansion is a welcome change, but fiscal and monetary policy issues must still be resolved.

The recent cyclical problems have been exacerbated by the convergence of several structural problems involving the future competitive position of both nations. Many of their basic manufacturing industries have become vulnerable to foreign competitors. Capital investment and research efforts need to be increased and overall cost structure must be adjusted to meet the increasing competition. Political leaders have adopted the rhetoric of allocating resources to industrial renewal, but specific proposals and a grand strategy have not been developed. Some critics have even claimed that the traditional work ethic and dynamic business characteristics have been lost because of growing affluence and the dominance of government intervention. Such claims ignore the long history of economic productivity and creativity of Germany and America and their unique abilities to restore economic leadership despite the destructive effects of wars and depressions.

Integration of National Interests and Policies

Both nations have similar economic interests and policies linked to the same cyclical and structural problems. They have fundamental comparative advantages and commitments to liberal economic principles tempered by political and social realities. Their economic vitality increasingly depends upon rationalizing the mix of fiscal and monetary policies and restoring stable international conditions, particularly continued access to foreign markets, raw materials, and flows of trade credit and investment capital.

Commitment to an Open Economic System Critics often attack the Federal Republic and the United States for "dogmatic liberalism" because they favor competitive marketplace policies and generally reject comprehensive government planning and controls. While they actively support the goals and technical functions of numerous international organizations, such as strengthening trade and investment, promoting technology and productivity, preparing codes of competitive behavior, providing trade and development financing, and alleviating balance-of-payments problems, both nations usually avoid "concerted action" programs for coordinating domestic economic policies to achieve regional and international objectives. Germany has consistently supported increased integration within the European Community without accepting the traditional arguments for increased government intervention.

The experiences of Germany during the 1930s and World War II, plus the discouraging examples of state-controlled economies in Eastern Europe, now provide fifty years of empirical evidence for evaluating the creativity and productivity of command economies compared with the overall results of market economies. Their continued skepticism about planned economies reflects deep concerns that competition might be curtailed, trade and financial protectionism might increase, wage and price controls and administrative regulations might be substituted for necessary fiscal and monetary policies, and national goals may become subordinated, even though the successful market economies will be expected to fund the operating budgets of international programs.

Despite criticism of potential German-American bigemony within the Atlantic Alliance, neither country is willing to give up its sovereign control of economic policies. The resulting tensions are unfortunate because economic problems are increasingly multinational. The annual economic summit meetings conducted by the leaders of large industrial nations have not helped much because controversial issues are usually avoided and the broad policy declarations are typically ignored by individual governments. The basic trends in the international economy appear to be moving toward increased government intervention, which will further isolate the Federal Republic and the United States, forcing them to decide between compromising their philosophical market orientation or continuing to compete on their own terms. Political issues will probably dominate these economic decisions, creating erratic pressures for short-term responses to election needs, rather than long-term goals.

Avoiding Protectionist Pressures

The many benefits of international trade and investment are always vulnerable to protectionist pressures, such as tariffs, discriminating nontariff regulations, cartelized orderly marketing agreements, financial subsidies, credit preferences, tax relief, and capital controls. These pressures escalate during periods of slow growth and high unemployment as governments strive to protect domestic economic interests and minimize balance-of-payments problems. These defensive barriers exacerbate the problems by creating a vicious circle of declining trade and investment. It is now fashionable to argue that classical free trade and investment theories are hopelessly obsolete since most nations rely on comprehensive government controls to arbitrarily restrict imports and promote exports. Protectionist intervention and subsidies are increasingly described as "fair trade" because they allegedly equalize multinational competitive disadvantages and retaliate for the nefarious actions of other nations. Advocates of protectionism admit that desirable trade and investment are reduced but argue that pragmatic compromises are inevitable and necessary to limit political and social turmoil.

Protectionist barriers are particularly disadvantageous for the Federal Republic and the United States because they are so dependent on foreign trade and investment for domestic economic vitality and they are frequently accused of being too idealistic and pious in supporting open and competitive rules of behavior. This criticism is ironic given the remarkable economic success of both nations and unfortunate trends toward more "voluntary" orderly marketing agreements to restrict imports and government export promotion programs to offset sluggish domestic activity. These compromises reflect the convergence of cyclical and structural adjustment problems, comparative labor costs around the world, balance-of-payments strains, historical links with regional trade partners, and intense sociopolitical pressures. It is difficult to defend somewhat abstract principles and criticize the destructive results of economic nationalism during the 1930s when the realities of current unemployment and financial bankruptcies and frequent political elections are dominant. Nevertheless, much of the postwar progress of the international economy is directly linked to the expansion of trade and investment. Germany and America have a special responsibility to promote the goals of free trade and investment despite the political attractions of protectionism. If they fail in this responsibility, economic progress, efficiency, and the beneficial exchange of goods and services will deteriorate rapidly.

The division of the world into a relatively small group of industrial nations dependent upon sustained access to energy resources and other commodities and a much larger group of developing countries interested in financial and technical assistance to accelerate their progress has complicated efforts to promote an open economic system. Industrial nations are being pressured to increase their development aid and support the stabilization of commodity export earnings by creating an integrated price support system and strict production controls. Marketplace developments eventually prevail over arbitrary government manipulation, as demonstrated by recent world oil prices and production trends, but efforts to cartelize economic activities often create chaotic conditions during the adjustment process. The Federal Republic and the United States have a major interest in the progress of developing nations as they already represent important markets for their manufactured goods and technical services and both have used foreign aid assistance to promote their commercial interests. In recent years, however, Germany has become more responsive in seeking political solutions to North-South trade and investment disputes leaving the United States increasingly isolated in international discussions.

Importance of Bilateral Trading of Goods and Services

As the two largest trading nations in the world, bilateral merchandise trade is naturally important as summarized in Table 2. The Federal Republic is now America's fifth largest export market, ranked below Canada, Japan,

TABLE 2   SELECTED U.S. MERCHANDISE TRADE FIGURES, 1973-1982[1]
(Millions of dollars)

	1973	1981	1982
Total U.S. merchandise exports	71,410	236,254	211,013
European Community (10)[2]	16,708	51,351	47,026
Federal Republic of Germany (FRG)	3,723	10,531	8,633
FRG share of total, percent	5.2	4.5	4.1
FRG share of European Community, percent	22.3	20.5	18.3
Total U.S. merchandise imports	70,499	264,143	247,344
European Community (10)[2]	15,816	41,424	42,349
Federal Republic of Germany	5,591	11,389	11,902
FRG share of total, percent	7.9	4.3	4.9
FRG share of European Community, percent	35.3	27.5	28.3
memo:			
Overall balance	911	−27,889	−36,331
European Community balance	892	9,927	4,677
Federal Republic of Germany balance	−1,868	−858	−3,269

[1] Balance of payments basis.
[2] European Community 1973 figures for nine nations; 1981 and 1982 figures for ten nations.
Source: U.S. Department of Commerce, Survey of Current Business, June 1982 Table 3, p. 48 and March 1983, Table 3, p. 52.

Mexico, and the United Kingdom, and also its fifth major supplier. The United States has become Germany's sixth largest export market, just behind its important Western European neighbors, and its fourth major supplier. The strategic nature of this bilateral trade is even more important than its absolute size, as most of the two-way exchange consists of sophisticated manufactured goods and industrial supplies, indicating that both nations have successfully developed technological advantages needed to create specialized markets in other industrialized nations. Only one-fourth of current U.S. exports to Germany are agricultural products, such as grains, soybeans, fruits and vegetables and other raw materials. Approximately three-fourths of the shipments involve a wide variety of specialized industrial machines, chemicals, electrical and electronic equipment, engines, office and electronic data processing equipment, motor vehicles and parts, aircraft, scientific, professional, and control instruments, and manufactured consumer goods. From the opposite direction, about 95 percent of Federal Republic exports into the American market are concentrated in industrial supplies, chemicals, iron, steel, and nonferrous metal products, industrial machinery, engines, professional, scientific, and optical instruments, motor vehicles (including $2 1/2 billion worth of passenger cars in 1981), and various manufactured consumer goods. It is significant that the general categories of mutual sales and purchases are similar, but a complementary pattern of exchange has evolved enabling both nations to exploit competitive advantages. In addition, a comparable group of impressive service industries has been developed to provide extensive exports and imports of tourist services, passenger and freight transportation, royalties and fees paid for exchanges of technology, special military goods and services transfers, and a diversified group of engineering, legal, accounting, advertising, education, communication, health, equipment leasing, construction, and entertainment services. In 1981, total U.S. exports of goods and services to the Federal Republic totaled $15.1 billion, and the return flows were valued at $20.2 billion, indicating the size and scope of economic cooperation that continues to grow.

Importance of Bilateral Foreign Direct Investment

The volume and strategic importance of bilateral direct foreign investment is another powerful integrating force (defined as the book value of equities and net outstanding loans in foreign affiliates). Foreign investments helped develop the U.S. economy and have contributed to the remarkable postwar recovery of the Federal Republic. From the host country's viewpoint, foreign direct investments expand the economic base, create jobs, introduce new products and services using advanced technology, and strengthen the balance of payments through capital inflows and the substitution of domestic goods and services for imports. Foreign investors are usually attracted by opportunities to maximize sales and profits by expanding into new markets, lower labor and materials costs, specific tax and financing incentives, improved access to local sources of energy, raw materials, and unique technology, avoidance of local-content rules and other import barriers, creation of a base for exporting to other markets, and occasionally as a means of transferring capital away from unstable political and social conditions to safer locations.

As summarized in Table 3, American companies have accumulated large foreign direct investments (the current market value of total assets is actually a much higher figure). Most of the commitments were made earlier in the postwar era when the dollar was particularly strong and the current earnings fortunately offset the chronic merchandise trade deficits enabling the United States to approximately balance its international current accounts. Investments in the Federal Republic have been concentrated in the manufacturing sectors, with additional interests in the petroleum and trade industries, following the general bilateral pattern of trying to exploit technological advantages. Germany now ranks third, below Canada and the United Kingdom, in the terms of direct foreign investment received from the United States.

Foreign direct investment in the United States has surged upward during the 1970s, particularly since 1978, and reached a total of $90 billion in 1981. The devaluation of the dollar and relatively low equity prices have made American companies particularly attractive in addition to the fundamental economic advantages of this huge economy. The Federal Republic has moved into fourth place behind Canada, the United Kingdom, and the Netherlands as a source of investments. This performance is particularly impressive because existing German assets were confiscated during World War II so that the current diversified array of manufacturing, trade, and financial investments summarized in Table 4 has been accumulated just since the mid-1960s.

TABLE 3   U.S. DIRECT INVESTMENT POSITION ABROAD AT YEAR END, 1973–1981
(Millions of dollars)

	1973	1980	1981
Total, all areas	103,675	215,578	227,342
European Community (9)[1]	30,920	77,402	80,492
Federal Republic of Germany	7,650	15,418	16,077
Petroleum	2,250	3,479	3,282
Manufacturing	4,449	9,657	10,312
Food and kindred products	244	790	839
Chemical and allied products	578	1,500	1,644
Primary and fabricated metal	291	600	644
Machinery, except electric		2,513	2,445
Electric and electronic machinery	1,683	877	770
Transportation equipment	1,299	1,925	2,432
Other manufacturing	345	1,452	1,538
Trade	372	1,084	1,112
Banking		707	703
Finance	474	375	529
Other industries	113	116	139

[1] European Community includes ten nations in 1981.
Source: U.S. Department of Commerce, *Survey of Current Business:*, August 1982, Tables 13 and 14, pp. 21 and 22 and October 1975, Table 12, p. 52.

TABLE 4 FOREIGN DIRECT INVESTMENT POSITION IN THE UNITED STATES AT YEAR END, 1973–1981 (Millions of dollars)

	1973	1980	1981
Total, all areas	20,556	65,351	89,759
European Community (9)[1]	11,977	77,952	51,191
Federal Republic of Germany	965	5,402	7,067
Petroleum	7	50	56
Manufacturing	593	2,093	2,917
Food Products	2	28	25
Chemical and allied products	425	1,798	1,855
Primary and fabricated metals	34	163	170
Machinery	51	402	605
Other manufacturing	82	−298	263
Trade	267	1,831	2,271
Finance	32	163	301
Insurance	40	692	764
Real Estate	17	168	183
Other	10	407	574

[1] European Community includes ten nations in 1981.
Source: U.S. Department of Commerce, *Survey of Current Business*, August 1982, Table 9 and 10, pp. 36 and 37 and October 1977, Table 15, p. 35.

Bilateral Financial Institution Cooperation

Parallel to increases in trade and investment, a comprehensive network of commercial and investment banking, insurance, real estate, foreign currency trading, and consulting services has developed. The growth of financial services was originally linked to the postwar expansion of exports and then evolved into working capital and project lending as foreign direct investment increased. This process accelerated in the 1970s as governments of developing nations arranged massive loans to pay for costly oil imports and domestic economic development. German and American banks have been major participants in the banking consortiums created to provide these large private and public loans. Because of their regional responsibilities, American institutions have frequently been the lead banks for Latin American loans and German banks have played the leading role in Eastern European credits; but the geographical interests of financial institutions in both nations have been diversified. The unfortunate combination of supply-side shocks, particularly the sharp increase in world oil prices, and the serious erosion of commodity exports caused by extended recession have recently forced several borrowers to reschedule debt service payments to avoid widespread default. Various "lenders clubs" have been formed to coordinate the difficult adjustment process while damage control programs limit the number of official bankruptcies. The challenge of the 1980s will be to complete these "work-out" programs while continuing to supply the additional international credit needed to finance future development. German and American financial institutions will continue to have lead roles in the international money and capital markets.

Importance of Stable Exchange Rates and Open Capital Markets

Both nations have historically preferred stable exchange rates and minimal government intervention in international flows of capital to reduce uncertainties and distortions in trade and investment caused by volatile currency movements and arbitrary regulations. This shared preference does not, however, include support for any immediate return to the fixed exchange rate system that prevailed prior to March 1973 when the existing managed float arrangements were adopted. Monetary officials are similarly skeptical that official intervention in international financial markets can correct a fundamental disequilibrium, although they do occasionally intervene to neutralize temporary disturbances. It is generally agreed that economic policies and resulting rates of growth, inflation, investment, and current account balances must become more compatible before stable exchange rates can become a feasible option. Both governments have also avoided widespread capital controls, although the United States did make a futile attempt to restrict foreign loan and investments during the 1960s. Efforts to frustrate underlying market forces are usually inefficient and ineffective, but pressures for official intervention will continue because of the diverging patterns of national cyclical expansions and the ominous international financial situation.

Competitive National Interests and Policies

Bilateral Economic Competition Intense bilateral economic competition naturally results from exports of goods and services to each other and to third markets. Export industries remain the most dynamic part of the German economy and their crucial role is finally being recognized in America. Beyond the general complementary characteristics of the two economies, there is considerable competition in selling specialized industrial equipment, chemicals, steel, automobiles, scientific equipment, and various professional services. German exporters begin with a regional advantage in selling to Western European countries within their common market and a unique relationship with Eastern Europe has been developed. American firms compete effectively in these areas and have expanded their efforts in Canada, Latin America, and Asia. The next competitive phase will involve increasing their markets in other developing countries and expanding contacts with China. The rapid expansion of German exports of goods and services to OPEC nations is a classic example of the potential competition as industrial nations attempt to create new markets for their high-technology goods and services and to solidify sources of necessary raw materials. Bilateral foreign aid assistance will continue to be an important part of such programs. Similar competition in foreign direct investment and financial institution activities will also characterize future German-American economic relations.

Despite the intensity of competition, both nations have avoided most protectionist abuses because of their liberal economic principles and the fundamental inportance of international activities to their domestic growth and stability. Powerful special interest groups have forced political leaders to employ the usual non-tariff import barriers and export subsidies and complaints from several basic industries have increased as the prolonged economic recession has curtailed trade and increased unemployment. Nevertheless, the Federal Republic and the United States remain strong advocates of free trade and their steel and agricultural product disputes are exceptions to the general pattern. They have also avoided disagreements about export credit subsidies and strategic goods exports to Eastern Europe except for the unfortunate pipeline sanctions debate in 1982. In general, they remain committed to internal industrial adjustments and technological development as the best way to preserve their international competitiveness.

The Role of Locomotive Economies Their success makes the Federal Republic and the United States prime targets for critics arguing that strong economies should accelerate internal growth to increase international development. This locomotive theory was promoted by the United States during the late-1970s, and partially accepted by Germany and Japan; but disappointing stagflation and sluggish trade conditions eroded support for such concerted action programs. The recent Williamsburg Economic Summmit meetings pledged to "promote economic recovery" by pursuing "appropriate monetary and budget policies," but explicit references to the discredited locomotive theory were avoided. Nevertheless, both nations, along with Japan and the United Kingdom, have now been designated by the OECD to lead the cyclical expansion expected in 1983 and 1984. Current disagreement about the mix and thrust of national fiscal and monetary policies will continue to be divisive.

The irony of traditional locomotive recommendations is that they would perpetuate the stop-and-go economic policies that have prevailed in the United States during the last twenty-five years: increased government spending and credit programs, tax reductions, and the rapid growth of money and credit. During 1983, government spending continues to rise at the double-digit pace that has persisted since the mid-1960s, the third stage of tax-rate reductions begun in 1981 will be completed, and the growth of various monetary aggregates continues at double-digit rate. With chronic budget deficits expected to continue in the $200-billion zone, before consideration of off-budget outlays and government credit programs, serious capital market strains are anticipated if private investment borrowing increases rapidly during this cyclical expansion. The devastating effects of high interest rates during the last several years have caused many critics of U.S. policies to plead for a different mix of tighter fiscal actions to reduce the prospective deficits and more accommodative monetary initiatives to lower interest rates and encourage trade and investment. Since it is generally agreed that lower long-term interest rates are a prerequisite for restoring and sustaining economic growth, the extraordinary level of real interest rates, after adjusting nominal rates for prospective inflation, has created a vicious circle in which capital investments are delayed pending fiscal and monetary policy adjustments even though sustained economic recovery is contingent upon the revival of such spending. As long as this paralysis continues, the United States will be criticized for restricting the scope and pace of international economic recovery. The Federal Republic may also be accused of insensitivity to regional and global priorities and it might even join the critics of its Atlantic partner if the pressures become more intense.

Competitive Exchange Rate Goals   It is sometimes argued that Germany should evolve away from its traditional alliance by leading a competitive bloc of European currencies aligned against the U.S. dollar to reduce its destabilizing influence. The Deutsche Mark had already appreciated within the fixed-rate system in 1961, 1969, and 1971 before the cumulative monetary crisis led to a joint floating of selected European currencies within the "tunnel" and "snake" arrangements adopted after March 1973. Some analysts now suggest that the process should be expanded beyond the guidelines set for intra-European exchange rate activity to gradually pool national monetary reserves to be used for concerted intervention to sustain the fixed rates and provide bridge assistance for balance-of-payments problems, including increased regional consultations leading eventually to formal coordination of domestic fiscal and monetary policies. The European Community has announced various initiatives to achieve these long-term goals since the 1960s, but recurring economic and monetary crises have disrupted the plans. In 1979, the European Monetary System was created to enforce discipline among participating nations and Germany accepted an increased reserve currency role despite its traditional concerns about international currency speculation and erosion of its internal monetary controls. Nevertheless, the anticipated stability has not resulted and nations with weaker currencies have had to leave the system periodically or impose politically painful domestic stabilization policies. On March 21, 1982, the European Community Finance Ministers announced the latest of a series of internal currency realignments, including another large appreciation of the Deutsche Mark. At least the risks of anti-American actions have been avoided and the anticipated stability may develop as the international economy improves.

Divergent National Interests and Policies

Domestic Economic Goals   Sovereign nations usually have different priorities concerning growth, inflation, unemployment, balance-of-payments targets, the organization of business and financial activities, and the scope of government planning and control. The Federal Republic and the United States currently share similar goals of stimulating domestic growth and employment, while protecting the recent progress made in reducing inflation, and improving international trade and financial conditions, but this harmony conceals previous disagreements and potential risks. Various international organizations have recommended that both nations concentrate on rapidly increasing their growth rates. The United States has been severely criticized because of its unbalanced combination of fiscal and monetary policies and the volatile behavior of the dollar in foreign exchange markets. Critics argue that the prolonged failure of fiscal policies to control government spending and credit and the erosion of tax revenues have created a series of large deficits, which have forced central bank officials to monetize chronic government debts to accommodate total public and private credit needs, causing serious inflation problems, or to restrict the growth of money and credit leading to high interest rates and reduced capital investments. High American interest rates have been blamed for the sharp appreciation of the dollar's exchange rate, which forces other nations to maintain high rates to prevent the outflow of funds into dollar investments and pushes up the cost of their energy and raw material imports. They also accuse the United States of disrupting the international financial markets and discriminating against debtor nations. The Federal Republic is similarly criticized within Europe for emphasizing anti-inflation monetary policies and continuing unwillingness to rapidly reflate its sluggish economy.

It is obvious that the timing of business cycles and political elections frequently cause national economic policies to be out of synchronization and that exogenous disruptions, such as bad weather, political and military crises, and protectionist actions, also distort economic stability. Both the Federal Republic and the United States are subject to increasing pressure to adapt their internal economic policies to the expansion goals of other nations. The disappointing results of similar fiscal and monetary initiatives during the 1960s and 1970s have so far restrained their responses to these demands, but the difficulties of harmonizing national policies are increasing.

East-West Trade and Finance Issues A second divisive issue involves the style and substance of East-West trade. The United States has frequently tried to manipulate economic relations with the Soviet Union as part of their continuing geo-political competition. The original economic aspirations of detente deteriorated throughout the 1970s and then collapsed when the United States restricted its grain exports to Russia and prohibited the sale of technical equipment to be used in building a Siberian natural gas pipeline. Efforts to extend the pipeline sanctions, to include the European subsidiaries and licensees of American companies, created an abrasive confrontation and U.S. Government officials eventually rescinded the regulations in exchange for a general agreement to consider alternative sources of energy and pledges to strengthen existing procedures used to control the transfer of strategic goods to the Soviet Union, the monitoring of financial arrangements, and harmonization of export credit policies. Legislation covering these controversial issues is currently being considered by the Congress.

The Federal Republic has a different appraisal of the potential risks and benefits of East-West trade based on its geographical and historical perspectives and the realities of domestic economic and political goals. Following the adoption of *Ostpolitik* policies in 1969, and the signing of the Eastern Treaties formalizing postwar political borders, trade and other contacts with Eastern Europe increased rapidly. The Federal Republic now accounts for approximately one-fifth of total East-West trade, with exports to Eastern Europe amounting to about 6 percent of its foreign sales and imports representing about 5 percent of foreign purchases. This relatively small volume of trade is approximately equal to transactions with the United States or Switzerland, but falls well below the totals for major European Community partners. Nevertheless, current and potential East-West trade is considered to be important to the entire West German economy, and to several key industries, as shipments of high-quality capital equipment and technical assistance, involving favorable financing arrangements based on low German interest rates, have made it the largest supplier by far of nonagricultural goods and services from the West. Long-term agreements have been signed to exchange German steel, industrial machinery and supplies, and high-technology goods and services for Russian energy resources and raw materials.

Most German officials agree that the *Ostpolitik* initiatives have served important functions beyond the economic rewards of increased trade. The original intent was to restore Germany's pivotal role by opening up political contacts in the East without disrupting the economic and security advantages of belonging to the Atlantic Alliance. They view these efforts as a positive bridge for achieving traditional regional interests rather than a move toward neutralism. The timing of the political and economic initiatives was somewhat unfortunate, however, because it coincided with popular journalistic analyses depicting the United States as a faltering power following the Vietnam and Watergate experiences, but the motivation was to promote German interests rather than to denigrate America. Both nations now appear to have overcome the rhetorical claims and adjusted to the differences in regional and global goals. The Federal Republic continues to emphasize the importance of its relatively modest East-West economic transactions and its commitment to the European Community and Atlantic Alliance as justification for its efforts to sustain three specific benefits. First, the increased trade and financial opportunities helped its economy, particularly certain heavy-industry sectors, during a difficult transition period when international recession and trade distortions were escalating. Second, political contacts were increased throughout Eastern Europe, and particularly with the German Democratic Republic, through expanded trade, improved transportation and communication links, increased emigration to the West, and reduced tensions along the restricted border which divides Germany into two nations. Regardless of how the "reunification issue" is finally resolved, it remains a political necessity to emphasize the importance of bilateral contacts. Third, increasing the scope and continuity of East-West activities demonstrates the independence of the European Community in conducting a regional foreign policy and the leadership role of the Federal Republic. Effective political cooperation will be required to avoid the risks of an unfortunate potential tradeoff in which the European Community might declare its autonomy by moving closer to the Soviet orbit. The Federal Republic is well aware of this danger after almost forty years of difficult coexistence experiences.

Regional Versus Global Commitments A third fragmenting force involves pressures on the Federal Republic to conform to the consensus policies of the European Community even though the results are sometimes contrary to its global interests and bilateral relations with the United States. Important geopolitical goals and risks justify the commitment to European integration. First, its regional neighbors comprise the major markets for German exports of goods and services and creation of a common market has contributed to the "economic miracle." The Federal Republic has consistently supported a liberal economic order and rejected the *dirigisme* of government economic planning and regulations, cartels, trade barriers, and capital controls. Enlargement of the European Community over time has expanded German economic interests. Second, the formal organization has enabled the Federal Republic to evolve into a position of regional political and security leadership commensurate with its economic power without seriously alienating other nations sensitive to the risks of renewed German hegemony. The institutions and consultation arrangements have provided a convenient forum for broader participation and Germany has responded with strong financial and moral support for regional programs. Third, the Federal Republic has wrapped itself in the cloak of European institutions in foreign affairs enabling it to maintain a low profile and avoid much of the abusive rhetoric directed at the United States. It has been possible to create positive contacts with Third World countries by participating in the Lome Agreements arranged by the European Community. Fourth, active regional participation has been responsive to domestic political pressures to the "best Europeans" and to fulfill perceived obligations to Spain, Portugal and Greece as they formally join the group. The evolving Franco-German exchanges and Eastern European initiatives have similarly benefited from regional support. Fifth, identification with the Western Europe bloc has contributed to its image of independence from the two superpowers without dissipating political contacts with the Soviet Union or substantively reducing economic and security arrangements with the United States. This demonstration of autonomy evidently fulfills a national image requirement, particularly at a time when the European Community is buffeted by internal problems linked to sluggish domestic growth and stagnant trade.

As the leading economy with the strongest currency in the European Community, the Federal Republic has a difficult challenge responding to the proliferation of bureaucratic regulations and the demands of other member nations committed to government intervention. In recent years, it has been asked to stimulate more regional growth by adopting expansive domestic policies, reducing its regular trade surpluses, helping to finance regional capital investments to assist underdeveloped areas, and supporting exchange rate stability through the European Monetary System, despite wide disparities in economic policies and results which have required frequent currency realignments to reflect marketplace realities. Germany has supported most of these proposed initiatives, often at considerable costs measured by budget contribution, but it has usually refused to manipulate domestic fiscal and monetary policies and has only reluctantly accepted part of the responsibilities of a reserve currency. The regional coordination of external policies has caused specific trade and investment disputes with the United States, along with general criticism of its mix of fiscal and monetary policies and the resulting interest rate problems. The most persistent disagreement, however, involves Europe's Common Agricultural Policy (CAP), which enforces a comprehensive set of administered prices, production guidelines, import restrictions, export subsidies, and development grants to promote and protect agricultural interests. The Federal Republic has strongly supported the CAP, through budget contributions and bureaucratic maneuvers, even though the *dirigiste* system is inconsistent with its support of an open and competitive economy. The acceptance of the CAP, and related budget financial burdens, demonstrates Germany's postwar emphasis on European integration as an important factor in creating strong markets for it exports of industrial equipment and supplies and the historical political clout of farmers in gaining special treatment, even though the agricultural sector now produces only three percent of its total GNP. The agriculture trade issue is rapidly becoming more abrasive as the United States seeks to exploit its comparative advantages while Europe defends existing arrangements despite increasing regional production and stagnant demand conditions. American initiatives for liberalizing agriculture trade rules were largely ignored at the November 1982 meetings of trade ministers. European officials argued that existing GATT regulations recognize the CAP procedures and that disruptive reforms to appease American interests are not worth the political and social turmoil that would result. American critics claim that CAP subsidies create excessive regional output that is increasingly exported to compete with U.S. sales in other areas, adding insult to the injury of being unable to penetrate European markets. Frustrations continue to escalate on both sides and careful management will be required to prevent specific arguments from deteriorating into unwanted disagreements about comprehensive economic, political, and security issues.

With the notable exception of agriculture trade concerns, the United States has consistently supported the European Community as an effective means of fostering stable political and security conditions even though it realizes that the process inevitably creates a stronger competitor. These persuasive arguments have drawn the United States into European economic and security affairs despite the problem of being an outsider and the frustrations of dealing with an institutional bureaucracy in addition to each member nation. Cooperation will become even more complex as internal goals and the world environment continue to change, but mutual interests will likely prevent divisive "continental drift." The Federal Republic has not had to choose between its regional priorities and the broader association with the United States and specific disagreements have eventually been resolved or ignored to sustain the beneficial alliance.

The German experience in balancing competing regional and global interests provides an excellent example. Throughout the postwar era, the United States has concentrated most of its attention on Western and Eastern Europe because of traditional links and its geo-political confrontation with the Soviet Union. This orientation has too often diluted necessary emphasis upon other areas of extreme importance to the United States, except during serious political and military crises. During the 1980s, America should significantly increase its response to opportunities and responsibilities in Latin America and the Pacific Basin. Both areas offer unique challenges to participate in the development of their abundant resources and large markets for goods, services, and capital. This expansion of American interest does not imply any erosion of the Atlantic Alliance. It simply recognizes the geopolitical and economic realities that make these areas so crucial to the future of the United States and recommends that it become more international and less insular. The United States should follow the example of *Modell Deutschland* as it cultivates its regional neighbors, creates an opening into Eastern Europe, and increases contacts in the Third World through the Lome Convention and aggressive bilateral trade and investment deals in the Middle East, Africa, Latin America, and Asia.

Relations with Third World Nations A fourth point of possible divergence involves the arrangements for dealing with trade, investment, financial, and public aid issues between industrial nations and the Third World. Since the substantive policies of the Federal Republic and the United States are similar, particularly support for international institutions and promotion of liberal trade and investment rules, the major differences seem to involve procedures and rhetoric. The Federal Republic has been active in multinational agreements, such as the European Community's Lome Convention contacts with a large group of developing nations, and has used foreign aid effectively to promote its national interests. The bilateral aid procedures used by the United States, and its relatively harsh rhetoric and unique size, have caused it to be somewhat isolated and criticized. Once again, the United States could learn some valuable lessons from the Federal Republic.

Conclusions

The preceding analysis leads to five general conclusions. First, economic prospects will depend upon the creativity and productivity of workers and managers, capital investments, technology, and international development as a foundation for restoring the output of goods and services, reducing unemployment, controlling inflation, correcting widespread structural problems, and avoiding destructive protectionist pressures. A cyclical recovery is now occurring, following four years of disappointing results, but doubts persist about the sustainability of the expansion. Serious structural problems affecting productivity remain and the obvious imbalance of fiscal and monetary policies, caused by increased government spending patterns and large budget deficits affecting the growth of money and credit and important interest rates, must be adjusted to avoid future cyclical distortions.

Second, powerful integrating forces will strengthen the links between these two world-class economies based on their similar commitments to liberal domestic and international economic principles, opposition to protectionism, mutually beneficial trade and investments concentrated in sophisticated manufactured products, industrial materials, and technical services, and the central roles of the U.S. dollar and Deutsche Mark.

Third, bilateral competition will escalate as both nations strive to expand their exports of goods and services, foreign investments, and financial activities. Policy differences will be inevitable because of specific national interests and problems. The Federal Republic has special regional priorities in Western and Eastern Europe extending beyond the bilateral alliance. The United States should become more responsive to opportunities and risks in Latin America and the Pacific Basin. This regional concern does not mean that the United States is carelessly turning away from its fundamental global priorities and the central role of Western Europe, or that the Federal Republic is about to reject the substance of the Atlantic Alliance in favor of political neutrality. To the contrary, the policy initiatives reflect a positive broadening of interests and a more realistic recognition of bilateral power and responsibilities.

Fourth, despite the unique strength of their domestic economies, both nations should become more responsive to the aspirations of other countries seeking economic development and the risks created by extended stagflation problems and repeated supply-side shocks involving oil, agricultural products, and other raw materials. At the same time, they should preserve their traditional values and liberal policies which have created political, social, and economic progress and provided a foundation for their military security alliance.

Fifth, bilateral relations will remain fundamentally strong even though the international environment is rapidly changing. Mutual contacts will be more complex and less predictable, but the benefits of cooperation remain the same. Imposing critics will cite specific disputes, and occasional anti-American incidents and neutralist rhetoric, to argue that the postwar Atlantic Alliance is disintegrating. A few will even claim that the United States is too powerful to tolerate the interests of others and that its economic hegemony is just as dangerous as Soviet military imperialism. These are serious accusations deserving careful analysis to avoid naive complacency, particularly during the transition of leadership to a new generation that did not personally experience the tragic results of political and economic policy blunders during the 1930s and 1940s, but such arguments ignore the basic calculus of bilateral benefits and dependence. This reality is clearly identified in the wise advice given by Dr. Arthur F. Burns, America's distinguished Ambassador to the Federal Republic of Germany:

> The reason for the survival and vitality of the Alliance derives from a fact which overrides every other—namely, that it is based on and represents the basic moral and political values that Western Europe shares with the United States and Canada.
>
> *Ambassador Arthur F. Burns speaking to the Deutsche Atlantische Gesellschaft, December 9, 1982.*

THE ECONOMIC RELATIONS OF THE FEDERAL REPUBLIC OF GERMANY AND THE UNITED STATES OF AMERICA

by Reimut Jochimsen

1. In the 1970s, the world economy abruptly found itself confronted with a slew of economic problems. Many states viewed these problems as a natural phenomenon — as the inevitable consequence of the finiteness of economic activity ("Spaceship Earth") both in terms of natural resources availability and environmental pollution control needs — rather than as the inevitable result of erroneous development which accumulated throughout the 1960s (e.g., the world inflation caused by the Vietnam War) and then erupted in the wake of the first oil price explosion in 1973.

The price/cost ratios in the world had widened, and the terms of trade impaired the bartering position of the raw materials producers — particularly of the oil-producing countries. The oil-exporting countries improved their foreign trade position at a single stroke: their terms of trade rose from 40 percent in 1972 to over 105 percent in 1974, reaching their present level of 184 percent. At the same time, the terms of trade of the industrial countries worsened from 112, to 98 and then to 90 percent (1975 - 100).[1]

Subsequently, real growth decelerated worldwide. This was over and above the deceleration which industrial economies had already been experiencing for some time, testifying to the fact that high real growth (particularly of the steady state type) always has been more the exception than the rule for socio-economic development in industrialized nations.

There was an alarming increase in average unemployment year after year. Inflation rates jumped (in some countries to double digit figures); fundamental balance of payments disequilibrium developed; productivity growth rates declined. The leeway for private as well as public sector demands shrank, and production facilities shriveled away as sectoral and regional production capacities diminished. The Bretton Woods System of fixed exchange rates was finally abandoned.

The 1970s became a decade of inflexibility and uncertainty. Inflation, interest, and exchange rates showed wide fluctuation spreads which were not always reconcilable with economic or political developments. The structural adaptation of economies to changed market conditions worldwide became the economists' undisputed magic formula for solving economic difficulties, especially labor market problems. This was especially true since flexible or floating exchange rates seemingly restored to national government the choice of inflation-free full employment policies with stable external balances. Nevertheless, distribution of the national product remained controversial both within a national framework initially, but eventually also on an international basis. A perfect example of this is the Third World's demand for a "new world economic order."

2. The economic turbulences brought about a change in the structure of the world economy. The U.S. is without a doubt still a dominant country which holds the key to solving many important economic questions, though its relative weight in the Western economies diminished from about 70 percent to less than 40 percent from 1950 to 1980.[2] New poles of differing though considerable weight began to emerge in addition to the dual polarity of the politically-dominant superpowers, the U.S. and the Soviet Union. The new factors included the stronger economic cohesion of the European Community, the stronger emergence of Japan in the world markets, the founding of the OPEC cartel, the closing of ranks among the threshold countries and the stronger voice of the Third World.

In some economic statistics, the European Community surpassed the United States in the 1970s. With its aggregate population of 270 million,[3] the group of 10 constitutes the largest self-contained domestic market in the world. It accounts for more than half of the free world's national product[4] and about 60 percent of its foreign trade.[5]

Despite the loosening of the international political nexus due to the pushing aside of workable institutions such as the International Monetary Fund, the reality of growing international economic interdependence emerged clearly during the 1970s. As the OECD puts it, economies now have to act as teams in order to be successful or to fail.[6] In 1979 the major industrialized countries, in reacting to rising oil prices by anti-inflationary means, all moved in the same direction at the same time, and the effect on each of them was greater than each one anticipated. They reinforced each other in powerful ways, but these same linkages also have a side-effect. They make it very difficult for any one country to depart very far from the general direction being taken by the industrialized countries as a group. One example is the failure of France's socialist government to speed up its economy and create jobs while most of its trading partners were mainly worried about inflation.

Following temporary phases of improvement, the structural adaptation problems still remaining at the beginning of the 1980s have not only brought about a three-year-old world economic crisis (which will hopefully be overcome soon), but have also caused manifold disruptions of trade. These issues were often debated so vehemently that it may have seemed almost impossible to find a common platform for consistent and relevant action. And it has proven to be of little help that every year there are intensive consultations at the highest levels, such as the world economic summit meetings since the mid-1970s or those of the OECD, GATT, and UNCTAD. The impetus for holding world economic summits came from Europe, incidentally mostly at the initiative of France and Germany, in an attempt to deal specifically with the post-crisis policies after the oil shock and the break-up of the exchange rate set-up.

Such summit meetings are held regularly in an aura of expectations which they cannot fulfill. They are nevertheless under such pressure to come up with results that when they do not, these summits are viewed as failures. Williamsburg is one example among several, but there have also been exceptions. At the May 8, 1977 London summit, a joint decision was made to combat worldwide inflation since inflation does not lower unemployment but, on the contrary, tends to be one of its main causes.

There is an increased need for stable, continuous, institutionalized arrangements for more solid policy-coordination among the major industrialized countries where both the U.S. and Europe have to play leading roles.[7]

3. Structural changes, the need to promote qualitative growth rather than quantitative expansion, and the challenge to affect their acceleration have been felt mainly in the regions of industrialized economies where basic and production goods industries dominate. These areas, like the old established smokestack industrial areas of the U.S. or Europe, are very sensitive to energy and raw material cost shocks. Conversion problems have been particularly difficult in the Midwest, but also in this country.

The Rhine-Ruhr basin is the heart of the State of North Rhine-Westphalia. From the early days of industrialization two centuries ago until very recently, its economy has been based primarily on coal and steel.[8] With almost six million inhabitants it still forms the hard core of industrial Germany and also the largest economic agglomeration in Europe. North Rhine-Westphalia has been contributing almost one third of West German exports and imports as production and income; thus, in terms of international exchange its contribution to world trade exceeds that of countries like Sweden, the Netherlands, or Canada.

It is here that the signals of the limits to growth because of environmental pollution and the exigencies of the changing energy scenario (including the economy needs of raw material inputs) were felt in their conflicting dimensions. On the one hand there is a "renaissance" of domestic and secure energies like hard coal; on the other hand there is a diminishing importance of heavy overhead investments. Both suffer even more from high interest rates and consequent stagnation.[9]

The older industrial agglomerations in the developed economies are facing similar challenges, and finding answers is becoming more urgent as the impetus to recovery and growth declines. Furthermore, the fundamental changes are necessary in areas where the process of modernization has never before been successfully undertaken and completed. In North Rhine-Westphalia, however, it appears that the fundamental elements of factor endowment, well-qualified manpower and infrastructural outfitting, ecological improvements, and emerging patterns of production are quite favorable for mastering this change successfully. The Rhine-Ruhr basin needed and still needs, however, a careful monitoring of the process as well as a state policy to aid and cushion the shifts and adjustments. All this calls for deliberate policy at various levels including the State, regionally, nationally, and European-wide; the policy will have to extend beyond monetary, trade, employment, and development policies on a national or international scale.

4. Both the United States and the Federal Republic of Germany pursue basically the same economic objectives. One of the most important is regaining a high level of employment with growth entailing as little inflation as possible, both within an integrated market economy based on competition, social security as well as democratic consensus. In addition, both countries are aiming at securing the external economic balance necessary for having the most liberal world trade possible and to increase investments abroad. At first glance, the economic policy successes of recent years are not particularly encouraging. There is insufficient economic growth everywhere. There has been an increase — in some cases drastic — of unemployment, particularly among youth and minority groups.

The long-term deviation from full employment and the limited regional, sectoral, and ethnic success of socio-economic integration of the young and women leads to tendencies of segmentation in the labor market, thus increasing the threats of an emerging socio-economic dualism.[10] Interest levels — with historically high real margins — are nowhere near a level commensurate with the needs of the economy; investments are much lower and shorter term oriented and employment is kept low. This puts an additional premium on cost reduction when capacities are not fully utilized. Nonetheless, the reduction inflation rates have made marked progress in the Western industrialized states, but this constitutes just one vital prerequisite for re-achieving new qualitative growth.

By the spring of 1983, the rise in consumer prices had decelerated to an average of 4.8 percent in the most important industrialized countries after peaking at 13 percent in mid-1980.[11] This marked deceleration is attributable primarily to the successes in combating inflation in those countries which previously had experienced a high rate of inflation, above all the U.S. and Great Britain. The deceleration is certainly also attributable to cyclical developments which contributed to the fact that prices for oil and raw materials have been dropping for some time. But as the expected upswing of the world economy sets in, it is unlikely that this component of the deceleration process will continue to make itself felt.

There are numerous indications that the three-year old economic recession seems to have bottomed out. Significant indicators, above all in the U.S., point to a gradual upswing. A worldwide upswing, however, appears to be just as uncertain as it does in other major countries, including Germany.

Continuing high real interest rates, substantial budget deficits in many countries, exchange rate irritations and the debt problems of many developing countries still cast a dark shadow on prospects for an early and thoroughgoing economic upswing. The major industrialized countries now stand at the crossroads of future economic development faced with a particular challenge and bearing a special responsibility. In addition to what certainly are necessary declaration and proclamations, concrete economic policy must be geared toward:

— bringing about a worldwide upswing by concerted determination and action;

— fostering further structural change and adjustment in the industrialized economies though without ruptures and collapses in the smokestack industries, and without destroying social peace and producing intolerable regional disparities;

— regaining the viability of the international monetary system;

— keeping access to markets open and securing the free flow of world trade; and

— achieving progress in the integration of the threshold and developing countries into the international economy.

Calling for more unity and cooperation in economic policy is undoubtedly an important prerequisite for overcoming the world's economic problems. This, however, cannot and should not absolve each individual country of the responsibility for above all putting its own house in order through action on a national scale. The world economy is a phenomenon made up of a multitude of national economies. Decisions to have specific countries assume the role of locomotive to pull others — as was given West Germany by the 1978 world economic summit meeting in Bonn — are completely out of place in the present economic situation.[12]

What is appropriate at the moment is for governments to construct and implement their national measures to achieve international effectiveness. In that respect, the United States has a significant leadership role to play in the future development of the world economy. There is nothing at all to criticize about the U.S.'s forceful and successful campaign against domestic inflation. What is open to criticism, however, is the one-sided monetaristic approach which has been taken for some time and the lack of consideration given its international repercussions, especially the effect it has on interest rate development and exchange rates elsewhere. The U.S. still appears to follow the habit of grossly underestimating the influences of the rest of the world on U.S. prosperity.[13]

5. The United States is the world's largest trading nation. Though far behind the U.S., West Germany is nevertheless ahead of Japan. These three countries together account for almost one-third of the total export volume in world trade.[14] The significance of world trade to the Federal Republic, however, is far greater than for either the U.S. or Japan. The export of goods and services in West Germany amounts to almost 30 percent of its gross domestic product; the export ratios for the U.S. and Japan are much lower, amounting to about 10 and 14 percent respectively.[15] Apart from manufactured goods, West Germany is even exporting slightly more goods than the

U.S. (in 1982: $156 billion vs. $152 billion).[16] West Germany is strongly integrated in the international exchange of goods and services.

This exceptionally strong interrelationship with the world economy also documents the country's exceptional sensitivity to extraneous economic influences. West Germany's per capita export figure is currently almost DM 5,700, compared with the U.S.'s DM 1,750 and Japan's DM 2,019.[17] None of the other major industrialized countries has such a high per capita export figure. In addition, it has been above all in important industrial sectors, and in the State of North Rhine-Westphalia in particular, that the external influences on domestic development have been most telling. The degree of dependence on exports is particularly high in the iron and steel producing industry, through which approximately 77 percent of all persons gainfully employed in this sector are either directly or indirectly dependent on exports (industrial average: 47 percent).[18] This testifies to the enormous importance of the machine building and tool making industries which export up to three-quarters of production, thus accounting for about half of total world exports. Comparable figures apply to the export of integrated plant and equipment schemes. In all branches of the German manufacturing sector the dependence on exports has been increasing, most strongly since 1976. According to the latest figures, in 1981 almost every fourth West German worker was employed directly or indirectly in the export sector. Though 70 percent of German exports go into the Common Market (20 percent alone to France), the remaining volume going to the U.S. (6 percent), Japan and Eastern Europe (5 percent) is still important.[19]

These figures illustrate West Germany's vital interest in international trade which is as unencumbered as possible by protectionism, regimentation and subsidization.

In this context the flow of goods between Germany and the U.S. plays an important role although the export figures do not reflect the complete extent of the economic ties between the two countries. As far as Germany's exports go, the U.S. currently occupies sixth position and with respect to imports fourth position. From the U.S. point of view the picture is similar.[20] It should come as no surprise that Germany's exporters focus prime attention on adjacent countries, above all within the European Community. But this picture would not be a completely accurate one without mentioning that the U.S. has for a long while been Germany's most important partner regarding direct investment. The year of 1975 saw an important break in this development with the shift in the D-Mark/dollar exchange rate. Since then, German investors have made far larger commitments in the U.S. than American investors in Germany. From 1976 to 1982, German direct investment in the United States amounted to just under DM 17 billion compared to DM 4 billion by U.S. investors in Germany. This is undoubtedly a further contribution toward the deepening and intensification of transatlantic relations — and not only in the economic sphere.[21]

6. A comparison of the German and U.S. economies reveals a good deal of common ground and similarities. At the same time, however, it highlights

divergent developments which should really come as no surprise considering the differing structural dimensions of a "big country," such as the U.S. and a "smaller one," such as West Germany. The most pronounced dissimilarity between the two is exemplified by the fact that over the last twenty years the American economy has developed increasingly into one geared to the service industries and the procurement of information.

The employment share of those economic sectors which no longer manufacture goods in the real sense of the word currently stands at 70 percent and a further increase to 80 percent is anticipated by 1990. In West Germany, on the other hand, this proportion is still much lower (55 percent), although account should be taken of the problems involved in drawing clear-cut demarcation lines between the service sectors and goods manufacturing industries. It should be remembered, however, that among the larger industrialized countries only the Federal Republic of Germany expanded its manufacturing sector in terms of production and employment not only quantitatively, but also in relative terms during the first two decades after World War II, a period in which the U.S. industrial sector has continuously lost in relative terms.[22]

On the other hand, between 1962 and 1982 the number of employed in the U.S. rose by 33 million to just under 100 million, an increase of nearly 50 percent. This means that since 1962, roughly 6 million more new jobs have been created in the U.S. than the total number of jobs existing in the Federal Republic.[23] The last ten years have seen 17 million more U.S. citizens finding work, a period during which employment stagnated in West Germany. Thus average job availability in the United States over this period has risen by between 1 and 2 million annually.

These new jobs have been created almost exclusively by the service industry. The tertiary sector in the U.S. doubled its workforce between 1960 and 1980 whereas its counterpart in Germany only recorded a one-third increase in the same period. From 1972-1982 alone, the American service sector created 15.7 million new jobs for wage and salary earners, although one should add that 2.5 million of these were in the government and administrative sectors.[24]

Employment in the U.S. manufacturing sector has been stagnating since the mid-60s, although undergoing a certain amount of cyclical fluctuation. The German manufacturing workforce, on the other hand, has shrunk by 1.1 million to 11.7 million between 1972 and 1983. The employment share attributable to the U.S. manufacturing industry fell from 37 percent in 1962 to 32 percent in 1972 and down to 27 percent ten years later, representing still about 27 million members of the workforce.[25]

The strong job growth in the United States is a remarkable phenomenon for the outside observer insofar as the longer-term average for overall economic growth in this country has turned out on the weak side. With an increase in employment of 2 percent per year[26] and an annual decline in the average working week of approximately 0.5 percent over the last ten years, the real national product has only risen by 2 percent. Thus, productivity progress in the American economy has been only slight. Between 1972 and

1982, the output per work hour amounted to just under 1 percent per year compared to almost three times this figure (average yearly productivity progress of 2.8 percent) during the two preceding decades.

Decelerating productivity progress in the U.S. has to be mainly attributable to meager growth of capital input. An important reason for the slowdown in capital input growth could very well be the bulge in the labor force. In 1982 there were 48 million employable persons in the United States, 77 percent more than in 1952. The employment ratio rose between 1952 and 1982 from 42 percent to 48 percent. The number of employable persons in the Federal Republic went up by only 11 percent over the same period. The 46 percent employment ratio in 1982 was no higher than in 1952, and in the intervening period it had even fallen short of this figure. The permanent labor surplus in the U.S. had held down wage increases. The last twenty years have seen hourly wages go up by a nominal 245 percent, only 10 percent in real terms; this is equivalent to a nominal yearly growth rate of 6.4 percent; 0.5 percent in real terms. By comparison, German hourly wage scales rose by a nominal 326 percent and by 89 percent in real terms, in other words an annual average increase of a nominal 7.5 percent or 3.2 percent in real terms.

Compared to the Federal Republic with its more rapid wage increases and shorter supply of labor, the rationalization pressure in the U.S. was not so high. At the same time there was often great leeway for absorbing rising wage costs. In the past twenty years, U.S. producer prices have advanced by an average of 5.6 percent per year compared to only 3.8 percent in West Germany. The fact that U.S. corporations were able to pass on a far larger portion of wage cost increase in the form of higher prices probably explains why corporate profits were not adversely affected by comparatively lower investment levels and lesser productivity gains. The last two decades have seen very little change in the profit/sales ratio for American industry, in marked contrast to development in the Federal Republic.

7. The German economy is presently characterized by a halt in the rise of the ratio of fixed asset formation to national product; indeed, technological progress is currently being made in large portions which require less expenditure both in terms of labor and capital.[27] This is not least a reflection of the necessity to maintain and — where possible — strengthen German product competitiveness both in the domestic and world markets, pressure which the U.S. is not subject to in the same measure, though in the U.S. too the old formula of trade as a luxury rather than a necessity no longer holds true as the international division of labor is progressing. The smokestack industries in particular suffer through this growing interrelationship.

8. This also focuses attention on one particular danger which poses an increasing threat to West Germany's position in international trade. The reference is to protectionism, the growing inclination to hinder accessibility to markets and to throw up barriers to trade. It goes without saying that countries as deeply involved in the international division of labor as the U.S.

and especially West Germany are dependent on the free functioning of international trade. Generaly speaking, countries are not only exporters but also importers. In 1982, West Germany imported goods worth nearly DM 380 billion. This puts it in second place in the world import rankings behind the United States.[28] In the past, open markets and liberalism in world trade were crucial prerequisites for growth and increasing prosperity both in a national and international context. Moreover, these two factors are likely to become even more crucial in the future.

Considerable progress was achieved in the liberalization of world trade during the three decades following the end of the Second World War, a development encouraged by the rapid growth in the industrialized countries and the pent-up demand for goods and services. These factors facilitated the structural adjustment inevitably connected with the removal of impediments to trade and service flows. This sustained liberalization of trade policy considerably intensified world economic interlinkage on goods and capital markets. In recent years, however, this enlightened attitude to trade has begun to evaporate rapidly, a direct function of rising unemployment figures and their regional concentration. The actual behavior of the industrialized countries both toward one another and toward the Third World bears very little resemblance to their repeated assurances of adherence to the free trade principle. The Williamsburg Summit also felt bound to make avowals of faith in the free trade idea. All participants agreed to "stem protectionist tendencies and, parallel to a strengthening economy, to reverse this sealing off process with the eventual aim of removing trade barriers altogether."

In practice, however, this story is quite different. The Federal Republic, though, is only a relatively minor transgressor. The agricultural sector, be it in the United States or in Europe, has always been the prime example of an industry which has never been exposed to international competition. We have already had the U.S. and the European Community on the brink of a trade war during the '60s and '70s. Moreover, the problem of EC agricultural subsidies and their effects both on bilateral and third-country trade has up to now defied satisfactory solution. Besides, protectionism within the EC for agriculture and within the steel and textile spheres is also an ample source of trade policy conflict between the United States and the European Community. To illustrate the point, the massive subsidies paid to some steel industries in Europe prompted the U.S. to impose anti-dumping levies on steel imports from the EC. A self-restraint agreement, now in operation until 1985, requires that European steel manufacturers adhere to "voluntary" export quotas.[29] The widespread fear in Europe at present is that the protectionist wave in the U.S. could swell — despite the thoroughly negative experience of the notorious Smoot-Hawley Tariff Act of 1930 which introduced the heaviest protective levies in the history of the United States and triggered a spate of retaliatory measures. Acute new impositions of countervailing duties, as the U.S. chose to enact in July 1983 in the field of alloy steels, demonstrate the problem of the U.S. dollar exchange rates. The rates are prohibitive to U.S. exports and inducive to imports of manufactured goods where substitutions appear to be possible, but in the field of high technology and other "intelligent" products, this still proves to be very difficult. And there appears no end to these mechanisms once set into motion.

The problems and points of controversy are not only confined to bilateral relations. Ties to third countries are also ridden with conflict. The Americans, for example, are calling for an easing of European controls on agricultural imports from the Third World; improved sales changes for agricultural produce from developing countries would undoubtedly enhance prospects for a solution to the debt crisis in the Third World. Indeed, U.S. imports emanating from non-oil producing developing countries are almost three times as high as the corresponding figure for the European Community.

Of late there as been a general deterioration in the trade policy climate. This appears to be the logical consequence both of the growing international interdependence as well as the general lack of growth. The problem is compounded by an insufficient level of effective aggregate demand internationally. This leads to an intensified struggle for market volumes and shares, first and especially for commodities which are staples, homogeneous, or easy substitutes, and second where production techniques are known and transferable as well as prone to further rigid rationalization, for example for steel, textiles, car making or grains. This deterioration in trade policy climate is typified by the increasing frequency of bilateral trade conflicts and the lengthening list of non-tariff impediments to trade in commercial, industrial, and agricultural goods. The menacing aspect of the current situation is, above all, the appearance of protectionism in new guises. It has numerous extremely sophisticated mechanisms in its repertoire. The wide range of "tricks" employed is a greater cause for concern than the classical customs barriers because the range obviously offers the inventive mind almost limitless possibilities.

Generally speaking, more attention is paid to the unavoidable adjustment costs arising from unfettered free trade than to the advantages which this could generate, be those benefits in the form of lower prices for the consumer, fiercer competition in the respective national markets, productivity progress or employment bonuses. Relevant, too, is the judgment (or prejudice) that the additional benefits which the already affluent Western industrial countries could derive from an intensification of the international division of labor appears to be only minimal. Coping with the structural change triggered by the stronger division of labor with the Third World countries is proving especially difficult. Compared to strengthening goods trade between the industrialized countries, the same process with the involvement of the developing nations intensifies the division of labor between industrial sectors. Job losses in one sector resulting from increasing import pressure can actually turn into additional employment opportunities in others as a consequence of an upsurge in exports.

In the present situation the free trade idea appears less attractive since the nature and effects of technological advance in this phase at the end of a Kondratieff long wave seem to merge with the end of a classical Wicksellian process of a switch away from extensive to intensive growth, with simultaneous advances of both labor and capital saving techniques.[30] The possible longer-term advantage of an optimum allocation of production factors is thus overshadowed by the question of whether those jobs which go by the board in the short and medium term can be recreated.

The free trade principle loses a good deal of glow when one looks at the poor growth conditions worldwide, stagnating overall demand, balance of payments disequilibrium and the dire straits of many sovereign borrowers, above all in the Third World. The best sort of structural policy under these circumstances appears to be erecting barriers to trade and service flow, thereby keeping the initial adjustment requirement to a minimum. Many countries regard this alternative as more advantageous than taking part in the international division of labor and the acceptance of the competitive challenges connected with this.

Nevertheless, protectionism for goods and for services is no permanent substitute for structural (sectoral or regional) adjustment. Those who still believe in the establishment of national self-sufficiency are laboring under a severe misapprehension. Import restrictions are not a suitable means of coping with structural change, that is to say of encouraging the necessary adjustment processes. Indeed, it can be empirically proven that import barriers eventually turn out to be ineffective and more of a liability than a benefit to domestic industries. This contention has been substantiated again through a study of the U.S. steel industry between 1969 and 1974 and of the controls imposed on color TV imports into the U.S. during the late '70s.[31] Import restrictions cannot prevent an ongoing erosion of competitiveness and market shares; such controls are bypassed sooner or later anyway, and before long the countries involved resort to retaliatory measures. Already existing structural weaknesses are not remedied, adjustment processes are delayed and the absence of competitive pressure hinders improvements to products and production processes as well as the achievement of higher productivity.

On top of this, protectionism on the part of the industrialized countries is likely to exacerbate the debt problems of many developing and threshold countries. Inflexible adherence to original debt schedules by the industrialized countries would in the end drastically cut export opportunities. Conversely, through the export of goods and services to the lender countries, the developing countries need to be in a position to whittle down the debt-servicing burden on an accumulated $700 billion borrowed abroad.[32] Sovereign debtors require export surpluses in trade with the lender countries.

Thus the future has to produce an internationally coordinated trade policy. In the first stage all countries should agree not to take any further protectionist measures. As a second step, there has to be a return to a longer-term liberalization plan geared to the gradual dismantling of world trade barriers. The liberal world trade system must not prove to be just a fine-weather setup which collapses during the first protracted slump period. To this end assurances with respect to the overall performance of industrial economies in terms of currency inflation and employment prospects need to be developed and enforced. It is not possible any longer, because of the state and intensity of the interrelationship and interdependency between the nations of the world economy, to solve trade policy issues alone.[33]

Furthermore, reading again the extensive literature on the great depression of the 1930s and its origins, causes and effects, one has to ask whether the lessons have been forgotten. In looking at the debt rescheduling problems of Third World countries one is also tempted to inquire whether the lessons to be drawn from the problems of the German reparations after World War I and the exigencies of real transfer of resources linked to trade and employment effects at home have been forgotten too.

9. Permit me now to make special mention of the present situation in the steel industry. This is of particular significance to me as Economics Minister in North Rhine-Westphalia, since our state manufactures roughly two-thirds of all German crude steel.

Excess capacity in the world steel industry coupled with a weak business cycle also caused a drastic slump in U.S. crude steel output. Only 67.4 million tons were produced in 1982 compared to approximately 110 million tons the year before.[34] This works out at an average capacity utilization for the year of less than 50 percent, the level even dropping to below 30 percent in December. The situation has, admittedly, improved a little since the beginning of 1983 (capacity utilization 57 percent). Besides unsatisfactory demand, the major steel corporations are feeling growing competition from the so-called mini-mills which have superior technology for producing the steel needed by the construction industry. These mills, over the last two decades, have been able to hoist their market share from zero to 20 percent. The U.S. steel industry also lays the blame for present difficulties on the volume of imports. For example, 11.1 million tons of rolled steel were imported into the U.S. during 1981, far outweighing the export volume of 2.1 million tons for the same period. The total production for that year amounted to 65.4 million tons.

This situation has prompted the U.S. steel industry to make repeated calls for protection against imports and to file anti-dumping suits against Japanese and EC suppliers. The most recent suits against EC exports culminated in October 1982 with the conclusion of a steel supply agreement covering the 11 most important steel products (excluding high-grade or alloy steel) exported by the European Community into the United States. On the strength of this agreement the American steel industry withdrew the suit.

Recently, the U.S. administration has also imposed restrictions on the import of high-grade steel in the form of customs penalties and import quotas. This was done as a surprise and without prior consultation (as the U.S. had agreed to do in 1982). These restrictions, which are to remain in effect for four years, are an additional severe blow to the German steel industry following last year's blows. The German government was disturbed by this decision and views it as a departure from the Williamsburg Accords which called for an end to protectionism.

10. East-West trade has also become quite a visible bone of contention in recent years. The contrasting extent of our two countries' trade with the Comecon states is naturally a relevant factor in this regard;[35] the U.S. trade involvement with these countries (1.9 percent) is well below that of the Federal Republic (5.6 percent).[36] This is not to overlook the fact that West Germany's significance as an exporter to Comecon has nevertheless diminished slightly since 1977 (when it stood at 7 percent), as has that of the U.S. (1977: 2.2 percent).

Germany's dominant position in trade with the East Bloc countries is partly explained by its geographical proximity and partly by its liberal handling of goods from this source which are subject to few import restrictions.[37] The U.S., on the other hand, subjects imports from most Comecon countries to heavy customs duties.[38]

Whereas the U.S. regularly achieves surpluses in its trade with Comecon, the European industrialized countries since 1979 have been showing an increasing trade deficit, mainly due to Soviet energy exports. This development has even partially affected the Federal Republic which until recently usually posted high trade surpluses with the East Bloc countries.

From a balance sheet point-of-view, one could argue that for several years now the Comecon surpluses in trade with the Europeans have been financing the former's deficit with the U.S. Nevertheless, with the exception of direct neighbors such as Austria and especially Finland, the overall economic significance of trade with the East tends to be over-estimated. The indebtedness and financing difficulties of most Comecon countries will probably mean a further shrinkage in the importance of export trade with Eastern European countries. There are, however, several industrial sectors which are considerably dependent on trade with the East Bloc. During 1981, Comecon customers purchased 1/4 of Germany's sheet pipe exports, 1/5 of its sheet iron and 1/6 of its machine tools and rolling mill equipment.[39] These are all products which are mainly manufactured in North Rhine-Westphalia. U.S. exports to East Bloc countries are, of course, largely made up of wheat shipments.

11. The controversies surrounding East-West trade have highlighted the following problems:

— Western dependence on trade with the East;

— The link between trade with the East Bloc and the latter's increased military strength;

— Suitability of East-West trade as a vehicle for economic sanctions;

— Western export and interest subsidies in trade with the East Bloc.

Is there a Western overdependence on trade with the East? As has been mentioned, there are certain sectors and corporations both in Germany and the U.S. whose dependence on Comecon trade is relatively heavy. What is more, this fact is not lost on politicians in these two countries. And it is actually both countries that are open to possible coercion. Regarding imports, however, any possible dependence is confined to the Western European countries and to West Germany in particular. The USSR is one of the three most important suppliers of raw materials to the Federal Republic: i.e., nickel, titanium, platinum, taladium, vanadium, thallium, asbestos and gold.[40] American criticism, in this regard, focuses on West Germany's alleged dependence on energy supplies from Comecon.

Does trade with the East Bloc facilitate its military buildup? In essence, the criticism is that Western imports release economic resources which would otherwise have to be employed in other sectors of the economy.

A high proportion of the Soviet national product goes to military expenditures. According to the U.S., the Soviets would be compelled to appropriate their resources differently if it were not for cheap imports of consumer and investment goods and technological know-how from the West, paid for in raw materials. Without these imports the USSR would be forced to meet these needs through commensurate cuts in military spending. Although there is some truth to this argument, one should not overlook the spirit of sacrifice latent in the Soviet Union. In principle, the argument also has to apply to the wheat shipments made by the U.S. According to the American Wharton Institute, the USSR in 1981 received 46 million tons of wheat from the West, paid for with 29.2 million tons of oil. The amount of oil necessary (mainly in the form of fertilizers) for the Soviets to cultivate this volume of wheat themselves would have been more than five times as much, namely 159 million tons.[41] The logical conclusion, then, is to discontinue both exports of industrial goods and agricultural produce to the Comecon countries. The Western industrialized states would also have to cease importing from East Bloc countries, thereby shutting off the flow of hard currency which would otherwise directly or indirectly aid Comecon's military buildup. Such a move would undoubtedly signal the end of all trade with the East Bloc and, moreover, would administer a severe blow to the international division of labor.

There is agreement in principle between the U.S. and its Western allies that no goods are to be exported to the Comecon countries which can be directly employed to strengthen the latters' armaments capability. This agreement on the export of strategic goods between the NATO countries and Japan has been operating since 1950 through the COCOM lists.

The COCOM lists contain those products which can be exported only with the express permission of the COCOM member involved and, where necessary, with the additional authorization of the COCOM Committee. But the actual composition of the lists has triggered substantial differences of opinion between the U.S., with its harder line for amending these lists substantially, and the remaining allies. Participants in the dispute whether or not to extend the list of embargoed products should consider whether such action ignores economic realities. An overly extensive application of COCOM principles beyond strictly strategic goods could very well lead to circumventions on the part of other companies and countries, calling for tight controls vis-a-vis third country trade. Indeed, this has very often been the case in the past. The dangers to the Federal Republic of an economic blockade triggered by extending the COCOM lists are all too obvious. Apart from losses incurred on the jobs and credit-repayment front, such a development would be severely detrimental to sustaining the status of *Ostpolitik* results, above all regarding inner-German relations.

12. Thus, it appears that East-West trade is hardly suitable for economic sanctions. Everyone recalls the embargo on wheat shipments to the Soviet Union imposed by President Carter at the beginning of the 1980s, following the Soviet invasion of Afghanistan. This embargo was lifted by President Reagan in April 1981. At the end of that year, Ronald Reagan himself reacted to the imposition of martial law in Poland by stopping exports of American technology and equipment to the Soviet Union, a move which posed a special threat to the laying of the gas-pipeline between that country and Western Europe. Europe's fierce opposition to this embargo was not insignificant in leading to its removal in November 1982. The decision to backtrack was certainly also encouraged by a study commissioned by the House of Representatives which clearly showed that in most cases, embargoes were of little use and tended more to disturb international trade relations, including transatlantic ties. The criticism was directed mainly at the attempt to block the gas-pipeline deal, through the extra-territorial application of U.S. law to the foreign subsidiaries of American firms and U.S. licensees abroad as well as through interference in already existing supply contracts. The West Europeans regarded the embargo measures as not exactly free of inherent contradictions. Nor could they completely rid themselves of the suspicion that U.S. Administrations are prone to imposing economic sanctions which hurt their own allies. The backlash from economic sanctions imposed on a country such as the USSR — which still must count as one of the most self-sufficient in the world — could very well damage the initiators far more than the recipients.

The basic consensus is undoubtedly that East-West trade — as other world trade — should be conducted according to free market principles. In other words, the Comecon states receive no exclusive privileges. German export and credit guarantees are not only granted to Comecon countries but also to all creditworthy states outside this Bloc and are financed via the premiums paid by the insurance policy holder. An increase in the premiums paid is presently being negotiated in the light of the greater risk involved.

The Federal Republic has always refused to grant interest subsidies, even in cases of public sector credits. In so doing, it has consistently adhered to the OECD consensus of July 1982 which stipulated that certain minimum rates — varying according to the borrower's per capita income — should not be undercut when lending to the public sector. In contrast, there are other European countries which, in the interests of their trade balance, grant considerable export subsidies.

Here too, it should be mentioned that the gas-pipeline deal between the Soviet Union and a group of West European countries will neither make the Federal Republic dangerously dependent on Soviet gas nor provide the Soviet Union with huge amounts of hard currency. The share of Soviet gas in overall German gas consumption will, admittedly, rise from a current 20 percent to around 30 percent by the beginning of the 1990s, meaning that natural gas will then account for between 5 and 6 percent of overall primary energy consumption in Germany. The share of overall energy supplies from the Comecon countries — besides Soviet oil and gas, especially Polish pit coal — should then increase from just under 8 percent to 10 percent.[42] Energy supplies from Comecon would then match Saudi Arabia's share but remain well behind the share accounted for by the OPEC countries overall. The currency earnings for the Soviet Union arising from the gas deal are usually grossly exaggerated. It is thought likely, from a present-day viewpoint, that the Soviet Union will not approach annual income of around $4 billion until the beginning of the 1990s.[43] The most recent turn of events revealed, however, that different answers can be offered to the question of whether the gas volumes will not be oversupplying European markets to the detriment of domestic resources, particularly hard coal.

13. Since President Reagan has assumed office, the world has had to adapt to a distinct shift in American economic policy. The new orientation was centered on a supply-side orientation of fiscal and economic policy, the main object of which was to eliminate obstacles to economic activity — especially investment activity — so as to revitalize the economy. For someone admiring Anglo-Saxon pragmatism and considering the self-imposed anti-ideological overture of the political approach, it has again come as a surprise to see how supposedly universally applicable recipes for complex and complicated policy issues have been handed out. Continental Europeans in general would not dream of following the war-cries of "Keynesianism versus Monetarism" or other magic formulas, considering the challenges and exigencies of employment and growth, of influences and distributions in the 1980s.

On the other hand, one of the unmistakable merits of "supply-side economics" is that it has reawakened consciousness of the shortcomings of the traditional economic policies of the 1960s and 1970s. Those policies, which focused on the demand side, have to be complemented by measures which also promote the supply side in order to have a favorable influence on allocation, efficiency, and growth of resources of an economy. It is no revelation, however, that (a) depending on their design, tax systems can either further or destroy incentive, and (b) that a supply-side policy in particular can have a certain positive effect on the availability of resources, namely, on capital formation.

It would, however, probably be much too one-sided to expect that a purely supply-side oriented policy would be able to master the existing problems without any consideration for the demand-side. Indeed, insulated supply-side policies will not work any wonders in strengthening growth and productivity, thereby lowering unemployment.

14. Up until the fall of 1982, Chancellor Helmut Schmidt's government had pursued an economic policy in West Germany which was geared toward correlating the requirements for strengthening supply conditions with the requirements for securing demand conditions. The assumption of power by the new conservative government in October 1982 strengthened further the position of the supply-side advocates in the Federal Republic. One look at the current economic situation, however, shows that the economy — especially the labor market — has yet to benefit to any great extent from the reorientation, aside from the beneficial effects of the traces of optimism which have been hammered into the headlines ever since. Looking at the insulated supply-side approach, the OECD uttered criticism of the West German economy, suggesting that the approach will bring about neither the self-sustained nature of the recovery nor the end of the vicious circle of cumulative downturn.[44]

Consideration has to be given to pursuing these general macroeconomic aspects of national policy to regain price stability, consolidation of public sector finances and full employment in an open international economy while still maintaining ordered international balances. In addition, there is the need, on the one hand, for structure-oriented industrial policies — particularly with respect to sectors and regions which have to undergo dramatic changes — and, on the other hand, for addressing new avenues of future technological advance. It is of utmost importance to understand that all policies designed to hold the line against long-term market trends are, of course, doomed to fail and will prove to be extremely and increasingly costly. Therefore, policies must not subsidize against structural change, but rather aid and cushion it.

It is essential to support and encourage new complementary or additional economic activities, particularly newly founded firms as well as small businesses. The newly established universities and technical colleges and the research centers in the Rhine-Ruhr basin are called upon to induce and promote spin-offs and facilitate the transfer of technology and innovation so characteristic of modern firms.[45] It should be out of the question at the same time to exclude the straight collapse of the traditional base structures. In terms of interfaces in important commodity markets it is important to retain, on a strictly redefined smaller basis, those elements of production structure which also warrant a certain basis for political and economic sovereignty in terms of energy supplies. Examples here are domestic coal and the manufacturing of machinery and equipment based largely on steel input from domestic sources. Basically similar principles should be applied to the strengthening of research and development efforts linked to technological strategies vis-a-vis the most advanced new industries.

The need is not for an imitation of the concerted action seen in "Japan, Inc." or MITI, nor is it for state planification *a la francaise*. Instead, a joint effort is required on the part of enterprises and business branches as well as the state to extend beyond traditional supply-side oriented policy measures, such as improvement of qualifications, research, development, technological transfer and support to small and medium-sized enterprises. We have to move beyond a catalogue of offers to more project-oriented, interlinked efforts. There is no one in a better position to discern technological advances and market inroads than the management of mobile and productive firms. The state certainly cannot substitute any wants or lacks in management decisions. However, certain important business activities need the complement of state support. For such a process of rapid transformation a high measure of consensus is needed politically as well as socially, to smooth over the consolidation process and help in the understanding and active shaping of the expansion of new products and production techniques. The active involvement of the Government in these processes in conjunction with the participation of the labor unions has been characteristic of the German postwar experience. This should remain the case in the future, but a new sense of direction is necessary. The new Federal Government's lack of active involvement is threatening the social consensus. This is demonstrated by the dismal prototypes of restructuring the steel and the shipbuilding industries and also by the Government's general employment policy.

15. The new Administration took office in Washington with the firm belief that its version of supply-side economics could and would solve all of the country's economic problems and simultaneously those of the international economy, as a kind of automatic side-effect. The expectation was that it would create economic growth, lower both inflation and unemployment as well as consolidate public sector finances, and stabilize both current account surplus and net capital exports. These high-flying expectations have not been fulfilled, and probably cannot be fulfilled by pursuing such a course. The idea that budget deficits of that extent can be "self- financed" by lowering taxes has so far proved to be an illusion, and probably will never be anything more. As a matter of fact, indications are that American budget deficits will continue to remain extremely high over the next few years at least. As it now looks, the rise in U.S. budget deficits and the stubborn refusal to reduce them will continue to constitute the greatest obstacle toward a substantial decline in the U.S. interest level, and will offset the positive effects of lowering inflation rates as well as hinder the U.S. recovery because of hidden Keynesian demand expansion. The tough, monetarist-oriented course pursued by the U.S. up to mid-1982 clearly brought down inflation sharply. At the same time, however, this development was accompanied by undesirable — and, in part, inevitable — side effects which have proven to be persistent:

— a deep recession with high unemployment which is now down somewhat but without a longer term outlook for a sustained boom;

— extremely high and sometimes widely fluctuating interest rates; and

— strong and erratic fluctuations of exchange rates.

The shift in America's foreign exchange policy ten years ago — from managed floating to conscious neglect of ironing out exchange rate fluctuations through limited intervention on the foreign currency exchanges ("benign neglect") — contributed to the latter development.

The recent strong upsurge of the dollar is contrary to the wisdom of conventional economics, if you concentrate on the DM/dollar relationship.[46] For approximately the last two years the current account of the DM has been in surplus, and the current account of the dollar has been in the negative. Price rises have been much smaller in West Germany than in the U.S. for at least the last ten years. German producer prices (Index 1975 = 100) have risen from 112.7 in 1979 to 135.1 in May 1983. The corresponding U.S. figures are: 1979 = 134.4, 1983 (May) = 172.5. That means that the U.S. price hike from 1979 to 1983 was 28.3 percent, while the German increase stood at 19.9 percent. The exchange rate showed a dollar rise of 48 percent with a corresponding rise in the real dollar rate of 58 percent. A large part of the explanation for this relates to the effects of movements in the capital accounts which offset all current account and purchasing power parity considerations. Why, though, does the dollar show such strength in attracting foreign capital?

Odd as it may sound to the traditional economist trained in equilibrium theory of either the Keynesian or the neo-classical type, this is the result of the fervent political position taken by the U.S. Administration. The Administration's policy is linked to international security policies accompanied by the passive acceptance of huge budget deficits which keep up the rate of interest. The complete turn-around of the benign neglect for the dollar from full-fledged passivity under Carter to dramatic activity under Reagan made the rest of the world indirectly more unstable and less secure. This objectively made it easier for the U.S. Treasury to finance the huge increases in armaments expenditures (or the cutbacks in taxation) by increasing net capital imports. They were attracted by extremely high interest rates which are pushed by budget deficits and corresponding deficits in trade. This seems to constitute a miraculously self-fulfilling prophecy: the more the U.S. follows a policy of asserting its strength, the easier its finance; this, however, works to the detriment of the functioning of an international economy of equal partners and to the detriment of the performances of the other industrialized democracies, the developing countries, and the instruments of international cooperation.[47]

The obvious interfaces between international economic relations and security policies exclude any possibility of easy solutions, but rather call for more coordinated efforts, based on mutual judgment in the West. The constituency of the U.S. President comprises, after all, the whole of the West, though there may not be many voters living there. All this exacerbates the international financial disturbances, requiring more rescheduling of debt which also strengthens the U.S. dollar and keeps interest rates up.

Throughout the recent strong surge of the dollar in mid-1983, German experts kept maintaining that in terms of both economic fundamentals and the recent performance in international trade and domestic economic policy, the competitiveness of the DM has grown vis-a-vis the dollar, as it has persistently within the European Monetary System. U.S. policy has tended to be one-sided, involving at the same time seemingly erratic impositions of egocentrism. This has been true both domestically with respect to the rising budget deficits and internationally with respect to fulfilling the Williamsburg promises *verbatim* and in substance. Unless changes are made, the U.S. economic policy is likely to oppress compromises promising elements of recovery and, even more importantly, of growth. The real rate of interest in the Federal Republic has now been standing at 5 to 6 percent for several years, impairing long-term investments and job creation and making a self-sustained take-off to an enduring recovery rather unlikely.

16. The economic policy "innovations" in the U.S. have amplified the worldwide disorientation of the financial and commodity markets which resulted from the imbalances created after the second oil shock. And it was, above all, during this phase of the world economic crisis that the pivotal role which the U.S. plays as a key currency country and pacemaker for the world economy became unmistakably clear because:

— in monetary terms, hardly any country in the world could escape the strong effect of the high U.S. interest rate level;

— in non-monetary terms, the worldwide recession and crisis of the developing countries was intensified;

— in terms of foreign exchange policy, a U.S. economic policy characterized by uncertainties and conflicting goals paradoxically did not weaken the dollar but strengthened it because the key currency of an insecure world economy was viewed as a refuge of relative stability.

The industrial countries — and not least the Federal Republic of Germany — have been able to uncouple themselves only to a very limited extent from Amerian financial market development — i.e., only to the extent to which progress in combatting inflation and improvement in the current account balance allow. In the present scenario of lower U.S. inflation rates and rising U.S. interest rates, the linkage has again become even stronger. It is high time that American economic policy takes this dependence and its ensuing responsibility for the world economy into consideration and acts on it.

17. The question of foreign exchange relations has thus again become a subject of debate, since the present system of flexible exchange rates

— tends toward exaggeration;

— experiences erratic fluctuations; and

— has been almost totally ineffective in fulfilling its function as a buffer to cyclical movements and inflation.

The latter, however, cannot really be viewed as a fault of the system itself but rather the result of erroneous strategies to adapt domestic economies or a consequence of international counter-measures. It goes without saying that no one will readily accept the decline in real income caused by shifts in the terms of trade. This means that exchange rates must also be supported by domestic interest rate policies. And despite its successful adaption of wages, Japan was not able to escape being drawn into the 1979-1981 world recession because other countries reacted to the devaluation of the yen by implementing protectionist measures. Calls for a return to a fixed parity system are inappropriate because the economic structures and achievements and, above all, the economic policy priorities of individual countries still differ too much. Experience with the European Monetary System — the EMS — and its seven realignments within four years, also shows that the compulsion to exercise discipline, which is considered to be such a great advantage of a system of fixed exchange rates, is no longer of much significance. Still, the EMS has been since its inception an indispensable, stabilizing element in the Western European economy.

It, therefore, seems all the more necessary for the strongly erratic fluctuations (which seem to be inherent in the system and which in part endanger the system) to be reduced. This could be achieved most thoroughly (1) if there were to be a vigorous narrowing of inflation differentials internationally, and (2) if benign neglect were to be replaced by a certain amount of cooperation in constructing international economic policy in terms of currency, trade, employment and development strategies. If these goals aim too high, there should at least be closer cooperation in exchange rate policy, not for the purpose of maintaining unrealistic exchange rates but rather with the goal of ironing out temporary erratic exchange rate fluctuations. In any case, central banks should work together more closely, if only to construct their monetary policies on the basis of the dollar, DM and yen circulation worldwide rather than domestically. Adequate consideration must be given to the innovations in financial techniques which the age of "on-line" electronic instantaneous communication has brought.

18. Thus the U.S. economy as well as U.S. policy may have to forego some of the inherent advantages of the role and function of the dollar in the international economy. The dollar economy is apparently having no problems with the internal and external balance of U.S. economic growth and performance, but other economies are suffering because they cannot survive persistent external imbalances.

The threshold economies in Latin America and France are experiencing this problem particularly drastically. It is probably correct to assume that the successful rescheduling of debts of Latin American countries as well as that of their developing economies is contributing both to persistent high rates of interest and to the rising value of the dollar which is so much in demand.

By continuing to run up huge budget deficits, the U.S. seems to be paying even less attention to the international repercussions it creates. This forces other economies to make even more adjustments. Growing mutual interfaces of economic, security, and political inter-dependencies make this shift in U.S. economic policy all the more necessary because a persistent world-wide economic crisis might very well endanger and even destroy the credibility of democratic institutions in Western industrial societies.[48] It would be highly desirable, therefore, if the Williamsburg concession by President Reagan to President Mitterand to reconvene a new "Bretton Woods"-like initiative would turn into reality soon.[49] It is the existential dimension of these issues for the survival of Western democracies in the 1980s — their ability to return to qualitative growth and to restore full employment — that calls for it. A European "decoupling from the dollar," by contrast, even if successfully achieved (and which the author cannot advocate) would mean stepping away from an integrated international economy based on free trade and capital movements as well as full employment and price stability with maximum welfare.[50]

NOTES

[1] *1982/83 Annual Economic Survey of the European Commission*, p. 3.16.

[2] "Der Streit Europa/Vereinigte Staaten/Japan," *Stichwort Europa*, 9/83, Commission of the European Communities, Generaldirektion Information Bruxelles.

[3] *Statistical Yearbook of the Federal Republic of Germany 1983*, Wiesbaden, 1983, p. 636 Tab. 3.1.

[4] Cf. Commission of the European Communities, Brussels.

[5] *Statistical Yearbook*, p. 672 Tab. 8.3, p. 675 Tab. 8.5.

[6] Cf. *OECD Economic Outlook*, Paris, July 1983, p. 15.

[7] See Institute for International Economics (editor), *Promoting World Recovery, A Statement on Global Economic Strategy by 26 Economists from 14 Countries*, Washington, D.C., 1982, p. 4 passim.

[8] Cf. Landesregierung Nordrhein-Westfalen, *Landesentwicklungsbericht 1982*, Düsseldorf, 1983. Der Minister für Wirtschaft, Mittelstand und Verkehr, *Zur Wachstumssituation in Nordrhein-Westfalen*, Düsseldorf, 1982.

[9] Cf. R. Jochimsen, *Politik für das Ruhrgebiet*, Gelsenkirchen, 1983, pp. 3-12.

[10] See OECD (ed.), *Education Policies and Trends, A Report by a Group of Experts*, Paris, 1977. Also R. Jochimsen, "The Changing World of Work," in H.S. Williams (ed.), *Education and the World of Work*, The Australian College of Education, Perth, 1980, pp. 25-36.

[11] Bank for International Settlements, *53rd Annual Report*, Basel, 1983, pp. 16 and 19.

[12] Cf. *OECD Economic Outlook*, Paris, July 1983, p. 12.

[13] *Ibid.*

[14] *Statistical Yearbook*, p. 671 Tab. 8.1, p. 675 Tab. 8.5.

[15] *Ibid.*, p. 729 Tab. 17.2.

[16] Morgan Guaranty Trust Company of New York, *World Financial Markets*, July 1983, p. 10 Tab. 7.

[17] *Statistical Yearbook*, p. 646 Tab. 4.1, pp. 675 f. Tab. 8.5.

[18] Cf. Wochenbericht des Deutschen Instituts für Wirtschaftsforschung, "Aussenwirtschaftsabhängigkeit der industriellen Arbeitsplätze in der Bundesrepublik," 1982, Heft 39, pp. 483-91.

[19] Statistisches Bundesamt (Federal Statistical Office), Fachserie 7, Reihe 1 (1982), p. 31.

[20] *Ibid.*

[21] See Circular Ordinances of the Federal Ministry of Economics, "Runderlasse," published in *Der Bundesanzeiger*, different years.

[22] *Statistical Yearbook*, p. 94.

[23] *Prognos Euro Report '83*; Industrialized Countries, Basel, 1982. *Statistical Abstract of the United States*, diverse yearbooks.

[24] *Ibid.*

[25] *Ibid.*

[26] Bank of International Settlements, *op. cit.*, p. 31.

[27] See G. Mensch, *Stalemate in Technology*, Cambridge, Mass., 1979. G. Mensch, W. Weidlich, G. Haag, *The Schumpeter Clock*, Cambridge, Mass., 1983.

[28] Statistisches Bundesamt, *loc. cit.*

[29] Ordinances (EEC) Nos. 2869/82 and 2870/82 of the Council of Ministers.

[30] Mensch, *Stalemate.*

[31] See A. Laffer's Study of the U.S. Steel Industry, 1969-1974.

[32] Bank for International Settlements, *op. cit.*

[33] See Institute for International Economics, *op. cit.*

[34] Statistisches Bundesamt, *Eisen + Stahl*, 4 Vj. 82.

[35] Cf. J. Stankowsky, "Die Bedeutung des Osthandels im internationalen Vergleich. Forschungsberichte des Wiener Instituts für Internationale Wirtschaftsvergleiche," Wien, 1983; author's calculations.

[36] Share of exports of Comecon as a percentage of 1981 overall foreign trade.

[37] In 1981 the share of the Federal Republic in overall OECD exports to Comecon made up 21 percent, whereas the corresponding U.S. share grew to 12 percent (the 1977 figures ran at 26 percent and 10 percent respectively).

[38] "Der Deutsche Osthandel 1982," Studie des Bundesministeriums für Wirtschaft, December 1982, Bonn, p. 16.

[39] *Ibid.*, p. 4.

[40] *Ibid.*, p. 23.

[41] Wharton Econometric Forecasting Associates, "Cooperative Advantage in Soviet Grain and Energy Trade," Washington, D.C., Sept. 10, 1982.

[42] "Der Deutsche Osthandel," p. 21.

[43] *Ibid.*, p. 22.

[44] Cf. *OECD Economic Surveys 1982-1983*, Germany, June 1983, p. 24.

[45] See R. Jochimsen, *Politik für das Ruhrgebiet*. Also *Landesentwicklungsbericht 1980*, by Landesregierung Nordrhein-Westfalen, Düsseldorf, 1981.

[46] *Financial Times*, August 11, 1983, p. 9.

[47] Lester C. Thurow puts the negative savings ratio of the U.S. economy for 1983 at minus 2.4 percent. See *Newsweek*, Nov. 28, 1983, p. 53. The Council of the United Nations University with headquarters in Tokyo, whose charter was adopted in December 1973 by the General Assembly to foster research into the most pressing global socio-economic problems of development, hunger and welfare, has decided to set up a "World Institute of Development Economics Research" (WIDER) in Helsinki, Finland, in an effort to enhance work in this field.

[48] See R.I. McKinnon, *Money in International Exchange: The Convertible Currency System*, New York and Oxford, 1979, pp. 27ff.

[49] International Economics Research Center (ed.), *Rethinking Global Negotiations, A Statement of North-South Economic Strategy* (New York: Columbia University, 1983).

[50] Samuel Brittan, "Decouple from the Dollar," *Financial Times*, August 11, 1983, p. 9.

AMERICAN FORCES IN THE FEDERAL REPUBLIC: PAST, CURRENT AND FUTURE

by Ernest May

At present, the people of the United States have as clear a commitment to fight for the Federal Republic of Germany as to fight for Pennsylvania or California. Its bond is a quarter million American troops sitting on several thousand nuclear weapons. These troops are dedicated to providing "forward defense" in accordance with a doctrine of "flexible response." Officially, the first term means "a coherent defense conducted close to the intra-German border with the aim of losing as little ground as possible and confining damage to a minimum"; the second means "mutually reinforcing strategic nuclear, theater nuclear, and conventional military forces that can respond effectively to any level of attack."[1]

This essay addresses two sets of questions. First: Why is the alliance what it is? Why are the troops where they are? Why in such numbers? Why with nuclear weapons? And why with "forward defense" and "flexible response" as their watchwords? Second: Will the alliance remain the same in the future? One justification for asking the historical questions is the simple fact that most people don't know the answers. Two-thirds of all Americans and three-fifths of all West Germans have been born since 1945. They cannot know even why the alliance exists unless someone tells them.

A justification for trying to peer ahead is that so many people seem nowadays to be saying that the time has come for a change. In the Federal Republic, Peter Bender has captured a large following with the argument that East-West ideological differences are no longer important and that a German-American partnership against Communism is an anachronism. Not long ago, the publisher of *Die Zeit* used *Foreign Affairs*, the house organ of the American foreign policy establishment, to warn that American Cold Warriors were laying "foundations of strife" with Bonn.[2]

Foreign Affairs has also published articles by Americans arguing for letting Germans defend themselves. So has its rival, the more professional *Foreign Policy*. And the snobbish literary weekly, *The New Yorker*, gave most of two issues to revisionist historian Richard Barnet for an argument very similar to Peter Bender's.[3]

To be sure, intellectuals have been calling for or warning of changes in the alliance almost from its beginning. In the early 1970s, for example, Karl Kaiser, the dean of the West German foreign policy establishment, wrote in

Foreign Affairs that ". . . the present crisis . . . appears to threaten the essence, indeed the survival, of cooperation both within Europe and in the Atlantic world." The sagest of Americans and Britons, as, for example, Professors William E. Griffith and Michael Howard, expressed similar concern. It is not clear that there is more uncertainty now than in the past. Indeed, poll data for the Federal Republic and the United States assembled by, respectively, Elisabeth Noelle-Neumann and John Rielly indicate that popular support for the alliance may be at an all-time high.[4]

What makes the present period seem different from most others is the fact that questioning now comes also from the practical people who engineer American-German political and military collaboration. Given intelligence data about the growing military strength of the Warsaw Pact, they are asking if the allies can long continue business as usual.

Back in the 1960s Secretary of Defense Robert S. McNamara asked how, with approximately the same number of men under arms, the Soviet Union could possibly have 175 divisions while the United States had no more than fifteen. By the time his systems analysts finished answering the question, long-accepted estimates concerning the Red Army's capacity to overrun Western Europe had come into doubt. Hence, during most of the period from the missile crisis of 1962 through detente and *Ostpolitik*, only people specifically paid to do so gave much thought to the possibility of a Soviet strike against Europe.[5]

By the mid 1970s, however, Washington and Bonn had begun to notice not only new Soviet strategic missiles but mounting numbers of troops, main battle tanks, and other such forces in Eastern Europe and European Russia. In 1975, Secretary of Defense James Schlesinger called attention to these numbers and also to evidence that Soviet military planners seemed to be thinking in terms of a Blitzkrieg.[6]

By the early 1980s official NATO publications portrayed the military balance in Europe as decidedly disadvantageous. In May 1982 the Secretary General of NATO issued a document citing the following comparisons of forces in place in Europe:[7]

	NATO	Warsaw Pact
Total Military	2.6 million	4.0 million
Divisions	84	173
Main Battle Tanks	13,000	42,500
Artillery, Mortars	10,750	31,500
Armored Personnel Carriers	30,000	78,500
Bombers	—	350
Fighter-Bombers	1,950	1,920
Interceptors	740	4,370
Reconnaissance Aircraft	285	600
Aircraft Carriers/Kiev Class Ships	7	2
Cruisers	15	21
Destroyers and Frigates Submarines	274	182
Ballistic Missile	35	52
Long-Range Attack	60	149
Other	95	57

No consensus existed as to the exact meaning of the figures. General Robert Close of Belgium interpreted them as signifying that the Russians could get to the Rhine in forty-eight hours. A number of West German and American defense experts voiced similar, though not quite such alarmist, opinions. In a searching analysis for the International Institute of Strategic Studies, Robert L. Fisher reasoned that logistic and transport constraints would slow down a Soviet offensive, and NATO would have time to deploy some reserves. Under both Harold Brown and Caspar Weinberger, the United States Department of Defense took Fisher's position as its own. Brown's former Under Secretary for Policy, Robert Komer, has said, however, that his relative optimism consists in the belief that the Soviets would need twenty to thirty days to overrun Europe.[8]

Others minimize the significance of the apparent imbalance. Alain Enthoven, who was McNamara's chief systems analyst, has continued to make the point that Soviet strength is easily overestimated, and journalists such as Andrew Cockburn and scholars such as John Mearsheimer have pointed out the many reasons why Soviet and Warsaw Pact forces are apt to be credited with capabilities which they may well not possess. A sober review prepared for the Brookings Institution in 1983 by William Mako concludes that, in reality, the NATO-Warsaw Pact troop balance in Europe may be about even.[9]

The fact of steady expansion and modernization in Soviet and Warsaw Pact ground, air, and naval forces is nonetheless undeniable. Whatever their specific judgments about the existing balance, the majority of practical planners have felt obliged at least to take the view expressed in the International Institute of Strategic Studies' reckoning of the military balance: "One cannot necessarily conclude . . . that NATO would suffer defeat in war, but one can conclude that there has been sufficient danger in the trend to require urgent remedies."[10]

In the resultant debate, at least four broad alternatives have been identified.

One is simple adherence to the principles of "forward defense" and "flexible response" combined with an attempt to maintain the balance that obtained in previous decades. That continues to be the official position both of the West German government and of the NATO Council. It is the essence of the existing NATO Long-Term Defense Program.[11]

A second alternative is to retain the principles but make the response considerably more flexible by widening the "firebreak" between conventional and nuclear warfare, whether the latter is envisioned as "tactical" or "strategic." During the late 1970s it became apparent that some American strategists were contemplating significant redefinition of forward defense. Despite subsequent denials, press leaks concerning Presidential Review Memorandum 10 of the Carter Administration provided one indication. One draft of PRM-10 was said to speak of NATO forces trying to stop advancing Warsaw Pact armies along the banks of the Weser and the Lech, thus ceding to the enemy about one-third of the Federal Republic. A contemporaneous U.S. Army field manual said "combat in Germany will automatically involve repeated, almost continuous battle for cities, towns, villages, and adjacent built-up areas."[12]

In the 1980s Americans inside and outside the government began to ventilate proposals for preparing to fight a protracted non-nuclear war without necessarily abandoning "forward defense." The Supreme Allied Commander, Europe [SACEUR], U.S. General Bernard Rogers, suggested that this might become more feasible if the allies were to increase by about twenty-five percent (another one percent of GNP on top of the currently promised three percent) their total spending on defense and were to devote most of this increment to conventional forces. A group of distinguished academicians and former officials assembled by the American Academy of Arts and Sciences issued a report saying that the goal could be realized at considerably less expense — $2 billion a year over ten years (give or take a billion a year) — if NATO invested in advanced weaponry able to identify, locate, and precisely and promptly target Warsaw Pact aircraft and follow-on forces. U.S. Army officers meanwhile developed the "Air Land Battle" concept envisioning air and airborne forces neutralizing a Warsaw Pact offensive by overleaping the front and striking the enemy rear. Professor Samuel P. Huntington of Harvard, earlier chief author of the final version of PRM-10, argued for NATO's responding to a Warsaw Pact offensive with conventional counteroffensives against Eastern Europe. At the core of all these proposals stood the proposition that, without renouncing the possible use of nuclear weapons in extremes, Americans and Germans should prepare to defend Europe using non-nuclear weapons only.[13]

A third alternative was most clearly stated by former Army chief of staff and Joint Chiefs chairman General Maxwell Taylor. Americans and Germans, he wrote in 1979, would simply have to acknowledge that they could not prevent Soviet military conquest of the continent. Resort to nuclear weapons, he asserted, would have no effect except to make conditions worse for everyone. The two powers, he argued, should maintain in Europe sufficient ready military power to cause the Soviets concern about the costs of an offensive, the extent to which they might find Europe a ruined prize, and the possibility that they would be leaving themselves vulnerable elsewhere. But, said Taylor, ready forces able really to hold the Russians back would cost far more than the allies were prepared to spend; and half-measures would have the effect probably of wasting in Europe American forces better saved for its eventual liberation. Though Taylor did not advocate withdrawing or even diminishing the American garrison in Germany and though he lent general support to the notion of modernizing NATO's conventional capabilities, he said ". . . it is an act of realism to acknowledge that our forces deployed in Europe . . . are capable of little more than symbolizing by their presence deep American concern for the area and exhibiting by their visible quality an ability to inflict painful damage if attacked." Though not openly adopted by any American official, this fourth alternative has had some degree of support from prominent civilian defense analysts and has received a not wholly unsympathetic hearing on Capitol Hill.[14]

The fourth possibility is dissolution of the alliance. While this alternative has so far been espoused only by a few intellectuals, their lines of argument are not altogether different from ones occasionally advanced in congressional discussion of possible withdrawal of U.S. forces from Europe.[15]

The present uncertainty stems from the question of whether interplay between popular debate on the ethos of the relationship and technical debate over strategy and force structure is likely to lead to some fundamental change. One can imagine Americans and Germans entering the next century with their alliance essentially as it is today. They would still be committed to "forward defense." They would still have non-nuclear forces probably but not certainly incapable of fulfilling that commitment. The avoidance of war and conquest would continue to hinge on an almost but not quite incredible threat of "flexible response," construed to mean possible early resort to battlefield and/or strategic nuclear weapons.

On the other hand, one can also imagine the final decade of the century finding the allies committed to and poised for protracted non-nuclear combat in Europe. Some combination of force increases, untried but promising technologies, and alterations in doctrine would provide hope (and threat) of checking a Warsaw Pact offensive somewhere at or past the West German frontier, but allied planning would assume that, in event of failure, large parts of West Germany could become battlegrounds in a large-scale non-nuclear war.

One can imagine thirdly a situation in which the alliance no longer offered the Federal Republic immediate military security. NATO organs might continue to serve for consultation and coordination. The United States and the Federal Republic might work together in many spheres, including the military, but the Federal Republic would be protected against coming under the control of the Soviet Union by, in some combination, its own resources, the inherent conservatism of the Soviet state, and fear in the Kremlin that conquest of Germany would result eventually in the Red Army's having to confront liberating armies comparable to those of 1943-45.

In general, one can pose the critical question in terms of three possible paths. As the alliance proceeds toward its jubilee, will its tendency be to remain a deterrent alliance in the present mold? Will it instead become more of an armed alliance — genuinely prepared for sustained non-nuclear combat? Or will it turn in some other direction — toward greater dependence on threats of strategic nuclear retaliation, toward an alliance based on promises of liberation rather than protection, or toward no alliance at all? With this context, one turns to history to ask what factors shaped the alliance and how likely it is that they will produce in future the same results as in the past.

Looking back at the early history of the alliance, one is reminded that it became a deterrent alliance in the current model only after the trial of a number of alternatives — no alliance at all; a short-lived promise-of-liberation alliance; an almost equally short-lived armed alliance endeavoring to match the Soviets in non-nuclear forces; and then, for a longer period, a deterrent alliance without (or virtually without) capacity for "flexible response."

At the beginning of the postwar era, Americans had no plans for alliances with any Europeans. They did not even expect to keep occupation forces in Europe for very long. Late in World War II, President Franklin D. Roosevelt told Soviet Generalissimo Josef V. Stalin that American troops would stay in Europe for no more than two years. Not until September 1946 — sixteen months after Germany's surrender — did Roosevelt's successor, Harry S Truman, authorize a clear statement to the contrary, letting Secretary of State James F. Byrnes say at Stuttgart that the United States might keep forces in Germany "for a long period."[16]

Distressed by the virtual Soviet takeover of much of Eastern Europe and, in Western Europe, economic weakness, political instability, and Communist revolutionary and subversive activity, the American government launched its European Recovery Program. In part, the premise was that peace and order in Western Europe were preconditions for peace for the United States. Another, newer premise was that the Soviet Union wanted to control Europe and perhaps all the rest of the world and that United States security required an effort to "contain" Soviet and/or Communist expansion.[17] President Truman and his chief advisers believed at the time that their goals could be best achieved by building up the economies of, and promoting democratic processes in, Europe and, to some degree, other threatened areas. His Secretary of State, General George C. Marshall, justified economic aid to Europeans in part in terms of "getting them to assume part of our burden," and from the outset be spoke of it as "essential that Germany be fitted into the picture."[18]

The formation of a formal alliance resulted from unexpected events of 1948. Led by British Foreign Secretary Ernest Bevin, Western European governments moved toward forming a defensive alliance of their own. It was intended to provide a sense of security against a possibly resurgent Germany and against the newer menace of the Soviet Union. Truman and Marshall were not at first enthusiastic. George F. Kennan, then chief of Marshall's Policy Planning Staff, voiced concern lest a defense build-up divert the Europeans from economic reconstruction and slow their progress toward political cooperation. A sudden and brutal Communist takeover in Czechoslovakia, followed soon afterward by Soviet closing of land and water routes to Berlin, seemed evidence, however, that Bevin's fears had not been misplaced. Heeding advisers other than Kennan, Truman and Marshall came around not only to supporting the European move but starting a modest military assistance program to speed their defense build-up. Now, however, the Europeans insisted the the United States had to become a formal partner. Mere presidential statements of support would not suffice, no matter how strongly they might be worded. Given the past history of American isolationism, they said, the Russians would not be deterred, and Europeans would not feel safe, without a security guarantee ratified by the U. S. Senate. When Marshall's Under Secretary, Robert A. Lovett, sounded out Republican leaders in the Senate and found them not wholly averse, the Administration bowed to these pressures.[19]

Owing partly to lawyers' urgings and partly to Canadian wishes, the guarantee took the form of a North Atlantic Treaty. Its final text said that each party would consider an attack on any one member as equivalent to an attack on all. It nevertheless contained escape holes, leaving to each signatory the right to decide for itself what action to take and, by referring to "constitutional processes," implying that any American decision to use force might require approval by Congress.

For the moment, the continued presence of American occupying forces in Western Germany and Berlin provided assurance that, if the Russians should be foolish enough to march against Europe, the United States would be militarily engaged from the beginning. The location of those forces and of British and French contingents also made it for the time being a moot point that Germany had no government and was not a party to the alliance. Truman now said publicly, moreover, that the United States would "keep occupation forces in Germany until peace is secure in Europe." But, during debate on the treaty and on contemporaneous Administration proposals for military assistance to Europe, key senators made it clear that they did not believe themselves to be making any kind of long-term military commitment. In an executive session of the Senate Foreign Relations Committee, Arthur Vandenberg of Michigan, the Republican leading the fight for ratification, said to Administration representatives: ". . . if this North Atlantic Pact is going to take on the. . . character of a permanent military alliance. . . there just ain't going to be any North Atlantic Pact, because you won't get the votes for it." When the Treaty Organization was put together in 1949, the United States successfully resisted formal membership in any planning groups other than those concerned with the Atlantic Ocean and North America. American leaders still did not envision permanently stationing ground forces abroad.[20]

The United States, to be sure, had a strategic air force and atomic bombs. The North Atlantic Treaty could therefore be seen as shielding Europe from Soviet attack primarily through nuclear deterrence. This was in fact the understanding of the NATO Council in January 1950, when "collective balanced forces" became the Organization's first shibboleth. But the few who at the time knew anything about matters nuclear assumed (a) that this represented a frail shield at best and (b) that the strategy could only serve until the continental United States became subject to Soviet counter-deterrence, for the weapons stockpile was small; rapid delivery capability was almost non-existent; the ballistic characteristics of existing bombs were such that they could not be reliably targeted on a particular city, let alone on any military objective; and experts had said from the outset that the Soviets would have their own atomic bomb within a few years. Once a Soviet nuclear test was detected and intelligence analysts began to predict that the Soviets would soon have a stockpile of 200 atomic bombs and a Long Range Air Force with perhaps a thousand B-29-type bombers, mutual deterrence seemed a condition likely to exist by the mid-1950s, if not earlier. In the spring of 1950 Joint Chiefs Chairman General Omar N. Bradley was talking publicly about Europe's needing urgently to build up military defenses because "atomic deadlock" was at hand.[21]

From 1948 and the decision to form an alliance through 1950 and the outbreak of the Korean War, whatever security West Germans and other West Europeans possessed against a Soviet threat resided first in the hope that the Soviets would be deterred by fear of American atomic reprisals and second in the near certainty that, if they were conquered, American armies would attempt to liberate them. The best-informed American experts estimated that a nuclear offensive against the Soviet Union could not prevent the Soviets from taking Europe. The rag-tag American, British, and French divisions doing occupation duty in Germany were not believed by anyone to be a match even for the thirty Russian combat divisions in eastern Germany, let alone for the full 175 divisions with which they were credited. American war plans of the period, such as they were, envisioned efforts to hold a line at the Pyrenees so that the model for the reconquest of Europe could be Wellington's rather than Eisenhower's.[22]

In 1950 the model of a promise-of-liberation alliance was replaced by a model of an armed alliance prepared actually to hold Western Europe against advancing Soviet armies. The Korean conflict served as the precipitant. Americans, Germans, and others interpreted North Korea's surprise attack as perhaps a rehearsal for one by East Germany against West Germany. For some time, Konrad Adenauer and other West German leaders had been complaining to U.S. High Commissioner John J. McCloy and other U.S. officials about the Soviet build-up of a paramilitary East German *Volkspolizei*, suggesting vainly that the Western powers do something similar. Though fear soon eased of any immediate East German or Soviet move against Europe, the Korean conflict nevertheless made Communist military action in Europe seem a much more likely contingency than had been the case earlier. At the same time, Washington, Paris, and London became much more aware of the anxieties of West Germans.

Korea also persuaded many West Europeans that the defense of Europe required German soldiers. From the time of the Berlin blockade, U.S. military planners had been saying privately that any hope of holding a line in Central or Western Europe depended on German troops being available. By the spring of 1950, before Korea, the U.S. Joint Chiefs had developed specific proposals. On both sides of the Atlantic, the press picked up many rumors on the subject. The prevailing view in Washington, London, and Paris continued nevertheless to be that expressed by French Foreign Minister Robert Schuman — that German rearmament was "unthinkable." Seeing a Defense Department paper which recommended such rearmament, Truman wrote across its face, "as wrong as can be." After the beginning of the Korean conflict, Schuman, Truman, and nearly every other Western leader changed at least his stated opinion.[23]

In addition, the Korean conflict produced a complete change in Truman's attitude toward military spending. Previously, he had been committed to holding down the U.S. defense budget. Year by year he had cut back outlays, pushing toward near prewar levels. Though successive Secretaries of Defense, service secretaries, chiefs of staff, and others protested the disparity between commitments and resources, Truman appeared to pay no heed. Then the North Korean attack turned him entirely around. He ordered the services to ask for what they needed, regardless of cost. As a result, he more than tripled current expenditures, and he obtained from Congress authorization to order great quantities of planes, ships, and other weaponry for future delivery.

Making NATO an armed alliance was not easy. Though French leaders came around to recognizing a need for German soldiers, they proposed incorporating them in a European army as a species of legionnaires. The more American and British leaders advanced arguments for creating anything like a German national military establishment, the more the French pressed for a permanent American garrison in Europe. In the alternative, said French President Vincent Auriol, the Americans would simply be playing the Russian game, setting the continent up for domination by *"un complot germano-russe."* The French argued incidentally the desirability of a "forward strategy" designed to develop a defense line "as near as possible to the Iron Curtain." They wanted to avoid any fighting on French soil, and they reasoned also that German soldiers would fight best on their own home ground.[24]

Out of intense, prolonged debate came a compromise. The Europeans were to create a European Defense Community into which German units would be brigaded, and there would be no independent German military establishment. The United States would meanwhile assign to duty with NATO and station in Europe some four to six divisions. An American general would be named Supreme Commander. A greatly expanded U.S. military assistance program would help the British and the European allies enlarge and modernize their forces.

The general concept was clear enough. Members of NATO set themselves the target of having by 1954 some ninety-six divisions and 9,000 modern aircraft, with more than a third of the divisions regularly on the ready. At Lisbon in February 1952 the North Atlantic Council not only agreed on these force goals but published them to the world.[25]

Just who was to do what, however, remained unclear. Europeans tended to assume that the United States was permanently committed to keeping sizable combat forces in Europe and would carry most of the costs of European defense. At almost the very moment of agreeing to the Lisbon force goals, the British and French cabinets were deciding to trim their own outlays for defense of the continent.

Americans, on the other hand, assumed that Europeans would eventually carry for themselves most of the burden of defending the continent. In a so-called "great debate" in early 1951, the Truman Administration successfully overcame congressional opposition to stationing U.S. combat divisions in Europe, but it did so by making a case that the need was temporary. Acheson, Marshall (on duty now as Secretary of Defense), and Supreme Commander-designate Dwight D. Eisenhower all emphasized this point. The Senate approved the action by passing a resolution which expressed its understanding that Europeans themselves would provide most of NATO's ground forces and that, "as soon as possible," NATO would use both German and Spanish manpower. The U.S. Joint Chiefs of Staff and their planners prepared papers arguing for West Germany's becoming independent, with freedom to develop its own nuclear arsenal. In that event, they said, the United States could pull back most or all of its Army contingent. As President, Eisenhower continued to evidence belief that the American garrison in Europe ought at least to be severely reduced. As late as 1957 he was still urging his Secretary of State to move in that direction — but to do so "quietly."[26]

In any case, the armed alliance had only a short life. Less than a year after Lisbon, the Truman Administration, too, was stretching out defense spending. The new Eisenhower Administration took office in 1953 committed to across-the-board reductions. Its "new look" in defense policy involved a declaratory doctrine of threatening to retaliate — if necessary, massively — against any Soviet or Soviet-sponsored aggression but, instead of responding at the point of pressure, as in Korea, to act at times and places of its own choosing. The rationale which permitted saying this and simultaneously cutting forces rested on the great increase in firepower supposedly available from "tactical" nuclear weapons, for the short interval between 1948 and 1953 had seen the development of high-yield nuclear warheads weighing less than half a ton and so configured that they could be fitted to ordinary fighter-bombers and even to field artillery. Coupled with the new declaratory doctrine went an operational doctrine which said that nuclear weapons should be regarded as virtually interchangeable with "conventional" weapons.[27]

In Europe, the result was — to substitute rapidly for the armed alliance previously envisioned — a deterrent alliance wedded, for practical purposes, to a doctrine of inflexible response. Implacable opposition in the French Chamber of Deputies had killed the European Defense Community. The Paris Accords of 1954 then substituted the arrangement under which the Federal Republic was to create an army but assign it to NATO. Even as German units came into being, however, total NATO troop strength dwindled. By 1957-1958 the alliance had no more than twenty ready divisions and relatively few mobilizable reserves.

After the 1955 "Carte Blanche" exercise produced a hypothetical total of five million German casualties as a result of using tactical nuclear weapons, the Adenauer government showed dismayed uncertainty, then it affirmed support for existing NATO strategy subject to the proviso that the Federal Republic share in "modern technological developments," then it pushed successfully for a new doctrine offering Germans higher hope for survival. Eventually, arrangements were made for the *Bundeswehr* to be equipped to employ its own tactical nuclear weapons provided that the United States released the requisite warheads. The solution to the dilemma of how to field such forces but not to have results similar to those of "Carte Blanche" was provided in 1957 by the NATO Council's officially adopting MC 70, which postulated that NATO ground forces would serve only as a "shield" or, as others put it, a "trip wire" or "plate glass wall," which, if merely penetrated, would lead to America's launching its strategic nuclear forces directly against the Soviet homeland.[28]

Year by year, Americans and Germans alike felt less and less faith in this shield. With rockets rapidly gaining in range and accuracy, American vulnerability became increasingly apparent. In 1955 a Technological Capabilities Panel headed by M.I.T. President James R. Killian reported to President Eisenhower that U.S. superiority to the Soviets in nuclear weaponry might last no longer than three to five years. After the Soviets launched their Sputnik spacecraft, another panel, this one headed by Ford Foundation board chairman H. Rowan Gaither, advised Eisenhower that American superiority was already a thing of the past. Though the texts of the Killian and Gaither reports and comparable documents remained secret, their substance speedily leaked into the news media. Meanwhile, defense analysts such as Albert Wohlstetter pointed out to both official and popular audiences the unlikelihood that *any* defense could be erected to protect population centers against ballistic missiles. The best a nation could do would be to safeguard its own missiles sufficiently to ensure its capability to a devastating "second strike."

The behavior of Nikita Khrushchev seemed meanwhile to testify that the nuclear sword inspired less and less concern in the Kremlin. During the Suez crisis of 1956, he took the side of Egypt and blustered about firing off nuclear rockets. Almost simultaneously, with seeming disregard for any possibility that the West might interfere, Soviet military forces marched into Hungary. In 1958, when a crisis had once again developed on account of mainland Chinese moves against the Quemoys and Matsus, inshore islands occupied by Nationalist Chinese, Khrushchev spoke of using Soviet nuclear might in behalf of his then ally. From Communist China's standpoint, the gesture came very late. Some analysts see this as having put the last, snapping strain on the Sino-Soviet alliance. Americans, however, saw little besides further evidence of Khrushchev's lack of fear of "massive retaliation." Europeans saw in addition what many interpreted as American willingness to risk *their* lives on account of worthless outcroppings of rock off the coast of China.

Hardly had the Quemoy crisis subsided when Khrushchev delivered what many regarded as an ultimatum concerning the future of East Germany and Berlin. He threatened unilaterally to sign a peace treaty with the East Germans if the Western powers failed within the next six months to "establish a sound basis for solution to the problem."[29]

For the next three years, crises alternated with periods of promising calm. Khrushchev let the six-month deadline pass. In fact, in 1959 he was touring the United States and, with Eisenhower, generating a "spirit of Camp David" which foreshadowed the subsequent Nixon-Kissinger detente. But 1960 brought fresh tension, with the Soviets shooting down an American high altitude reconnaissance plane and Khrushchev breaking up a summit meeting.

The subsequent year saw the Soviets confront the new American President, John F. Kennedy, and the NATO allies with the terrible *fait accompli* of the Berlin Wall. And in 1962 they attempted — this time unsuccessfully — to achieve as another *fait accompli* a Cuba converted into an advanced base for Soviet strategic missiles.

Except perhaps for the Soviet backdown in the Cuban missile crisis, all this seemed to testify to Soviet lack of dread of American strategic nuclear might. And from a German perspective it was more noteworthy that the American nuclear sword had not preserved access to East Berlin than that it had perhaps prevented the emplacement of Soviet IRBMs and MRBMs in Cuba. All in all, the period from the mid-1950s to the mid-1960s gave both Americans and Europeans ample reason to question whether the threat of nuclear devastation served as a serious restraint on the Russians.

Creative thinking about this state of affairs followed several tracks. Sometimes it followed more than one track at the same time. A first led toward making the American strategic threat more credible to the Russians. As early as the mid-1950s some Americans had been arguing publicly, others privately, that it would make more sense to say that the prime targets for American nuclear weapons were not Russian cities but Russian nuclear weapons and other military forces. It would be more credible that the United States would dispatch bombers and missiles against such targets, for it would in fact be more sensible to do so in the event a war actually occurred.

A second track led toward making the strategic threat not exclusively an American threat. While the United States government might be willing to destroy Chicago for the sake of Hamburg, a West German government might calculate differently. In France such reasoning (and the return to power of General de Gaulle) produced the *force de frappe*. In West Germany it produced some faint-hearted talk of a comparable venture, some serious consideration of forming a German-French axis independent of either superpower, but, above all else, an impulse to work out some collaborative arrangement with the Americans such as to quiet the Russians without disquieting tbe French.

A third track led back to the concept of an armed alliance. If the Soviet and American strategic forces now cancelled one another out, ran the argument, conditions were those envisioned back in the 1950s. The answer was to match Russian and East European divisions with equivalent numbers of NATO divisions. After "Carte Blanche," various American officers at NATO headquarters had proposed schemes for strengthening ready forces along the central front so that they could hold a line for some significant period. Some of these schemes envisioned fighting with "conventional" weapons; resort, if that failed, to "tactical" nuclear weapons; and only if that, too, failed, resort to the strategic arsenal. Eisenhower's last Secretary of Defense, Thomas Gates, evidenced interest. Under Secretary, subsequently Secretary, of State Christian Herter meanwhile made a public admission of the growing incredibility of the strategic nuclear threat. He could not, he said, "conceive of the President involving us in an all-out nuclear war unless the facts showed clearly that we are in danger of devastation ourselves. . . ."[30]

After 1960, with Kennedy as President and McNamara as Secretary of Defense, the United States became once again an outright advocate of NATO's becoming an armed alliance. Taking mutual deterrence to be virtually a fact, Kennedy and McNamara assigned strategic forces the mission of maintaining invulnerable second strike capability. Without quite saying that Europeans should not expect the United States ever to use strategic forces except for such a purpose, they urged the European allies to join the United States in rebuilding conventional armed forces and so deploying them as at least to permit NATO to wage war for a few days or weeks without itself having to employ any nuclear weapons at all. Given the revised estimates of Soviet and East European conventional strength, this could be represented as a more attainable goal than it had seemed in the early 1950s. Though these Americans spoke of "flexible response," Europeans understood them to be speaking of non-nuclear warfare only, and they were not tempted. The result might be to spare the United States, but it offered Europe no choice except one between ruins and chains.

It took years for Americans and Europeans to adjust these differences. In the meantime, as a result of Britain's developing its own nuclear forces and forming a special partnership with the United States and General de Gaulle's vetoing British participation in the European common market, Britain became more separate from the continental members of NATO. Continuing work commenced by his predecessors, de Gaulle developed and displayed the French *force de frappe*. Not long afterward he took France out of NATO. To a greater and greater extent, NATO became primarily an alliance between the United States and the Federal Republic.[31] And it was this NATO which in 1967 became formally a deterrent alliance committed to forward defense and flexible response much as those phrases are understood today.

The long and difficult transition was successfully bridged, it should be said, in part because of the ingenuity of a "cabal" of Americans who dedicated themselves to holding the alliance together. The key figures were Gerard Smith, Robert R. Bowie, Henry Owen, and J. Robert Schaetzel.[32] As an alternative to the Federal Republic's developing its own strategic nuclear deterrent or combining with the French to create a European deterrent or allowing itself to become part of some type of nuclear free zone, they proposed creation of a multilateral force (MLF). This MLF was to consist of nuclear-armed warships (originally submarines, then surface vessels) manned with crews of mixed nationality, with NATO governments jointly in control. While the United States would still be able to fire its own nuclear weapons, it would not be able to fire those of the MLF without the consent of its allies.

Though cockeyed schemes abound in the nuclear realm, the MLF, if judged only by military criteria, may deserve first prize. Politically, however, it was a creation of genius. Very few people in either Washington or Bonn liked any of the available alternatives. The MLF had just enough plausibility to serve them as a life preserver while they swam in search of something more desirable. In combination, the passage of time, the retirement of Adenauer, the arrogance of de Gaulle, the development of a supposition that the Soviets would be content with strategic parity, and some signs of change within the Eastern bloc then permitted the American and West German governments to reach the compact which has, with relatively little change, persisted ever since.

Though with occasional alterations in the size, deployment, and equipment of their forces, the two allies have since 1967 maintained an approximately constant military posture. They have kept available on site several thousand nuclear delivery vehicles with the warheads stored under American control, to be released if authorized by the President. Regular meetings of a NATO Nuclear Planning Group have given Germans and other Europeans greater understanding of nuclear technology and some sense of influencing broad American policy with regard to nuclear weaponry.

The two nations can thus be said to have chosen this form of relationship — a deterrent alliance with a doctrine of flexible response — after having tried and discarded every one of the alternatives now proposed as a substitute.

The question now is whether the alliance will keep this shape in years ahead. Many factors could lead one to conclude that it will not — that in the late 1980s or in the 1990s the allies will try instead to rebuild an armed alliance or turn in some alternative direction.

The first such reason is the simple fact that it is very hard to make a logical case for the current version of the alliance. Consider the "Hegelei" to which the West German Ministry of Defense has had to resort when attempting to explain matters to the public:

> The initial tactical use of nuclear weapons must be timed as late as possible but as early as necessary, which is to say that the doctrine of Forward Defense must retain its validity. . . . The intent is to persuade the attacker to reconsider his intention, to desist in his aggression, and to withdraw. At the same time, it will be impressed upon him that he risks still further escalation if he continues to attack. Such further escalation would mean that strategic nuclear weapons would be used. . . .[33]

The shrewd and sarcastic American defense analyst, Morton Halperin, has captured the inherent illogicality of alliance doctrine by summarizing it as follows: "We will fight with conventional weapons until we are losing, then we will fight with tactical nuclear weapons until we are losing and then we will blow up the world."[34]

Those who attempt to defend this doctrine against well-informed skeptics usually have to adopt one or both of two hypotheses. The first is that the chances of the Soviet leadership's actually launching a non-nuclear war are so small as to be almost inconsiderable. Concern about their satellites, the quality of their material, the loyalty even of their own troops would continue to deter them, according to this hypothesis, almost regardless of how much the numerical balance might seem to tip in their favor. The second, often associated with former British Defense Minister Dennis Healey and hence dubbed by historian Michael Howard as "Healey's theorem," is that a "microscopic degree of credibility" is all the nuclear deterrent requires to be 100 per cent effective.[35] Either or both of these assumptions can, however, be borrowed to argue for any of several quite different patterns of relationship, including those implicitly or explicitly advocated by Peter Bender and Richard Barnet or by Maxwell Taylor.

A second reason why the next generation might decide not to keep the present form of alliance is that its members do not hold the deep assumptions which cause some of their elders to attach high value to a firm alliance even though the price of firmness is ambiguity and illogicality.

For it is quite obvious that the molders of the alliance shared three strong fears, all of which were products of their experience. First, having seen Mussolini and Hitler and having equated Stalin with them, they feared sudden, opportunistic totalitarian aggression. Second, they fear Germany. Indeed, a strong case can be made not only that other Europeans have seen NATO as more a shield against Germany than against the Soviet Union but that this view was shared in Washington. Acheson has been interpreted as believing that NATO would have been needed even had there been no Soviet Union. John Foster Dulles, Secretary of State during most of the Eisenhower Administration, testified that the purpose of the alliance was "to solve the problem of Germany" — to deter the Germans from playing East against West. To Willy Brandt, Dulles was to say in the late 1950s that, while the United States and the Soviet Union agreed on very few things, one was that they would "never permit a reunited and rearmed Germany to roam around in the no-man's land between East and West."[36] Thirdly, recalling American behavior in the interwar years, the designers of the alliance feared an American return to isolationism.

In some degree, this combination of fears has continued to animate the allies. Though both American and West German images of the Soviet Union changed after the end of the Stalin era, commentary on the invasions of Czechoslovakia in 1968 and Afghanistan in 1979, especially on the American side, contained many notes reminiscent of the late 1940s and early 1950s. These notes have become more prominent in the rhetoric of the Reagan Administration. Persisting American concern about independent action by Germany was best evidenced probably by the nervous reaction to Schmidt's description of the Federal Republic in 1981 as a *"Dolmetscher"* or interpreter between East and West. Nor has it been confined to Americans, for leaders of German opinion such as Hans Peter Schwarz and Karl Kaiser have publicly cautioned that one important function of the alliance is to keep in check fears and ambitions which in previous decades made Germany a menace to Europe's peace. And apprehensiveness about American "neo-isolationism" rises to the surface every time a move commences in Congress to reduce the American garrison in Germany.[37]

Increasingly, however, these are old men's fears, not shared or even understood by the young. While its brutality is doubted only by those indifferent to evidence, the Soviet regime can easily be viewed nowadays as quintessentially conservative, using its armies to keep discipline inside its own empire but in no way disposed to risk external conflict. Younger Germans think of their own country as a complacent middle power, not a potential threat to anyone.[38] Younger Americans probably have a similar image of Germany. It is hard otherwise to explain the popularity of the long-running television series, "Hogan's Heroes," which portrayed the Wehrmacht as an aggregation of good-natured bumblers. And in Germany and the United States alike, people schooled in and after the 1960s do not often debate about whether the United States will turn inward. They are apt instead to discuss how America's imperialism differs from Russia's, if at all. There is at least some possibility thus of a moment arriving when the Federal Republic and the United States are both led by men and women who simply do not hold the basic assumptions which gave the alliance life.

A third factor which might lead one to forecast a major change is closely related. It is that both nations face a break in the continuity of their foreign policy leadership. On the American side key makers of policy and key leaders of public opinion were for a long time the very men who made the alliance — Acheson, Lovett, McCloy, Kennan, et al. Of their number only Paul Nitze, Kennan's successor as head of the Policy Planning Staff, remains alive and not in retirement. Because these men were themselves comparatively young, their aides or disciples are also out of public life or very nearly so. Lucius Battle, who was Acheson's personal assistant, and Robert R. Bowie, who was McCloy's legal adviser, have both recently retired. On the German side something similar is happening simply because the early leadership of the Federal Republic consisted either of relics like Adenauer and Kurt Schumacher or of youngsters little contaminated, if at all, by the Third Reich. The former have long been gone. The latter — Schmidt, Franz Josef Strauss, Herbert Wehner, Egon Bahr, et al. — are near to being so. Thus, if there should be a sea change in public attitudes, there may be few people around in either country able to explain how much trial and error, and how much pain, went into the alliance's fashioning.

On the other hand, one can also identify forces that will probably work toward keeping the alliance as it is.

One such force is the Soviet Union. If its past behavior is a guide, it will periodically act in ways which cause Germans and Americans to feel that they had better stick together. Aged, hidebound, and informed and advised by people who toady to their preconceptions, the members of the Politburo seldom perceive until too late the consequences for relations with the West of decisions made in a different context. Objectives such as suppressing dissent within their empire or disciplining the East Germans or putting the noses of the Chinese out of joint take precedence, and they do things which make West Germans and Americans just nervous enough to conclude that the time is not quite ripe for fundamentally modifying their relationship. This seems all the more likely to continue in view of indications that Soviet leaders may actually feel somewhat ambivalent about the possibility of the Federal Republic's detaching itself completely from the United States.[39]

A second force is American inertia. The United States government does not easily gear itself for basic changes in foreign policy. For both philosophical and institutional reasons, American officials prefer to work at margins. Debate and action concerning troop levels are likely therefore to concern incremental reductions or alterations. One result will be to give everyone in Washington, Bonn, and other capitals plenty of time and opportunity to frustrate or reverse undesired changes.

Contributing to inertia is the crass fact that a lot of people in both countries have a stake in keeping things as they are. Certain manufacturers and suppliers, even certain tradespeople and landlords, stand to lose if the existing terms of the alliance alter. More importantly, major elements in the bureaucracies of the two countries are apt to see any change as being full of danger. In the U.S. State Department, for example, the European Bureau is supreme. Thirty-five years ago, this was not the case. High-flyers like Dean Rusk and John D. Hickerson preferred the bureau that dealt with UN affairs. A major reason for the higher status gained by the Europeanists has been the amount of high-level business generated out of NATO. The Europeanists would not like to see this change, and, of course, they hold a disproportionate number of key jobs elsewhere in the Department. Like conditions obtain in Bonn.

In the U.S. Defense Department, any major change in current alliance understandings could open for debate longstanding and extremely delicate arrangements which give the Army a certain proportion of the total defense budget, tactical air a certain proportion of the Air Force budget, and so on. And these arrangements have all the more power because they have environed the lives of so many senior officers. While these officers may not have experienced the creation of the alliance or the torment that produced compromises on "forward defense" and "flexible response," they have given so many speeches about the vital importance of the alliance that they have probably come to believe it to be so.

But the foremost reason why the alliance may keep its present form is that leaders in both countries are unlikely to see any alternative as being equally safe and equally feasible. They know that since the Berlin blockade the Soviets have not posed a direct military threat to any part of Europe outside their recognized sphere. While American and German leaders do not know why this is so, they do know that the alliance has been in existence all that time. It may therefore have been a factor in making the Kremlin behave cautiously. Given that Westerners have no idea what considerations govern debates in the Politburo, experience thus makes an argument for keeping things as they are and making the alliance neither less of a deterrent nor more of a threat than it has been up to the present.

However silly "forward defense" and "flexible response" may seem when held up to the light, these principles, coupled with the continued presence of 200,000 to 250,000 American troops and 6,000 to 7,000 nuclear weapons, have held West Germany and the United States together. The leaders of the Federal Republic have not been seriously tempted to pursue an independent "balancing policy."And that perhaps accounts more than anything else for the fact that, despite many minor conflicts, the period since 1945 can be classified as one of general peace. For nothing — nothing — could so disturb and endanger international relations as a German state offering to play makeweight in the balance of power. The possibility that pressure for serious change could push the Federal Republic into independence ought to serve in both Washington and Bonn as an irresistible argument for making changes very, very slowly, if at all.

The future of the alliance will be decided by people who did not live its history. Chiefly because of faith that they will nevertheless take instruction from experience and be fearful of change because of the possible awful consequences for the allies and for humankind, I venture the prediction that the United States and Germany will continue into the next century with a relationship somewhat like that of the present. There will be a lot of American troops in the Federal Republic, but there will not be enough of them and of other NATO troops to seem a convincing conventional shield. There will also be a lot of nuclear weapons in the Federal Republic or near by, but it will not be clear how, if at all, they might ever be used. And though the litanies may alter, the allies will remain committed to a defense doctrine so ambiguous and impractical as to enable politicians on each side to pretend that their country will be defended at the expense of the other. It may not be an ideal condition, but it is probably the best to be had.

NOTES

[1] Federal Republic of Germany, Office of the Ministry of Defense, *White Paper 1979: The Security of the Federal Republic of Germany and the Development of the Federal Armed Forces* (Bonn: Ministry of Defense, 1979) p. 126; statement of Secretary of Defense Caspar Weinberger, 97th Congress, 2d session, United States Senate, Committee on Armed Services, *Hearings on Department of Defense Authorizations for Fiscal Year 1983*, p. 178.

[2] See William E. Griffith, "Bonn and Washington: From Deterioration to Crisis?," *Orbis*, XXVI (Spring 1982), pp. 117-133; David Gress, "What the West Should Know about German Neutralism," *Commentary* (Jan. 1983), pp. 26-31; Jeffrey Boutwell, "Politics and the Peace Movement in West Germany," *International Security*, VII (Spring 1983), pp. 72-92. The piece by the publisher of *Die Zeit* is Marion Gräfin Dönhoff, "Bonn and Washington: The Strained Relationship," *Foreign Affairs*, LVIII (Summer 1979), pp. 1052-1064. She has written a book on the same theme.

[3] David Calleo, "Inflation and American Power," *Foreign Affairs*, LIX (Spring 1981), pp. 805-811; Klaus Bloemer, "Freedom for Europe, East & West," *Foreign Policy* (Spring 1983), pp. 23-38; Richard Barnet, "Annals of Diplomacy: U.S.-German Relations," *New Yorker* (Oct. 10, 1983), pp. 53-105 (Oct. 17, 1983), pp. 94-167.

[4] Karl Kaiser, "Europe and America: A Critical Phase," *Foreign Affairs*, LII (July 1974), pp. 725-746; William E. Griffith, "NATO: Alliance in Disarray," *Reader's Digest*, CV (Aug. 1974), pp. 56-60; Michael Howard, "NATO and the Year of Europe," *Survival*, XVI (Jan./Feb. 1974), pp. 21-27: Elisabeth Noelle-Neumann, "Are the Germans 'Collapsing' or 'Standing Firm'?" *Encounter* (Feb. 1982), pp. 76-81; John E. Rielly, *American Public Opinion and U.S. Foreign Policy, 1983* (Chicago: Chicago Council on Foreign Relations, 1983).

[5] William W. Kaufmann, *The McNamara Strategy* (New York: Harper and Row, 1964), pp. 84-86; Alain C. Enthoven and K. Wayne Smith, *How Much Is Enough? Shaping the Defense Program. 1961-1969* (New York: Harper and Row, 1971), pp. 132-137.

⁶ United States Department of Defense, *Annual Report of the Secretary of Defense for Fiscal Year 1976 and Fiscal Year 1977.*

⁷ 97th Congress, 2d session, United States Senate, Committee on Foreign Relations, *Hearing: NATO Troop Withdrawals,* pp. 21-68.

⁸ The key works are: Friedrich Wiener, *The Armies of the Warsaw Pact Nations: Organisation, Concept of War, Weapons and Equipment* (translated by William J. Lewis; Vienna: Carl Ueberreuter, 1976) [originally published in 1974 as *Die Armeen der Warschauer-Pakt-Staaten*]; Robert Close, *L'Europe sans Defense?* (Brussels: Arts et Voyages, 1976); Johannes Steinhoff, *Wohin treibt die NATO? Probleme der Verteidigung West-Europas* (Hamburg: Hoffmann and Campe, 1976); Johann Adolf Graf Kielmansegg, "Probleme eines kriegerischen Konflikts, insbesondere in Mitteleuropa," Karl Kaiser and Karl Markus Kreis (eds.), *Sicherheitspolitik vor neuen Aufgaben* (Frankfurt: Metzner, 1977), pp. 295-350; 95th Congress, 1st session, United States Senate, Committee on Armed Services, *Report of Senator Sam Nunn and Senator Dewey F. Bartlett: NATO and the New Soviet Threat;* Robert Lucas Fisher, *Defending the Central Front: The Balance of Forces* (Adelphi Paper No. 127; London: International Institute of Strategic Studies, 1976). See Hans Peter Schwarz, "American Security Policy in an Era without Great Alternatives," in Karl Kaiser and Hans Peter Schwarz (eds.), *America and Western Europe: Problems and Prospects* (Lexington, Mass.: Lexington Books, 1977), pp. 189-234. For the positions of Brown and Weinberger, see the sections on NATO in their successive *Annual Reports.* Komer's comment is in 97th Congress, 2d session, United States House of Representatives, Committee on Foreign Affairs, Subcommittee on Europe and the Middle East, *Hearings: NATO's Future Role,* p. 43. Different but extremely thoughtful reviews of the context are: Stanley Hoffmann, "NATO and Nuclear Weapons," *Foreign Affairs,* LIX (Winter 1981-82), and Gregory F. Treverton, "Managing NATO's Nuclear Dilemmas," *International Security,* VII (Spring 1983), pp. 93-115.

⁹ Alain C. Enthoven, "U. S. Forces in Europe: How Many? Doing What?," *Foreign Affairs,* LIII (April 1975), pp. 513-532; Andrew Cockburn, *The Threat Inside the Soviet Military Machine* (New York: Random House, 1983); John J. Mearsheimer, "Maneuver, Mobile Defense, and the NATO Central Front," *International Security,* VI (Winter 1981-82), pp. 104-122 and "Why the Soviets Can't Win Quickly in Central Europe," *Ibid.,* VII (Summer 1982), pp. 3-39; William P. Mako, *U.S. Ground Forces and the Defense of Central Europe* (Washington, D.C.: The Brookings Institution, 1983).

¹⁰ International Institute of Strategic Studies, *The Military Balance, 1981-1982* (London: International Institute of Strategic Studies, 1981), p. 121.

¹¹ For a searching review of the Long-Term Defense Program, see Richard Burt, "The Hidden Nuclear Crisis in the Atlantic Alliance," in David S. Yost (ed.), *NATO's Strategic Options: Arms Control and Defense* (New York: Pergamon, 1981), pp. 46-59.

¹² On PRM-10 see David N. Schwartz, *NATO's Nuclear Dilemmas* (Washington, D.C.: The Brookings Institution, 1983), pp. 213-215; the Army field manual is quoted in Mako, *U.S. Ground Forces,* pp. 34-35.

¹³ Bernard Rogers, "Greater Flexibility for NATO's Flexible Response," *Strategic Review,* XI (Spring 1983), pp. 11-19; *Strengthening Conventional Deterrence in Europe: Proposals for the 1980s. Report of the European Security Study* (New York: St. Martin's, 1983); U. S. Department of the Army, *Operational Concepts for the Airland Battle and Corps Operations 1986* (Fort Monroe, Va.: U.S. Army Training and Doctrine Command Pamphlet No. 525-5, 1981); Samuel P. Huntington, "Conventional Deterrence and Conventional Retaliation in Europe," *International Security,* VIII (Winter 1983-84), pp. 32-56.

¹⁴ See Earl Ravenal, "After Schlesinger: Something Has to Give," *Foreign Policy* (Spring 1976), pp. 71-96, and 97th Congress, 2d session, United States Senate, Committee on Foreign Relations, *Hearing: NATO Troop Withdrawals,* and United States House of Representatives, Committee on Foreign Affairs, Subcommittee on Europe and the Middle East, *Hearings: NATO's Future Role.*

¹⁵ Maxwell D. Taylor, "Changing Military Priorities," *AEI Foreign Policy and Defense Review.* I (April 1979), pp. 2-13; Steven L. Canby, "Territorial Defense in Central Europe," *Armed Forces and Society,* VII (Fall 1980), pp. 51-67; testimony by Jeffrey Record, *NATO's Future Role,* pp. 15-56. See the statements by Senator Claiborne Pell in *NATO Troop Withdrawals,* p. 68.

¹⁶ See John Backer, *The Decision to Divide Germany* (Durham, N. C.: Duke University Press, 1978), pp. 144-145.

¹⁷ See John L. Gaddis, *The United States and the Origins of the Cold War, 1941-1947* (New York: Columbia University Press, 1972) and *Strategies of Containment: A Critical Reappraisal of Postwar American National Security Policy* (New York: Oxford University Press, 1982).

[18] United States Department of State, *Foreign Relations of the United States* [hereafter *FRUS*] 1947, I, pp. 772-775. See Timothy P. Ireland, *Creating the Entangling Alliance: The Origins of the North Atlantic Treaty Organization* (Westport, Conn.: Greenwood Press, 1981), pp. 54-55.

[19] See Robert E. Osgood, *NATO: The Entangling Alliance* (Chicago; University of Chicago Press, 1962), pp. 32-47; *FRUS 1948*, III, pp. 7-18, 40-42, 82-88, 122-123.

[20] Truman's statement is in *Public Papers of the Presidents: Harry S Truman, 1948* (Washington, D. C.: Government Printing Office, 1963), p. 52, Vandenberg's in United States Senate, Committee on Foreign Relations, *Historical Series: The Vandenberg Resolution and NATO*, p. 242. See Ireland, *Creating the Entangling Alliance*, p. 137.

[21] See David Alan Rosenberg, "The Origins of Overkill: Nuclear Weapons and American Strategy, 1945-1960," *International Security*, VII (Spring 1983), pp. 11-18; John Prados, *The Soviet Estimate: U.S. Intelligence Analysis and Russian Military Strength* (New York: Dial Press, 1982), pp. 18-22; Lawrence Martin, "The American Decision to Rearm Germany," in Harold Stein (ed.), *American Civil-Military Decisions* (Birmingham, Ala.: University of Alabama Press, 1962), p. 649.

[22] See David Alan Rosenberg, "American Atomic Strategy and the Hydrogen Bomb Decision," *Journal of American History*, LVI (June 1979), pp 62-87.

[23] The fullest treatment of the subject will be the Harvard Ph.D. dissertation by Thomas Schwartz, "From Occupation to Alliance: John J. McCloy and the Allied High Commission in the Federal Republic of Germany, 1949-1952," which will probably be completed in 1985.

[24] I draw on Jennifer Laurendeau, "Presidential Transition and the EDC," a manuscript portion of a prospective Harvard Ph.D. dissertation comparing the U.S. presidential transitions of 1952-1953 and 1960-1961. The quotations are from Vincent Auriol, *Journal du Septennal. 1947-54* (7 vols; Paris: Librairie Armand Colin, 1971), VII, p. 361, and Andre Beaufre, *NATO and Europe* (New York: Alfred A. Knopf, 1966), pp. 24-28.

[25] Osgood, *NATO*, pp. 87-88. The development of these goals can be traced in the JCS 2073 series in Records of the U.S. Joint Chiefs of Staff, 1945-1953 (University Microfilms).

[26] Ireland, *Creating the Entangling Alliance*, pp. 208-214; JCS 2124/108, Sept. 24, 1953 (microfilm); transcript of March 28, 1957, John Foster Dulles-Dwight D. Eisenhower Telephone Conversations (University Microfilms).

[27] See Glenn H. Snyder, "The 'New Look' of 1953," in Warner R. Schilling et al., *Strategy, Politics, and Defense Budgets* (New York: Columbia University Press, 1962), pp. 379-524; Ricbard G. Hewlett and Francis Duncan, *Atomic Shield, 1947/1952* [*A History of the United States Atomic Energy Commission*, vol. II] (University Park, Pa.: Pennsylvania State University Press, 1969); Rosenberg, "Origins of Overkill."

[28] Gordon A. Craig, "Germany and NATO: The Rearmament Debate, 1950-1958," in Klaus Knorr (ed.), *NATO and American Security* (Princeton: Princeton University Press, 1959), pp. 236-259; Catherine McArdle Kelleher, *Germany and the Politics of Nuclear Weapons* (New York: Columbia University Press, 1975), pp. 1-155; Schwartz, *NATO's Nuclear Dilemmas*, pp. 31-61. Subsequent paragraphs draw heavily on Kelleher and Schwartz and, to a lesser extent, on Hans-Peter Althaus, "Einfluss und Rationalität westdeutscher Sicherheitspolitik in der NATO, 1955-1965," Inaugural Dissertation, Rheinische Friedrich Wilhelms-Universität zu Bonn (1974), and Helga Haftendorn, *Abrüstungs und Entspannungspolitik zwischen Sicherheitsbefriedigung und Friedenssicherung: zur Aussenpolitik der BRD. 1955-1973* (Düsseldorf: Bertelsmann Universitätsverlag, 1974).

[29] See Eberhard Schulz, "Die sowjetische Deutschlandpolitik," in Dietrich Geyer (ed.), *Osteuropa-Handbuch: Sowjetunion, Aussenpolitik, 1955-1973* (Cologne: Bohlau Verlag, 1976), pp. 255-259.

[30] Quoted in Kaufmann, *The McNamara Strategy*, p. 26.

[31] See Philip Windsor, "Germany and the Western Alliance," *Adelphi Paper* 170 (London: International Institute of Strategic Studies, 1981).

[32] In addition to the works of Kelleher and David Schwartz, see John D. Steinbruner, *The Cybernetic Theory of Decision: New Dimensions of Political Analysis* (Princeton: Princeton University Press, 1974), a fundamental theoretical work which also happens to use the MLF as its central case.

[33] Federal Republic of Germany, Ministry of Defense, *White Paper 1975/1976*, pp. 20-21.

[34] Quoted in James A. Kuhlmann (ed.), *Strategies, Alliances, and Military Power: Changing Roles* (Leyden: A. W. Sijthoff, 1977), p. 307.

[35] Quoted in Reed, *NATO's Theater Nuclear Forces*, p. 31.

[36] David McLellan, *Dean Acheson: The State Department Years* (New York: Dodd, Mead, 1976), pp. 145-148; Ireland, *Creating the Entangling Alliance*, p. 139; Willy Brandt, *People and Politics. The Years 1960-1975* (Boston: Little, Brown, 1976), p. 79.

[37] Renata Fritsch-Bournazel, "Germany's Role in Europe: Historical and Psychological Dimensions," Wilson Center, International Security Studies Program, *Working Paper No. 44* (August 1982), pp. 18-19; Hans Peter Schwarz, "The Roles of the Federal Republic of Germany in the Community of States," in Karl Kaiser and Roger Morgan (eds.), *Britain and West Germany: Changing Societies and the Future of Foreign Policy* (New York: Oxford University Press, 1971), p. 221; Karl Kaiser, "The New Ostpolitik," in Wolfram Hanrieder (ed.), *West German Foreign Policy. 1949-1979* (Boulder, Col.: Westview, 1980), p. 153.

[38] See Elisabeth Noelle-Neumann, *loc. cit.*, and Wolf Michael Iwand, *Politische Aspekte des Amerikabildes in der Überregionalen westdeutschen Presse* (Frankfurt am Main: Akademische Verlagsgesellschaft, 1974).

[39] This evidence is more fully described in Ernest R. May, "Soviet Policy and 'the German Problem,'" *Naval War College Review* (Sept.-Oct. 1983), pp.18-36.

SQUARING MANY CIRCLES: WEST GERMAN SECURITY POLICY BETWEEN DETERRENCE, DETENTE AND ALLIANCE

by Josef Joffe

The Setting of German Security

West Germany is the product, the pillar and the problem of the Atlantic order.

The Product: A child of the Cold War, the Federal Republic was created from the ruins of the Third Reich because the new conflict between the United States and the Soviet Union demanded sturdy allies rather than closely guarded wards. Once the United States committed itself to the defense of Western Europe *circa* 1947, the logic of total victory had to yield to the imperatives of far-flung coalition-building. Instead of Nuremberg, there was NATO; instead of a super-Versailles, there was the stunning *renversement des alliances*; instead of long-term victimization, there was the windfall offer of community with the victors.

Given the war-time hatred Nazi Germany had mobilized against itself, the transformation was even more miraculous than the rehabilitation of France after 1815. Only four years after the collapse of the Hitler empire, one part of the Reich suddenly found itself reincarnated as the "Federal Republic of Germany." One year later, in 1950, American *fiat* opened the way for West German rearmament. In 1955, only a decade after unconditional surrender, the second German republic joined the ranks of NATO.

The Pillar: Today, the Federal Republic is the pillar of the Atlantic order because, by virtue of geographic position and critical mass, it alone among the European powers could change, and even unhinge, the postwar status quo. A settlement by default, the European status quo rests on a twin-foundation: the Continent's partition into two hostile spheres of influence and a closely watched balance of power with the two Germanys at its fulcrum.

France's withdrawal from the integrated command structure of the Alliance in 1966 is almost forgotten because, apart from the shift of SHAPE to Belgium, it made so little difference to the larger order of things. Conversely, Spain's accession to NATO in 1982 was practically ignored because it, too, did not perceptibly affect the balance. Imagine, however, a West Germany that would either switch allegiance or turn neutral. The consequences would be momentous.

With its army of 500,000, Western Europe's largest, the Federal Republic holds the front-line of NATO's defense. As narrow as it is, West Germany territory provides vital strategic space. The country plays host to thousands of American nuclear weapons and to hundreds of thousands of Allied troops.[1] Shifting that potential into the Soviet camp would at best reduce NATO to an American bridgehead centered on France and off-shore England; at worst to sheer oblivion. Even a neutral West Germany, armed or not, would have a similarly unsettling effect. Unarmed, the Federal Republic would invite domination by the East while bottling up Western defenses behind the Rhine. Armed, especially if armed with nuclear weapons, a neutral West Germany would act as a perennial source of anxiety for all of its neighbors, as a tempting target of manipulation, or both. In either case, Europe's astounding postwar stability would become a dream of the past.

The Problem: Precisely because West Germany is the European pillar of the Atlantic order, it is also its latent problem. The problem of its critical mass in the military balance is reinforced by the Federal Republic's complicated position in the political balance. Alone among NATO's members, West Germany brought to the Alliance a burdensome legacy of revisionism stemming from the nation's partition. Whereas all the other member states had banded together in defense of the status quo, Bonn was officially committed to its transformation on behalf of reunification.

Given that tension, NATO was historically dedicated to a dual perception. Formally, the Alliance was founded to contain and hobble the might of the Soviet Union; tacitly, it was extended to constrain and harness the strength of a resurgent half-Germany. Indeed, as the demise of the European Defense Community in 1954 demonstrated, it was only the United States' and Britain's commitment to permanent entanglement in the affairs of Europe that finally gained France's grudging consent to the rearmament of its ancient rival and nemesis. Moreover, the Federal Republic's entry into NATO was predicated on an unprecedented policy of self-denial. Among its key elements was Bonn's categorical renunciation of nuclear weapons and its contractual vow "never to have recourse to force to achieve the reunification of Germany."[2]

Today, and given the FRG's sterling record as model ally and model European, the preoccupation with German power, both real and potential, has receded from the consciousness of the West. So has the issue of revisionism in the aftermath of a "New *Ostpolitik*" (1969-1972) that enveloped the unresolved business of World War II in a series of pledges affirming the "inviolability" of Europe's postwar borders.

Still, the problem persists, if also in a different and more subtle guise. Yesterday's legal and direct challenge to the status quo has yielded to a political and indirect approach to the national issue. If reunification is impossible, then its absence must become tolerable, perhaps even to the point where the goal itself becomes superfluous. That requires increasing interaction with (and liberalization in) the German Democratic Republic (GDR) which, in turn, is tightly linked to the overall pace of evolution in Eastern Europe and the Soviet Union. The breathtaking gamble of *Ostpolitik*, in effect, rests on a finely-tuned trade-off between reassurances and "subversion," between cooperation and cooptation. Reassuring the Soviets will allow them to relax the heavy grip of imperial control. Reassuring the regimes of the East will lower the risk of partial liberalization. And both, buttressed by economic rewards, will combine to maximize opportunities for the interaction between states, societies and individuals. It is a policy of many small steps which is to pierce the barriers of partition. In the end, though, it poses the stark question of "who 'Finlandizes' whom?" Can bloc ties be loosened in the East without paying a higher price in the same coinage in the West?

Although firmly embedded in the West, *Ostpolitik* has evidently complicated the calculation of West German interests and its relationship with the Alliance because it hinges on an irreducible level of collaboration with the East. To protect its ties with the GDR, Bonn must protect its ties with Eastern Europe, and to do both, it cannot afford to alienate the Soviet Union. During the 1970s, the decade of detente, the Federal Republic could discharge that triple task with relative ease, but even then the Schmidt government resented Jimmy Carter's human rights campaign as a gratuitous (and pernicious) affront to the Kremlin. In the wake of the Afghanistan invasion and the Polish putsch, frictions between the United States and its foremost European ally became inevitable, even nasty.

Indeed, the much-bemoaned Atlantic crisis of the early 1980s was, *au fond*, the German-American crisis writ large because the onset of Cold War II drove the two key protagonists of the Alliance into opposite directions. Responding to the logic of great-power rivalry, the United States quite naturally proclaimed the "indivisibility of detente" while calling for resistance on a global scale. Following the logic of its national and regional mission, the Federal Republic acted as if detente could (and should) be compartmentalized while denigrating the wider implications of the Polish putsch and the Soviet foray in Southwest Asia. Given their hefty and unique stake in regional tranquility, the Germans were condemned to oppose America's call to arms more vigorously than any other European power. For confrontation meant choice rather than balance, discipline rather than freedom of maneuver. It meant the recentralization of alliances and hence the abrupt closure of access to the East. No wonder, then, that the Germans strained obsessively to insulate Central Europe against the shock waves of the Soviet-American clash while trying to snatch as many pieces of detente as possible from the jaws of the rattled giants.

The lessons of Afghanistan and Poland are hardly ephemeral, since they have demonstrated some *structural* reasons for conflict between the two key members of an alliance where regional and global concerns do not necessarily mesh. On the part of the United States, the crisis dramatized the limits of great power tolerance in the face of small-power deviation. For its part, the Federal Republic came close to invoking the very limits of allegiance when it was suddenly forced to choose between its security interests and its Eastern vocation.

Trying to strike an equipoise when the times demanded priorities, the government of Helmut Schmidt inevitably appeared to assume the role of arbiter, if not roadmaster, of East-West relations in Europe. In the West, especially in the United States and France, the pose inevitably resurrected long-buried anxieties about *les incertitudes allemandes* — about an ally that was *of* the West, but *with* the West only at his discretion.

Historically, Germany has repeatedly confronted the fateful choice between East and West. To recall Germany's special geographical fate, however, does not confirm what familiar analogies such as Rapallo or the Hitler-Stalin pact are meant to suggest: that there are irreversible forces which will always draw Germany to the East, even to the point of abandonment and betrayal of the West.

In the first place, there are just as many forces that have repelled Germany and Russia from one another, embroiling them in catastrophic wars. If anything, the analogies of 1922 and 1939[3] highlight the *unique* conditions of radical collusion between the two nations. Both cases represented not destiny but classic instances of pre-emptive diplomacy — where each power, in a surprise maneuver, sought to forestall the other's inclusion in a coalition directed against itself. And therein lies perhaps the more appropriate lesson: Germany has tended to turn East whenever it was (or felt) isolated, frustrated and humiliated by the West. Conversely, the FRG's accommodation within a stable Western community, one that offered a shelter as well as a legitimate outlet, has acted as sturdiest guarantee of diplomatic reliability. The "pillar" will become a "problem" only when the balance between the country's Eastern mission and Western obligations is unhinged — whether by allies who ignore the FRG's needs, or by domestic forces which ignore the limits of German power.

German Defense and Its Dilemmas

Shaping the ambiguities of the West German role in the Atlantic order, history and geography have also defined some enduring dilemmas for the country's security policy. These dilemmas are familiar enough, but they bear restating because, paradoxically, they explain the astounding continuity of German defense policy since World War II — the recurrent problems as well as the recurrent responses. Normally, dilemmas make not for stability but gyration, and in prior incarnations, Germany was no exception. Indeed, there are few nations whose security policies have fluctuated so widely and wildly as Germany's — from the status quo policy of a Bismarck to the hegemonial ambitions of Wilhelm II; from the impotence of the Reich in the first Thirty Years' War to the megalomania of the Nazi empire in the second. The postwar setting of German policy, however, made for a narrow range of choices, hence for tightly circumscribed compromises, hence for the stuff from which orthodoxy is born.

Autonomy vs. Alliance — Rearmed by American *fiat* under the watchful eyes of its European neighbors, the Federal Republic's are the only armed forces that are totally integrated in the Alliance. (There is no General Staff, and in theory, national command authority in wartime stops at the corps level.) Subordination was the very condition of self-assertion. If other nations raise armies to protect their sovereignty, the Federal Republic offered an army to gain it. As early as 1948, when West Germany was but a tripartite occupation zone, chancellor-to-be Konrad Adenauer cautiously broached the issue of a German defense contribution, clearly intending to use it as a wedge toward sovereignty.[4] Or as he put it later to U.S. High Commissioner John McCloy: "Once our defense contribution becomes a reality, demilitarization and neutralization are out of the question."[5] From the very beginning, then, West Germay's peculiar condition determined the unique tasks of its armed forces. Their main function was that of a straightforward bargaining chip in the silent battle for sovereignty and community, with the Bundeswehr acting as an admissions ticket to the West.

Once the FRG had joined the Alliance, the country's armed forces had to act like a principal's net worth in a joint business venture — as visible token of West Germany's weight in Atlantic councils. Or as Adenauer put it in retrospect: "It became obvious to me that in this day and age our policy would only have as much strength (*Kraft*) as there was strength to back it up. Without strength, no policy. Without strength our words will not be heeded."[6]

Such a calculation explains why Adenauer almost risked his flourishing personal relationship with President Eisenhower and his Secretary of State Dulles[7] to fight the notorious "Radford Plan" of 1956, the first in a long series of sudden strategy shifts the United States has since then sprung on its unsuspecting allies. Named after the then Chairman of the Joint Chiefs of Staff, the Plan foresaw a drastic reduction of American forces (by 800,000 men) to be compensated by the massive deployment of tactical nuclear weapons, particularly in the European theater. Although the cuts were not executed, the shift toward tactical nuclear weapons soon entered into NATO strategy.

For Adenauer, the Radford Plan posed a double-horror scenario. In the first place, he saw it as smokescreen for American troop withdrawals from the Continent, hence as prelude to the "decoupling trauma" which would continue to haunt Germans and Europeans in changing guise ever since. Even more importantly, the idea of substituting nuclear firepower for men on the ground threatened the very premise of Adenauer's defense policy. If troops were to be devalued by weapons, then the political capital of West Germany's projected 12 divisions would dwindle fast, and with it, German influence in an alliance where a denuclearized FRG could not emulate England and France (which had already embarked on a nuclear weapons program of its own).

Little wonder, then, that Adenauer only months later reversed course by 180 degrees. Since tactical weapons were to assume a hefty burden in Western defense, the logic of German policy (armed strength equals political influence) demanded that the FRG acquire at least surrogate nuclear status. By December 1956, the Government made known its interest in receiving battlefield nuclear weapons. In March 1958, after he had gained an absolute majority in the 1957 elections, Adenauer forced a bitterly contested vote through the Bundestag which authorized the acquisition of delivery weapons for the Bundeswehr and the stationing of American nuclear warheads on German soil.

The price of influence-through-integration was exorbitant. Throughout the 1950s, rearmament and nuclear weapons polarized West German society like no other issue then and thereafter. Popular opinion was clearly hostile to both, with solid majorities opposing both the draft and the acquisition of nuclear weapons under American control. Rearmament, NATO membership and nuclear weapons reactivated the Social Democratic Party's pacifist and neutralist reflexes that it had barely buried in the early postwar years, pushing the party into protracted, fundamentalist opposition. (A generation later the same tendencies would re-emerge in response to the deployment of American intermediate-range nuclear weapons.) And finally, Adenauer's nuclear choice of 1958 provided the Soviet Union with a cause or pretext for organizing its own campaign against German nuclear weapons which culminated in the Berlin crisis of 1958-1962. Here, too, the past would haunt the future, with Soviet threats against INF deployment in West Germany echoing the pressure campaign of the late 1950s.

Significantly, there were vociferous critics even among the *Wehrmacht* officers who were rebuilding the FRG's armed forces in close agreement with Adenauer's purposes. In 1955, Colonel Bogislaw von Bonin — formerly a member of the *Amt Blank*, the precursor of the West German defense ministry — went public with an attack that limned the abiding tensions between autonomy and alliance:

> Current plans will not solve the problems of our security. Moreover, the rearmament of the Federal Republic . . . may render hopeless the achievement of reunification anytime soon. Our presumptive opponent will surely perceive a rapidly improvised draft army as preparation for war.[8]

The so-called "Bonin Plan" proposed a small volunteer army of 150,000 with a strictly defensive posture based on fixed anti-tank positions which would not provoke the Soviet Union. And significantly, the idea of defensive autonomy refuses to fade away. The reasons are easy to fathom. If geography had cursed the FRG with maximal exposure to aggression, prevailing NATO doctrine had made the country uniquely dependent on the reliability of its allies. NATO's "layercake" forward-defense in West Germany rests on the instantaneous involvement of five foreign armies "up front" and two more in the rear[9]; out of 10 deployment sectors along the intra-German border, the Bundeswehr holds only three.

Mortgaging the FRG's physical survival to the loyalty of many sovereign allies, "forward-defense" imposes a heavy psychological burden on the foreordained victims of any war in Central Europe. Therefore it is hardly surprising that von Bonin's intellectual and political descendants continue to spawn strategic designs that would implicitly seek to tilt the autonomy vs. alliance dilemma in the direction of greater German self-reliance. The emergence of precision-guided munitions and their apparently devastating effect in the Yom Kippur War[10] have spawned new variations on the von Bonin Plan which are based on small, mobile commandoes equipped with sophisticated anti-tank weapons.[11] In part these designs reflect the perennial and universal temptation to view sudden technological break-throughs as a panacea for many strategic complaints. More profoundly, however, the idea of stopping a superior enemy with an inferior but more fleet-footed force that might need neither allies nor a provocative nuclear armory also offers insurance against the vagaries of Alliance politics and a lever for radical arms control in Europe (which, in turn, would mute German security dependence even further).

Indeed, one might speculate that it is precisely West Germany's unique dependence and exposure, hence the specter of entrapment in somebody else's conflicts, that has galvanized the inchoate peace movement of the 1980s. Perhaps it is not nuclear weapons *per se* that have inspired pacifist nationalism, but *foreign* nuclear weapons. Renegade officers like former panzer general Gert Bastian (a prominent Bundestag deputy of the Greens until 1984 when he bolted from the party and continued in Parliament as an independent) are surely no pacifists. Nor is former Defense Ministry staffer Alfred Mechtersheimer, another well-known spokesman of the peace movement, hailing from the Right, who sees the Alliance as a prime threat to West German security:

> Military alliances guarantee the escalation and extension of war. A pre-eminent threat to the Federal Republic stems from the concentration of nuclear weapons systems like landbased nuclear strike-aircraft [on its territory]. Capable only of a first strike, they are the targets of pre-emptive nuclear attacks. . . . The task is to reverse the fateful nuclearization of Central Europe by political means. The Bundeswehr's military function must be redefined. The goal is the defense of the homeland (*Heimatverteidigung*), not repulse (*Abwehrkampf*).[12]

Given iron-clad policy dilemmas, revolts are bound to happen, along with the visionary search for bold conceptual departures that promise radical transcendence. Transcendence is certainly the message of a peace movement that seeks salvation in unilateral disarmament, the exorcism of nuclear weapons and the dismantling of alliances.[13] Yet after thirty years, the real puzzle in need of solution is the continuity of German policy, not the bouts of fitful disaffection. In the coinage of national aspirations blocked and of autonomy lost, the West Germans have certainly paid the highest price for membership in the postwar "stalemate system."[14] Why, then, did they not revolt more often and more thoroughly?

The best, albeit slightly circular, answer is "realism buttressed by satisfaction." In the first decade of the Alliance, the West Germans traded (nonexistent) autonomy for partial, if also real, sovereignty and admission to the Western community. That was a massive pay-off which established the permissive condition for everything else. Even thereafter, limited autonomy in matters of national security was ironically a blessing in disguise.

For the first time in history, Germany (or a part of it) was neither too weak nor too strong, neither prey nor threat. Unlike the Second Empire from 1871 onward, it did not have to labor under the twin burden of projecting the main threat to Europe's order and of managing its stability from a lonely position at the center. Unlike the Weimar Republic, the FRG did not have to play East against West in order to escape from manipulation and impotence. From Frederick the Great's Prussia to Hitler's "Reich of the Thousand Years," Germany's offensive capabilities had always exceeded its defensive strength. Now the situation was exactly reversed. As the Federal Republic's security was essentially provided by others (notably the United States), it could neither threaten nor be threatened. Instead of embarking on an autonomous defense policy — historically the most important source of conflict among nations — the Federal Republic could reap the fruits of tutelage.

In the first place, the Federal Republic is surely a net importer of security because it is part of an alliance that, ultimately, rests on a unilateral guarantee by the United States. To price that "import" is evidently a matter of freewheeling speculation.[15] How much would it cost to replace 200,000 American troops, several thousand nuclear warheads and the commitment both symbolize? Yet it stands to reason that the FRG invests less in its defense than would a country of similar importance and vulnerability *without* a superpower guarantee. For West Germany, the key allocation issue has not been: "How much do we need to spend for an adequate defense?" but, at first, "How much must be contributed to regain sovereignty?" and thereafter, "How much must we contribute to maintain the American guarantees?"

Limited freedom has entailed limited choices and thus fewer strains on the West German economy. Forced to foreswear nuclear weapons (and amply compensated by the American wherewithals of extended deterrence on German soil), the FRG could devote to civilian uses those billions that France and England lavished on their national deterrents. Disabused of all global pretensions, the FRG could reap the belated fruits of the Versailles settlement which, in 1919, had relieved the Weimar Republic of all colonial possessions. Without colonies or global responsibilities, there were no faraway wars to be fought. West Germany could enjoy the comforts of a cocooned civilian power while the United States, France and England squandered their blood and treasure in military intervention around the globe. Historically, the FRG has devoted smaller fractions of its GNP to defense than France or England, let alone the United States.

Finally, because the Bundeswehr did not (and could not) serve the traditional functions of armies (like power projection and intervention), the West Germany body politic was spared the society-rending strife of an

Algerian war that contributed to the fall of the Fourth Republic and threatened to topple the Fifth. Nor was the Federal Army involved in a Vietnam-type operation that discredited not only an entire generation of American leaders but also the very idea of military power and preparedness for years to come.

Perhaps, there may even be an element of causation in the benign correlation between alliance and democracy during the postwar era, as there may have been a link between Germany's endemic insecurity and its antidemocratic evolution from the 18th to the mid-20th century. From Frederick the Great onward, Prussia and the Reich could only compensate for geographic and demographic disadvantage by extracting a maximum of military strength from a resource base that could never quite match the reserves of Germany's many potential enemies. Frederick did so by perfecting a highly efficient authoritarian state apparatus that could impose a thoroughly modern draft system on a tiny population. The Wilhelmine Empire could repeat Frederick's feat on a grander scale by harnessing nationalism to industrialization while wielding the *Primat der Aussenpolitik* against rising claims for mass and middle-class participation. (A normative theory of domestic politics, that 19th century contribution of German historiography postulated the strict subordination of factional politics to the paramount demands of national strength.) The experience of insecurity and victimization contributed heavily to the demise of the Weimar Republic; discrediting a frail democratic system, it legitimized those who would mobilize Germany for the sake of total war.

The Federal Republic, on the other hand, labored under none of these burdens. For the first time, Germany did not stand alone. Its security was provided by others, and alliance was the passport to international respectability (and, of course, economic prosperity). In that setting, the habits of pluralism and consensual politics could flourish, and anti-democratic forces would not, because there was no supreme existential threat that could be manipulated in the cause of a behemoth state. Democracy requires many conditions, but one of them is surely a feeling of security.

Such blessings are not easily foregone, and since they are the fruits of West Germany's on balance, comfortable role in NATO, neither will the Alliance forego them. On the other hand, it is precisely that sturdy equilibrium of costs and profits that will mute, if not foreclose, any activist departures. The Federal Republic is not likely to shed its dogged resistance to any expansion of its role beyond present confines. In a characteristic restatement of continuity, CDU Minister of Defense Manfred Wörner put it in the bluntest of terms: "For the Federal Republic of Germany, deployment of forces outside the NATO area is out of the question."[16] Instead of dispatching forces-in-being to the Gulf the FRG is prepared, again in Wörner's words, "to relieve U.S. forces in Europe for missions elsewhere . . . on the basis of a formula still to be defined."[17]

Nor is it likely that the Federal Republic will expand its military role *in Europe*. It is a compliment to the Atlantic system, and one of history's nicer ironies to boot that, forty years after total prostration, Germans today worry not about discrimination and impotence but about too much power in the European scheme of things. Outlining the virtues of equilibrium-minded modesty, former Defense Minister Georg Leber brushed aside pressures for German muscle-flexing by declaring: With a larger German army, "inner-European problems would arise with certainty because of the excessive weight that such a German army would then have among the other West European powers. And I must protect Europe against that."[18] It was the first time in almost a hundred years that a German leader could echo Bismarck's reassuring words: that Germany belonged to those nations which were "saturated . . . pacific and conservative."[19]

Deterrence vs. Defense   Once upon a time, there was a Golden Age of NATO which, in the strategist's vernacular, was known as the age of "massive retaliation." It was the age of America's quasi-monopoly in nuclear weapons, when the United States could threaten to rain nuclear devastation on the Soviet Union without fear of retaliation. It was therefore the only time when the United States could safely extend deterrence on behalf of its non-nuclear allies. Invulnerable to a Soviet counter-strike, the United States did not have to risk Washington for the sake of Bonn. Indeed, nuclear weapons could inhibit even the most limited forays because they spelled Armageddon for the aggressor and no risk for their possessors.

Like all Golden Ages, this one, too, probably never existed. If at all, it spanned only a brief and shrouded period: from the early 1950s when the United States could carry several hundred nuclear bombs into Soviet territory via foreign-based bombers to about 1957 when the Soviets began to deploy long-range bombers of their own. As soon as the United States was a target itself, "extended deterrence" was bound to become brittle. And although it took the Soviet Union another 15 years to reach "parity," American leaders began to *assume* mutual vulnerability as early as 1957 when the Soviet Union launched its first intercontinental missile, closely followed by Sputnik, in 1957.

If NATO should ever dissolve, future historians will probably mark 1957 as the beginning of its demise. From this time onward, the United Stated *did* run the risk of sacrificing Washington for the sake of Bonn, Rome, Brussels, *et al.* Its commitment could never be certain — hence, the endless conundra of "extended deterrence" that have racked the Alliance ever since.

In the 1950s, both France and England began to take out their own nuclear insurance in the form of independent deterrents. For historical reasons, that road was blocked for Bonn. Yet for geographical reasons, the Federal Republic depends more than any other Alliance member on the undiminished hold of deterrence because it is most vulnerable to attack and least able to sustain its consequences once deterrence has failed.

Apart from Norway, the FRG is the only NATO country in Western Europe that abuts on the territory of the Warsaw Pact, sharing a 1,000 mile border with the GDR and the CSSR. The FRG's shape is a defense planner's nightmare. At its "waist," the distance between the Federal Republic's eastern and western borders measures a mere 225 kilometers. A third of West

Germany's population and a quarter of its industrial potential are located within a 100-kilometer strip east of the inner-German border. If that strip is doubled, it encompasses two-thirds (40 million) of the population. Hamburg is one tank hour (40 kilometers) to the west of the Lauenburg checkpoint; Dortmund, the beginning of the Rhine-Ruhr industrial heartland, is but a hundred miles from the East German border. In short, the FRG cannot trade space for time.

That, logically, leaves two basic strategic preferences: deterrence over defense, or offense over defense. The latter has in fact been Germany's classic strategy from Frederick's Prussia to Hitler's "Reich of the Thousand Years." Given Germany's vulnerable frontiers and the number of its potential foes, demographic and geographic disadvantages had to be overcome by the concentration of forces, pre-emption, and the speed and deftness of maneuver which would carry the war into the enemy's territory from the very beginning. (Today, a classic instance of the Prussian posture is embodied in Israel's military doctrine and performance.)

Political realities, however, forbid what pure strategic logic might demand. "Cross-border" operations will surely occur once war has broken out, and they are even vaguely outlined in NATO's MC 14/2 document that forms part of the Alliance's doctrinal repository since December 1957. Still, by training and deployment, by doctrine and political intent, NATO is a defensive alliance that will probably not survive the attempt to turn pre-emption into a component of its official posture. If anything, NATO's *defensive* rationale has acquired even more weight during the decade of detente, making for an interesting historical shift. Originally, NATO's super-defensive purpose was implicitly directed against a "revanchist" Federal Republic; today, it is the very backbone of a West German *raison d'etat* (and *raison de nation*) that will not sacrifice the imperatives of detente to the logic of pure strategy. (The shift is in fact nicely reflected in a verbal reform of the 1970s — from *Vorwärtsverteidigung* [i.e., forward defense with its offensive connotation] to *Vorneverteidigung* [i.e., "defense up front" which implies a stance *at*, but not a thrust *across* the border].)[20]

If the FRG cannot find security in an Israeli-type doctrine (even though geography might demand it), what about its opposite, viz. the idea of a rear-based "mobile defense" that has lately intrigued both American and German experts.[21] Proponents of "mobile defense" would like to "defend in depth," compensating for NATO's lack of conventional power with fleet-footed maneuver through an extended defensive space. Again, there is some sound military logic that attends these strategic concepts. Given the tightly compressed "layercake" of NATO's forward defense close to the inner-German border, what is there to stop a Warsaw Pact attack short of the Rhine once that line has been punched?

Unfortunately, "there are no historical examples of a maneuver-oriented defense that has defeated an armored offensive."[22] Secondly, such a strategy poses a horrendous risk, as it literally invites the attacker to forge through a thinly-manned screening line into the defender's hinterland. If his momentum is not absorbed, there is no second chance on a territory such as

West Germany's which, at its narrowest, is but 225 kilometers wide. Third, there are the terrifying psychological costs of a rear-based mobile defense. Even Schlieffen's disciples lost their nerve at the beginning of World War I as they watched the Russian mobilization steamroller gather speed, starting to shift their troops eastward before France was crushed. Would their successors react with more *sangfroid* as Soviet armies surged into the West German heartland?[23]

Hence, the key weakness of any rear-based strategy: It might possibly work for NATO (as a whole) but not for its West German glacis. Athwart the front line, the Federal Republic will carry the brunt of any attack; it will be the main battlefield and victim. Even a limited war will be a general war for the Federal Republic. "Forward defense" at, or close to, the German-German border may not be a planner's dream; it is still a more pleasant prospect than the nightmare of a fluid battle that would sacrifice German space for the sale of ultimate allied victory.[24] And it would also undo the historical compact that underlies the Federal Republic's membership in NATO: The country must be sheltered from attack, not liberated *ex post facto*.

If defense, even a successful one, would hardly be different from defeat, then deterrence must carry the main burden of West German security. That burden was comfortable enough while an American near-monopoly in nuclear weapons promised balance minus the terror. Yet as the glory days of "extended deterrence" gave way to real or assumed "peril parity" by the end of the 1950s, West Germany became entangled in a set of horrifying double-binds. They were afraid that the United States would *not* use its nuclear armory, and they were afraid that it *would*. They began to fear the dwindling credibility of the American deterrent, and they began to fear American attempts to restore it. They worried about *too much* arms control, which might sacrifice German interests on the altar of superpower comity, and they worried about *too little* arms control, which might endanger German interests on the battlefield of superpower confrontation.

These double-binds are evidently rooted in the familiar paradoxes of nuclear strategy where the evil to be halted by deterrence is forever dwarfed by the possible consequences of its failure. We cherish the pacific end, and we loathe the murderous means. To assure the peace, we court limitless disaster, and by acquiring the instruments, we build not only a sturdy shelter but also a tempting target for nuclear devastation.

In the German case, these deadly conundra have always been aggravated by the extra burden of existential dependence on a faraway ally, the United States. Since the American guarantee is ultimately expressed in the language of the atom, American nuclear doctrine inevitably came to embody the very essence of America's commitment to West German security. A change in doctrine, no matter in which direction, inevitably carried an ominous message for the German-American relationship that spelled "decoupling." And since American strategy would perennially shift in response to changing realities of the Soviet-American balance, it was bound to trigger endless cycles of German anxiety.

Paradoxically, two strategic reforms as profoundly different as the Radford Plan (1956) and "flexible response" (1962) were both seen as first steps toward abandonment. To Konrad Adenauer, the substitution of tactical nuclear weapons for men on the ground (implying the early resort to nuclear strikes) looked like the first step toward the reduction of the American presence in Western Europe, hence toward "decoupling" and, ultimately, Soviet-American collusion. "I can only hope for one thing," lamented Adenauer in September of 1956,

> . . . namely that American policy will not turn toward Russia. . . . The Americans are political businessmen. When they withdraw from Europe they will demand a political payment from Russia. . . . Then something is going to happen which we do not want. . . . Coexistence. . . . And what is going to happen to us? We should go along. We are not going to do this; Europe is not going to do this.[25]

Yet only half a dozen years later, the shift toward "flexible response" (which implied the opposite, i.e., the *delay* of a nuclear response in favor of improved conventional options) also evoked the specter of "decoupling." It meant a "nuclear pause," a raised "nuclear threshold," and consequently the prospect of prolonged conventional devastation in the absence of American readiness to retaliate swiftly with the full weight of its nuclear panoply. "We have reason to believe," warned Defense Minister Franz Josef Strauss, "that the New Look (sic) of the American defense conception — the strengthening of conventional forces and the simultaneous raising of the nuclear threshold — will be interpreted fallaciously by Khrushchev as a renunciation of the nuclear deterrence strategy."[26] And his successor Kai-Uwe von Hassel postulated that "nuclear battlefield weapons must be made ready for employment in an *early phase* of a recognizable attack on Europe.[27]

Similarly, both the American reluctance to deploy intermediate-range nuclear forces (INF) in Western Europe (as under Carter) and the apparent eagerness to do so (as under Reagan) looked like a "decoupling" maneuver. Chancellor Helmut Schmidt's fabled speech before the International Institute for Strategic Studies in the fall of 1977 *could* be read as a German demand for long-range nuclear hardware.[28] First and foremost, however, it was a convoluted signal of German nervousness in the face of superpower negotiations that threatened to sacrifice German interests for the sake of a speedy SALT II agreement.

"SALT," as Helmut Schmidt put it, "neutralizes [American and Soviet] nuclear capabilities. In Europe, this magnifies the significance of the disparities between East and West in nuclear, tactical, and conventional weapons. . . . We in Europe must be particularly careful that these negotiations do not neglect the components of NATO's deterrent strategy."[29] Decoded, that message to the United States read: "You must not allow the Soviet Union to keep and strengthen a Eurostrategic arsenal (like the SS-20) that threatens *only* Western Europe because that unlinks our fate from yours."

The second part of the message drove home West Germany's *political* decoupling trauma: "Do not forget that your allies are more important than your adversaries." The West Germans, at that point, were not so much concerned with *obtaining* fancy new missiles than with losing the *option* which would inevitably symbolize the devaluation of Alliance priorities for the sake of "Big Twoism." And that threat was well-foreshadowed by Soviet insistence on cruise missile range limits, on non-transfer and non-circumvention clauses in the context of SALT II.

Three years later, the threat was not too much, but too little SALT; not Jimmy Carter's reluctance to part with cruise and Pershing II missiles, but NATO's December 1979 decision to deploy them in Western Europe. For the ruling Social Democrats, beset by a burgeoning peace movement on the left, and intent on saving detente from the post-Afghanistan chill, SALT became hope incarnate because SALT II would lead to SALT III which, in turn, would merge the INF with the strategic arms talks, and thus postpone deployment to a hazy future. Or as Willy Brandt, the former chancellor and present chairman of the SPD, put it in retrospect: "At the time, we German Social Democrats intended to facilitate the ratification of SALT II. Thereafter the problem of European strategic missiles was to be discussed under SALT III."[30]

If the Social Democrats (in power until 1982) were haunted by the missiles' impact on regional tranquility, the West German peace movement chose to portray INF deployment as a conspiracy against the Federal Republic while confusing the purposes of deterrence with the consequences of its failure. Pastor Heinrich Albertz, the former SPD mayor of Berlin, told the 250,000 demonstrators who had assembled in Bonn on October 10, 1981 that West Germany was destined to become the "shooting gallery of the superpowers." Or as one spokesman of the extreme anti-nuclear faction in the SPD put it in an imaginative syllogism: "Since NATO defines as 'theater' those countries that do not produce nuclear weapons but only function as the locus of deployment, NATO strategy signifies certain death for the population of the Federal Republic whose territory contains over 6000 TNF [theater nuclear forces] warheads."[31] Willy Brandt, using more oblique language, asked: ". . . who could rule out that an attempt to control it would be made if nuclear war broke out? . . . . [W]e in Europe would not live to see the results, for the decision would only come after we had been blasted away."[32]

If that be paranoia, it is paranoia with a venerable tradition that reflects West Germany's enduring condition as a nuclear "protectorate" of the United States. Behind the indictment of the peace movement lurks, once more, the specter of "decoupling" — if also in a more malign guise than the ghosts which tormented Adenauer and his successors. If Adenauer was obsessed with the nightmare of abandonment, the spokesmen of the peace movement regard INF deployment as abandonment-plus: as a great power plot to turn Germany into a neatly demarcated arena for nuclear proxy war, with the two Germanys as its battlefield and victims.

And to complete the vicious cycle that is driven by West Germany's nuclear dilemmas, those who find themselves at extreme odds with the peace movement ironically employ similar language to articulate similar fears. When a group of prominent American citizens and ex-officials published its "no first-use" proposal in *Foreign Affairs* in 1982,[33] the swiftest and most massive counterattack came from West Germany, the country that stands to lose most from a doctrinal shift which would loosen the link between conventional aggression and the escalation to general war.[34] Representing a bipartisan, middle-of-the-road consensus, the German foursome devoted its most painstaking efforts to reading between the lines of *Foreign Affairs*, and the exercise left them rattled.

Predictably, they fastened on the American authors' "redefinition" of United States' "extraordinary [security] guarantee"[35] and read it as implied "withdrawal from present commitments of the United States."[36] Moreover, "if the ideas of the authors were followed," the four West German critics remonstrated, "conventional conflicts in Europe would no longer involve any existential risk for the territory of the Soviet Union and . . . would be *without such risk for the territory of the United States as well.*"[37] No wonder, then, that the four Germans perceived the *Foreign Affairs* foray of McGeorge Bundy *et al.*, as fuel for the worst of West German suspicions: as prod to greater conventional efforts on the part of the Europeans which, at last, would permit the United States to retract safely behind its nuclear umbrella on the opposite shores of the Atlantic.

In short, there is no end of a lesson — whether driven home by the detractors or the defenders of NATO's strategic orthodoxy. The worst nightmare for *both* is a European war that, to recall the phrase of the German *Foreign Affairs* authors, "would be without existential risk for the territory of the Soviet Union or the United States." And for that nightmare, there can be no conclusive therapy because the territories of the United States and the Federal Republic are separated by the gulf of geography and sovereignty. Or as Gaullist logic has it: *le nucleaire ne se partage pas*, which is French for saying that, ultimately, nuclear weapons protect only their possessors.

The identity of fate between nations, which is but another word for "extended deterrence," can never be more than approximate — even if tangibly buttressed by 200,000 American troops on German soil, armed with nuclear weapons that embody the risk of general war. This is why these cycles of anxiety will continue to haunt the German-American relationship. There must be neither too much nor too little stress on the atom; deterrence must reign but its means must be mute; the country must offer neither a target nor a battlefield. Nobody could have expressed the Federal Republic's irreducible ambivalence more drastically than the former Chief of Staff of the Air Force, General Johannes Steinhoff:

> I am in favor of retaining nuclear weapons as political tools but not permitting them to become battlefield weapons. . . . I am firmly opposed to their tactical use on our soil. I cannot favor a

nuclear war on German territory while the two superpowers observe safely at a distance.[38]

Deterrence vs. Detente   In the late 1950s, when Adenauer opted for tactical nuclear weapons in the face of widespread domestic revulsion and mounting Soviet hostility, he sent a telling signal to Moscow: He refused to accept American medium-range missiles capable of reaching Soviet territory. These first-generation systems were eventually deployed throughout Europe,[39] but *not* in West Germany, and they were withdrawn in the course of the1960s as the United States acquired the technology to hit the Soviet Union without resort to foreign bases. Yet in 1979, Adenauer's successor Helmut Schmidt would claim "from hindsight" that withdrawal had been the "wrong step. They should have been modernized rather than dismantled."[40]

Together, these two messages delineate the outer limits of West Germany's nuclear dilemma within the larger scheme of East-West relations in Europe. Konrad Adenauer, though viscerally anti-Soviet, did not want to cross the line that separated the European battlefield from the Soviet homeland. Helmut Schmidt, though second to none in his detente-mindedness, believed throughout his intellectual and political career that European security could not tolerate the profound strategic assymmetry that a Soviet sanctuary imposed. This explains his unceasing reference to the (regional) peril that (global) parity had wrought, hence his strong intellectual commitment to a "Eurostrategic balance"[41] — by arms control if possible, by counter-armament if necessary.

Yet the defense-intellectual Schmidt would soon clash with the diplomatist Schmidt and thus with the political limits that Adenauer had accepted with his tactful "no" to American medium-range nuclear weapons. As the INF drama unfolded, those limits were redrawn as much by Soviet pressure as by internal resistance within Schmidt's own party. The SPD had gained power in 1969 as the party of detente and *Ostpolitik*, and it was thereafter doubly-chained to the perpetuation of both. The party understood correctly that it could only flourish at home as long as an international climate based on arms control and East-West cooperation legitimized the detente-oriented Left rather than the Conservatives. And correctly, the SPD understood that its freedom to maneuver in the interstices of bipolarity — the policy of small steps toward evolution in Central and Eastern Europe — was also irrevocably tied to a permissive international milieu.

INF deployment in Western Europe, particularly in West Germany, was not likely to buttress detente — which, at any rate, would soon succumb to the blows meted out on the faraway battlefield of Afghanistan. By late1978, when the Carter Administration had finally come around to granting the Europeans the gleaming new missile hardware they apparently so ardently desired, Helmut Schmidt was fully caught between the horns of the deterrence/detente dilemma his predecessor Adenauer had dimly foreseen 20 years earlier.

Schmidt's response was at once logical and practical: a tortuous balancing act that might just have succeeded if his party had not abandoned him in revolt and if global detente had not been mortally wounded by Angola, Afghanistan and the "Committee on the Present Danger." The weights on the tightrope were distributed as follows: In the first place, the Federal Republic had to dispel the dreaded specter of "singularity" that could cast Bonn into the unacceptable role of America's "continental sword." That was continuity *par excellence*. Most comfortable when marching in lockstep, Bonn had thoroughly absorbed the lesson of the scuttled Multilateral Force (MLF).

Launched in the early 1960s, the idea of an MLF was the first attempt at multi-nationalizing "extended deterrence." It was to consist of a missile-bearing surface fleet, armed with 200 *Polaris* and manned by mixed contingents from NATO countries. Anybody could buy a share, but control over the nuclear weapons was to be strictly confined to the United States. Among other reasons, the MLF was sunk because it suggested a German-American "axis," especially in the final phase when the potential membership had shrunk to two: the U.S. and the Federal Republic. Fifteen years later, the remedy was well-foreshadowed by the Schmidt government's doxology on the ill-fated "neutron bomb." Bonn would accept enhanced radiation weapons only if all the other members agreed, and if they would not be stationed in the Federal Republic alone.[42] And so with INF.

Secondly, the Alliance's INF posture had to combine maximum coupling with minimal provocation. As a result, a small number of systems, i.e., 572, was proposed as opposed to the 2,000 that some Pentagon planners were suggesting as a "real" military option. In addition to provoking the Soviets, so high a number would have suggested a separate "Eurostrategic" balance which was anathema to the idea of "coupling" Europe's to America's strategic arsenal. Hence also a lion's share for the slow-flying cruise missile (464) which did not pose a first-strike threat, but only a small number of Pershing II's (108) which were swift and precise yet not capable of reaching Moscow.

Third, nobody must have cause to accuse the FRG of extending a covetous hand toward somebody else's nuclear trigger. Conscious of the aborted MLF, which was dropped in 1964 not the least because it (wrongly) evoked too much of a German say in matters nuclear, Helmut Schmidt flatly rejected any ownership or control over the cruise or Pershing II missiles (such as a "dual-key" system).

Fourth, and most importantly, deployment was to open a uniquely promising avenue toward arms control. For once, negotiations would precede deployment. The Alliance had four years to trade away its non-existing missiles for the destruction of a steadily growing arsenal of real SS-20's. If arms control could not serve as a substitute, it would at least provide an indispensable alibi for deployment. At a minimum, another negotiating link would be tied with the Soviets that, in the perilous times ahead, might symbolize detente through its very existence. Thus, the "dual-track" decision of December 1979 was born.

The Brussels package shows Helmut Schmidt's guiding hand throughout. It was the West German Chancellor who persuaded Jimmy Carter during the quadripartite summit at Guadeloupe in January 1979 to accept the arms control-deployment link. (France was represented by Valery Giscard d'Estaing, and Britain by James Callaghan.) It was Helmut Schmidt who harnessed Italy's stationing commitment in the service of the "non-singularity" principle. And it was Helmut Schmidt who — in the summer of 1980, after the outbreak of Cold War II — turned Leonid Brezhnev's icy "no" to INF negotiations into an at least half-hearted interest.

Yet within his own party, the Chancellor had already lost the battle when he returned from Guadeloupe. By January 1979, the anti-missile movement in the SPD was no longer spearheaded by a left-wing fringe but by one of the party's foremost leaders, Herbert Wehner. Unable to sway Schmidt *in camera*, Wehner took his case to the media in a series of well-orchestrated interviews. Basing INF on German soil would turn the Federal Republic into a kind of "stationary aircraft carrier."[43] A few days later, Wehner vowed: "I want to help prevent a drop in the political temperature between the Soviet Union and the West European nations, in particular the Federal Republic, below the freezing point. What we have tried so hard to develop in the past ten years — a contractual relationship — ought not to be destroyed by a lack of patience in regard to disarmament talks."[44] Finally, the SPD parliamentary leader warned darkly: "This new weapon [Pershing II] signifies an American-West German axis. And that is impossible."[45]

The battle lines drawn in January 1979 would inexorably harden in the years to come, as the SPD moved from the subtly, perhaps too subtly, balanced "two-track" approach toward a single track of unconditional negotiation. Perhaps, it was Helmut Schmidt's personal tragedy that he could not achieve against his own party what his finely honed instincts for the requisites of military stability had taught him. (He resigned from the leadership of the party after his ouster from the Chancellorship in October 1982.) Perhaps he had also underestimated the Soviet Union's stake in preserving the quasi-imperial advantage over Western Europe it had gained in a fit of American absent-mindedness when the U.S. withdrew its *Thor, Jupiter* and *Mace* during the 1960s without exacting the removal of those Soviet SS-4's and SS-5's that, originally, had been deployed to hold Western Europe hostage for want of long-range systems that could hit the continental United States. That stake is by no means on the small side. Militarily, SS-20's provide an impressive counter-deterrence panoply that, even without recourse to the Soviet strategic arsenal, robs NATO of the "escalation dominance" on which "flexible response" is ultimately based. Politically, SS-20's serve as silent symbols of a favorable "correlation of forces" that promises the highest returns vis-a-vis the one key European country — the Federal Republic — which cannot seek refuge in an independent deterrent.

Perhaps, and that may be the most profound lesson of the INF drama, Schmidt foundered against circumstances which were beyond the Federal Republic's control. Throughout postwar history, nuclear weapons in and for Germany have imposed the most fearsome choices on the Federal Republic. They represent the focus where the global, the regional, the inner-German and the domestic dimensions of West German foreign policy clash with merciless regularity. On the global level, nuclear weapons pose the question of West Germany's place between the superpowers: how to tighten the existential link with the United States required for "extended deterrence"; how to preserve a political link with the Soviet Union required for "extended detente."

Regionally, nuclear weapons forever threaten to unhinge the Federal Republic's complex role in the European order. In the West, and especially in France, Bonn attracts concerns about its "true" intentions when it appears too avid in the search for collective nuclear arrangements (as in the case of the MLF) or, conversely, too reluctant to shoulder the nuclear burden (as during the protracted battle over INF). In the East, the nuclear connection serves as a useful imperial tool for the Soviets, allowing them to wield it as a means of recentralization which compresses West Germany's access to Eastern Europe and the GDR. The "palisade of missiles" Moscow threatened in the event of INF deployment was thus a doubly-ominous metaphor. It spelled "counter-counter-deployment" and a new tilt in the regional nuclear balance as well as a latter-day "iron curtain" that would sever the ties of interaction across Europe's and across Germany's divide. Finally, nuclear weapons in Germany, whether in the 1950s or the 1980s, have regularly triggered domestic revolt. Although unflagging in its support for the Alliance and a strong defense, German public opinion has never taken kindly to the idea that the Federal Republic plays prime hostage (and potential victim) to deterrence in Europe.

To simultaneously assure deterrence and detente, one as vital as the other, from a dependency position at the European center will tax West Germany's diplomatic skills and domestic stability no matter who stands at the helm in Bonn. Helmut Kohl, Chancellor since the fall of 1982, is not beset by a deeply-rent party as was Helmut Schmidt. Nor are the Christian Democrats' electoral fortunes as closely tied to a cooperative East-West climate as was the SPD. Indeed, historically, the CDU/CSU has rather profited from an anti-communist consensus. Finally, the Conservatives do not look for votes on the Left; they, therefore, may have fewer qualms about wielding the coercive powers of the State against the veto claims of a street-based protest movement.

Yet even so, and in spite of the deployment that began at the turn of 1984, Helmut Kohl and his cohorts cannot escape from the claims of a divided nation in close proximity to the Soviet superpower. Within a year of his accession to the Chancellorship, Helmut Kohl had shifted from the orthodoxy of the "zero option" (no missiles on either side), from stout vows of deployment to the more cautious search for a "compromise" (equal limits for both, but a Soviet monopoly on ballistic missiles) that paid due respect to Soviet pressures centered on the 108 Pershing II's scheduled for deployment in Germany alone.

Striking a balance between deterrence and detente will require an extraordinarily fortuitous constellation beyond West Germany's control. In the end, nuclear weapons are the preserve of the superpowers, and therefore their relationship provides the limiting condition for the moves of all the other players on the multi-dimensional chessboard that is Europe. Managing the balance will require a United States that does not foresake the needs of its allies as it shifts between the poles of militant containment and arms control *a deux*. If one — the politics of early Reaganism — embroils the allies in conflicts they would rather not shoulder, the other — world order politics *a la* Carter — reduces them to spectators in a global game where their own security interests form part of the stakes.

On the other side, it will require a Soviet Union that would accept "extended deterrence" as a natural part of the European order, even as it continues to play out its ancient game for primacy on the Continent. In sum, it will require a degree of predictability on the part of the United States and of wisdom on the part of the Soviet Union that is not the strong suit of either.

Conclusion: Security and Society

Throughout the Western World, notably in its northern, Protestant parts, a gathering protest movement began to challenge established security policy at the turn of the 1980s. Some observers have interpreted this phenomenon as a kind of sea change that spells an irrevocable break with the past and the ultimate triumph of democracy's forward march. Accordingly, the realm of national security — the last domain where a disembodied *raison d'etat* could still hold sway — has been irrevocably breached by the forces of mass participation.

> Pandora's Box has been opened. For good or ill, nuclear strategy in Europe has been a "leadership decision," taken by an informed few — a tiny nuclear elite — on behalf of an only-intermittently-interested many. . . . That no longer applies in Western Europe. The Pandora's Box of the nuclear age is public participation in nuclear policy-making; and the true message of the protest movements . . . is that the lid has opened.[46]

That is a bold diagnosis, and were one to follow such a widespread line of reasoning, one would arrive at even more tenuous conclusions. First, one might surmise that the change is secular and thus here to stay. Second, one might conclude that the West's traditional elites have finally lost their authority over national security — out of lassitude, perhaps, or sheer demoralization. Third, a vociferous, militant protest movement, bypassing the institutional routines of majority rule, may have acquired a permanent veto power over security policy.

Based on the single experience of the 1980s peace movement, these would be bold conclusions, indeed. For we have to ask not only why peace movements arise but also why they vanish, as did the anti-nuclear movement of the 1950s. The West has experienced only two protest movements in the nuclear age, and so paltry a number may be a very shaky base for generalization. Still, if we go back in history, short as it is, a very different set of conclusions emerges. Rather than a true sea change, the revolt of the 1980s seems to spell merely another *wave* of populist protest against nuclear weapons.

In the first place, there seems to be a distinct generational flavor to the anti-nuclear revolt. In Europe, the rise of the 1950s and 1980s peace movement is separated by about a quarter century, and perhaps it is not sheer happenstance that this period spans the normal generational cycle of 25 years. Every generation must come to grips with nuclear weapons on its own. In each case, in 1957 and in 1982, a new generation had to learn to live with "the bomb" that could not be banished from the earth but might one day incinerate it. To accept the horrifying paradoxes of deterrence — that more is never enough, that we must threaten to destroy the world in order to save it — goes against the very grain of a Western teleology that sees all problems as temporary and all evils as mere steppingstones on the path to ultimate salvation. It should come as no surprise, then, that the young — whose very life experience is progress incarnate — will regularly revolt against so powerful a symbol of doom as nuclear weapons.

But moods alone do not yet make for movements. So, secondly, there have to be triggering events, concrete and tangible, which convert a vaguely felt malaise into the push and pull of personal revolt. And there were at least three common crisis factors present at the creation of both anti-nuclear protest waves.

First, both peace movements were paralleled or preceded by momentous shifts in the nuclear balance. Khrushchev's rocket threats against Paris and London during the Suez Crisis of 1956 were the early harbingers of a new age; one year later, the West was shocked to learn that the Russians had launched an intercontinental ballistic missile ahead of the Americans. Before 1957, "assured destruction" had been pretty much a one-way threat — the comfortable monopoly of the United States. Now, Western societies were suddenly, and for the first time, brought face to face with their *own* vulnerability to the nuclear firestorm.

What Suez and Sputnik did for the first time, the relentless Soviet build-up during the 1970s did for the second peace movement. Matched by the breathtaking expansion of the Soviet strategic arsenal, the three-generation jump[47] from the half-forgotten SS-4 and SS-5 to the SS-20 missile in the European "theater" drove home the depressing realization that all of Western Europe, though a serene island of seemingly permanent detente, was an immovable target and a hostage to Soviet nuclear might.

Rapid technological change, the shift from older to newer and "better" weapons systems, yielded a second trigger event. We live most comfortably with "the bomb" when we are allowed to forget its existence. Forgetfulness and repression cease to function, however, when new weapons intrude on the mind. In the late 1950s, the European-wide deployment of American medium-range systems ("Thor," "Jupiter") and of so-called "tactical nuclear weapons" (thousands of them) literally brought the abstractions of deterrence down to earth. It is again no accident that the first peace movement flourished most luxuriantly in West Germany. A country the size of Oregon, the Federal Republic came to host more nuclear weapons per square mile than any other nation in the world. And the bulk of these tactical weapons was short-range, meaning that they would explode not in faraway reaches of the Soviet Union but on densely populated home ground.

Similarly, at the threshold of the 1980s, yet another generation of nuclear weapons punctured the veil of repression we normally spread over death, taxes, and the accoutrements of "mutual assured destruction." Many of the new weapons entering the arsenals of the 1980s were smaller, more precise and hence ostensibly more "useable"; and "warfighting" suddenly seemed to edge out "deterrence" as the doctrine of the day. "Neutron bombs," Pershing II and cruise missiles abruptly reminded the West Germans (as well as the Dutch and the British) that nuclear terror was the price of an unprecedented peace *cum* prosperity, that survival — in Churchill's legendary words — was indeed the "twin brother of annihilation."

The third trigger factor was more properly political and perhaps the most important of them all: the breakdown of detente. New generations of nuclear weapons are scary because they suddenly cast a glaring light on the murderous premises of our security. A surge in Soviet power awakens us to our ever-present vulnerability. But sharply deteriorating East-West relations add urgency to the *Angst*. Rightly or wrongly, democratic societies instinctively recoil from the sound and the fury of international tension because they habitually equate the noise with the real war.

In 1958, right after the famous post-Stalin "thaw" and the arrival of huge numbers of battlefield nuclear weapons, there came the long ice age of Khrushchev's "Berlin Ultimatum" which would continue to send shivers of World War III through Western Europe until 1962. A similar chill descended at the threshold of the present decade which was ushered in by such unassuring events as the Iran hostage crisis, the Soviet invasion of Afghanistan and the war of nerves over Poland. Put differently, the new "Euromissiles" — the cruise and the Pershing — intruded on the collective unconscious of the West precisely at a time when "detente" gave way to "neo-containment" in the wake of Afghanistan and sundry Soviet adventures elsewhere. Both events seemed to make war more likely, inexorably turning attention away from the obvious sturdiness of the "balance of terror" and toward the unthinkable consequences of its collapse. It did not matter that nuclear weapons had kept the peace for almost 40 years. Indeed, the very success of deterrence in keeping the superpowers at their best behavior now spelled its greatest danger as many in the West succumbed to "proof-by-reverse induction": fail it must because it has endured so long.

Third, in addition to generational change and trigger events, there must be a leadership to harness psychology to politics. In both historical cases, protest did not spring fully-clad from the depth of an *Angst*-ridden subconscious. What looked like a spontaneous clash between leaders and led, between old and young, was in fact an *intra*-elite struggle played out on a populist stage — where one part of the political establishment sought to outmaneuver the other.

Nowhere was this more evident than in the case of West Germany, in the 1950s as well as in the 1980s. In 1958, West German public opinion was solidly arrayed against the government's nuclear choice.[48] During the spring of 1958, hundreds of thousands took to the streets to protest the impending deployment of tactical nuclear weapons on West German soil. Yet the movement was led and controlled by an SPD (and its ally, the German Trade Union Federation) that, after three lost elections, saw the nuclear issue as a promising vehicle toward governmental tenure.

The connection between party and movement was less direct in the late 1970s and early 1980s, not the least because the SPD was then no longer in opposition. Yet the struggle against ER (enhanced radiation) and INF weapons began as a struggle *within* the party long before the huge peace marches of 1981 and 1982 would converge on Bonn. It was spearheaded by those who, like Willy Brandt, Herbert Wehner and Egon Bahr, saw "neutron bombs," Pershing II and cruise missiles as a grievous threat to arms control, detente and *Ostpolitik*. Domestically, they hoped once more to convert that banner into ballots during the 1980 elections, and thus to repeat the successful strategy of 1969 and 1972. *Within* the party, the nuclear issue would also help to shift the balance of power toward the left around Willy Brandt, who had been forced to yield the Chancellorship to Helmut Schmidt in the wake of the Guillaume spy scandal in 1974. The German peace movement was probably born in July of 1977 when Egon Bahr delivered his famed broadcast against enhanced-radiation weapons: "Is mankind turning mad? .... Our scale of values has been turned upside down. The object is the preservation of matter; mankind has become a secondary consideration. . . . The neutron bomb symbolizes the perversion of thinking."[49] It was a deliberate call to arms, directed as much against Helmut Schmidt as against Jimmy Carter, dedicated as much to detente with the Soviets as to undercutting the ascendancy of the Schmidt wing within the party.

This does not mean that the SPD "founded" the peace movement, let alone that it could control the hundred-thousands who would eventually take to the street. Movements, once galvanized, have a life of their own, and if anything, the Social Democrats have ever since been trying to contain and to channel the protest potential with some desperation. The point is more complex. In explaining the rise (rather than the course) of protest movements, we must look at the politics behind the populism. We must ask why politicians take up certain cudgels at certain times to clobber or cow their opponents. And we must look not only at the actors in the noisy drama, but also at the authors of the script which shaped the terms of the debate long before the play became a free-for-all. In the beginning there is always politics, and its protagonists are neither young[50] nor of the grass roots but professional politicians who seek to rouse and to ride forces that promise victory in the battle for domestic power. That, in fact, is the name of the democratic game.

Why and when do protest movements disappear? Such movements fail because they fail. Behind this tautology lurks a simple insight into the nature of populist politics. Grassroots movements try to mobilize maximum numbers at maximum speed; by necessity they become a motley crowd. Yet pastors and pacifists, "Greens" and "Reds," Leninists and idealists, ecologists and feminists are factions; they do not make a coalition. For a while, they manage to submerge their political differences for the sake of the great single-issue — for the battle against tactical nuclear weapons as in the 1950s, for the fight against Pershing and cruise missiles as in the 1980s.

Yet what happens when that objective — the glue that holds it all together — is frustrated as it was at the end of 1983 when the INF deployment in West Germany began on schedule? Unlike entrenched political parties, populist movements have a hard time surviving in the cold. Established parties grouped around stable coalitions are *geared* for life in opposition. They have organizations, they have a base, and they dispense patronage and positions. Even after defeat in a national contest, they can seek cover in local and regional power bastions where they can regroup for a counter-attack four years later. For political parties, defeat does not spell the end but a new beginning.

Not so for ad hoc groupings like the West German peace movement of the 1980s. How do they inspire their cohorts and gain new recruits after failure? The stretch-out of the deployment until the end of the decade might still offer successive rallying points. Yet if the call to stop the missiles did not rouse the masses yesterday, will the call to stop the *next* batch prove more galvanizing tomorrow? In the meantime, initial failure poses the pressing problem of organizational cohesion. The first response is the communal huddle and the collective soul-searching: Where did all of us go wrong? Not far behind comes the intra-mural reckoning: Who lost the battle? The third stage is likely to bring the bitterness and the beginning of break-up as the diverse factions, faced with their clashing needs, either retreat into the solidarity of their own fold or, conversely, strike out to impose uniformity by capturing the entire organization.

In the wake of the initial INF deployment, much of what might have been predicted did come to pass. Early in 1984, the best-known spokeswoman of the German peace movement, Petra Kelly, withdrew from the "Krefeld Appeal," leaving behind the charge that this large umbrella organization of the anti-missile forces had fallen prey to communist subversion. At the same time, her prominent colleague and mentor, Gert Bastian, left the Greens, accusing his old flock of running a "dictatorship of incompetence" that was too soft on communism and too hostile toward the United States. And by early 1984, the Movement was desperately searching for new banners — such as "acid rain" or American "imperialism in Nicaragua."

While seeking to regroup, the West German peace movement was also threatened from without — notably by a Social Democratic Party which, in opposition since 1982, was driven by electoral logic to contain and to absorb the potential of the Greens and sundry protest groups to the left of itself. Might the Social Democrats provide the organizational corset that the peace movement, by its very nature, cannot generate and maintain on its own?

West Germany's electoral history suggests a different outcome. Put differently, the electoral battles of the past were not won at the extreme of the political spectrum, and the vast and sluggish political center of the West German body politic shows no signs of breaking up during the 1980s. Twice in the postwar period, the Social Democrats have tried to convert anti-nuclear sentiments into victory at the polls, and twice they failed — during the crucial regional elections in North Rhine-Westphalia in 1958[51] and the federal elections of 1983. The mid-1980s are of course not like the late 1950s when the party was already on the road to Bad Godesberg, the watershed convention of 1959, where the SPD shed its residual Marxism and its reluctance to embrace rearmament, NATO and nuclear weapons. By the middle of the 1980s, the SPD had barely halted its leftward drift, yet having been routed in the 1983 national contest (the worst showing at the polls since 1961), the SPD is not likely to forget the advice of its old taskmaster Herbert Wehner. Asked why, at the height of the anti-nuclear campaign in 1958, the Social Democrats had stuck to their ancient anti-populist instincts by refusing to endorse a general strike, Herbert Wehner replied: It was dangerous to "rouse moods and to mobilize people with whom Social Democracy could not continue to make common cause after a certain point and who would obstruct even further its access to the so-called common man."[52] Populism does not have a proud tradition in Germany.

There are more tangible reasons which lend weight to Wehner's warning. That the SPD should have failed twice in the space of one generation to mobilize anti-nuclear sentiment for electoral gain may suggest some deeper truths about the nature of West German society. While the social pulse-takers have had little trouble in extracting anti-missile majorities from their samples, the polls also and invariably demonstrate stable majorities in favor of the Alliance and the United States as well as the low "issue salience" of nuclear weapons. "Issue salience" refers to the importance citizens attach to a certain issue — how much does it matter in the overall context of their concerns?

Even though aversion to them may be widespread, nuclear weapons are a perfect instance of "low issue salience." During the late 1970s and early 1980s, West German voters have consistently ranked defense and foreign policy issues below unemployment, inflation and social security — the triptych of their main concerns. Another way to illustrate this point is a poll first taken in 1981 and then repeated in 1983 which sought to measure West German reactions to NATO's "two-track approach." In 1981, 21 percent of the respondents took a negative view, 36 percent a positive view, and 42 percent confessed either ignorance or indifference. The following two years witnessed the flowering of the peace movement, with 250,000 marching on Bonn in the fall of 1981 and another 200,000 returning for an anti-missile demonstration in the early summer of 1982. The surge of the movement was paralleled by a massive anti-nuclear campaign on the part of key segments of the print and electronic media, with nuclear pacifism virtually monopolizing the terms of the public debate. Yet when the identical question was posed in 1983, the response had barely changed: 22 percent took a negative view; 38 percent took a positive view; and 39 percent still reported that they either did not know or did not care about NATO's "two-track approach."⁵³

Together, these two polls suggested not only a large bloc of indifference and ignorance but also a fascinating degree of immunity on the part of the many to the activism of the few. Perhaps the most profound reason for the failure of the peace movement to convert attitudes into action is the *shallowness* of anti-nuclear sentiments. In the fall of 1983, for instance, the pollsters descended on the town of Schwäbisch-Gmünd to plumb the community's nuclear *Angst*. The obscure locale in the southwest of Germany was chosen for a good reason: an American army base next door which, at that point, was being readied to receive a batch of Pershing II missiles. Predictably, almost 6 out of 10 respondents opposed the deployment. But just as predictably, only 15 percent of those polled would "actively support" the peace movement.⁵⁴ If there is so vast a gap (44 percentage points) between opinion and behavior even on the part of the foreordained victims, then nuclear weapons do not offer the appropriate rallying point for a genuine mass-based revolt. Nuclear weapons mobilize counter-elites, but twice in postwar history the revulsion against them has proven too shallow to allow the peace movement (and the SPD) to moblize the "man in the street" against the government's nuclear choice.

History offers additional reasons why orthodoxy prevailed in the German body politic. The previous analysis suggested that similar trigger events were present at the creation of both peace movements, i.e., the deterioration of the nuclear balance, the intrusion of new weapons and the breakdown of detente. If this theory is correct, one should expect that the converse, i.e., the restabilization of the balance, the psychological absorption of new weapons and the return to detente would exert a calming effect on ruffled sensibilities. The Cuban missile crisis was an obvious watershed. To the rattled Western mind, the happy ending at the brink was doubly reassuring. It revealed that statesmen laboring in the shadow of the apocalypse do not behave as recklessly as their forefathers in 1914. And to those who would have yielded to Khrushchev's pressures in Cuba and Berlin for survival's sake, it demonstrated that it helps to be well-prepared when moving toward the edge of the nuclear unknown.

With the global balance so palpably restored, the feat of nuclear weapons receded throughout the West. The new weapons became "old weapons," and were forgotten once more. But there was another factor, perhaps even more weighty, which helped to mute nuclear *Angst*: the global detente that followed the reassertion of Western strength in Cuba and Berlin. In the wake of deadly confrontation, the United States and the Soviet Union took their first steps toward taming the menace of the storm by linking Washington and Moscow through the vaunted "Hotline" in 1962 and by concluding a limited test-ban treaty in 1963. By then, the peace movement had vanished throughout Western Europe.

Modest as they were, these steps pulled the sting out of nuclear despair. They symbolized the power of human action over brooding terror. If the weapons could not be banished from the earth, they might at least be rendered impotent. And the lesson transcends the events of yesteryear. Precisely because nuclear weapons cannot be exorcized, they require a doctrine of salvation. Arms control and detente, no matter how sterile by the standards of the true believer, have provided that doctrine — a vital myth that elevates hope over an intractable reality. Presumably, the peace movement of the early 1980s could not have flourished without the denigration of arms control and detente that accompanied the frightening surge in the quality and quantity of nuclear weapons. Conversely, the movement would not have receded as quickly by the mid-'80s without the calming moderation in our tone and language.

In conclusion, peace movements are not hardy perennials because they depend on very narrow soil and climate conditions. History suggests why they arise, history also points to the political setting in which they disappear. That they were contained twice in the space of one generation may suggest a third moral: the sturdiness of the multiple balances which have determined the narrow limits of West German choices in matter of security. Will those balances — between autonomy and alliance, between deterrence and defense, between deterrence and detente — continue to withstand recurrent stress?

Pourvue que ca dure, Napoleon's mother once cautioned. *Ca dure*, one might answer, as long as the Atlantic order endures of which West Germany is the product, the pillar and the problem.

NOTES

[1] Among them are 213,000 American troops. The FRG provides about half of NATO's ground forces in Central Europe, half of its ground-based air defenses, and 30 percent of combat aircraft. In the Baltic, the FRG accounts for 70 percent of naval and 100 percent of naval air forces.

[2] This pledge was appropriately flanked by a declaration of France, Britain and the United States which was certainly aimed against their new partner. "They will regard as a threat to their own peace and safety any recourse to force which . . . threatens the integrity and unity of the Atlantic alliance or its defensive purposes. . . . They will act . . . with a view to taking other measures which may be appropriate." "London Conference" (September 28 October 3, 1954), in Council on Foreign Relations, ed., *Documents on American Foreign Relations 1954* (New York: Harper Brothers, 1954), pp. 115-17.

[3] For those fond of historical analogies, the Weimar Republic's Locarno-Politik (1925-26) might actually provide the more fitting echo from the past. In the Locarno Treaties, the Weimar Republic pledged itself to respect the redrawn borders in the West; at the same time it joined the League of Nations which, because it excluded Soviet Russia, was the functional equivalent of an anti-Soviet alliance. Berlin, however, reserved a special status for itself: the right to participate in League sanctions (against Russia) only if "compatible with its military situation and [if it] takes into account its geographical position." One year later, the Russo-German Treaty of Berlin made Germany's special status explicit when each nation bound itself not to join economic or financial boycotts directed against the other. See Annex F, Locarno Treaties, in Fritz Berber, ed., *Locarno: Eine Dokumentensammlung* (Berlin: Junker und Dunnhaupt, 1936), p. 63.

[4] Cf. Gerhard Wettig, *Entmilitarisierung und Wiederbewaffnung in Deutschland, 1943-1955* (Munich: Oldenbourg, 1967), p. 245.

[5] Konrad Adenauer, *Erinnerungen*, vol. I, (Stuttgart: Deutsche Verlags-Anstalt, 1965), p. 457.

[6] As quoted by Dieter Schröder in *Süddeutsche Zeitung*, January 7, 1960.

[7] In the summer of 1956, the Chancellor dispatched one of his trusted associates, Felix von Eckhardt, to the United States to mobilize, *inter alia*, the leadership of the Democratic Party against his Republican friends and the Joint Chiefs of Staff.

[8] Bogislaw von Bonin, *Opposition gegen Adenauers Sicherheitspolitik*, ed. Heinz Brill (Hamburg: Verlag neue Politik, 1976), p. 22.

[9] These are the troops of Denmark, Holland, Great Britain, Belgium and the United States, on the immediate front line, and of Canada and France in the southwest corner of the Federal Republic. (Dutch and Belgians are not physically present in peacetime; they are supposed to move forward into their assigned sectors prior to hostilities.)

[10] In fact, the impact of precision-guided anti-tank weapons has been vastly exaggerated. "The true lessons" of the Yom Kippur War "may be extracted from the knowledge that, of the approximately 3000 Arab and Israeli tanks destroyed or damaged . . . at least 80 percent were knocked out by other tanks." Kenneth Rush, et al., *Strengthening Deterrence: NATO and the Credibility of Western Defense in the 1980's* (Cambridge: Ballinger, 1982), p. 129.

[11] See in particular, Horst Afheldt, *Verteidigung und Frieden* (Munich: Hanser, 1976), whose ideas are currently reattracting the attention of the SPD. For an updated version see his *Defensive Verteidigung* (Reinbek: Rowohlt, 1983). Less radical but with similar implications, Hans-Joachim Löser, "Raumdeckende Verteidigung gegen raumgreifende Operationen," *Europäische Wehrkunde*, September 1977.

[12] "Weder Abschreckung noch Verteidigung: Zur militärischen Funktion der Bundeswehr damals und heute," *Friedensanalysen*, Vol. 14 (Frankfurt: Suhrkamp, 1982), p. 250. Before switching to the peace movement, Mechtersheimer was a member of the Christian Social Union (CSU), the more conservative Bavarian affiliate of the Christian Democratic Union (CDU). On the left, Karsten Voigt, a foreign policy spokesman of the SPD parliamentary group, in 1983 began to speculate about a "two-key" system for American INF in Germany, an idea that former SPD chancellor Helmut Schmidt had explicitly rejected during NATO's High Level Group deliberations on missile modernization.

[13] See for instance the apt comment by an anonymous Hamburg journalist quoted in the *Washington Post*, July 31, 1983, p. D2: "We have a hard time coming to terms with our history and with our geography, too. Germans don't like the fact that they are on the front line between East and West. If we could, we would move our country out of Central Europe."

[14] The term was coined by Stanley Hoffmann who continues: "Dreams are (its) victims." *Gulliver's Troubles, Or, The Setting of American Foreign Policy* (New York: McGraw-Hill, 1968), p. 55.

[15] A simple but misleading cost assessment might be: a weighted fraction of those vaunted $90 billion that the United States is said to spend annually on NATO. Yet how much would have to be subtracted in terms of the FRG's manpower and equipment contribution to Alliance security? What is the dollar value of the real estate Bonn provides in the form of foreign bases and maneuver areas?How much of these $90 billion (a dubious figure to begin with), actually help to protect *American* interests? Obviously, the dissolution of NATO would not lead to a net saving of $90 billion, as American troops would not be disbanded but merely relocated while losing the strategic (and cost) advantage of deployment near likely theaters of conflict like the Gulf.

[16] Manfred Wörner, "The Security Policy of the Federal Republic of Germany in the 1980's," *Germany: Keystone to European Security*, special issue of the American Enterprise Institute's *Foreign Policy and Defense Review*, Vol. IV, 1983, p. 45.

[17] *Ibid.*, p. 46.

[18] As quoted in Walter F. Hahn, *Between Westpolitik and Ostpolitik* (Beverly Hills: Sage, 1975), p. 70.

[19] In a letter to the British Prime Minister, Lord Salisbury, of November 22, 1887. *Gesammelte Werke*, Vol. 14, Pt. 2, Wolfgang Windelband and Werner Frauendienst, eds. (Berlin: Deutsche Verlagsanstalt, 1924-1935), p. 890.

[20] For a more detailed critique of offensive alternatives to NATO's "flexible response" strategy (such as "deep interdiction" and "conventional retaliation") see my "Can Europe Live With Its Defense?" in Lawrence Freedman, ed., *The Troubled Alliance* (London: Heinemann, 1983).

[21] For two rather diverse German views, see Franz Uhle-Wettler, *Gefechtsfeld Mitteleuropa* (n.p.: Bernard & Graefe, 1980) and Hans-Joachim Löser, "Vorneverteidigung in der Bundesrepublik Deutschland?," *Oesterreichische Militärzeitschrift*, No. 2, 1980. For American perspectives on maneuver-oriented defense, see Steven L. Canby, "Mutual Force Reduction: A Military Perspective,"

International Security (Winter 1978), and William S. Lind, "Military Doctrine, Force Structure and the Defense-Decision-Making Process," *Air University Review*, (May/June 1979).

[22] John J. Mearsheimer in his superb critique, "Maneuver, Mobile Defense, and the NATO Central Front," *International Security* (Winter 1981/82), p. 108.

[23] I have expanded these points in "Can Europe Live With Its Defense?" in Lawrence Freedman, ed., *op. cit.*

[24] Predictably, the West Germans reacted with great anxiety to PRM-10, the Presidential Review Memorandum of 1977 that suggested that NATO forces might have to fall back to the Rhine before regrouping for a counter-attack.

[25] In a conversation with an American journalist in London, September 28, 1956, as cited in Arnulf Baring, *Sehr verehrter Herr Bundeskanzler Heinrich von Brentano im Briefwechsel mit Konrad Adenauer*, (Hamburg: Hoffmann und Campe, 1974), p. 202.

[26] As quoted in *Die Zeit*, September 1, 1961.

[27] "Organizing Western Defense," *Foreign Affairs* (Jan. 1965), p. 211 (emphasis added).

[28] Helmut Schmidt's IISS speech was so subtly balanced that, in retrospect, it could mean all things to all people. On the other hand, there was the demand for a *comprehensive* American arms control concept that would give due weight to European concerns: "Strategic arms limitations confined to the United States and the Soviet Union will inevitably impair the security of the West European members of the Alliance vis-a-vis Soviet military superiority in Europe if we do not succeed in removing the disparities of military power in Europe parallel to the SALT negotiations." On the other hand, there was a muted call for compensatory armament (in the face of the growing Soviet SS-20 threat): "So long as this [the restoration of a balance through negotiations] is not the case, we must maintain the balance of the full range of deterrence strategy. The Alliance must, therefore, be ready to make available the means to support the present strategy." "The 1977 Alastair Buchan Memorial Lecture," October 28, 1977, *Survival* (Jan-Feb 1978), pp. 3-4.

[29] Ibid., p. 3.

[30] "Willy Brandt's Plea: It's Not Too Late for an Arms Deal," *Washington Post*, August 7, 1983, p. C2.

[31] Oskar Lafontaine, "Die Begriffe der heutigen Sicherheitspolitik stimmen nicht mehr," *Blätter für deutsche und internationale Politik*, No. 11, 1981, p. 1323. (Mr. Lafontaine is the mayor of Saarbrücken and chairman of the Saarland SPD.)

[32] Willy Brandt, *op. cit.*

[33] McGeorge Bundy, George F. Kennan, Robert S. McNamara and Gerard Smith, "Nuclear Weapons and the Atlantic Alliance," *Foreign Affairs*, Spring 1982.

[34] Karl Kaiser, Georg Leber, Alois Mertes and Franz-Josef Schultz, "Nuclear Weapons and the Preservation of Peace," *Foreign Affairs*, Summer 1982. (Karl Kaiser is a member of the SPD and Georg Leber was SPD Minister of Defense from 1972 to 1978. Alois Mertes, a member of the CDU, has been Deputy Minister of Foreign Affairs since 1982. Franz-Josef Schultz was Commander-in-Chief of Allied Forces Central Europe from 1977 to 1979.)

[35] McGeorge Bundy, et al., p. 759.

[36] Karl Kaiser, et al., p. 1161.

[37] Ibid., p. 1162, emphasis added.

[38] As quoted by Alex A. Vardamis, "German-American Military Fissures," *Foreign Policy* (Spring 1979), pp. 94-95.

[39] 60 *Thor* missiles were deployed in England, 45 *Jupiters* in Italy and Turkey. A number of B-47 bomber wings capable of reaching the Soviet Union were based in North Africa and Spain. 96 *Mace*, a primitive predecessor of today's cruise missile with a range of 2000 kms, were stationed in West Germany.

[40] In an interview with the *Economist*, October 6, 1979, p. 49.

[41] The quotation marks are meant to stress that this "balance" must be neither a truly "separate" nor a truly "equal" one, because such features would inevitably signify the "decoupling" of Europe from America's strategic arsenal.

[42] Cf. Helmut Schmidt, as reported by *Süddeutsche Zeitung*, April 13, 1978.

[43] As quoted in *Der Spiegel*, January 29, 1979, p. 36-37. Using the same simile a few weeks later, he added: " . . . and one has to shoot at such a carrier." As quoted in *Die Welt*, March 8, 1979.

[44] As quoted in *Neue Ruhr-Zeitung*, January 31, 1979.

[45] As quoted in *NRC Handelsblad*, February 3, 1979.

[46] John Barry, "Just Who is Deterred by the Deterrent?" *The Times*, August 18, 1981, p. 12.

[47] Deployed in the late 1950s, the SS-4 and SS-5 were liquid-fueled, stationary and equipped with a single warhead. The SS-20, deployed as of 1976, is solid-fueled, mobile (hence almost impossible to destroy) and comes with a triple-warhead.

[48] In a poll taken in 1958, 52 percent of the respondents favored a general strike to prevent the deployment of tactical nuclear weapons. (*Jahrbuch der öffentlichen Meinung, 1958-1964* [Allensbach: Verlag für Demoskopie, 1951], p. 375.) When the issue was posed in terms of being nuclear missile launchers on West German soil, opposition jumped to 83 percent. (See pamphlet by the Emnid polling institute, *Raketenbasen in Deutschland*, Bielefeld, March 1958.)

[49] In an article in *Vorwärts*, July 17, 1977. The attack recalls Helmut Schmidt's sentiments expressed during the Bundestag debate on the acquisition of tactical weapons on March 22, 1958: "Do you remember the NATO maneuvers *Carte Blanche* and *Black Lion*? There is a new [nuclear] staff exercise going on at present — this time called *Blue Lion*. I have been told that the officers involved in the preparations for this exercise were reduced to tears [when thinking about] the day-to-day consequences of the reality behind the exercises."

[50] Significantly, many of the personages that have provided the 1980s peace movement with intellectual and ideological leadership are well into their fifties and beyond: SPD Chairman Willy Brandt, the former Chancellor; Egon Bahr, the former Secretary-General of the SPD; Erhard Eppler, the former chairman of the Baden-Würtemberg SPD; Heinrich Albertz, the former SPD mayor of West Berlin; Hellmut Gollwitzer, a prominent Protestant theologian; Gert Bastian, a retired general who represented the Greens in the Bundestag.

[51] Touted as a test-vote on West Germany's nuclear armament by both SPD and CDU, the *Land* election of North Rhine-Westphalia marked the end of the SPD's anti-nuclear campaign in the 1950s. Even though the heavily industrialized *Land* was a traditional stronghold of the SPD, the CDU gained an absolute majority in the election.

[52] As quoted in Günther Gaus, *Staatserhaltende Opposition: Gespräche mit Herbert Wehner* (Hamburg: Rowohlt, 1966), p. 26.

[53] Emnid poll, as cited in *Der Spiegel*, No. 6, 1983, p. 90.

[54] Poll cited in *Der Spiegel*, No. 42, 1983, p. 59.

POLICY IMPLICATIONS OF DEVELOPMENT AND THE PRESENT STATUS OF U.S.-GERMAN RELATIONS: A GERMAN POINT OF VIEW

by Kurt H. Biedenkopf

This year Americans and Germans commemorate the 300th anniversary of the arrival of the first German settlers in the United States. Thirteen families from Krefeld settled in Pennsylvania and founded Germantown. German-American relations, therefore, not only are 300 years old but predate the existence of the United States and have, in various ways, influenced subsequent American development. German-American relations thus have deep roots in American history.

They have also influenced German history significantly, although only more recently. For Germans in the 18th and 19th centuries, the U.S. existed mainly as a country of immigration and seemingly unlimited opportunities for those who could not find any at home. It was only in the 20th century that the U.S. established an increasingly important influence in Europe and thus on German affairs: first, by entering World War I as a consequence of unrestricted submarine warfare declared by Germany; then — after a period of isolationism — as the leading power of allied forces in the Second World War; and ever since as a dominant factor of Germany's political fate after World War II.

We are here concerned with this latest period, which is roughly identical with the grown-up life of my generation. For this generation — which is also that of Chancellor Helmut Kohl — no single influence on political development has been and continues to be more important for the life and affairs of my country than the influence of the U.S. on postwar Europe.

Any effort to define policy implications of present U.S.-German relations should keep this singularity of the relationship in mind. The influence of the United States on Germany's development and destiny during the last 40 years has been singular not only for my generation but also for my country. The U.S. has played a dominant role for all of Western Europe, yet no other European country has been influenced as much by the United States as has Germany.

It is therefore not surprising that both Germans and Americans should periodically concern themselves with the substance, the quality, the structure and the climate of this relationship. For Germans, it has been an existential one since the Federal Republic's foundation in the Western part of divided Germany. To the United States, guardianship for the democratic fledgling, stewardship for the young democratic state and, finally, partnership with the well-established, economically strong and politically stable middle power in Europe were of major importance in the framework of their European interests and their relationship to the Soviet Union. On the one hand, West Germany during this period had developed into one of the most reliable allies of the U.S. On the other hand, however, West Germany's geographic location in Europe, its special situation as the country most affected by the military, political and ideological division of Europe and its role as a cornerstone in the structure of military defense against the Soviet Union, where this defense was most important to the U.S., made the country an object of continued close attention and observation. Although free Germany's integration into the Alliance of Western States could not conceivably have been more complete, the stability and duration of this integration have never really been taken for granted. A potential for suspicion and skepticism remains. No amount of "good behavior" has so far been able to eliminate it. A certain ambivalence in the relationship between the U.S. and postwar Germany is the result. It surfaces whenever issues arise that lend themselves either to questions about German reliability or to speculation on the future course of German politics and objectives in the heart of Europe.

The close and dominating relationship that exists between the U.S. and the FRG is the exception rather than the rule among nations. That a country with 60 million inhabitants — with one of the strongest and best developed economies in the world — should rely for its defense and thus stake its political future on the willingness of another nation to mortgage its own existence to defend this future is, historically speaking, unusual. It is indeed — as is nuclear deterrence itself — without historic precedent.

1. To those who participated in the development of the relationship on both sides of the Atlantic, it seems quite normal. Measured against its major objectives — namely, to keep the peace in Europe and protect freedom from Soviet expansion and oppression — it has clearly been very successful. True, it has not brought Germany closer to national unity. The country's national identity which was lost because of the division of Germany after World War II has not been reestablished — and there is little likelihood that it will be in the foreseeable future. But then those who shaped German policy during the last three decades have knowingly opted for freedom over the vague possibilities of reunification under uncertain conditions. They decided for integration into the Western Alliance and the European Community and against reunification under Soviet terms or even control. To them, as to the overwhelming majority of Germans today, this choice constituted a basic foundation of national and political existence.

2. Even though all this is true, a realistic assessment of future policies must take into account that the present character of relations between West

Germany and the U.S. is exceptional. The structure was shaped under exceptional political conditions and was meant to answer the obvious military and political threat to free Europe which was exerted by the Soviet empire and which Europeans at the time were unable to meet on their own.

To accept full American protection in the framework of the Alliance, therefore, seemed reasonable and the only alternative to Soviet hegemony in all of Europe. That the U.S. would assume special responsibilities within this Atlantic Alliance also made sense: economically it was by far the strongest member of the Alliance; militarily it controlled nuclear arsenals vastly superior to those of the Soviet Union and out of reach for all European members; and politically the preservation of a free Western Europe was in the overriding U.S. interest.

Conditions such as these are never permanent. In fact, those facts which supported the original decisions to construct the Atlantic Alliance have all changed, yet the structure of the Alliance continues to exist. It remains as the institutional answer to assumptions that may no longer be valid, to experiences which we shared during the past 30 years that may no longer be applicable to present and future needs. We still assume that Europe is unable to protect its freedom against a Soviet threat and to maintain peace on the Continent; we continue to consider U.S. willingness to respond to any Soviet attack with all-out nuclear force, if necessary, as an indispensable precondition for the freedom of Western Europe and therefore as existential to our survival as free nations.

3. Yet voices are growing in number that question the validity of these basic assumptions of the Alliance or challenge them outright. At the time of the Polish coup, when the U.S. asked their European partners to cooperate in imposing economic sanctions against the Soviet Union (thus exercising the special responsibilities, as they saw them, resulting from their leadership position in NATO), Jacques Chirac is quoted as saying: "Can we seriously say that this Europe of 250 million people must depend on the U.S. for its defense? This is not serious; it is not reasonable." U.S. Ambassador to the Federal Republic Arthur Burns, in his first major address in Bonn in December 1981, warned European leaders that the current European atmosphere and statements of some European leaders could set off a backlash in America.

> There may well be a growing sentiment in America to turn back upon itself and let Europe depend for its security and freedom upon its own resources or upon Soviet good will. Isolationism is by no means the alternative that my country seeks. But many Americans are wondering whether Europeans are sufficiently mindful of the fact that the Atlantic Alliance has made a free, prosperous and peaceful Western Europe possible during the last 30 years.

American troops, he added, "will not stay if they are not welcome" in Western Europe. The *Wall Street Journal* in March 1982 voiced the sentiments of many Americans:

The most pertinent argument against U.S. involvement in NATO is the most obvious. Thirty-five years after World War II, Europe is capable of looking after itself. Western Europe has approximately 250 million vigorous inhabitants possessing sophisticated technology, excellent management skills, a capacity for capital formation and a claim for some mutuality of interests. Unified they match about 80 million Russians plus about 170 million disparate peoples under Russian rule. It is appropriate for Western Europeans to forge an alliance among themselves.

In making his statement, Ambassador Burns made two things clear: (1) the United States does not have an alternative to its present engagement in Europe and the Atlantic Alliance; (2) the U.S. — as a consequence — does not consider its engagement in NATO to be of such paramount importance for the protection of its own national interests that it excludes the consideration of alternative ways to serve this interest. If this interpretation is not totally wrong — and careful scrutiny of opinions at political, mass media and academic levels in the U.S. during the last two years indicates that it is not — then this in itself constitutes a dramatic departure from the assumptions we continue to make in the framework of the Alliance.

4. There are those who suggest that things can be straightened out and we all can return to the days of mutual understanding if we only tried, consulted with one another more often and increased mutual exchange of people on all levels of society. Others — in the U.S. and in Europe — feel that the present Administration's new ways of defining U.S. positions and identity, its new language and willingness to discuss defense options unacceptable to Europeans, have contributed significantly to the present strains in the Alliance. Remedy this practice, they suggest, and the strains will pass away. Still others, mostly in the U.S., look upon the Europeans' lack of understanding for U.S. positions as a major source of misunderstanding.

Even if it were true that discussing realities in harsh terms may make it harder to accept the results, it does not in itself invalidate those results. To discuss the realities of the doctrine of flexible response must indeed be intolerable to those in West Germany or elsewhere for whom the difference between tactical and strategic nuclear weapons offers no consolation when it comes to the use of the former to avoid the application of the latter. But what is discussed here is well established NATO doctrine shared by all since its adoption in the 1960s.

Neither tough language nor the possible deterioration of mutual understanding within the younger generations of responsible citizens on both sides of the Atlantic can explain the problems the Alliance is facing today. At the core of the matter, what we experience is the growing contradiction between realities of our times and their demands on the one side and institutions that embody past realities and experience, on the other side.

5. To this, as far as the Alliance is concerned, is added a new outlook on needs and priorities in Europe and the U.S. It is expressed mainly but not exclusively by members of the younger generation. They see the situation as exceptional and question the permanent stability of an arrangement that

assumes American readiness to sacrifice its very existence for the protection of freedom in Western Europe. Many of them consider such an assumption unwise or even irresponsible. What many of us might take as an ill-advised departure from proven patterns of action seems to the young generation like a return to an evaluation of our Atlantic relationship that is guided by well-proven rules of conduct between nations. For them, relying on the common heritage of culture and religion as the sole foundation of a long-term relationship between nations seems rather sentimental and signals a certain lack of realism. They, it seems, prefer clear answers to equally clear issues of national interest — congruent if possible, divergent where necessary, honestly and unsentimentally defined in any case. Common heritage and culture, they may argue, will facilitate this task, but they cannot substitute for it.

There is a lot to be said for this position. It does not negate the benefits we have drawn from the Atlantic Alliance, nor does it suggest dissolving NATO. Instead, it calls for a reappraisal of the structure of our Atlantic relationship in light of changed conditions, facts and interests. This, it seems to me, is a fair and reasonable demand. If it is met openly and without efforts to avoid issues or questions that are felt to be improper by those whose vested interests in existing institutions, time-honored experience or established wisdom are at stake, then we will not only have a fruitful and creative dialogue across the Atlantic, within Europe and between the generations. We shall then also have a real chance to come up with answers that can find majority support similar to the answers that we found in the 1950s to the problems and issues of that decade.

There are three areas of policy in which such a reappraisal to me seems most urgent: (1) the present structure, objectives and purposes of NATO; (2) economic and social development on both sides of the Atlantic and its relevance to the Alliance and its members; and (3) the changing outlook on values, objectives and purposes of modern Western society. Not all of what is involved in these areas directly relates to the Alliance and U.S.-German relations, but the questions that are of relevance to these issues are bound to influence in one way or another the cohesion of the Alliance and the substance of our dialogue.

1. Discussion about reforming NATO is by no means new. Many efforts have been made in the last 35 years to modernize NATO's institutions, its forms of cooperation and its structure to comply with new needs or changes in underlying assumptions. Still, it seems to me, the more recent debate on the future of NATO reaches deeper. Two reasons can be identified that could account for the different quality of the debate. First, reduction of economic growth-rates in the face of increasing demands on public funds has brought defense spending into direct and increasingly intensive competition with social and economic demands for public spending. The resulting conflicts have not only increased the political burden of proof that must be met when military spending is increased in the face of cuts in social

outlays. They have also sharpened public awareness of the cost of defense and have contributed to the erosion of confidence in the expertise of those who in the past were largely entrusted with defense decisions.

As a result, to maintain public consensus for defense spending and the underlying strategies has become more complicated and difficult. Members of the Alliance react to this change differently. The readiness of some to bear existing or increased defense burdens has lessened. As a consequence, their estimates of the danger facing Europe and the Alliance differs from other members of the Alliance. A lack of agreement on this vital issue within NATO is the result.

The second reason for a changed debate relates to parity. The arrival of parity between the United States and the Soviet Union in both strategic and tactical nuclear systems — in the face of continued Soviet superiority in conventional fighting power — has thrown grave doubts on the continued validity of the present NATO doctrine of flexible response. In addition, the creation of readily available mobile forces by the U.S. to meet its responsibilities and defend its national interests — and what the U.S. considers those of its Allies — in areas of the world outside of NATO territory has affected the division of labor within the Alliance. The implied terms of the change are that the U.S. should bear virtually the entire burden of global defense at large but that the Allies should sustain a much greater part of the defense of their own regions.

Such developments lead to substantial division and disagreement on some fundamentals which require agreement if the Alliance is to function. More important, however, the basic assumption of NATO has come into doubt: that the U.S. is still willing to risk having a nuclear exchange with the Soviets that could mean trading the destruction of Chicago to save Bonn. To many the American nuclear "umbrella" today seems purely imaginary. Surely the President of the U.S. can still answer a Soviet attack on Europe with a strategic nuclear response. Yet, as Irving Kristol observed in the *Wall Street Journal* (March 12, 1983), "The people of Western Europe have perceived that any such reaction by any U.S. President is very, very unlikely — would, indeed, be stupid. Their governments continue to say otherwise, but they are speaking into the wind, with hollow voices."

One could argue that doubts about the readiness of the U.S. to answer Soviet military aggression with strategic nuclear weapons, thus involving U.S. territory, have plagued NATO before. Indeed, the doctrine of flexible response owes its existence to doubts that massive retaliation was a proper response to local military conflict in Europe. Today's doubts, however, are not those voiced by experts; they are the consequence of public debate. In the 1960s nuclear strategy in Europe was decided by an informed few — John Barry called them a "tiny nuclear elite" — on behalf of an only intermittently interested public. Public acceptability of the doctrine hung upon the opinion of those few.

Today we have public participation in the determination of nuclear policy. It seems that the nuclear elite can no longer give clear leads or guidance in the present debate because within the elite itself there is disagreement on what policy to follow. The role of conventional defense as a possible alternative to early use of nuclear weapons is one of the issues. Many warn that to rely on conventional defense would in effect leave Europe unprotected. Others, like U.S. General Bernard Rogers, press for an increase in conventional deterrent to avoid an early choice of "going nuclear or capitulate." They feel that Europe could raise the threshold to nuclear exchange substantially if it were only willing to shoulder that burden. Kristol, with whom I fully agree on this point, defines the issue when he states:

> If we were all unwilling to shoulder that burden, then we are simply unworthy of the liberties we seek to preserve. A nation or an alliance that prefers mass annihilation to higher taxes or a diminution of social services will, when the crunch comes, surely decide that appeasement is preferable to both.

It is both the number of basic issues in dispute within NATO and the new quality of their debate that makes common defense of the Alliance one of the most urgent areas of concern. The U.S.-German dialogue alone cannot supply the answers, but in shaping future Alliance policy both sides will have great influence. The way we conduct our dialogue and organize our cooperation should recognize this importance.

2. Trade between Europe and the U.S. is the lifeblood of a free international economy. Both sides of the Atlantic have drawn immense benefits from applying free market principles not only to their domestic economies but to international trade and commerce. Again it was the United States which particularly fostered this prosperity after World War II. West Germany benefited especially from the American decision to assist German reconstruction and thus build up and support the creation of a social-market economy. The idea of open markets protected from restraints of competition by law, as it was first embodied in antitrust legislation, owes much of its success in postwar Germany to U.S. postwar policies between 1947 and 1955. As in defense, the United States with the economic power made postwar recovery in Europe possible and allowed the exhausted "Old Continent" to draw on the resources of the new continent for its revival.

Yet, as is true for defense, conditions also have changed in economic relations within the Alliance. Again, two changes can be singled out as the most significant.

(1) West Europe's economic strength has increased until it practically equals that of the U.S. Although GNP and other indicators of economic performance still show the U.S. ahead in many ways, the margin has become insignificantly small. For all practical purposes, Europe has reached a stage of economic development which permits us to speak of equals on both sides of the Atlantic.

(2) Reduced growth rates, growing problems in the markets of the Third World, and increased difficulties with the rising debts of developing countries have drastically reduced opportunities for expanding national economic activities. International competition for existing markets has therefore be-

come more intense. Protectionism, as a consequence, is on the rise both in Europe and between Europe and the United States. "Political markets" such as steel or farm products have an increased chance to be permanently protected for political reasons.

As a consequence of both these changes, economic considerations have become more important for Alliance policy. One issue is the problem of burden-sharing. Since West Europe's economic potential roughly equals that of the U.S., the redistribution of defense burdens to match the change must become an issue. Increased awareness of the political importance of social programs in the U.S., even in relation to defense, has led to similar questions. It is less accepted in the U.S. today than it used to be that the United States should carry a disproportionally large share of defense costs while Europeans not only continue to perfect social systems but criticize American policy for its lack of respect for principles of social justice. In short, the social dimension of economic policy and the relation of both to defense efforts have entered the picture and further complicate matters.

Questions of burden-sharing have, of course, not only sharpened public attention in the U.S. They have also initiated discussion in Europe on how to define defense burdens and what to include in their determination. One of the questions raised recently concerns the cost to Europe's economy of American monetary policy and its results for interest rates, capital movement and exchange rates. The consequence of public debt in the U.S. for international economic development has been under debate for some time. There is, of course, no readily available alternative to the dollar's role as the most important lead currency. Yet those who try to redefine the "basket of criteria" to determine justice in burden sharing tend to include such indirect burdens as may result for Europe from American national policies. Even if one may not agree with the inclusion of such additional criteria, the validity of the issue cannot be questioned. The web of interdependencies has become more dense. Future dialogue will only lead to acceptable answers if this is accepted.

In addition to these primarily commercial problems, there are growing differences on the strategic dimension of international trade, especially with the East. The extended dispute on the gas pipeline deal with the Soviet Union bears witness to these differences. It was simply the last link in a sequence of controversies over the proper use of trade relations with the Soviets and their satellites for strategic purposes. The wisdom and effect of economic sanctions as an answer to undesired international activities is another subject of debate.

The reasons for these differences are numerous. Economic rivalry and the difficulty to console domestic interests with the consequences of open international markets is one of them. What lies at the heart of much of the dispute, however, is the difference in evaluation of the effects of economic relations with the Soviet Union on its political and strategic behavior. Is it, as Europeans tend to believe, more desirable to have expanding economic relations with the Soviets, or should it be our objective to weaken the Russians economically in order to reduce their military capabilities? Are we more interested in stable economic conditions within Russia to secure political stability in Europe, or are we aiming at "economic warfare" to weaken the Soviet potential for aggression? What are the net gains of sanctions, if any?

As in defense policy, a reappraisal of these and other related issues is in demand. The United States, despite its economic strength and the continuing importance of the dollar as a world currency, no longer dominates the Alliance economically. Some U.S. policies, such as the extra-territorial extension of its laws and administrative decisions, are more or less incompatible with Alliance partnership. They reflect the experience (in economic as well as political relations) of a continent which up to recently did not need to take much notice of the necessity to trade and cooperate in the same economic environment with others — as has been the century-old practice for European countries.

Such reappraisal will make clear that the American and European economies are beset by basically the same kinds of problems (unemployment, rapid increase of cost of existing social programs without corresponding increase in effectiveness, insufficient capital formation in production, growing public deficits, etc.). Solutions to these problems should therefore be sought jointly. To me the overhaul of existing economic doctrine on both sides of the Atlantic is almost as important for the future cohesion of the Alliance as the reexamination of military doctrine. Without such an overhaul we certainly will not be able to find answers to the existing economic difficulties. I agree with those who say that present economic theory will not supply answers to our problems but has rather become the source of them. Long-term democratic consensus on defense, however, requires reasonably sound economic conditions. Our common efforts should therefore concentrate on developing more adequate answers to the economic challenge.

3. Much emphasis has, thirdly, been placed on what is called the change in the value system, both in the U.S. and in Europe. The common cultural, historic and religious heritage of the U.S. and Europe are for good reason considered of great importance to the cohesion of the Alliance. Changes in their composition therefore deserve close attention.

Many changes during the last 35 years took place initially in the U.S., and they presaged similar change in Europe a few years later. But the influence of the American way of life went beyond these phenomena. The English language, English literature, culture, art, and of course the sciences have assumed an almost dominating role in Western Europe. Above all, the development of the social sciences was subject to strong American influence.

This development has been criticized periodically in Europe, especially in France where efforts were made to balance American influence on French culture and science in order to avoid what was considered undue foreign influence. Fortunately, the possibilities for governments in free and open societies to control and restrain such "foreign influence" are small, but the underlying issue is relevant to U.S.-European relations and should not be taken lightly. For the foreseeable future, if ever, Europe will not be able to match U.S. military strength. European economic performance may be equal to that of the U.S. but it will never surpass it substantially or outweigh

American military preponderance. If for no other reason, cultural identity will therefore be of great importance to Europe, and it will also be needed to solve the basic problem facing Europe and the Western World, namely to develop a peace in Europe which ultimately rests on security other than that supplied by a policy of nuclear deterrence.

The perception of changing values in the U.S. and Europe affects consensus on political objectives and priorities. It is therefore important to find out what really takes place and to identify both the changes and their causes correctly. It is my impression that important explanations and operational answers are still missing. The discussion of work ethics in the U.S. and the ostensibly diminishing willingness to work in Germany are good examples. Both assume a decline in the willingness to work, to adhere to the discipline demanded by a highly developed division of labor. Both draw pessimistic conclusions for the future productivity of our economies and the preservation of our standards of living. I have considerable difficulty with such theories. To me they do not account sufficiently for the consequences that a revolutionary expansion of personal income and wealth benefiting a large majority of private households must have on the way people live and on the priorities they set for themselves. What we are witnessing, in effect, is an entire population learning by trial and error how to live under conditions of mass affluence. As in other areas of national policy we should not try to measure and comprehend this phenomenon with standards that were developed when affluence was relevant only for certain minorities rather than for the majority of the population. The meaning of this should be the subject of our dialogue.

Another important phenomenon in the "value area" is the reentry of religion into politics. For most of the 20th century religion had little influence on the development of society and the conduct of its political affairs. Although religious standards were occasionally raised in political arguments, the real effect of religious thinking on popular consensus for important political issues was small. The scientifically-organized and enlightened society seemed to have no need for actively cultivating and renewing religious norms and rules of conduct. The churches themselves have repeatedly observed this and deplored what can be called the "privatization" of religion.

Recently there are signs of a reversal of this development. The most important single incident is official church participation in the debate on moral and ethical aspects of nuclear deterrence. To me this engagement and its political consequences are one of the most important changes in the political scene on both sides of the Atlantic. The actual effect which utterances of church authorities may have on our present public debate is less important than that the officials are participating in the discussion of subjects which fall outside the traditional areas of political concern to churches. The political process is apt to be altered significantly by this. In substance the renewal of church participation in the political debate on nuclear arms or the protection of the environment could mean an end to almost total reliance on scientific and "rational" problem solving.

Science and technology and the priesthood of experts in all their fields had promised almost uninhibited progress. Today we are becoming aware of the price tag. And many, in realizing the enormous consequences of progress in nuclear armament or encroachment of the environment seem ready to withdraw from the priesthood of modern times the sole right to lead society and decide its future. In looking for new authority to help them fill the vacuum created by the shaken faith in the experts, they turn to religion and its body of norms and commandments for guidance and stability.

The purpose of this paper does not permit us to discuss in greater detail the possible ramifications of this change. However, they are surely worth our attention. If a few years ago someone in the U.S. would have suggested that the U.S. Catholic bishops would approve a national pastoral letter addressing itself to the "dynamics of the nuclear arms race" and that the Administration would make efforts to influence the letter's content because of its possible effects on public opinion and consensus, he would have met with disbelief or downright rejection. Yet we are now, in my opinion, witnessing just the beginning of a new kind of involvement by the churches. Decision-making by elected government officials will certainly be influenced by it. Our dialogue should concern itself with the consequences.

4. Although the three areas outlined above can be identified separately they are of course part of a larger whole. In addition there are problems facing future U.S.-European relations that particularly concern the Federal Republic. They have their roots in its geographic location, in the division of the country and in the special situation in Berlin. The future of the free part of Berlin obviously rests on American presence in the former German capital and on U.S. willingness to guarantee free access to and from the city. Nowhere in Europe is the need for continued U.S. engagement more obvious — and nowhere is reality further apart from normality — than in the case of Berlin. The continued existence of the Berlin problem will therefore give U.S.-German relations a unique quality. This quality, however, is not restricted to protection of Berlin's freedom. In one way or another it influences all the U.S.-German relations. The United States has a special interest in maintaining freedom in Western Europe. But the Germans — unless they should separate themselves from the fate of Berlin — have an overriding national interest in the preservation of Berlin's freedom. For the protection of this interest they need the U.S. This need will guide German policy vis-a-vis the U.S. as long as the abnormality of divided Berlin continues to exist.

This abnormality, in turn, focuses our attention on the second issue which gives a special character to U.S.-German relations and sets them apart from relations to other European countries or members of the Western Alliance: the division of Germany. Helmut Kohl during his recent visit to Moscow made it quite clear that Germans will not cease to regard unification of all Germans in freedom as a major national objective. True, the Federal Republic of Germany has opted for Western integration. But Germans are paying a considerable price for this decision. Roughly one quarter of the population and 40 percent of the territory of the whole of Germany in its postwar boundaries are under foreign control. The long-term effects of this are difficult to estimate. I am certain, however, that it will be of importance to future German policy. The Chancellor's conviction, that reunification as envisioned by the German constitution (the "Basic Law") is a historic obligation for all Germans, is shared by a large majority of the population despite the nearly impossible chances to achieve reunification in the foreseeable future.

To secure the freedom of Berlin, the FRG needs the United States. To ease the situation of a divided Germany and make life more bearable for its citizens in the Eastern part, the FRG needs to cooperate with the Soviet Union. The existence of both needs contributes in part to the ambivalence in the U.S.-German relationship I previously mentioned. The Federal Republic will never be in a position to mediate between the superpowers' European interests or bridge the gap between East and West. All West German governments since 1949 have recognized the limitations placed on their foreign policy by the fact that the country must suffer the burden of East-West confrontation through its own divided national identity.

There is, however, a special German interest — apart from general considerations of peace and security — to reduce and eventually overcome the antagonisms that make up East-West confrontation in Europe. If German reunification — and each single step in this direction — requires the cooperation of both the U.S. and the Soviet Union, continued antagonism between the superpowers is detrimental to this major objective of West German policy. It is for this reason that the Federal Republic watches any increase in East-West antagonisms and confrontation with added alarm. A bipolar situation in Europe is undesirable for all concerned. But it means an added burden on Germany; a reduction of tension in Europe means added opportunities to reduce the abnormalities resulting from national separation, barbed wire fences and the wall around Berlin.

Nonetheless, it is not only Berlin, a divided country and long-term policy of reunification that add special quality to U.S.-German relations apart from West German participation in European-U.S. relations. There also exists in the United States special sensibilities and sensitiveness toward Germany that are worth examining. One of the sources has to do with the Nazi period and holocaust. The normal irritations that may arise in the relationships between nations are often amplified in the German case because of these factors, which stem in part from the American Jewish population and in part from Americans who continue to see the FRG as a country under special U.S. stewardship and hence feel disappointed by expressions of German independence or emancipation from past dependencies. U.S.-German relations have never been free from such emotional distortions. To recognize their existence is necessary if we want to overcome them. With the postwar generation of Germans assuming political responsibility, the chances to reduce these special sources of irritation are good.

The key to future U.S.-German relations lies in Europe, not Germany. It is Europe that must develop a political identity of its own and that must assume corresponding responsibilities. As I have tried to show, the present relationship between Europe and the U.S. is not a stable one. It can be explained and presently justified as the result of an extraordinary historic situation — the postwar period and East-West confrontation in this time — to which equally extraordinary answers had to be found. To continuously apply these answers in the face of dramatically changed circumstances, however, is not a feasible long-term concept. What we have today, with NATO in its present structure and with the NATO decision of December 1979 to negotiate with the Soviets and be ready to deploy medium-range nuclear missiles if negotiations fail, may make sense under current political conditions, but whether it can serve as a basis for long-term policy is another matter.

In the long run it seems rather unlikely that the American population will continue to accept the notion that Europeans are unable to organize their own defense and shoulder responsibilities for areas of the world, such as the Middle East or the Mediterranean, which are of vital importance to them. To be sure, there are no indications of an immediate reversal of present U.S. policy or a sudden refusal on the part of the majority of the U.S. electorate to continue to protect European security. A majority of the American people continues to support the present U.S. role in Europe. This, however, should not mislead us to believe that nothing needs to be done. Rather, efforts to reform the present defense structure and search for long-term alternatives must take place at a time when we are not pressed by the need for immediate action. It is only then that we can hope to be ready with alternative structures to secure peace and freedom in Europe, if and when the present ones will no longer be able to do the job.

What is often referred to as a period of transition means, in effect, maintaining existing structures and attaining policy objectives with them while, at the same time, new ones are developed to facilitate the orderly transition from the old to the new way of solving the same problem. This is not an easy task. Working on alternatives to existing policies signals to the general public that those responsible consider the present structures no longer adequate. Yet until new ways are found and agreed upon, popular support for the present way of doing things must continue. Political leaders have to generate public support for political instruments which they feel have to be replaced. In the face of the difficulties this creates, it is even more important to make clear that we are not about to change our basic policy and structures with which we try to attain them. And the majority support for the basic objective of securing peace and freedom must be maintained.

The present structure of defense in Europe resulted from U.S. acquiescence to Soviet control of Eastern Europe during the 1950s because the alternative seemed to be war. The resulting arrangement was then and is today considered to be a stable one. But developments in Poland and elsewhere in Eastern Europe signal change. What has been and probably still is a structure securing stability in Europe may thus soon become a source of instability in Europe, and thus the cause of war. The situation of both the U.S. and the Soviet Union has changed. It is therefore only fair to say, as William Pfaff observed in a recent reflection in *The New Yorker*, that

> ... we have a positive interest, as does the Soviet Union, in replacing this system, which can no longer be relied upon, with an agreement that would substitute political for military guarantees of security to both sides in Europe.... A new attempt to find a political settlement in Europe would be time-consuming and complicated to negotiate and would possess a real cost in destabilizing the existing security arrangements. It would presume a minimal willingness to accommodate on the part of the Soviet government.

But it also would

> ... represent an attempt to capitalize intelligently upon the Soviet Union's waning power to control the insurgent nationalism of Eastern Europe, and upon the inevitable and approaching end to America's guardianship of Western Europe — and thus to turn to constructive use what cannot be avoided.

I agree with this analysis. It takes notice of the need to develop new instruments and structures to secure peace and stability in Europe while the present ones still serve their purpose. The argument that NATO has secured the peace in Europe for the last 35 years is certainly a valid one. NATO has kept the peace! But this does not make sure that it will or even can do so in the future. Given the dramatic changes in underlying conditions, a good argument can be made — and actually is being made — for the need to reform and develop new ways to serve the old purpose: to keep the peace and protect freedom.

Obviously the Federal Republic will have to play a prominent part in this process. As one of the leading European powers it must not only contribute substantially to the "Europeanization" of defense efforts. The FRG will also have to make contributions relative to its economic and political resources to European integration, to the gradual elimination of poverty in southern and south-east Europe, and to the needed changes in economic structure throughout Europe.

In turn the Federal Republic will expect from Europe support for its national objective of gradual reunification. European governments have always held that such a process can only take place in the framework of a reunification of Europe. The division of Germany is, in all consequence, a division of Europe. To overcome this division is a European political objective, and it must be a European objective to extend the order of peace which the Western European countries have to those of Eastern Europe.

To the Federal Republic of Germany the acceptance of these European political objectives is an inseparable condition for its own integration in the European community of nations. Without such acceptance, a contradiction between the long-term goal of reunification and European integration of the free part of Germany would become unavoidable. Thus the special German interest in this part of European policy and its willingness to support European unity even when the Community's attraction to other member nations may seem to decline.

There are many who regard German or European reunification as impossible to achieve and therefore unsuited to serve as a political objective governing European policy and the reform of Europe's defense structure. I do not share this view. Even if it seems pragmatic, it ignores the historic dimension of the problem and is therefore not, in the real meaning of the word, a political point-of-view. In his address to the CDU convention in Cologne in May 1983 Franz Josef Strauss reminded his audience that he had been brought up to believe there existed a historic antagonism between France and Germany, an *Erbfeindschaft* passing from generation to generation, and that it would have been absurd at the time to suggest it could be overcome. Today, he continued, we are friends and allies and only a fool could even consider the possibility of military conflict between us. "I am convinced," he said, "that Marxism will loose the struggle between the systems if we ourselves remain convinced of our free system, and if we carry this conviction across into the East." "This," he stated, "may sound utopian. But all important goals of mankind had to begin as utopian if they were to end as reality."

U.S.-German relations will, of course, be affected by this long-term objective. For many reasons, they will remain special and unique for a long time to come. But West Germany's main political goals require a European policy. To reduce confrontation and superpower antagonism in Europe is something only Europe acting as an entity can accomplish. Only Europe, utilizing its resources and capabilities can overcome the bipolar power structure that exists today and threatens to reduce all major world problems to an East-West dimension. Only Europe can break up the duopolistic situation involving continent-sized nations armed to their teeth and becoming ever more deeply involved in the duopolistic process of reacting to reactions, of imitating one another militarily and strategically without a reasonable chance to stop the process.

To envision such possibilities means opening the floor for questions. And agreement about the right questions to ask must stand at the forefront of our quest for new structures and institutions. It is the definition of these questions — indeed, the readiness to have them asked — that should concern us most as we continue our dialogue.

This chapter has outlined several questions relevant to U.S-German relations, and to some of the questions we have suggested possible answers. As the dialogue continues, though, one thing is certain. We shall continue to work on the fulfillment of an age-old dream: namely, the dream that led those 13 families on their long and strenuous voyage across the Atlantic and to Germantown — to have peace and liberty.

SUSTAINING THE AMERICAN-GERMAN RELATIONSHIP IN A TIME OF STRATEGIC AND ATTITUDINAL CHANGE

by James R. Schlesinger

Sustaining the ties that bind together the democratic societies of the North Atlantic I take to be the irreducible minimum for the preservation of what we, sometimes hopefully, sometimes propagandistically, refer to as the Free World. When the latter term is not being used in its all-inclusive sense of those nations not subservient to the Soviet Union, it is evident that the democratic societies of the North Atlantic, characterized by free institutions, represent the real heart of the Free World. That those ties have been subject to increasing, though not irreparable, strain during the last decade is as evident as it is regrettable.

At base, those strains may be said to reflect a dramatic alteration in the military balance which has had two major consequences. First, the United States is no longer universally regarded as able to provide unqualified military protection for Western Europe — as it could for some thirty years after World War II. The enhanced responsibilities and efforts thereby imposed upon the Western European countries quite naturally lead to a desire for a stronger voice in the determination of the common policies of the West. Second, the global reach of Soviet power, reflecting the change in the military balance, leads to troubles in the Third World. Many, if not most, Europeans fear that such tensions reflecting superpower rivalries will feed back into Western Europe and disturb the *modus vivendi* that they believe they can maintain with the Soviet Union. That concern is perhaps at its greatest in regard to the Middle East, reflecting European dependence on somewhat insecure sources of crude oil. Yet it also reflects troubles in Latin America, Africa and other parts of Asia.

In addition, American political practices and attitudes have been undergoing change that has increasingly and painfully come to the attention of Europeans particularly since 1975. The image of the United States, powerful, possessing national unity, and steady in its foreign policy objectives, has given way to a perception of the United States as divided, erratic and unpredictable, plagued by an 18th century constitution, and occasionally provincial. Belief that the United States could behave irresponsibly has come as a shock to Europeans, who, whatever their own practices, long assumed that the United States should be immune to this ailment.

Within Europe these new doubts have been both obvious and most important in Germany, where earlier confidence in the United States had been highest. At the political level they have been openly expressed by former Chancellor Helmut Schmidt.

Despite these new strains, the desirability of pooling political and military strengths across the North Atlantic remains as high, if not higher, than it ever was. Without the stiffening presence of the Western superpower, the European democracies could not long withstand pressure from the East. Both their independence and their institutions would gradually crumble over time. While the United States could for the foreseeable future preserve its independence and its institutions within the Western Hemisphere, the character of this society would undergo unwelcome and painful changes in the event of Soviet domination of Western Europe. It would become a more small-minded and less tolerant society, as the domain of freedom shrank around the globe. For all of us, therefore, the stakes in the Atlantic connection remain high. For free Europe — despite some occasionally silly chatter — these bonds are indispensable.

In the past, significant differences in basic attitudes between the United States and continental Europe have been less important than they are now. When interests are regarded as virtually synonomous, underlying differences of attitude may be ignored. In periods of strain, however, when the goal is to knit together a relationship somewhat frayed, those subtle differences deserve careful study. To understand the present discontents and future prospects, one must understand the past. For the discontents of the present will be burdened by memories of a happier period in the relationship between the United States and Germany. America will be burdened with the memory of the more tranquil postwar Germany — a more deferential partner, absorbed by the *Wirtschaftswunder*. Germany, in turn, will be burdened by the memory of the earlier American Colossus, only mildly challenged elsewhere and capable of dealing with such challenges. It will recall an America possessed of national unity, supreme in its power and self-confidence, normally generous and outward-looking in economic affairs, and an all-powerful protector. It will, in short, recall the postwar America, confident in its nigh-on-universal mission, before its own time of troubles and before the global reach of the Soviet Union.

It is necessary for me to touch upon the underlying American attitude toward foreign affairs, a subject already discussed with great erudition by Gordon Craig. These attitudes are very deep-seated and reflect the American experience of growing to world power in continental isolation, presumably guided by manifest destiny and with little need to adjust its aspirations to those of other serious contenders. The attitude is quite different from that of continental Europe, with its historic focus on power, nurtured by dynastic rivalries and by reasons of state, and with its memory of the ups and downs of political fortunes. Only memories of figures like Gladstone are able substantially to comprehend these underlying American impulses. In a phrase, the American impulse in foreign affairs is quintessentially "idealist-romantic."

Since its emergence on the world scene in this century the United States has oscillated in its moods. There are the periods of missionary zeal in which we Americans, through our goodwill and energy, have sought to remake other nations in accordance with our own lights. Alternatively, the United States has gone into periods of withdrawal, reverting as it were to the aboriginal isolation that was a physical fact of life down to the end of the nineteenth century. The missionary zeal does not disappear, but it does become passive. It has been a time-honored American belief that by establishing a model society here in North America, other nations would be induced to emulate our practices — through the persuasive power of good example. This belief in the uncontaminated beacon, reflected in liberal isolationism, is best exemplified by a figure like Robert LaFollette. Conservative isolationism, a generalized disdain for the contamination in world affairs, was exhibited in the 1920s and '30s.

Whether Europeans view this American impulse with irritation, amusement, or simply perplexity, they would be ill-advised to disregard either it or its implications for their policies and their security. As I have indicated, that impulse is very deep-seated, tracing back to the New England Puritans. An early New England divine, the Reverend Samuel Danforth, in his election sermon in 1670 referred to that mission as the "Errand Into the Wilderness." From the New England model, it had been hoped, would come the guiding light for the reformation of all Christendom. Imagine the consternation, indeed the despair, of the second generation of Puritans, when it became evident after the Puritan Revolution in England that the New England model not only was not followed, it was consciously rejected. That constituted but the first of many such American disappointments. Nonetheless, that visionary impulse, increasingly in a secularized form of democratic reform, has served to energize American foreign policy over the past century.

The missionary zeal that has driven American foreign policy in its active periods is most clearly illustrated by the figures of Woodrow Wilson and Jimmy Carter, and to an extent by the rhetoric of Franklin Roosevelt. At least in its early stages, the Reagan Administration reflected a different set of impulses. It did not wish to withdraw fron overseas involvement, as had the Republican administrations of the 1920s, but it was restless with the restraints on American independence of action imposed by other players in the international scene, including our allies. That phase, sometimes referred to as global unilateralism, has hopefully now ended.

All Europeans should take seriously this fundamental missionary zeal of the American society in both its active and passive phases. In the American society, foreign policy, in part, wells up from below and must certainly be sustained from below. The underlying beliefs of the American public are rarely conveyed to Europeans, however, when they talk with American diplomats or even American scholars. But it is necessary to bear in mind that the American people are now moved by concepts of *Realpolitik* or even of national interests, as defined for them by elites. Unless our foreign tasks can be combined with that American missionary zeal, they will have tough going. Therein lies a primary reason for the difficulties in achieving national unity today.

American support for Europe, though difficult for many Europeans to understand, ultimately rests on no sophisticated appreciation of national interests or the balance of power, but rather a simple, yet invaluable belief that the European democracies are populated by good people who deserve our protection.

This simple attitude is frequently ignored or misunderstood by European leaders, who will suggest in all seriousness that American national interest (as they define it) will force the United States to retain its forces in Europe in order to provide protection. The ultimate example is provided by a recent French foreign minister, who — pressing Cartesian logic beyond its limits — observed that the Europeans could insult, torment, or humiliate the Americans, and still the Americans would be obliged by the national interest to provide protection for Europe.

Therein lies a grave misconception. European definitions of our national interests be damned, one can almost hear the visceral American response. In the pursuit of righteousness, the American society will do unwise as well as wise things. European statesmen should recognize there is more of Savonarola than there is of Richelieu in the American makeup.

At no time has the idealistic strain in American foreign policy been better illustrated than in the post-World War II period. The reconstruction of the European nations, friend and foe alike, was facilitated by the Marshall Plan. Given the extent of the devastation, the opportunity for economic reconstruction was, of course, even greater in Germany than elsewhere. But even more important, what better fields of endeavor for the American missionary zeal than the ruins of Hitler's new order? What better opportunity would there be to demonstrate American virtue than to lead the erring sinners to the light and (despite the teaching of history) to create in Germany a new society based (if only unconsciously) on the American model. Germans — in their fear, hunger, and despair — proved responsive. They had not the fractiousness of the French, the complacency of the British, or the lighthearted lack of seriousness of the Italians. Indeed, the expectations developed in the early postwar period continue to influence attitudes today. Americans are still more astonished when Germany rebuffs proffered policy guidelines and goes its own way than when other European states do the same.

Particularly after Korea, American attention turned gradually from reconstruction to rearmament. German rearmament began in 1955. Given its exposed position, it should be noted, no government in the Alliance was stronger than the German government in its embrace of the full logic of reliance on the nuclear deterrent. Indeed, by 1961, when Robert McNamara began the initial efforts to strengthen conventional forces within the Alliance, the German government offered the most vigorous resistance on the grounds it would weaken overall deterrence.

Over the years, the weight of the German military role within the Alliance has become ever more significant — despite the postwar constraints on the German political role. Britain was economically strained and was preoccupied elsewhere. The French withdrawal from the NATO military organization, the removal of NATO headquarters and military bases from France, and the non-coherence of French military strategy (to put it most politely) with that of the rest of the Alliance inevitably increased the importance of the Federal Republic of Germany.

When I became Secretary of Defense in 1973, I was determined (despite all of the difficulties of the post-Vietnam period) to strengthen German-American bilateral cooperation within the framework of the Alliance. I was also determined to strengthen the conventional capabilities of the Alliance, thereby shoring up the deterrent. Despite the prophecies of those who felt that American forces would be reduced under the pressures of the Mansfield Amendment, our deployments were strengthened. Two American brigades were added to our force structure in West Germany — one in the North, outside the existing American zone of responsibility.

I had benefited, if only vicariously, from McNamara's earlier, if abortive, attempts to strengthen the conventional deterrent. I therefore proceeded in such a way that the strengthening of the conventional forces would not be taken by the German government as weakening in any way the nuclear deterrent. By analogy to America's own strategic forces, I developed the concept of the NATO Triad, in which all three legs of the Triad — conventional, tactical nuclear, and strategic — were regarded as mutually supporting. Thus, the strengthening of the conventional leg would be understood as synergistically increasing the deterrence efficacy of the two nuclear legs. Finally, I attempted better to tie in America's strategic forces to deterrence in Europe through the concept of selective strikes. In all this, I was vigorously supported by George Leber, then the German Defense Minister, and ultimately, though more ambivalently, by Helmut Schmidt.

West Germany had become, through the press of circumstance, inevitably and indisputably the European bastion of NATO. In strengthening German-American bilateral cooperation, I was prepared, despite some nervousness among our diplomats, to describe the German position in precisely that way — *the European Bastion of NATO*. The passing of the simplicities of massive retaliation and of the tripwire concept, the newly-endorsed strategy of flexible response and the need for forward defense made such an acknowledgment overdue. I revert to these actions of a decade ago in this paper because it points to the need for the continuous adjustment of the Alliance military posture, as the power of the Soviet Union and the position of the Warsaw Pact alter. I shall return to this subject later.

The old order changeth, as Tennyson tells us — sometimes yielding place to the new with surprising speed. Certainly that was the case in the transformation of American foreign policy in the five-year period after World War II. The initial decisions — bringing the boys home, the sudden termination of Lend-Lease, the rapid demobilization, the end of the draft — all bore the earmarks of the primordial American policy of disengagement from the affairs of Europe. That policy had earlier been interrupted only by brief and intermittent crusades to remove from the world scene leaders so evil that they would disrupt the international order. But, with success in the crusade, America, duty done and believing that the international order was normally self-sustaining, felt it could withdraw to the Western Hemisphere.

In 1945, it appeared that the cyclical process would be repeated. Yet, starting with the Greek-Turkish aid program in 1947 and reaching its climax after the onset of the Korean War, American policy was revolutionized. The United States — acting in response to demands, indeed beseeching demands, from European leaders — began to deploy forces in Europe *on a permanent basis* to deal with the perceived threat from the East.

In its early years the North Atlantic Alliance, whatever the formalities, represented an extension to Europe by the United States of a unilateral guarantee of protection. For a quarter century thereafter that guarantee was not seriously doubted. A Charles de Gaulle could feel such confidence in the power balance that he could rhetorically question the American commitment to European defense for his own domestic purposes — and still feel utterly secure in its protective cover. However, it should be noted, the unilateral guarantee that underlay European security has imposed a growing psychological burden on the effective functioning of the Alliance, as the strategic situation has changed and as the Alliance has matured.

Nonetheless, given the altered constellation of forces that emerged at the war's end and the clear possibility of the extinguishing of the European democracies, the transformation of American policy should not be regarded as adventitious. With the changed balance of power, that transformation merely made permanent the underlying, if more episodic goals of the United States in both world wars. America is, by and large, a creation of European culture — a reflection of European hopes and of European failed hopes. The American Revolution was fought to preserve the liberties of Englishmen. America's political institutions are British institutions — reflecting largely British experience and British political theorists, though there is to a lesser degree some continental flavor drawn from the Enlightenment philosophers. America is, as General de Gaulle once remarked, "the daughter of Europe." It may be a daughter surprisingly robust, muscular, and even crude. Of late, according to European tastes, it may exhibit more of an element of *machismo* than is desirable. Nonetheless, a sense of filial responsibility makes the postwar transformation of U.S. policy less than wholly surprising.

I have mentioned the speed with which the old order can sometimes change. Sometimes, indeed, the speed of change is greater in accepting new responsibilities than it is in adjusting aspirations to a reduced position of power. In making such adjustments during the last decade the American public has been a little reluctant to abandon those expectations built up during America's period of dominance — and that has caused considerable disquietude in Europe (as well as elsewhere). The preponderance enjoyed by the United States during the decades of the 1950s and '60s in military, economic, and political matters represents a unique episode in world history, ultimately based upon transient conditions. Yet the expectations of the American public still reflect to a considerable degree the attitudes fostered by that period of preponderance — and frustration occurs when those expectations are not fulfilled. In the past decade such frustrations have caused problems for the Alliance from the American side.

The association of the democracies of the North Atlantic, I suggested earlier, remains an indispensable instrument for the preservation in the world of a substantial arena for our free institutions. Yet, it is an association of sovereign states whose perspectives, interests, and internal pressures are certainly not identical. That implies some broad constraints on common action. It also underlies the inherent limitations of the Alliance, not always understood.

It is my basic belief that preserving cohesion among the allies should remain our first priority, transcending all the lesser disputes about military or economic instruments. It is my ultimate fear that a tendency to pitch expectations too high and to demand too much of the Alliance could eventually undermine its necessary vitality. The Alliance, with all of its defects, remains an indispensable element for stability on the world scene.

NATO, it must steadily be recalled, is a defensive alliance. It provides mutual protection for the territories of the signatory parties, should they come under attack. That is a substantial pledge, but it is all that is pledged. The Alliance creates no arrangements and establishes no policies for Central America or Afghanistan. Indeed, all that lies south of the Tropic of Cancer is explicitly, if artificially excluded. I emphasize this limited territorial reach in light of the pernicious belief that an alliance with defined purposes is failing if there is an absence of common purpose outside of the area of definition.

One occasionally encounters the belief in Europe that the United States — a world power within the Alliance — is somehow behaving irresponsibly if it takes actions elsewhere in the world that result in any increased tension in Europe. Of equal and perhaps greater importance is the belief in the United States that, if our allies fail to support our position or our requests in Afghanistan or Central America, somehow the Alliance has become meaningless. Such attitudes must be resisted. If they are not resisted, based as they are on unreasonable expectations, they will ultimately undermine the indispensable political cohesion of the Western democracies.

One scarcely needs to be reminded that mutual irritations of this sort have been commonplace during the past decade. Open expression of such irritations had been reduced by the coming into power in several capitals of governments with less diversified attitudes on major East-West issues. But those irritations still exist — and not below the surface. To past disputes over Iran, the Moscow Olympics, Afghanistan, Middle Eastern policy, the falling American dollar, and the failure of the United States to deploy missiles in Europe as a counterweight to the SS-20, we have more recently added disputes over Poland, gas pipelines, trade credits, American deficits, interest rates, the rising American dollar, and the deployment of those American missiles in response to prior European requests. Differences of view are unavoidable, but no such difference should be allowed to take a life of its own. The combination of too high expectations and too little forbearance among the allies has too frequently resulted in the transformation of what were expected to be common measures bringing pressure to bear on the Soviet Union into issues of disunity for the West.

Given the present balance, I would argue for the transcendent importance of the political role of the Alliance. Above all else, it must be respected, preserved and nurtured. No subsidy will add so much to the economic strength of the Soviet Union, no military deployment or measure will add so much to the confidence in the deterrent or the strength of our military posture, that such secondary issues should be allowed to threaten Alliance political cohesion.

From the American perspective, preservation of a free Europe remains a most important, perhaps the ultimate, foreign policy objective. That objective is sufficiently momentous in itself that Americans should rein in their expectations regarding common purposes outside of the area of the Alliance. Yet, in moments of strain and irritation, I find far too few who continuously bear in mind this paramount consideration. The unity of the Alliance should not be sacrificed because of European attitudes on, say, Nicaragua or the Palestinian problem.

The achievement of common goals and common actions outside of the NATO territory, while desirable, still remains secondary. Such common actions are not required by the Alliance itself. If common action is to be achieved — as we should continuously strive to do — it will require the further nurturing of the political relationships born in the Alliance context itself. Nonetheless, disappointments are inevitable, and hopes should not be pitched too high. Achievement of the original purposes of the Alliance is in itself a substantial accomplishment that continues to merit our close attention. Partly as a result of the success of the Alliance over the years, attention has been diverted to less stable areas of the globe, where inherently there exists a greater diversity of interest. Consequently the danger exists that the necessity of Alliance cohesion, now mandatory as a consequence of the shift in the power balance, will be forgotten.

The political role of the Alliance is all-important. Alliance cohesion must be nurtured and preserved. That calls upon all of us to recognize the need for and the ultimate limits to coalition politics. It severely circumscribes unilateralism, which can be pursued by *any* of the allies only at peril.

The questions of deterrence and defense continue to lie at the heart of the German-American and European-American relationships. In the absence of a movement toward European unification (including defense) or a major buildup of European forces, and of a coherent strategy, the capacity of Europe to resist pressures from the East without the stiffening presence of the Western superpower will remain inadequate. With all the problems in both forces and strategy, the deterrent posture established by NATO has been sufficient to maintain the peace in Europe for almost forty years — putting aside Soviet moves to keep insubordinate satellites in line. Disputes among the allies over economic issues or over actions taken in the Third World tend to draw attention away from this fundamental reality. Yet, past success should not be the basis for present complacency. The questions remain: Will our military posture remain sufficient in the future, and can that posture be sustained?

If one takes a long-term view regarding NATO forces and strategy, one could argue that it is a history of periodic failures — with patchwork covering of the failures to achieve force objectives. At the Lisbon conference of 1952 a force goal of ninety divisions was established — a target that has never been approached, even after the onset of German rearmament. One might suggest that the failure of the Lisbon targets is representative of the problems that continue to haunt the Alliance.

The arrival of the Eisenhower Administration in 1953 led to an abandonment of such goals. The Administration was committed to budget reductions. The "New Look" in strategy featured significant cutbacks in planned conventional forces and the embrace of a strategy involving immediate nuclear retaliation against major Soviet aggression. The stated premise of the strategy was that the West could never match the "hordes" of Soviet manpower — a premise political in nature and taken in flat disregard of the relative bases of population in the two blocs. Tactical nuclear weapons were produced in the 1950s and began to move to Europe. The strategy of the Alliance was engraved in 14/2 featuring immediate nuclear response.

The strategy has always been questioned by many in the military services, such as Maxwell Taylor, and by almost the entire community of defense intellectuals. It was a strategy that provided satisfaction only so long as the United States possessed overwhelming nuclear superiority — and the Soviet Union had failed to develop an adequate nuclear counter-deterrent. Yet it was strategy that provided political, psychological, and budget ease — at least in the short run. In the longer run, however, it promised significant political and psychological difficulties whenever the publics of the several countries began to examine the implications of the strategy — if deterrence failed. Even by the end of the 1950s, there was some pullback from the pristine logic of the strategy, when General Norstad began to introduce a "pause" — presumably permitting the Soviets to come to their senses — before a full nuclear response.

The Kennedy Administration, influenced by the concerns expressed within the defense community during the 1950s, sought to move rapidly away from dependence upon immediate nuclear response. Secretary McNamara made substantial efforts to improve conventional forces — and also to alter the formal strategy. Then, as now, McNamara wished to avoid "first use" of nuclear weapons. Then, as now, there was vigorous resistance from Europe, and particularly from West Germany, to any change that would weaken the nuclear deterrent. There were force improvements, however modest. After the withdrawal of France from the integrated command structure, a new strategy, 14/3, featuring "flexible response" was adopted. Yet, it was adopted more in the vein of giving the Americans what they wanted in verbal form, without any serious commitment to undergo the exertions to give that strategy life.

Ironically, at that point the United States became primarily absorbed by the Vietnam conflict. Its conventional capabilities in Europe were weakened and the attempts to breathe life into the new strategy were consequently seriously compromised. As I indicated earlier, I returned to the task in 1973. With the necessary doctrinal modifications, there was a far better response. In the following decade, major force improvements took place. Nonetheless, during the entire period the military posture of the Warsaw Pact continued to improve even more rapidly.

A shift to full conventional defense and deterrence, designed to avoid any reliance on the threat of nuclear retaliation in the event of conventional assault, implies a sizable shift in the military and budgetary burden within the Alliance. For such a buildup to succeed the European allies would be required to make major commitments to military expenditures, which many have felt to be beyond the political and budgetary capacity of the European states. Thus, the embrace of a strategy of full conventional deterrence has always been halfhearted — even by such as the Dutch, who have been most uneasy with reliance on nuclear weapons.

The ultimate effect, however ironical, has been that the United States has for a quarter century taken the problem of European security far more seriously than have the Europeans themselves. Underlying such differences are a number of elements. Europe, with its memories of World War II, has found the thought of conventional warfare on the continent abhorrent — even more abhorrent until recently than nuclear deterrence, which was presupposed to avoid the possibility of war altogether.

To create the conventional forces necessary for full conventional deterrence would have required a far greater relative effort by the Europeans than by the Americans. While both Europeans and Americans have sought to take the easy way and find a cheap strategy, that tendency has been even stronger in Europe than in the United States. But even more important has been a substantial difference between Europe and the United States regarding the nature of the threat from the East — and the scope of the measures needed to deal with that threat.

Particularly over the last two decades European fears regarding the Soviet threat have gradually become attenuated. Curiously enough this has occurred during the very period that major Soviet expansion of both conventional and strategic forces has taken place. By contrast, the Americans have more consistently held to the view, first expressed in the late 1940s, that whenever the Soviets reached parity in nuclear strength, they might feel free to explore or to threaten the use of their conventional forces against Western Europe. And, of course, many Americans have steadily expressed the fear that under such circumstances the political will in Europe would crumble — the so-called process of self-Finlandization. For these reasons, the United States has steadily, if unsuccessfully, pressed its European partners to match the Soviet buildup.

The underlying irony remains that the United States has been far more concerned about European security than have the Europeans. To date, it should be noted, there is no *evidence* that the American fears are correct. The day of nuclear parity has certainly arrived. Nonetheless, under the present leadership, the Soviet Union has shown no greater tendency to exploit its conventional military advantages than at an earlier date. European leaders have taken note of internal Soviet political weaknesses and the disarray that has existed in Eastern Europe. They are inclined to believe that the long-run advantages lie with the West — and that there is no reason to sound the tocsin.

The upshot has been that the United States has regularly, if intermittently, pressed Europe for twenty years to create a high-confidence deterrent for the protection of Western Europe. The Europeans have just as steadily failed to yield to such pressures. European leaders, with a different assessment of the threat, have in practice believed that a low-confidence deterrent would be adequate. They have steadily shrugged off American pressures for the enhanced expenditures and enhanced forces necessary to achieve a high-confidence deterrent.

Only time will tell whether they are right. That will depend upon the nature of the Soviet leadership and of Soviet policy in the next generation. Nonetheless, a great deal of political capital has been expended over the years by the United States in the attempt to persuade the Europeans to do what they do not wish to do. It seems to me that the United States should accept the reality of the disparate views of the threat and of the means necessary to meet the threat. There will never be a full conventional capability in Europe until such time as the Europeans are imbued with the conviction and are prepared to make the effort necessary to establish such military capabilities. In the interim, the Americans should cease expending political capital in the fruitless attempt to persuade the Europeans to do what they do not wish to do. A new consensus within the Alliance is a prerequisite for the level of effort that would be necessary.

No vast expansion of military expenditures can be contemplated at this time. Nonetheless, one should not be defeatist about attempts to upgrade the conventional deterrent. While we will not match force levels of the Warsaw Pact, improvements in conventional forces and in the overall deterrent are possible within the constraints of projected budgets. Some of these have been emphasized by General Bernard Rogers in recent years. I myself would emphasize the mal-deployment of forces and the layer-cake arrangements along the central front, as particularly demanding of correction. These deployments are a residue not only of the occupation years, but of the period of the nuclear superiority of the United States and the dependence of the Alliance upon the threat of nuclear retaliation.

There is a new consensus, I believe, within the Alliance. It is not a consensus regarding the need for increased expenditures or about the magnitude of the threat. But it is a consensus regarding the desirability of the Alliance diminishing its reliance on early recourse to nuclear weapons. Thus, it supports improved conventional deterrence — so long as such improvements take place without major increases in military budgets.

The Alliance should therefore develop plans which reflect this new consensus. In my judgment, it is difficult if not impossible effectively to elaborate substantial changes within the formal councils of NATO. The time is ripe, I feel, for the allies to create a new body of "wise men" for the first time since the 1950s. If they have sufficient weight and authority, they can elaborate the relatively simple measures that could substantially improve the conventional posture of NATO — and thereby the confidence that all of the allies have in the overall deterrent. While they will continue to resist what they regard as frenetic attempts by the Americans to increase expenditures and expand force levels, the European allies would certainly prefer to increase the level of confidence in the deterrent, if it can be done at reasonable cost. Authoritative judgments reached by a body of wise men, separate from the traditional channels, can be fed back into both the several national governments and the formal NATO processes.

The German-American relationship must be understood in the context of the overall European-American relationship, including the all-important element of collective security. Yet the German-American relationship has special attributes that set it apart from the overall context. In the German-American relationship are special strengths and special weaknesses. The German role is central in European security, so that its actions and its attitudes will be more carefully watched than other NATO partners. The Federal Republic of Germany is, of course, the most vulnerable member of the Alliance, given its proximity to Soviet forces and to Soviet-controlled domain. The Federal Republic, therefore, has a correspondingly greater interest both in the efficacy of security arrangements and in avoiding increases of the level of tension in Central Europe. It is in West Germany that the bulk of the American forces are stationed. Consequently, Americans are particularly sensitive to changes in German policies or attitudes. In this connection, one should recall that West Germany has had imposed upon it in the past a special burden of offsetting the negative attitudes towards Europe in the United States induced by what was seen as French irresponsibility. Were West Germany and France simultaneously to become too fractious, or excessively independent-minded, I fear that the American support for the European security arrangements would rapidly wane — irrespective of so-called national interests.

Until such time as European unification should take place and Europe hypothetically develops adequate security arrangements of its own, it is overwhelmingly in the national interest of the European nations to keep the Americans sufficiently satisfied that they remain fully committed to the purposes of the Alliance. Taking the basic security benefits of the Alliance for granted to the extent that treatment of the Americans, because of other issues, becomes cavalier or captious would constitute a great disservice to the European or to the German cause. In this connection the Federal Republic has a special and weighty responsibility. The arrival in power of the Kohl government, given its style and its attitudes, provides a splendid opportunity to cement the German-American relationship — indeed to restore it, at least in part, to the happier and more stable mode of yesteryear.

Nonetheless, the initial responsibility rests with the United States, which remains the leader of the West, though its primacy is now reduced. Earlier I expressed concern regarding the reluctance of Americans to accept that the expectations built up in the period of American paramountcy must now be curbed — and the fear that such a process might be slower than the American acceptance of international responsibilities after World War II. The initial tendency of the Reagan Administration was simply to reassert American primacy. It felt that troubles within the Alliance were a reflection of the weakness of previous administrations. It consequently ran the banner of liberty up the flag pole and expected the allies to rally around. It failed to take into account the changes in attitudes, political relationships, and the balance of power that have occurred in the last fifteen years. To the Administration's surprise, the allies not only did not rally around, they became both worried and skeptical. Happily, however, since its early days the Administration has learned some valuable lessons in this respect.

For the future I offer the following admonitions:
1. The day in which the United States could "manage" the Alliance is now over. The European nations will *insist* that their preferences be dominant with regard to issues affecting the European continent and the tone of its relations with the East.

2. Europeans are not interested in posturing about East-West relationships simply to gratify emotions or ideologies regarding the contest between freedom and the police states, or whatever. They understand that they will have to co-exist on the Eurasian continent for a long, long time with states that do not satisfy their preferences. They do not seek, therefore, nor will they accept any unnecessary tempestuousness in those relations.

3. The United States can no longer set Alliance strategy for the defense of Europe. That strategy will ultimately depend to a large extent on the efforts the Europeans themselves are willing to make. While the United States may regard this as inconvenient and frustrating, in light of its world mission, it will have to accept this fundamental reality.

4. Alliance strategies must be designed in ways and couched in terms that take European sensibilities into account. This is particularly the case since a rising generation in Europe has little recollection of the dangers and the common actions taken to stabilize Europe in the postwar period. Indiscreet or reckless talk that ignores those changes in conditions and attitudes carries the risk of further and unnecessary separation of Europe from North America.

5. The great triumph of Western policy since World War II has been the stability that it has brought to Europe. Europeans wish to enjoy that stability and are not likely to forfeit it lightly. The logical conclusion is that

Americans must accept *some* divisibility of detente. So long as the Soviet Union wishes to support insurrections in the Third World, detente of the sort envisaged in 1972 will remain unattainable. Yet Europe will not accept the clash of rivalries in the Third World spilling back into unnecessary tension on the European continent itself.

6. While some divisibility of detente is acceptable, necessary, and even desirable, there are limits to that process. Americans quite rightly will insist that the pursuit of improved relationships with the East not be carried so far that it undermines the purposes or the investments made by the United States in collective security and the protection of Europe.

7. With reasonable luck the structure of international politics can be preserved in an era in which the United States no longer possesses paramount military power. The United States must accept an altered role as *primus inter pares* and not look nostalgically back upon its period of paramountcy. This implies a greater tolerance on the part of the United States for diversity — and no insistence that other nations must share our missionary or ideological zeal.

8. In sum, all this requires a new attention by Americans to the requirements of coalition politics. Arms control negotiations, for example, must be framed on the basis of what will hold the Alliance together. Alliance cohesion overall is more important than individual military or economic measures despite their substantive importance. Disputes that divide the Alliance, while possibly justifiable in small functional ways, are not worth the cost. Unilateral actions must be viewed with care — to ensure that they are worth any strains that they impose on Alliance relations.

Substantial as are these constraints in guiding future American policies, one must be aware of the constraints on German policy that can be violated only at risk. One must bear in mind the special role of Germany in Europe and the special role of Germany in eliciting continued American support for European security. Let me therefore provide a second list of admonitions:

1. The German polity cannot be sustained in the absence of a framework of European security and the continued involvement of the United States in that security. The restoration of German self-confidence, the search for a German identity, the revival of German nationalism must all be channelled in such manner that they do not bring into question fundamental Alliance ties. If the search for German independence of action were to lead to the point of undermining German security, it would surely have backfired.

2. The support of the American public for our engagements in Europe must be earned anew in each era. That support has rested and will rest in the future on the belief that Europeans generally and Germans in particular deserve American support. The American public has little appreciation for the niceties of the national interest. Unless the American public believes that its efforts are both deserved and appreciated, they will ultimately cease. Too much loose chatter, particularly at the official level, regarding the games that the superpowers supposedly play, with the implication of the desirability of German equidistance from both superpowers will, I fear, ultimately result in that expressed desire being satisfied — to the detriment of Europe

and of Germany. Whatever the irritation about the American role elsewhere in the world, the support of a sustaining American presence remains indispensable for the foreseeable future. A climate of opinion that pretends that this is not the case, that Germany or Europe would be better off to distance itself from the United States in matters concerning Europe, will undermine the requisite support for our European engagements within the United States.

3. The adjustments of the military posture of the Alliance, particularly on the central front, require continued updating. As the nation most concerned, the Federal Republic of Germany must take a leadership position within Europe in modifying and improving the Alliance military posture. Attention must be devoted to improving the conventional balance. Mere handwringing about excessive dependency on the threat to employ nuclear weapons is not enough.

4. Indiscreet comments can flow both ways across the Atlantic. Semipublic criticism of the United States and its leadership was elevated to a fine art in the last years of the Schmidt government. Perhaps the Chancellor felt that, given his experience and capabilities, he could handle issues facing the Western world better than could the American presidents. Indeed, such a belief might have had some justification. Nonetheless, while less fundamental than the critique from Gaullist France in its halycon days, the criticism, in its volume and acerbity, was scarcely productive. Its continuation would have served severely to undermine the relationship.

We all know that the attitudes of the Kohl government are both realistic on security issues and friendly to the United States. One trusts that the friendliness of the Kohl government will not be exploited in such a way that it undermines its authority in Germany. We may hope that American attitudes themselves have now become more realistic. The German-American relationship remains critical to the preservation of collective security in Europe and freedom in the world. Between now and the end of the century we will face many challenges. Let us hope that we can continue effectively to respond to such challenges.

CONCLUSION: GERMAN-AMERICAN RELATIONS AND "THE RETURN OF THE REPRESSED"

by Fritz Stern

In the life of nations as of men there occur moments of crisis which jolt people into greater awareness of self and into greater recognition of earlier, barely noticed subterranean changes. The prospect of deploying new American missiles of intermediate range on German soil — in accordance with the double-track decision of 1979 — constituted such a crisis for the West German polity. The debate over deployment brought so much to the fore: the prominence of the peace movement and the fear of so many West Germans that an uncontrolled arms race could lead to the incineration of both Germanys, a fear fed by a growing distrust of America's capacity for leadership; a recognition of uniquely German, of uniquely national, interests, of which one felt less and less inhibited to talk. Deployment stirred up thoughts of national destiny, and West Germans lived through what Freud called "the return of the repressed." In 1983, the German question reappeared — in all its intractable complexity.

There has been some skepticism — even among experts — about the military values of these new weapons; of their political shock value there can be no doubt. The issue of deployment dramatized and intensified changes in the spiritual and political life of the FRG. The previously existing consensus on issues of defense and foreign policy broke down — at least for the present. By voting against deployment, the Socialists, now happily ensconced as an opposition party, repudiated Helmut Schmidt, who had helped mold the original NATO decision, and tacitly began a re-examination of the FRG's foreign policy. The Greens want a break with the FRG's NATO alignment. Perhaps a new and as yet unspoken consensus may be emerging: a common commitment to the national interest, to the reassertion of German interests. But the parties spoke in different accents and placed somewhat different values on existing alignments.

The Reagan Administration seemed largely oblivious or scornful of these changes, as it was of the general deterioration of the Alliance. As deployment began in November 1983, and did so without the oft-predicted violence, Washington thought that good sense had triumphed over some kind of politically tainted wooliness, that the Soviets, so anxious to stop deployment, had suffered a major defeat. The Administration welcomed the ever-amiable Helmut Kohl as the replacement for the ever-instructive, ever-acerbic Helmut

Schmidt. As for the opposition to deployment or the peace movement in general, officialdom in Washington looked upon these as signs of incipient appeasement in the FRG, in Western Europe, indeed in the U.S. as well. Beneath the still friendly rhetoric between governments, misperceptions, parochialism, and polarization seemed on the increase; a negative dialectic was beginning to be at work, a reciprocity in mistrust, which no amount of inter-governmental harmony could fully banish. The rifts in the Alliance were greater than ever before.

The deployment issue, moreover, coincided with the end of the two great miracles of postwar Germany: (1) the economic miracle that had brought the FRG from ruin to unprecedented prosperity, that made it survive the oil shock better than its neighbors, but that finally ended in stagnation and high unemployment; and (2) what I regard as the political miracle. The political miracle is that from Konrad Adenauer to Helmut Schmidt, the FRG was governed with greater political talent, stability, and prudence at every level of government than any previous epoch in German history had achieved. The Kohl government began with great promises, but inspires little confidence, and this at a time when the Lambsdorff affair threatened to expose pervasive corporate but not personal corruption and where the Woerner-Kiessling affair suggested a kind of moral indifference in Bonn that to many citizens was an affront. These affairs have added to the Germans' *Unlust* (dissatisfaction) with their present politics, and the only hopeful sign is the choice of Richard von Weizsäcker as the next President of the FRG; he at least will again present the FRG — and, in time, perhaps the world beyond — with a voice of the greatest integrity and intelligence.

Deployment dramatized the deepest issue. It suddenly made Germans realize their dependency, the limits of their autonomy, the extent of their vulnerability. It also made them feel a certain chilly isolation: many Germans feared that the new missiles added to Germany's insecurity rather than security.[1] They thought themselves misunderstood: as they became more conscious of the special vulnerabilities of the FRG, they thought that the great protector, the U.S., was heedless of them — and that circumstances had left the West Germans exposed and dependent.

In the last year or so it became ever more acceptable to speak of German interests, to emphasize German needs, and above all to speak with a new urgency about German-German relations. In muted form these themes had been there since the mid-1970s; in the election of 1983, the Socialists ran on the slogan: "In the interest of Germany."[2] Disappointed in the West, disturbed by economic dangers, many West Germans turned to the other Germany and the consciousness of partition has become ever greater. Here was the strongest nation in Europe west of the U.S.S.R. with a uniquely deep national grievance. That the grievance was originally self-inflicted mattered little. The German question reappeared, so many voices and acts pointed to "the return of the repressed." A chronic, half-forgotten pain suddenly became sharper and less tolerable.

None of this was necessarily ominous. None of it could be understood in isolation. In part the Germans were responding — along with many

Europeans and Americans — to the new emphases in American policy under President Reagan. The currents pulling the allies apart seemed stronger, and hence the Fall of 1983 was a propitious time for a conference on German-American relations. The results, partly embodied in this volume, speak for themselves; the rest was atmosphere and informal talk which further enhanced the value of the meetings.

The organizers of the conference assumed that we would discuss our bilateral relations from the vantage point of our two countries and in the context of domestic and world politics. German-American relations are a part of the Alliance and part of the East-West antagonism. In actuality and without deliberate plan, we did not give equal time or thought to the two countries. We talked longer and more intensely of changes within the FRG: an unacknowledged tribute to the fact that in this century and before Germans have often asked decisive existential questions — for themselves and by implication for the civilization to which they belong. A century ago, Nietzsche asked how our civilization could survive the death of God and live in a world that had lost its faith without realizing that it was thus bereft. In the late 19th century many Germans railed against the inadequacies of bourgeois, capitalist society, and German Expressionists sensed the senselessness of the modern world even before the Great War made their personal anguish a collective trauma. The German answers in the political realm have been disastrous, but the questions were fundamental — and are still alive today. Are there questions coming out of Germany now that presage new uncertainties in that country, in Europe — and in consonance or in response, in the U.S. as well?

The conference began by taking an American-German look at the past, as evident in the penetrating essays by Gordon Craig and Richard Löwenthal. Implicit, I think, in papers and subsequent discussion is the assumption that the American past is better known than the German. We know America's past, even as there is worry about its future; the rise from remote and homogenous colony to independence, defined in exemplary and universal principles, to industrial giant, still thinking of itself as blessed by a kind of exceptionalism, to global preeminence. All that in a short historical span is perhaps more precarious and more discontinuous than we realize, but the facts, we think, are known. Perhaps people underestimate the burden that global responsibility has put on this nation and on its institutions, which were devised with supreme wisdom for a small and isolated country. An American historian, reflecting on this country's style in foreign policy, recently wrote that there has been a "persistent irrationality in [U.S] postwar foreign policy. A central element of the American response to the outside world in this period has been an unthinking anticommunism . . . ," which he attributes to domestic strains and pressures in a profoundly changing society.[3]

In the first decades after the Second World War, we thought that "our" Germany was also known. We had helped to create the Federal Republic at the height of our power and political will. Under the threat of our new rival, the U.S.S.R., that since its creation in 1917 has rattled this country, we quickly switched from a Morgenthau spirit of vengefulness to the generosity of the Marshall Plan, a splendid act of practical, self-serving idealism. The FRG was created when the discrepancy between victor and vanquished was at its greatest. And in those years when American power shone at its brightest and German impotence was compounded by moral bankruptcy, many Germans — with what may have been undue haste — grabbed at what they took to be the American essence, as revealed in American vitality and informality, in American dress and manner, in literature and art. In a recent book describing changes in America over the last three decades and hence in the perception of America, Marion Countess Dönhoff, the most respected writer-editor in the FRG, recalls how,

> after the [German] collapse and the long years of moral
> perversion, intolerance and spiritual emptiness, the United
> States, with its modern, open society, with its unfettered debates,
> its optimism and its confidence in the future, appeared to those
> of us who at that time had the chance of getting to know
> America more closely almost as a revelation. . . . Students,
> scholars, politicians who in those years got to know America
> returned with the impression that that society was nothing less
> than the model of the modern society.[4]

Inspired by America (as glorified perhaps by distant and impoverished observers) and driven by necessity, the postwar Germans created miracles of their own. The economic miracle, a product of inherited skill, hard work, and the influx of foreign aid and refugees from the East, ushered in a quarter of a century of unprecedented growth and prosperity. With that growth came the pacification of German society; the much-vaunted class conflict was transmuted into new collaborative schemes and into a general *embourgeoisement*, and the old working class, still discriminated against, especially in access to education, lost its embattled sense of isolation. A kind of cultural miracle occurred as well: a young German elite embraced an American and western orientation. That generation of Germans turned its back on that old German dream, so well described by Richard Löwenthal, that Germany should describe a *Zwischenkultur*, something different from western soul-destroying capitalism and eastern youthful barbarism, a dream that under Hitler had finally been realized — as a gigantic nightmare. The new Germans who flocked to America as students and apprentice-Americans, who were the first Germans to come in droves and to return, were the moral counterpart to Adenauer's calculated policy of anchoring the new Republic to the West and most especially to the bastion power of the West, the U.S.

Adenauer represented the beginning of what I have called the political miracle, Bonn's almost unbroken succession of effective and responsible leaders from Adenauer to Helmut Schmidt, each appropriate to the historic demands of his time. Chancellors were matched by political talent at other levels as well and it seemed as if the FRG — for all its faults, beginning with its purposely bungled de-Nazification policy — sought to make up for past deficiencies. Politicians had an almost Weberian sense of vocation, and thus Bonn gradually earned the respect and trust of its own citizens and of most of the outside world. In the Fall of 1982 conditions changed and *The Economist* noted at that time:

> The West Germany that is preparing to get rid of Helmut Schmidt is a more worrying place than it has been at any time since 1945. In acquiring one sort of self-confidence — as western Europe's economic giant no longer in need of having political allowance made for it — it has lost another: the sort that goes with knowing exactly who you are, and where you stand in the world.[5]

There have always been inter-governmental disputes between Washington and its allies. In February 1951 Marion Dönhoff noted American disappointment over England's rapprochement with what we then called Red China and Europe's unwillingness to shoulder more of its own defense burden, and a little later she wrote about the Soviet effort to drive a wedge between Western Europe and the U.S.[6] The basic themes have changed relatively little. On the governmental level there has been the perennial complaint about lack of consultation, but the disputes were generally resolved and bilateral relations seemed safely grounded in national interest and in sentiment. Today more intractable differences may become harder to reconcile and the popular consensus that existed on both sides is in question. There is less non-governmental commitment to German-American closeness or to the Alliance than there used to be.

For many people it took the jolt of the peace movement and the dispute over deployment to realize that the old days of the Bonn Republic as a kind of *Klein-Amerika* are over. Even discounting the present nostalgia, it is fair to say that the early years of German-American friendship were relatively harmonious. Successively, millions of GIs served in West Germany and found it congenial. At the end of the 1950s, the Social Democrats — in opposition ever since the founding of the "provisional" state — dropped their last dogmatic ties to Marxism and embraced the FRG's full integration into NATO: a wide centrist consensus had been achieved. Perhaps Kennedy's "Ich bin ein Berliner" had such an electrifying effect because it reciprocated the tacit identification of so many Germans with America. (Even today, one of the leaders of the Greens said: "We have all become Americans.") The liberal Establishment in America took a strong, almost proprietary, interest in the Alliance and most especially in German-American friendship.

America is not historically minded — the Europeans, who once were, have also lost much of their historical sense. But an America that is ever ready to celebrate something new is sometimes blind to change. Thus with our relations with the FRG. Many assumed that the FRG would forever remain our most compliant client; they did not see that Helmut Schmidt's critical, sometimes contemptuous style was a kind of world-historical metaphor for the FRG's maturity and increasing assertiveness. The last two

American administrations assumed the status quo *en permanence*. The alliance would remain the guarantor of peace; we accepted that it would always be "a troubled partnership," but never doubted that the alliance — already unique in its longevity in peacetime — would continue because it corresponded to the national interests of all concerned.

We assumed that the West Germans were "ours," even as the sovietized East Germans were "theirs." We knew that the Germans needed our protection, that in Josef Joffe's felicitous phrase, they were "net importers" of security. And in the process we forgot that Bonn was intended as a *provisorium*, that the Federal Constitution anticipated the time when the two Germanys would be reunited "in peace and freedom." We also forgot that NATO was originally intended to contain the Soviets openly — and the Germans, discreetly. We forgot to reckon with changes that were occurring in the FRG, in its place in the world, both in absolute terms and relative to our own standing in the world.

For several decades we forgot "the German question," as did so many Germans. We assumed that Adenauer's original option for western integration and indefinite postponement of the reunification would last forever. We did not anticipate that once the FRG had become the most powerful country in Europe west of the U.S.S.R., that once it had become somewhat disenchanted with the dream of Europe or the model of America, it would recall Germany's historic unity, it would remember that it uniquely is a powerful state with the deepest national grievance. People assumed too readily that the division of Germany had become a tacitly accepted fact — and one of great convenience to Germany's neighbors and allies. Tacit renunciation of reunification inspired other forms of preserving "the substance of the nation," and *Ostpolitik* gave the FRG the chance and context to improve German-German relations. These relations are growing ever closer — and on every level. At a time of overall contraction, trade between the two Germanys is increasing, as are various forms of close economic cooperation. To a surprising extent they are insulated from the coldness between the superpowers — indeed the coldness has strengthened collaboration between the two Germanys. The process of collaboration has built up its own dynamic, with risks and rewards for both sides. German-German relations have entered an entirely new and fascinating phase.

Most non-Germans probably underestimated the permanence of the German question. We are unprepared for "the return of the repressed," and yet that return is palpable and readily acknowledged by all parties in the FRG. Kurt Biedenkopf makes that same point unambiguously and, a few months ago, Richard von Weizsäcker wrote that "a curious ambivalence marks this German question. On the one hand, it has existed with ever greater vitality. There is hardly a serious political controversy in which sooner or later this question does not emerge."[7] In his book *German History Moves On*, Weizsäcker argues that the overcoming of partition is not the same thing as unification. It is, however, an effort to diminish the barriers of partition, and he himself has done a great deal to demonstrate the possibilities of German-German contacts. Like many other West Germans, he attended the celebration of Luther's 500th birthday which was held in East Germany, in the Marxist-Socialist state, which in recent years and with some success has tried to appropriate some of the German historic patrimony. Luther was symbolic; the GDR's debt to the West amounting to nearly $8 billion is symptomatic. The two Germanys are closer today than they have ever been, and some West Germans have come to think that the GDR, that curious amalgam of old-fashioned, small-town life with socialist exhortation and drab austerity, is perhaps more "German" than the Americanized consumer society of Bonn. The appeal of austerity — from a safe distance — is still great.[8]

It is hard to account for the suddenness with which a pervasive fear of nuclear weapons has gripped the West; the much-touted end of American nuclear superiority may have frightened Germans more than they realized or admitted. It is equally hard to account for the timing of the FRG's greater concern with German-German relations. Disappointments elsewhere — the deep crisis in Brussels, for example — quickened the concern. German interests remain anchored in the West; economic well-being and security depend on integration with the West. Most Germans confirm that the Alliance remains an historic necessity, but as public opinion polls show and as private conversations confirm, there is little passion behind the commitment either to Brussels or to the Atlantic Alliance. Many Germans probably see the inevitability of existing ties but it would be myopic to assume that the same number would subscribe to Richard von Weizsäcker's assertion that the FRG's political order demands the closest association with the other western democracies: and that that tie is "final and irrevocable."[9]

This was the assumption of our Washington conference. Papers and discussion evoked the rationale of the FRG's western integration: existing needs require existing ties. But the mood has changed, West Germans are disenchanted with America and disturbed by Reagan's intransigence; Germans feel alone — and a pervasive, contagious *Angst*. In a New Year's article entitled "Fear Not," Helmut Schmidt defined the sources of *Angst*:

> It is a fear of unemployment, of the natural conditions of life.
> . . . There is a growing fear that our total society, that our state
> or its leadership might not have the necessary understanding and
> the needed decisiveness to deal with these dangers, to
> circumscribe them and to avoid them . . . . [The rise to great
> power of] inexperienced people or, worse, of dilettantes . . .
> arouses further fear. In me, too.

This fear, present everywhere in the west, is worse for Germans because they lack a clear sense of national identity and still suffer from the legacy of Hitler.

Schmidt calls today's fear irrational, "It sits in our soul, it does not come from reason." It is spreading in the FRG and it alarms Germany's neighbors. "Once again 'the restless Germans' — thus speak many Frenchmen and other European neighbors." If Germans allow this impression to spread it will become a self-induced political liability because it will lead other nations to contain "German freedom of action and legitimate German interests."[10]

"The restless German, the incalculable German": these are epithets that Germans use as taunts for their political opponents. A critic of the Alliance is quickly dubbed "restless" — and warned that too many critical voices will make the rest of the world nervous and thus will jeopardize the trust so carefully built up during years of loyal obedience. In his defense of deployment to Parliament, Hans Dietrich Genscher warned that the Western neighbors were troubled by "a new kind of unpredictable German neutralism. . . . Theirs is the concern that in a state of somnabulence we Germans might proceed to withdraw from the Western community, captivated by the illusion that we can best solve our national problems through neutralism."[11]

The fear of the "restless" German could have salutary effects, too: the spectre of a neutralized Germany already prompts greater French solicitude for the FRG. A new Franco-German condominium — far closer than anything we have seen so far — could evolve in the next decade, based on common needs and on a common mistrust of the two superpowers, a condominium that would establish an entirely new pattern of military and economic integration. More or less secret talks on greater military cooperation have been underway for some time. A much closer Paris-Bonn entente that would prove the basis for a more independent Western and Central Europe is a distinct if remote possibility — especially if the European Community should fade into ever greater insignificance.

In our conference there was virtual unanimity about the health of the Bonn regime. We too rejected the notion that Bonn resembles Weimar — not even in this period of difficulty. We did not believe that the FRG would detach itself from the Alliance, would drift into neutralism, despite the fact that there are some Germans, the Greens for example, who favor such a course. Next year the Socialists will debate whether the FRG should remain in NATO or not. At the same time we recognized that the U.S. has to take German interests more seriously. The West Germans have outgrown their nonage and feel at once their strength and their grievance. Neither country should be lulled into complacency by the ritualistic invocation of our everlasting friendship.

Bilateral relations will become more difficult, as will relations within the Alliance generally. We discerned some of the major issues that will bedevil our relations — always remembering that they come against a background of different moods and sentiments in the two countries.

"A reunited, neutralized Germany" — that has been a recurrent dream of some Germans — and a nightmare for Germany's neighbors. It seemed an option in the early 1950s (Stalin's famous note of 1952), Henry Kissinger feared it in the beginnings of *Ostpolitik* around 1970, and it has resurfaced now. Most Germans and most Europeans would reject it — if for different reasons. The Germans would reject it because it is unlikely and unwelcome: a neutralized Germany would be too vulnerable to Soviet threats or blandishments, the Austrian example notwithstanding. Europeans reject it because a united Germany, with its immense economic strength, would pose too great a threat to Europe's stability. Still, there is a vision that attracts a growing number of people everywhere: the dissolution of both blocs and a reintegration of Europe, a Europeanization of Europe; Germans hope that in the wake of such a reintegration some closer bond between the two Germanys could emerge as well. For the time being — and in the absence of any sign that the Soviets would want to play so daring a game — neutralism is a kind of dream. German interests, economic and political, would argue against neutralism but sometimes people act not out of interest but in pursuit of some kind of collective national dream and such dreams must also be taken seriously. Heinrich Heine recognized the role of dreams:

> It's only when dreaming his ideal dreams
> That a German boldly expresses
> The German thoughts he bears so deep
> In his loyal heart's recesses.[12]

The conference grappled with questions concerning the Peace Movement, the appearance of the Greens in German politics, and the leftward drift of the SPD. To some Americans, these changes are alarming — and not made more palatable by the fact that they have their analogues in other countries as well, America included. The peace movement exists everywhere in northern, largely Protestant, Europe (in southern, largely Catholic, Europe, the main peace group seems to be the Roman Catholic Church); the Greens' anarchic concern with ecology, with a defense of nature against the mindless greed of a driven, achievement-bent society, is neither new nor exclusively German. But all these changes have a specific German element to them; they speak of a new concern for *German* interests.

In the FRG, as elsewhere, the peace movement is a response to the new cold war and the new arms race, though the fear of nuclear power in any of its guises is real enough. But in the FRG there is the added fear that the two Germanys would of necessity become the battleground of the two superpowers. Germany would be devastated first, perhaps Germany would be sacrificed while the superpowers protected themselves from the ravages of nuclear war. Given the many scenarios for European conflict and possible strategies for responding to them, as illuminated in Josef Joffe's essay, it is no wonder that some Germans feel bleakly as if the future was *Deutschland unter alles*.[13]

There are many reasons why the West Germans — with their 1,000-mile border with the East and the 4,000 nuclear warheads of foreign provenance on their soil — should become frightened by confrontation politics and by facile talk of winning a nuclear conflict. A great many Germans — not just among the Greens or the disgruntled but among the most pro-American groups — are disillusioned and troubled by American foreign policy. They remember the facile remarks of the early Reagan Administration and may not as readily register the more nuanced statements of the last few months. They may not grasp the real difference between the Administration's rhetoric and actual policy. Germans charge us with the absence of a realistic strategy; they worry that the replacement of the old elite by a rough-and-ready group of self-made men from the Sun Belt bodes ill for American-European relations, even as it might be symptomatic of America's greater concern with the Pacific. They despair of our political capacity and consistency, even as Americans despair of European abdication, of what Nietzsche called and dreaded, namely European Buddhism, a collapse of will.

The Europeans must understand the depth of irritation that many Americans feel at European passivity. They cannot ignore the recent speech by Lawrence Eagleburger, then Undersecretary of State and an old Europe-hand, who warned that continued European parochialism would force a shift in U.S. foreign policy toward greater concentration on the Pacific area and toward still greater collaboration with Japan. Henry Kissinger's call for a radical restructuring of NATO also reflects the fear that the continuation of the status quo, including the self-injuring European dependency on American protection, could encourage an American neo-isolationism, a new kind of backlash. He has harsh words for all; his analysis of the present inadequacies will dismay only those who wish to live in ignorant comfort, but whether the Europeans will respond to these appeals or to what the French like to call the logic of events remains to be seen.

German disenchantment goes beyond America's present stance in foreign policy. "Model America" vanished long ago, and while many Germans still admire American vitality and may still hope for some kind of dramatic regeneration, they are fearful that the domestic problems — economic, social and racial — will further distort American leadership abroad. Many Europeans — and Americans — share some of these misgivings; the Germans have the special experience of the disappointed lover, of a people who succumbed too completely to an earlier hold which the American dream has on Germans — and to their anxiety that that dream is being tarnished or destroyed.

Many Germans are anxious and some are angry. They resent their own dependency, especially at a moment when they wonder whether this imported security may not actually be a concealed risk. In their dubiety and anger they rediscover that they enjoy only limited sovereignty; the Allies withheld certain normal attributes of sovereignty from a state which has yet to have a regular peace treaty. The Allies, for example, retain their rights in Berlin and the West Germans forswore the development of their own nuclear weapons. The FRG's formidable *Bundeswehr* is entirely integrated into NATO. As Germans begin to think of alternate strategies for themselves, as they begin to spin dreams about the dissolution of both blocs and the Europeanization of Europe, they discover that the prohibitions on sovereignty correspond to still deeply rooted apprehensions about the Germans. The Soviets are not the only ones in Europe who would resist a reunited Germany; the Western nations have similar reservations and memories. In short, the Germans are discovering all sorts of things about themselves, and to generations that have been brought up largely ahistorical, these reminders are especially perplexing. In their present mood and after the agitation over deployment, a strident tone is sometimes struck. I recently heard a leading

German writer lament the fact that Germans were still living under an occupation power, that the U.S. was the *Besatzungsmacht* — a term that to his generation and mine instantly recalls the German occupation of most of Europe during the Second World War. Rhetoric matters, and these are deliberately wounding epithets that express anger and resentment.

The conference debated long and ardently whether the peace movement should be regarded as ephemeral or likely to be enduring. A high point of the conference was Jürgen Moltmann's evocation of the fears especially of the young that the spiritual void of the world is covered up by ever greater concern with military hardware and the response of the "realists" who failed to see the relevance of these yearnings and thought them dangerous manifestations of the "better-red-than-dead" syndrome; it was James Schlesinger who welcomed the presentation of what he considered to be genuine and important views and it was Gordon Craig, a celebrated historian of military affairs, who admonished the conference to take these sentiments seriously.

Some argued that the nuclear threat had engendered similar movements before; after all, in the 1950s Helmut Schmidt (following his entire party) was one of the most passionate opponents of German rearmament and nuclear weapons. Others believed that this time the peace movement was different, as it is in the rest of the world: it is more pervasive, it is better organized, and above all it has the growing support of both Christian churches. (Jürgen Moltmann's essay and Kurt Biedenkopf's observations make clear that the confrontation between state and church is likely to become graver with time.) At a time of nuclear imbalance, the threat of nuclear devastation and the absurdity of a continued arms race seem greater and world leaders of moral and practical authority — religious and secular — have demanded, passionately and cogently, that alternatives to the present policy of ever greater militarism must be found and adopted. The peace movement in the FRG, which today encompasses the Greens, large numbers of the socialist party, and many churchmen and professionals, may spread — unless the present course of arms escalation gives way to successful steps in arms reduction.

The peace movement has attracted a following in the other Germany as well — and again largely through the agency of the churches, the only possible forum for opposition. (The GDR is predominantly Protestant and hence it has been the Protestant churches that have spoken for peace and thus encouraged a peace movement in a country where "peace" had been the monopoly of state propaganda.) Here is an additional tie between the two Germanys and an element of what might be called a new common consciousness of the German nation. It has become customary for many Europeans to speak of the two superpowers as if the term connoted not only equal power but some rough moral equivalence as well. In the two Germanys this sense of being at the mercy of the two superpowers (one of which, no doubt, is still held in far greater fear than the other) is probably spreading.

It would be easy to extrapolate from present discontent to alarmist diagnoses of betrayals and desertions. Easy but entirely misleading. There is a great leap from dreams and resentments to political reality.

The conference grappled with some of the dominant issues likely to beset the Alliance in general and German-American relations in particular. Some complaints surface regularly: the Europeans complain about lack of consultation and specifically the Germans charge that during the Geneva talks the famous "walk in the woods" was never divulged to German officialdom — presumably out of fear that Bonn would pressure Washington to pursue this course. That both Schmidt and Kohl urged the U.S. to be more forthcoming in the Geneva talks is well-known, and their demarches had some effect — in the short run, on Reagan rhetoric, in the long run perhaps on the substance of policy.

The conference agreed that the single greatest irritant in our bilateral relations was the divergence in our respective assessments of the intentions and capabilities of the Soviet Union. Divergent assessments lead to divergent policies. Put simply, the Reagan Administration entered office with the doctrinaire conviction of what Carter had acquired empirically and at the end of his term: that detente had worked in America's disfavor and that dealing with the Soviets constructively was well-nigh impossible. President Ronald Reagan probably does see the Soviet Union as "the source of all evil," and believes that detente gave it a choice to build up military superiority. In this view the Soviets are sneaky and strong, aggressive and expansive, ever on the prowl; they are godless to boot and not like us. Their every move in the Middle East or in Central America is seen as yet another tentacle or part of some nefarious scheme to spread their odious influence into ever new areas. Early on, the Reagan Administration decided to restore the military balance that had existed before detente, to challenge the Soviets to a new arms race, which, one hoped, would ruin them economically. Meanwhile Washington looked for ways to punish the Soviets for all manner of wrongdoing, whether in Afghanistan or Poland, whether in the Middle East or in the shooting down of a Korean plane. American bellicosity in rhetoric — fortunately not matched in action — aroused fears everywhere, and American attempts to place the Soviet Union in some kind of moral quarantine — well provided with American wheat, however — seemed to Europeans a dangerous and ultimately immoral variant of a moralistic policy.

Most Germans see the Soviets as heirs of Russian history and imperialism, still backward in all respects save the military realm. They see the regime as marked by essential conservatism and rigidity. They are much more impressed by the fears the U.S.S.R. is prey to: fears that go back to the devastation of the Second World War, with the loss of 20 million Soviets, fears of a country that sees itself "encircled" (Germans should know that countries seized by this apprehension can act most irrationally, as German policy before 1914 demonstrated).

But other considerations enter West Germans' perceptions as well: for practical purposes the U.S.S.R. is the FRG's neighbor, and it holds the key to German-German relations; it is a superpower and the FRG knows itself to be a middle-size power, no larger than Oregon, as German leaders are fond of pointing out. They probably fear Soviet intentions less than Washington does, but they have a perfectly clear sense of Soviet capability. Different interests also dictate different perceptions: the Germans want to believe in detente, which in the guise of *Ostpolitik* brought them so many tangible and intangible gains. They want to continue to cultivate their relations with the U.S.S.R., expand their expanding trade (the more important in a period of recession), seek cooperation, not confrontation, with a power that could impose its own sanctions on the FRG — by creating new difficulties in Berlin or infringing on German-German relations. Most Germans wish for relatively relaxed relations with the U.S.S.R., under the umbrella, of course, of American protection.

The U.S.S.R. continues to treat the FRG as its greatest prize in Europe; disappointed by its failure to prevent deployment, it nevertheless continues to pursue a policy of simultaneously wooing and intimidating the Germans. Fears are hard to gauge and public expressions not altogether reliable indexes: it could well be that the West Germans (and the Europeans) fear the Soviets more than they like to admit and that the U.S. — both its public and its leadership — is slightly less afraid of them than we admit. Fears are genuine and and functional: they justify policy.

In the past there have been sharp differences between the U.S. and the FRG on what policies to adopt vis-a-vis the Soviets. Disputes over the Olympic Games and the pipeline, Poland and selective sanctions are cases in point. This is the area of maximum friction and is reflected in public debate as well: Americans are irritated by what they assume to be a soft and selfish line of the Germans; worse, they suspect appeasement and desertion. They see Germans exploiting American-delivered security in order to woo the Soviets. Americans would like to see German support for American efforts outside the NATO field, in the Middle East, for example. Instead of receiving help, they find that the Germans, always in the safe company of other European nations, criticize our efforts in the Middle East, berate Washington for its insistence that the Soviets must be contained and challenged everywhere. In his speech of September 13, warning his parliamentary party against rejecting deployment before the Geneva talks were concluded, Helmut Schmidt also said what I suspect most European politicians would say: "I have never seen the Soviet Union as our enemy and I pray to God that no German gets the idea to think of it as an enemy."[14] On this central issue, then, there has been a great deal of disagreement. Like so many other issues, this too is an Alliance issue, not a bilateral one, though the Germans have had and always will have a special stake in detente, or at least in reasonable relations between the superpowers.

The FRG and the U.S. are the world's largest trading countries; Germany's economy is decisively dependent on exports, America's increasingly so. As Sidney Jones points out in his paper, the integration of our two economies and the pattern of cooperation will continue, as will heavy reciprocal investments. But competition will get fiercer as well. In the last year or so the American economy has moved with great swiftness from recession to recovery; the German economy has remained almost stagnant and a strong recovery is not in sight; unemployment is high, both for cyclical and structural reasons.

It is inevitable that the U.S. and the FRG should compete for markets: it is also inevitable that both countries will be increasingly hurt by the export triumphs of newly developing nations, particularly those in East Asia, where capitalism seems to have found its last and most congenial home. After decades of "the economic miracle," the Germans are frightened by the prospect of protracted stagnation. As Reimut Jochimsen reminds us, the U.S. and the FRG cherish the same belief in the free market and in free trade, but the cry for protection is becoming ever stronger. So far free trade has withstood most protectionist pressure but tacit breaches have occurred and more are likely to occur. Meanwhile the Germans continue to criticize American economic policy; they object to our high interest rates, which drain German capital needed for domestic investments. They deplore the high dollar which hurts oil-importing countries even as it hobbles American exports. Like many Americans, they are alarmed by the huge budget deficit which saddles the future with ever greater indebtedness; they find it paradoxical that a conservative government should pursue so reckless and irresponsible a policy. For all their criticism, they realize, as do we, that we are bound together in the economic realm, that reciprocal recriminations could lead to new conflicts and to the much-dreaded possibility of protectionism. The agricultural issue between the two countries is already becoming more abrasive and steel and other disputes threaten the essentially open climate of bilateral economic connections.

In the economic realm, too, the Germans are skeptical of American leadership. Inescapably our economic policies and fortunes will have instant and profound effect on the FRG as on all other industrial countries. The country that invented Bretton Woods and the Marshall Plan now forges its economic policy according to its own economic needs and domestic exigencies. Helmut Schmidt once spoke of the inevitability of American economic leadership. By that he meant that no other country could provide the needed leadership — if America abdicates its responsiblity, then the world economy, already endangered by the huge indebtedness accumulated all over the world, would face still greater risks.[15] Our conference shared Sidney Jones' optimism that "the basic calculus of bilateral benefits and dependence" would compel both countries to seek ways of resolving inevitable conflicts.

The conference devoted much time to questions of security, as evident in the essays by Josef Joffe, Ernest May, James Schlesinger — and Jürgen Moltmann. The inclusion of the latter should remind us that after all the military capabilities are duly quantified and all the war games played, the intangibles, such as morale and will, are still the essential elements. The core of the Alliance — and of German-American relations — is security. There is general agreement that in the immediate postwar period the U.S. unilaterally, and after a few years the U.S. in NATO, provided the necessary shield for Europe — and thus for 39 years preserved the peace. (The earlier record for lasting peace in Europe was 44 years — and ended in 1914.) Containment and deterrence remain the goals of the Alliance, but the credibility of deterrence has become ever more controversial. In its present state and with its present strategic plans, the Alliance has many critics; some would argue that it provides risk and security in roughly equal measure.

The Alliance holds together nations of a common civilization and a common commitment to the democratic process. The Alliance serves economic interests as well — but its *raison d'etre* was and remains a common effort to provide security. But it is in the field of defense that the changes of power have been most striking, as James Schlesinger makes clear. The U.S. has lost its paramount position, the Soviets have grown stronger, as have the Europeans; in fact the Europeans have become too strong to be so weak. The historic nations of Western Europe, once so jealous of their sovereign statehood, collectively represent great power and great potential and their continued dependency on the U.S. is bound to be injurious to their pride and sense of self, the more so as they have professed to have lost much faith in the strength or wisdom of American leadership. What I have once called semi-Gaullism, a doctrine without the General and without much hope, stalls Europe.[16] As the most vulnerable and the most powerful of the European allies, West Germans harbor a particular unease about security: they want American protection and they want detente but increasingly fear the use of nuclear weapons on which deterrence has always rested. Their own consensus regarding defense has broken down.

On both sides of the Atlantic, observers call for a build-up of conventional forces that would themselves serve as a sufficient deterrent and would obviate the dreaded use, first or last, of nuclear weapons. Militarily such an effort at conventional deterrence is probably feasible, but its huge expense makes Europeans shy away from it. What the Europeans failed to do in prosperity, they are unlikely to do in times of trouble. Meanwhile they criticize the U.S. for not having a citizen army, which in addition to other virtues would increase Allied conventional capability. Americans believe that the Europeans should do much more for their own defense, and James Schlesinger, himself very much a partisan of the Alliance, notes that "for a quarter of a century [the United States] has taken the problem of European security far more seriously than have the Europeans themselves." Over 200,000 GIs remain in Germany — as unambiguous evidence of our resolve to defend Europe. Many Germans would want even more men — and fewer missiles or none. If European carping persists, if the Europeans fail to make a greater defense effort, then the United States, divided in its views and taxed by the increased use of its military all over the world, may decide to reduce or withdraw its European contingents.

The Germans are nervous on two familiar scores: on the one hand, they ask the old Gaullist question of whether the American deterrent is really credible, i.e., would an American President risk a nuclear attack on the U.S. in order to protect the FRG, sacrifice Chicago in order to revenge Hamburg? Some Germans argue that the new missiles heighten rather than reduce insecurity; they see these missiles as necessary and instant targets for the

Soviets, since the Pershings could reach to the suburbs of Moscow, to the very point, ironically enough, where once before Russians fought for their survival. On the other hand, the Germans realize that for all the real strength and excellence of the Bundeswehr, the presence of American troops — itself astonishing four decades after the war — as the guarantor of America's resolve to keep Germany inviolable, is essential. More than the other Europeans, the Germans know that their security rests in American hands, they know it, they depend on it, they resent it.

Germans fear too much or too little security. They fear foreign nuclear weapons and foreign fingers on the trigger. Germans have developed their own anxiety, their own fear that reckless American action could ignite the whole nuclear arsenal. They hear other voices of concern. Thus W. Averell Harriman wrote on New Year's Day:

> This is the grim result of Reagan Administration diplomacy. If present developments in nuclear arms and United States-Soviet relations are permitted to continue, we could face not the risk but the reality of nuclear war. . . . But blaming the Soviet Union [for the present situation], which has been the single-minded indulgence of this Administration since the first day it took office, is not a strategy or a policy. . . . It will not be easy to undo these three years of nuclear irresponsibility, or to free both nations from excessive pride, or to control new weapons while we set about the task of controlling all weapons.[17]

Or John B. Oakes, former senior editor of the *New York Times*, who argues that:

> President Reagan's consistent elevation of militarism over diplomacy creates a clear and present danger to the internal and external security of the United States. Presidents have been impeached for less . . . . Mr. Reagan exacerbates it [the Soviet threat] by striving for an unattainable superiority in every phase of nuclear overkill.[18]

The warnings are legion and non-partisan and include honored statesmen listened to on both sides of the Atlantic, like George F. Kennan.

In their apprehensions, the Germans are not alone. But in a newly felt estrangement or isolation, in the absence of the earlier comforting miracles, the Germans, like so many other western nations including the U.S., have turned more inward, thereby augmenting their fears and estrangement. Some Germans, as I mentioned earlier, dream of a new dispensation in Europe. Last September, Rudolf Bahro, a popular figure who left the GDR and is now a leader of the Greens, spoke of "our aims — to withdraw both parts of Germany and Europe from the two military blocs and to neutralize Europe."[19] In December, Rudolf Augstein, publisher of *Der Spiegel*, wrote "that if the Soviet Union, contrary to every expectation, offered authentic unification of the two German states — not merely a loose confederation —

we, the West Germans, like the Germans of the German Democratic Republic, would respond to our submerged national impulse. The problem, meanwhile, is to survive until we get to that point."[20] Survival is threatened, he believes, by the possibility that the two superpowers would, in a confrontation, "use German soil as their battlefield." Other nations have also turned inward and seek to protect their immediate interests; in a similar mood the Germans turn to the other Germany.

The U.S. must understand this mood and its causes. The Alliance cannot be saved by amiable rhetoric. A troubled FRG and a divided German nation in the heart of Europe remain a permanent challenge to the status quo. On the other hand, the Eagleburger-Kissinger remarks should make Europeans recognize American interests and American impatience with Europe's lagging contributions to defense. To speak of the possibility of a new American isolationism is not a scare tactic vis-a-vis the Europeans. It is part of a realistic assessment of the possibilities of estrangement, as Kurt Biedenkopf's remarks on burden-sharing make clear.

The Europeans are more aware of the German question than we are; they worry about "whither Germany," and thereby deepen Germany's sense of relative isolation. Our bilateral relations are both separate from and an integral part of the Alliance: if the latter drifts apart, if it slides into a "progressive divorce," as the French foreign minister remarked, then German-American relations will suffer as well. Bonn has always striven to avoid conditions in which it would have to choose between Europe and America. Its ties to Europe grew stronger as its trust in the U.S. diminished, but the crisis in Brussels complicates relations among the European allies. The trouble is that Europe's search for greater autonomy, its much-vaunted wisdom that comes in the form of *Realpolitik*, is not accompanied by the political will to construct a credible autonomy, to become truly independent. A carping Europe with the pious wish to be equidistant from both superpowers, is going to succumb to semi-Gaullism, i.e., a Europe that has the wish but not the will to be independent. Gaullism as reverie rather than as a summons to action is a prescription for resentment. Gaullism on the cheap is worse than the whole of the General's audacious vision.

We cannot count any longer on an automatic affinity between Western Europe and the U.S., but the realities of our interdependence and of the integration of all our economies allow for considerable optimism. The machinery of the Alliance in the economic, political, and military realms will probably remain intact. If everything goes wrong, the alternative might be a sullen, isolationist America and a Western Europe in suspense, adrift and will-less.

The conference came down on the side of optimism — but then we were all committed to the cause, to the Alliance, and had been for decades. We found persuasive reasons for optimism. We concluded that Bonn, that improvisation without a final peace treaty and with only a Basic Law because a formal Constitution would have bespoken permanence, proves the old adage *c'est seulement le provisoire qui dure*. Bonn is already more than twice as old as Weimar and it has survived economic crises and unemployment, terrorism and street violence, the rise and fall of a neo-Nazi party, all manner of shocks. Its roots have grown deeper, the habits of liberality have become stronger. Limited autonomy has had its domestic advantages: the FRG has had a narrowly circumscribed freedom of action in its foreign policy, and hence that potentially divisive issue has been muted in West German politics — until now, perhaps.

We took note as well of the disappearance of the old generation on both sides of the Atlantic; the generation that built the Marshall Plan and received its aid is now virtually gone. The party system in the FRG still requires of potential ministers a long-term education, whereby they gather political experience; in the last decade or so, the American system has produced political novices and the Europeans in particular lament the disappearance of the old Eastern liberal Establishment; they bemoan the absence of knowledgeable interlocutors. The reference here is to "the best and the brightest," and there are many Americans who view their eclipse with some degree of *Schadenfreude*.[21]

The conference understood that intergovernmental relations remained cordial though there too the prospects were for mounting problems under ever more precarious economic conditions. These problems have been elaborated in the essays of this volume. I have tried to say something about the reappearance of the German soul in world politics, at present in domestic politics and fastened on the overriding necessity for peace. That soul — those strivings of the German spirit which in the past have fused idealism and nihilism with little room for practicality — has often had a calamitous effect on the outside world. This time the German soul combines a universalist appeal — against war, against nuclear lightheartedness — with a nationalist note that speaks to the division of the country. German preoccupation with self may be the contemporary analogue to nationalism, and the world is leery of anything that resembles German nationalism because of its aggressive past, its unsatisfied present, and its unpredictable future. History would suggest that an FRG that feels itself isolated abroad and beset at home is most likely to be volatile or unpredictable.[22]

As mentioned before, the conference spent little time on the changes within the U.S. A growing number of Europeans and Americans think alike and both regard the present scene as alarming. European trust in American leadership, as measured by recent polls of the Atlantic Institute in Paris, is declining. Meanwhile a new American impatience with European passivity is building up and the spectre of a Mansfield Amendment revisited is not simply a device to scare recalcitrant Europeans. It would take no great imagination to project a future where the Atlantic does become a divide and where the old allies succumb to sullen parochialism and the Europeans discover — too late — what dependency is all about. At the moment, the dividing line runs within, not between, our countries. But a kind of international polarization could occur, whereby American insistence on a hard line toward the Soviet Union could feed European suspicions and procrastinations, which in turn could intensify American charges of appeasement and surrender.

Reason and collective self-interest prescribe a different course. But material difficulties and new fears could induce irrational responses, to the detriment of all. In democracies generally and in the U.S. in particular, foreign policy is not an insulated charge of a few, and hence both in the FRG and in the U.S. there will have to be a greater commitment to the Alliance by all the groups of a civil society, i.e., by business and labor, by the professions, by scholars and writers. The message should be clear and the conference intoned it repeatedly: our values and our interests demand that the remaining, embattled democracies must hold together and learn to live with their differences; they must aid other nations who seek to escape the clutches of authoritarianism. Interest and sentiment should tell us that there is no escape from our friendship, that at present there is no alternative to an Alliance that protects the future. To our German friends one would want to say that between the 1890s and Hitler's end, their penchant for utopianism, their restlessness, has in some fields been one of their most attractive traits; in politics, it has been calamitous. To which Germans might reply that American moralism has been attractive and dangerous as well. By and large, in the last four decades, the two countries have shown a healthy sense of realism and prudent self-interest — with a dash of intermittent generosity rare among nations. They need to cling to that recent, undramatic achievement.

NOTES

[1] Part of the Soviet response to the new American missiles was the stationing of new and modern Soviet missiles on GDR territory — to be paid for by the GDR — which is a perpetual debtor to the FRG. In a curious way, these twin developments made some Germans on both sides of the divide feel as if the nation had been put in double jeopardy, both equally endangered by its respective superpower. But it also enhanced their consciousness of common danger, common fate.

[2] It is perhaps worth noting that our language has changed as well. It was customary to speak of West Germany; we now usually speak of Germany or of German, when we mean the FRG. A tacit upgrading of the FRG, a belated denial of the existence of the other Germany, or an unacknowledged wish expression? There is an analogous process, annoying to many Europeans, whereby people on both sides of the Atlantic speak of Europe when they mean Western Europe. These rhetorical nuances and the responses to them have their own political importance.

[3] Robert Dallek, *The American Style of Foreign Policy. Cultural Politics and Foreign Affairs* (New York, 1983), p. xvii.

[4] Marion Gräfin Dönhoff, *Amerikanische Wechselbäder. Beobachtungen und Kommentare aus vier Jahrzehnten* (Stuttgart, 1983), p. 77.

[5] *The Economist*, September 25, 1982.

[6] Dönhoff, *op cit.*, pp. 29-36.

[7] Richard von Weizsäcker, *Die Deutsche Geschichte geht weiter* (Berlin, 1983), p. 7.

[8] Such a view of the DDR can be gleaned from Günter Gaus, *Wo Deutschland liegt. Eine Ortsbestimmung* (Hamburg, 1983), a current best seller in the FRG. Gaus is the former head of Bonn's Permanent Mission in East Berlin.

[9] Weizsäcker, *op. cit.*, p. 11.

[10] Helmut Schmidt, "Fürchtet Euch Nicht," *Die Zeit*, (North American ed.), December 30, 1983.

[11] Hans-Dietrich Genscher, Bundestag Debate, November 21, 1983, in *Statements and Speeches*, vol. IV, no. 19 (November 25, 1983), published by German Information Center, New York.

[12] *The Complete Poems of Heinrich Heine. A Modern English Version*, by Hal Draper (Boston, 1982), p. 514.

[13] A summary of the new critical thought on defense can be found in Rudolf Steinke and Michel Vale (eds.), *Germany Debates Defense: The NATO Alliance at the Crossroads* (Armonk, N.Y. 1983).

[14] Helmut Schmidt to the Social Democratic Bundestagfraktion, September 13, 1983, as printed in *Informationen der Sozialdemokratischen Bundestagfraktion*, Bonn, September 14, 1983.

[15] Helmut Schmidt, "The Inevitable Need for American Leadership," *The Economist*, February 26, 1983.

[16] Fritz Stern, "Germany in a Semi-Gaullist Europe," *Foreign Affairs*, vol. 58, no. 4 (Spring 1980), pp. 867-86.

[17] *New York Times*, January 1, 1984.

[18] *Ibid.*, January 9, 1984.

[19] *Ibid.*, September 30, 1983.

[20] *Ibid.*, December 9, 1983.

[21] Henry Kissinger regrets the elite's disappearance but his explanation for it has an amazingly facile and self-exculpatory quality to it: "The international Establishment, which had been responsible for the great achievements of our foreign policy, collapsed [in the late 1960s] before the onslaught of its children who questioned all its values." Henry Kissinger, *White House Years* (Boston, 1979), p. 65.

[22] I recently heard a leading FRG official, charged with special responsibility for German-German relations, remark: "The German dynamic will not stop until reunification has been achieved." An honest and honorable avowal — and yet how to convince the other powers of Europe, East and West, that the dynamic will *stop* then?

9534